THE TRADE UNION MOVEMENT IN NIGERIA

Complimentary Review Copy

Author / Editor: Wogu Ananaba

Title: The Trade Union Movement in Nigeria

Publication date: June 4, 1970

Price: $ 9.50 (hardcover) $ (paper)

AFRICANA PUBLISHING CORPORATION

101 Fifth Avenue, New York, N.Y. 10003 (212) 691-5252

APC

THE TRADE UNION MOVEMENT IN NIGERIA

BY

WOGU ANANABA

APC

AFRICANA PUBLISHING CORPORATION · NEW YORK

Published
in the United States of America 1970
by Africana Publishing Corporation
101 Fifth Avenue
New York, N.Y. 10003

Library of Congress catalog card no. 72-106044
SBN 8419-0039-6
Printed in Great Britain

CONTENTS

TABLES

FIGURES

PREFACE

A young man or woman leaves school and gets employment in either the workshop, the big departmental store, the banking or insurance house, or any of the offices, public or private. On taking up an appointment he or she is told of certain basic entitlements like free medical treatment, paid leave, overtime pay, etc. How did these things come about? Did the employer give them of his own volition and as proof of his kindly disposition towards the worker? Or were they fought for and won by the united action, the sweat and toil, the sacrifices – physical and financial – the broken heads and fractured arms, and sometimes the lives of Nigerian workers?

A new entrant to wage earning employment in Nigeria is often confused, when he hears or reads from the Nigerian press about workers' organisations being referred to as Adebola's faction, Imoudu's faction, Goodluck's faction, or Anunobi's faction. So also are foreign visitors and curious observers of the Nigerian trade union situation. What is faction in Nigerian trade union movement? How did it begin, and why does it persist?

This book tries to answer these questions. It is a brief history of the Nigerian trade union movement from the first trade union founded in 1912 to the fruitless merger efforts of 1966. It has been produced in response to an appeal made to me in 1961 by a group of Nigerian newspaper reporters, who heard my lecture in Port Harcourt on the subject to the first trade union seminar ever organised for women workers by the Trades Union Congress of Nigeria in co-operation with the International Confederation of Free Trade Unions. I was further encouraged by an assignment given to me the following year by Joseph P. O'Donnell, Executive Director of the Harvard University Trade Union Programme, to write a paper on the same subject. In a sense this book is a development of that paper.

It is difficult for one of the makers of history to escape the accusation of bias if he is to write on such a subject as I have chosen. I have tried to present the facts as I know them. Greater attention has been paid to those events which influenced or affected trade union development in general.

This book does not pretend to be perfect. But with all its imperfections it provides a basis for further research on the history of the labour movement in Nigeria. To that extent, I hope, the worker, the union leader, the industrial relations officer and the teacher in labour relations will find it a useful companion.

I wish to place on record my deep appreciation and gratitude to all those who helped in one way or the other in producing this book. Special tribute must be paid to the authorities of Makerere University College Library in Kampala, Uganda, and the National Archives at the University of Ibadan where the greater part of the research work was done. In particular I must pay tribute to the late L. C. Gwam, Principal Archivist of the National Archives, for his advice and co-operation. My thanks also go to the Secretary and Personnel Manager of the Nigerian Coal Corporation for supplying the list of the Iva Valley Martyrs and allowing me to visit the scene of the Enugu Blood Bath. I must also thank my colleagues in the trade union movement, past and present, for their co-operation, encouragement and advice. Mention must be made of stalwarts like T. A. Bankole, A. C. Macaulay, A. A. Adio-Moses, N. A. Cole, N. A. Oti, S. O. Oduleye, E. C. Okei-Achamba, L. L. Borha, O. Zudonu, N. O. Eshiett, N. F. Pepple and B. M. Udokporo.

Finally, let me express my thanks to Messrs. A. Arthur Gulanyago and F. A. K. Bernard, and Miss Agnes Adenowo for the magnificent work they did in Kampala and Ebute-Metta in typing the manuscript.

WOGU ANANABA

38 Falolu Road
Surulere
November 14, 1966

1

THE EARLY WORKERS

Paid employment is a comparatively new development in Nigeria. When it started, and who started it, is not easy to say with accuracy. There is little doubt, however, that very few Nigerians, if any, worked for wages before the advent of Europeans. The reason is not far to seek. The economy of the various states which make up modern Nigeria was basically a subsistence economy, and custom had established the practice that people should serve their parents, family and village heads, and the community without remuneration. Peasant farming, which was the main occupation of the people, was carried out on a co-operative basis. On a given day people went and worked for a particular individual. Throughout that day the man they served was responsible for their food and drink. On another day the man returned the service, and so it went on until everybody in the group was served.

Another reason for the non-existence of paid employment before the advent of Europeans is the total absence of a standardised or universally accepted currency. Until the introduction of the bar, the copper bar, the cowrie shells and the manilla, trade was carried on by barter. These early currencies varied in value, and were not universally used. Their sterling equivalents and the areas where each of them was commonly used are given in Dr. K. O. Dike's impressive book *Trade and Politics in the Niger Delta 1835–1885*.

It is probable that wage employment started with the activities of the early European explorers, who needed guides and carriers for their exploits, and would, therefore, not hesitate to engage any person offering his service. In his *History of Nigeria*, A. C. Burns, former Chief Secretary to the Nigerian Government, reports that, before he died in his attempts to discover the estuary of the Niger, Mungo Park engaged two guides, Amadi and Isaac. Amadi is reported to have been paid off at Yauri.[1]

Paid employment gained momentum after 1830, when Richard Lander and his brother John solved the mystery of the River Niger, and this 'served as an invitation for traders to penetrate the hinterland'[2] and trade in Nigerian products, particularly the palm oil. Macgregor Laird, the enterprising Liverpool merchant, took the lead. Trade in palm oil was a very lucrative venture, and after 1830 had largely displaced the slave trade as the main source of wealth in the Niger Delta. Dr. Dike reports that 'in the thirties the price of palm oil varied from £33 to £34, and in 1834 the trade was worth £450,185'.[3] For over 50 years after, the ambitions of European merchants and Nigerian middlemen to make the best from it dominated politics in the Niger Delta.

The competing European merchants did not just buy and go: they set up permanent trading posts along the Niger and the Benue. In the Delta alone, no less than 2,500[4] Europeans and Africans were employed by 1871. The number of persons engaged in paid employment increased after 1886, when the Royal Niger Company was chartered and given powers to 'administer, make treaties, levy customs and trade in all territories in the basin of the Niger and its affluents'.[5] Twenty-five years earlier, a few people had been employed in Lagos following the cession of Lagos and the setting up of an administration. These and the small staff of John Beecroft, who was appointed first Consul in 1849, formed the nucleus of public servants in Nigeria.

The great commercial activity engendered by the palm oil trade led to rivalry in the recruitment of labour. In Lagos, Calabar and the Niger Delta, where Christian missions had established schools, representatives of competing firms canvassed for employees among the pupils in elementary schools and the students of the handful of secondary schools then in existence. Elementary and secondary school products had little difficulties, therefore, in getting employment. Sometimes some of them abandoned schooling to take advantage of the glittering prospects and enhanced social prestige attached to white-collar jobs, which were then available in abundance. Manual labour was more difficult to recruit. Frequently European merchants recruited labour from the Gold Coast (now Ghana) and from Liberia and Sierra Leone. These non-Nigerian workers were commonly known as 'Kroo labourers'.

Generally of good physique and hard working, the Kroo labourers were very much liked by their employers. Sir L. H. Gallwey, Acting High Commissioner for Southern Nigeria, commended them in his report for 1899–1900 when he said: 'The labour chiefly employed by the Public Works and Marine Departments and by the commercial firms is Kroo labour. It is difficult to know how we could get along without this Kroo labour. . . . The Kroo boy also figures largely as a domestic servant. . . . The Kroo boy as a rule does an honest day's work and is always cheerful over it.'[1]

A deep thinker has said that there is something bad in the best of us as there is something good in the worst of us. This analogy is apt with the Kroo labourer. Although he was a likeable fellow, his stubbornness and sometimes his criminal tendencies often put his good qualities in the shade. Much of the trouble-making tendency of many Nigerian manual workers are believed to have been learnt from the Kroo labourers of old.

Many Kroo boys did not always give their correct names when requested to do so. A story has been told of a gang of Kroo labourers, who had an encounter with a medical practitioner in Lagos in the second decade of the twentieth century. Dr. G. M. Grey was going to work one morning. When he came to the old Carter Bridge he found that every available space had been occupied by Kroo boys hauling drums of palm oil to the depot of a nearby commercial firm. He sounded the horn of his car to announce his presence and to see if the men could make way for him. He tried many times without avail, and passed only when all the casks had been hauled across. Then he stopped and parked his car. He walked up to the man responsible for blocking the road, and asked for his name. The man laughed and said 'My name is Black Man Trouble'.[7] Dr. Grey was disarmed as he too was caught up in laughter. The incident was typical of the Kroo labourer who, though hard-working and likeable, would not scruple to make things uncomfortable for people if he wanted to do so.

Whether the conduct of some of the Kroo boys accounted for some of the inhuman treatment meted out to them by some British supercargoes on the Niger Delta in the nineteenth century is a matter for conjecture. Dr. Dike reports that 'many natives of the Gold Coast employed in the Delta by British firms were maltreated by the supercargoes, and as the Courts of Equity were dominated by the latter they rarely got justice from that quarter. Hence Gold Coast natives were in the habit of appealing against their decisions in British courts in their own country. As a result supercargoes were sometimes arrested at Accra and Freetown on the homeward voyage and heavily fined for actions brought against them by Africans they had sentenced in the Delta.'[8]

The recruitment of indigenous manual labour was first carried out through the agency of local chiefs, who invariably picked slaves or their children or the offspring of hated wives. There were good reasons for doing so. The average Nigerian parent did not take kindly to the incursions of the white man. He did not understand him or any of his motives. Everything the white man did tended to be suspect. Moreover, people had heard of the fate of prominent Nigerians like Jaja of Opobo, Pepple of Bonny and Kosoko of Lagos, following their opposition to British ambitions in Nigeria. In a situation such as this, it would hardly be in keeping with normal human behaviour that parents would be disposed to offer the services of the children they loved and were anxious to bring up as worthy successors. This would appear to explain the common experience in most Nigerian communities that the first group of people to receive education or acquire training and industrial skill were not the children of the ruling classes but the products of the outcast, the underdog or the slave.

Paid employment increased more than ever after 1900 when, for economic and strategic reasons, the British Government decided to revoke the Charter of the Royal Niger Company and take over the administration of the Protectorates of Northern and Southern Nigeria. The decision brought many things in its train. There was an urgent need to open up the extensive hinterland so as to facilitate commerce and achieve the chief objective of occupation – to provide an outlet for British manufactured goods and a source of raw materials for British factories. Opening up the hinterland meant, among other things, constructing roads, which in 1900 were almost non-existent. Even if roads had existed, there was still the need for a means of fast transportation in the form of trains to make contact with the coast, and convey heavy, bulky raw materials from the hinterland. It has been reported that the need had been seen as far back as 1878, when attempts were made by private firms to construct railways, but these attempts were frustrated by the opposition of the administration. A supporter of the project has been quoted as saying, apparently in disgust:

> Think of the benefit it would be to England in increasing markets for manufactured goods and receiving additional produce in return; . . . it would civilise the savage and prepare him for the missionary.[9]

The importance of the railway was also emphasised by Lord Lugard in 1901. Said Lugard in his Annual Report on Northern Nigeria for 1900–1:

> So vast an area as Nigeria comprising in all 380,000 square miles (of which Northern Nigeria contains about 320,000) cannot be commercially developed except by railways. I do not here dwell

on the political reasons which urge the construction of a railway in this vulnerable part of the Empire as a portion of the scheme of Imperial Defence. By railway construction alone can we achieve the rapid concentration of troops and supplies, which would supercede the necessity for greatly increased local force (involving an immense and unremunerative expenditure) to guard our frontiers. Railways are also essential for purposes of internal administration.

In 1898, after years of hesitation, it was decided to begin the construction of the Lagos Government Railways, funds for the purpose having been raised from the British Treasury. Along with railway construction went the construction of telegraph lines and harbours. The daily wage of labourers in Lagos at the time was 9d.; labourers working outside Lagos earned 1s. and received an additional 3d. subsistence allowance; headmen earned 1s. 3d. Since there were no trains or cars, European officers travelled by means of carriers, who received 2s. a day and an inducement addition of 5s., called head money.

It was possible to pay wages in sterling because by this time silver coins had begun to circulate in Nigeria. Partly because they were comparatively lighter in weight and were not subject to fluctuation in value (a disability from which the older currencies suffered constantly) and partly because of the influence of the administering authorities, people tended to show a preference for them. J. Mars reports that UK silver coins began to circulate in West Africa as far back as 1872, and the net importation to the British West African colonies between 1872 and 1911 totalled £6,675,514,[10] of which about 38 per cent went to Nigeria. The circulation of the silver coins was stopped after the commission of thc West African Currency Board in 1912.

Although by present-day standards the wages of labourers in 1898 were very low, yet they represent a fair wage when compared with the rates for identical positions in Lagos thirty years later. Wages in Lagos during the Great Depression of 1929–32 were much lower. It is, of course, debatable whether the wage rates of that time were a disincentive for people to come and take up paid employment, particularly if they were required to work away from their homes or familiar environments. Sir George C. Denton, Lieutenant-Governor for Lagos in 1898, makes the point that people refused to come forward because they disliked working away from their homes. Reporting on the difficulties encountered in getting Lagosians to work for the Gold Coast Railways he says:

> To obtain carriers to go out of the Colony is most difficult. Recently, to quote an instance, as much as two shillings a day was offered with head money of 5s., and yet very few carriers were prevailed upon to go to the Gold Coast. . . . The fact is that the Lagosian does not like foreign service.[11]

The wage rates in Lagos were by no means the same as rates prevailing in other parts of the country. Gallwey quotes the prevailing rates in the Niger Coast Protectorate as follows:

> The wage of local labourers is somewhat high compared with the East, and is roughly at the rate of about 9d. to 1s. a day. . . . This is excessive because the native of the Protectorate, with very few exceptions, is not fond of work, and it is very difficult to get out of him anything like the worth of the money paid.

Referring to the wages and conditions of employment of Kroo labourers, Gallwey adds:

> His wages vary, except in very few exceptions, from 30s. (as a headman) to 10s. per month; he is, of course, in addition to this supplied with rations of rice and beef. . . . The drawback to Kroo labour are, first of all, the expense of bringing him to the Protectorate – his passage costing 25s. each way – and secondly, the boys are very much averse to remaining away from their country for more than a year at a time.[12]

Two facts have been established by the conclusions of Denton and Gallwey about the attitude to work of the early Nigerian worker. The first is that unwillingness to work away from one's home is not peculiar to Nigerians. Gallwey himself admits that even the highly praised Kroo labourer is not an exception to this rule. It may be added that this characteristic trait of man is not peculiar to Africans. The scheme in the highly industrialised countries of taking industries to depressed areas is an attempt to find a solution to this common problem. The second fact is the marked difference in the conditions of employment of foreign and indigenous labour. Kroo labourers were paid the same wages as local labourers, and in addition were given rations, which apparently were denied local labourers. This discrimination in favour of the former would appear to have offered sufficient inducement for hard work. The so-called unwillingness to work of the early Nigerian worker must, therefore, be looked at from another angle.

Several factors were at work. The unsophisticated Nigerian coming from his village to enter the workforce for the first time could not reasonably be expected to conform immediately to the rigid discipline of paid employment, or to have the same productive capacity as others who had had some experience of industrial life. Paid employment at that time, and even today, invariably involved working away from one's home or familiar environments, and generally under very bad conditions. The thought of one's home and one's family and friends, coupled with the problems of social adjustment, created a considerable disquiet in the new entrant. When this is matched with the discrimination in conditions of employment, the incentive for hard work is nil. A situation like this might have been ameliorated by a little patience and humanity on the part of European supervisors, foremen, engineers and administrators. But the early European officials were more interested in painting pictures of primitiveness, of savagery, of lack of interest in work as a justification for continued employment of Kroo labour.

The reward of using tact, patience and understanding in handling Nigerian workers is amply illustrated by the experience gained during the construction of the railway in Eastern Nigeria. Lord Lugard reporting in 1914 cites the examples of three Railway officials: James, Hargrove and Graham. James is reported to have explained to the chiefs along the Imo Valley the advantages which the railways could bring to trade, and through these chiefs to have collected thousands of labourers on 'the assurance that they would be regularly paid a weekly wage, and relieved by others after a definite period. Hargrove, by similar explanation to large audiences of the leading men of each district, disarmed opposition to the acquisition of land for which full compensation was agreed.' Graham is specially commended for his tact in handling his workers. Lugard says: 'He maintained his reputation as the most skillful labour master in Nigeria, and in an incredibly short time transferred a mob of naked savages of the lowest type into willing labourers working on piece work task and cheerfully doing a fair day's work.'[13]

Although increased Government activities created more job opportunities, what actually encouraged most Nigerians, particularly the illiterate and unskilled, to come forward to take up paid employment was the high standard of living enjoyed by the early workers, and the fact that, contrary to expectation, almost all the people whom the various communities thought would never be seen again returned and were much better off. When they were being given away to Europeans or their agents, people regarded them as good riddance, and very little hope was entertained of seeing them again. It was a surprise, and in many cases a pleasant surprise, that most of them returned after some years, bringing back with them money and property far in excess of anything they might have acquired at home. The enhanced social status of the former underdog or outcast thus became a source of inspiration and sometimes of envy. Those who had never thought of leaving home summoned courage to take a leap into the unknown, having seen paid employment as a means of amassing wealth.

The administration itself used various methods to force people out. This was done apparently after some other alternatives had failed. As early as 1901 Lord Lugard had suggested that Indians, who would be prepared to earn less money, should be imported into Nigeria as an alternative to employing local labour on higher wages, which he considered to be 'preposterous'.[14] The suggestion was made after he had taken the initiative to make drastic cuts in the wages of local labour and announced his intention of making further cuts. In 1907 Sir Percy Girouard, who succeeded Lugard as High Commissioner for Northern Nigeria, reported that 'the important experiment of introducing artisans and senior clerks from India has proved a complete success so far as the artisans are concerned, but in the case of the clerks it proved unsuccessful'.[15]

Partly because of the failure of his scheme and partly because of a change of heart, Lugard in 1915 made another suggestion, which appears to be a more objective approach to the problem of getting a contented and disciplined workforce. Reporting on the Blue Book of 1914 he says:

> In my judgment the creation of an absolutely free labour market, the conception of the definite money of a fixed task (for which the individual is personally paid without the intermediacy of any chief or task master) are most potent methods for the eradication of the service status so ingrained in the tribes of Africa, and for creating that sense of individuality by which alone the root principles of slavery can be abolished. Well arranged labour camps with adequate housing, and a market in which supplies of imported food can be purchased at reasonable prices; the entire prohibition of trade liquor (although in the centre of the 'liquor zone'); and the substitution of coinage for the archaic forms of currency were all means employed to the same end.

As the workforce increased, some of the problems emerged which often do when people from different places and with different backgrounds come to work together. How the workers set about tackling them is what we shall now consider.

REFERENCES

1. *History of Nigeria*, page 80.
2. James S. Coleman, *Nigeria: Background to Nationalism*, page 41.
3. K. Onwuka Dike, *Trade and Politics in the Niger Delta*, page 51.
4. Ibid, page 198.
5. Coleman, op. cit., page 41.
6. *Colonial Reports (Annual) – Southern Nigeria, 1899–1900*, page 26.
7. Interview with A. C. Macaulay on February 3, 1963.
8. Ibid, page 198.
9. Coleman, op. cit., page 55.
10. *Money, Public Finance and External Payments*, page 178.
11. *Colonial Reports (Annual), Lagos, 1898*, page 27.
12. *Colonial Reports (Annual) – Southern Nigeria, 1899–1900*, page 26.
13. *Nigeria: Report on The Blue Book, 1914*, page 34.
14. *Colonial Reports (Annual) – Northern Nigeria, 1900–1901.*
15. *Colonial Reports (Annual) – Northern Nigeria, 1906–1907.*

2

THE FIRST TRADE UNIONS

Trade unions generally emerge from the efforts of workers to seek an improvement of existing conditions through collective action. These conditions may relate to wages, hours of work, and other conditions of employment. There is some doubt as to whether this was the reason for founding the first trade union in Nigeria, the Southern Nigeria Civil Service Union, which was inaugurated on August 19, 1912. The Union later changed its name to the Nigerian Civil Service Union after the creation of modern Nigeria in 1914 by the amalgamation of the Protectorates of Northern and Southern Nigeria.

Dr. T. M. Yesufu is of the opinion that 'the Union was thus not formed by a group of dissatisfied workers, who wanted a platform from which to fight for amelioration of grievances or for the improvement of specific conditions of employment'. He goes on: 'It would appear that the main reason for its formation was merely to match the existence of such institutions elsewhere.'[1] This conclusion is apparently based on two premises. First, the initiative to found the Union did not come from Nigerians; it came from a Sierra Leonian named Henry Libert, who was transferred from Freetown. In those days interterritorial transfer was a feature of the public service in the British colonial territories of West Africa. Libert convened the inaugural meeting, the principal purpose of which was to 'consider ways and means of inaugurating a League of Civil Service Officials'.[2]

The second premise is closely connected with the first. As Yesufu rightly points out, ignorance on the part of the convener and the participants of the purposes and philosophy of trade unionism made it impossible for Libert and his colleagues to say anything at the inaugural meeting about what impelled them to think of coming together. It took about three months for this to be done 'apparently after some information had been received from Sierra Leone'. But saying this is not necessarily supporting the argument that civil servants had no grievances. They had. They were dissatisfied with their rates of pay and the limited openings for Africans for advancement to positions of responsibility.

In 1912 the point of entry into third class clerical position was £2 a month, and the maximum salary for Africans was £20 10s., a situation which shows no improvement in wage rates since 1899. Gallwey quotes the prevailing wage rates for skilled and clerical positions as follows: native clerks £24–£250 per annum; engineers £36–£96; artificers £35–£150; tailors £30–£70 and carpenters £36–£50.[3] Yesufu himself admits that 'consideration of the conditions of service of union members was not, however, in practice entirely neglected . . . although it would appear that the most important matter about staff conditions of service, upon which the union was stirred to action, was that of leave rights'.

Civil servants were treated like indentured apprentices. They signed agreements with the Colonial Government – agreements which laid much emphasis on the obligations of the employees and said little or nothing about their rights. A typical example of these agreements is one dated September 18, 1918, between Adesola Collinwood Macaulay and the General Manager of the Nigerian Railway 'acting for and on behalf of the Colonial Government'. It says:

> In consideration of the commencing salary of £2 payable at the end of each month the servant agrees to enter into the service and employment of the Nigerian Railway, and to perform to the best of his ability all such works as the proper Railway Authorities shall require him to do, and to conduct himself honestly, faithfully and properly in the course of such service as well as to the Railway Authorities, and all the other servants, as to all people lawfully using the premises of the said Railway.[4]

Civil servants suffered many other disabilities. For example, they were fined for lateness and unauthorised absence from work, and the fine was deducted from the meagre salary. The fine varied in amount, but half a day's pay was commonplace.

From 1916 to 1919, the main preoccupation of the Civil Service Union was agitation for 'war bonus', some sort of relief payment to reduce the hardships arising out of the First World War. The demand was called 'war bonus' partly because the Union could not think of a more appropriate name and partly because European civil servants, who took part in the Cameroons campaign, were then agitating for payment of war bonus. The CSU agitation was rewarded when 'war bonus' calculated at the rate of 30 per cent of the pre-war salary was awarded and paid to African staff as an addition to prevailing salaries.

A fresh agitation for wage increase led to the appointment of a Salary Revision Committee composed of Donald C. Cameron, Central Secretary to the Government, and Dr. Henry Carr, the only African holding in the Education Department what was then known as a 'European post'. The Cameron–Carr Committee completed its work in August 1919, and made some recommendations on wage increases. For some unexplained reason the Report was not published, and its recommendations were not implemented. Delay led to frustration. Another Committee headed by Acting Government Treasurer Bratt was appointed in response to renewed agitation. Little is known about the Bratt Committee and its report, but Sir Hugh Clifford, in his address to the Nigerian Council in 1920, claimed that the Bratt Report and the Cameron–Carr Committee Report were considered together, and it was found that the rates recommended were inadequate for the conditions prevailing at the time. For this reason another Committee was appointed under the chairmanship of Dr. Rice, Director of Medical Services. The Rice Committee did its work with considerable dispatch, and on September 20, 1920, issued an interim report recommending, among other things, that in order to give immediate relief to the workers the existing war bonus be doubled. The recommendation was accepted, and the arrears were paid with effect from January 1, 1920.

No further improvement was made in the salaries of the African staff until about the second half of the 'twenties, when the Civil Service Union began a new agitation for wage increase and for Africans to be appointed to European posts. That Africans could hardly rise above the position of a clerk had been a perennial subject of grievance and of political agitation. There were not only 'European posts' but also European rates of pay. An African of proven ability who possessed the requisite educational qualification might be appointed to a European post, but he did not receive the salary for it. A typical example is the condition prevailing in the medical profession. An African holding the same degree in medicine as a European would be appointed as a 'Native Medical Officer' on three-quarters of the salary of his European colleague, who entered the service as a European Medical Officer.

In 1902 the salaries of medical officers were revised as follows:

	Existing Salary	*Increase*[5]
Principal Medical Officer	£800–£1,000	by £50 a year
Senior ,, ,,	£600–£700	,, £20 ,, ,,
European ,, ,,	£400–£500	,, £20 ,, ,,
Native ,, ,,	£300–£350	,, £10 ,, ,,

Thus a medical officer was graded and paid not because of the work he performed and his ability to do it, but because of the colour of his skin.

Resistance to racial discrimination in the public service had been going on much earlier. Commenting on this subject in its issue of February 14, 1919, the *Nigerian Pioneer* said that African civil servants 'are then left with no other alternative than that it is a policy of the Government to repress the natives to a position of inferiority in every department of service'. Racial discrimination was one of the subjects discussed by the inaugural congress of the National Congress of West Africa, founded in 1920. It was decided to send a delegation to the Secretary of State for the Colonies to demand, among other things, the abolition of racial discrimination in West Africa.

The demand for Africanisation of certain posts was granted rather grudgingly, and on the specific condition that where an African was appointed to a European post he should earn 75 per cent of the salary attached to it – an extension of the existing practice in the medical profession. The reason for this strange condition is yet obscure. Timothy A. Bankole, one of the surviving pioneers of trade unionism in Nigeria and the President of the first trades union congress, claims that officialdom believed that, no matter what his qualification and experience might be, an African could not discharge his responsibilities with the same efficiency as a European.[6]

In 1919 a new trade union (the Association of European Civil Servants in Nigeria) was formed. It was accorded official recognition in October of that year. Shortly after getting recognition it made representations, which led to the appointment of a Salaries Review Committee to investigate and report on

(i) the regrading of all branches of the European Public Service in Nigeria with the exception of the West African Medical Staff and the West African Frontier Force, which are being separately dealt with;
(ii) revision of salaries of all grades throughout all the Departments of the European Public Service with the exceptions noted above;
(iii) revision of travelling, detention, bush and transport allowances;
(iv) any recommendations of a general character which the Committee may consider it desirable to lay before Government with regard to matters affecting such Public Service in the course of its enquiry may be brought to its notice.

As a result of the Committee's recommendations, European Civil Servants were granted concessions ranging from the payment of one year's pensionable emoluments to the estates of all confirmed officers who died in the service, to placing no limit whatsoever on the amount which a European civil servant might draw as travelling allowance.[7]

Until the depression of 1929, Nigerian labour history was more or less the history of the Civil Service Union. There had been isolated cases of attempts to organise other sections of the public service, particularly the manual workers and railway employees. In 1931 the first known attempt to organise workers in the private sector was made in the inauguration of the Nigerian Union of Teachers. From the outset, the NUT was composed of teachers from government and voluntary agency schools, and it has maintained this all-embracing character ever since. Another union founded in 1931 is the Railway Workers' Union, of which more will be said in the next chapter. Five years later, the unestablished employees of the Marine Department founded the Marine Daily Paid Workers' Union, which in 1937 changed its name to the Nigerian Marine African Workers' Union. The Railway Workers' Union and the Nigerian Marine African Workers' Union were attempts by manual workers in the public service to set up permanent organisations, and the reasons for founding them were dissatisfaction with existing wage rates and conditions of employment.

At this juncture it is perhaps worthwhile to examine the strength and weakness of the early trade unions before the depression. The CSU was hardly a trade union as trade unions are known today: it was more or less a petition-writing body, heard only when a crisis was developing or an important official was retiring or proceeding on transfer or coming to assume duty. There seems to be no reliable record of its membership, and its financial position can, at best, be a matter of guesswork. Yesufu reports that the inaugural meeting decided that 'all native officials should be eligible for membership of the Union, but that at present it is only intended to limit it to officials down to and including those of the rank of first class, although the interests of all will be watched alike'. Perhaps the limitation of membership to the rank of first class accounts for the very few people who attended its meeting at any time. For one thing there were very few first-class clerks at the time, and the number of Africans in higher positions could easily be counted. Since the Union was not known to have held any mass meetings during the period, it is even more difficult to determine how much popular support it commanded. Its strength lay, perhaps, in the fact that its leaders (Nylander, Joseph McEwen, N. A. B. Thomas and I. O.

Gilbert) were among the most influential and highly respected members of the African Civil Service. This fact, more than anything else, would seem to have won it recognition. Its weakness lay in the fact that it was aristocratic to a fault. It did not just abhor strikes, but it lacked the courage even to make threats in furtherance of its demands.

What has been said of the CSU with regard to membership can also be said of the Association of European Civil Servants in Nigeria. Being a racial organisation, its activities and membership were naturally limited to the small privileged group it represented. Since its members earned far more than those of the CSU it is probable that it was in a healthier financial position. No one, of course, expects top civil servants ever to dream of striking, and their decision from the outset not to employ the strike weapon in furtherance of any demands is understandable. But although the members were a minority, they were a minority which knew their mind. Being comparatively well educated, they were better able to present their case in a convincing manner. Moreover, the colour of their skin was an asset and a passport for quick attention. This is clearly seen in the remarkable speed with which their grievances were treated in 1919.

REFERENCES

1. *An Introduction to Industrial Relations in Nigeria*, page 34.
2. Ibid.
3. *Colonial Reports (Annual) – Southern Nigeria, 1899–1900*, page 26.
4. Interview with A. C. Macaulay on February 3, 1963.
5. *Colonial Reports (Annual) – Lagos:* Report for 1903, page 12.
6. Interview with T. A. Bankole on February 27, 1963.
7. Address by H.E. the Governor to the Nigerian Council, 1920, page 62.

3

THE EMERGENCE OF IMOUDU

It is often believed that the inauguration of the Railway Workers' Union marked the beginning of militant unionism in Nigeria. This belief seems to be built on the fact that most Nigerians first witnessed protest demonstrations and sit-down strikes from its activities. Signs of militant unionism had indeed been noted earlier. Coleman reports that 'in 1921 the artisans employed on the Government railroad, who had joined with other technical workers to form the Mechanics' Union, struck against a threatened reduction in wages. They won the strike.'[1]

Some couple of years earlier, the clerical employees of the Nigerian Railway had become so thoroughly disgusted with the humdrum, unadventurous policies of the Civil Service Union that they withdrew from the Union and set up their own organisation called the Association of Nigerian Railway Civil Servants to handle matters affecting Railway office employees. One of the foremost leaders of the Association was A. J. Marinho, the accountant who later became one of the leading stars in Lagos politics after 1947. His experiences in the public service undoubtedly influenced his political activities. He joined the Nigerian Secretariat in 1906, and was transferred to the Nigerian Railway in 1914. In 1921 he was promoted Assistant Chief Clerk, and became an Accountant in 1934. It took him twenty-five years (1921–46) to move from £300 to £630 per annum. Eight months before his retirement in 1947, he was promoted Senior Accountant. In an editorial captioned 'Marinho's Promotion: an Eye Wash', *The West African Pilot* said: 'If Mr. Marinho had been a non-African; if the pigmentation of his skin had been anything but what it happens to be, we are sure that he definitely would have been the General Manager of the Nigerian Railway today. . . . Of what use, we ask, will his present position be to him when he is due to retire next February, and what is worse being an extention of time? How is he to enjoy his much deserved lift?'[2]

The Association of Nigerian Railway Civil Servants distinguished itself by its performance in the 'workers' train' dispute of 1919. Soon after the commencement of train services, Railway employees were granted the concession of free train service to and from work. The concession was a step in the right direction, because Lagos was then grossly lacking in public transport facilities. There was only one rickety bus plying from the island to the mainland, operated by Mrs. C. C. Obassa and popularly known as Anfani Bus. In 1919 the Railway management suddenly withdrew the free train concession, and this infuriated the workers, who threatened to go on strike. The Association sent a protest deputation to the management, which eventually reconsidered its decision and the train service was restored.

The militant unionism of the last two or three decades is a product of the depression of 1929. The depression adversely affected trade and commerce, and consequently the national income. Government activities had been increasing since the beginning of the century, and this meant a heavy financial burden. The great capital works like the construction of railways, harbours, roads and telegraph lines then in progress, coupled with expanding educational and health services, meant an even heavier burden on the lean treasury. Attempts had been made with varying successes in Lagos and in Western Nigeria to improve the financial situation of the country by the introduction of direct taxation. A similar attempt in Eastern Nigeria sparked off the historic Women's Riot at Aba, Owerri and parts of the old Calabar Province, and had the effect of delaying the introduction of direct taxation for some time. It was clear that, despite the precarious financial situation, government must continue to function, and essential services must be maintained. A panacea was found in mass retrenchment of public employees, in the conversion of some permanent posts to daily paid jobs, and in the reduction of working days in the month.

These sweeping changes set in motion a chain of reactions. The Civil Service Union petitioned the Secretary of State for the Colonies for protection of members of the African Civil Service. Not much came of the petition. The manual workers of the Nigerian Railway, including artisans, craftsmen, locomotive engine drivers, permanent way men and labourers, felt that the 'obedient servants' in the Nigerian Secretariat and the General Manager's office were not the type of men to save them from the threatening holocaust. They therefore decided to set up their own organisation. Their grievances were aggravated by the fact that:

(i) while most of them were on daily rated jobs, their colleagues in the offices were on monthly contracts of employment;
(ii) the economy measures introduced meant that their wages

would no longer be calculated on a daily but on an hourly basis and this, they suspected, would reduce their pay packets;

(iii) the economy measures also meant that some of them would not be paid on Saturdays, and this meant a further reduction of their pay packets and their purchasing power.

The office employee did not suffer any of these disabilities. Thus, while the circumstances leading to the Government's strict economy measures might be understood and appreciated, the application of these measures in a manner that favoured only a section of railway workers did not make sense to the men in the loco workshop.

The Railway Workers' Union was formally inaugurated in 1932, but the incident leading to its formation took place the previous year. The Railway Management had posted a notice announcing the date of commencement of the hourly system of calculating wages. The day previous to the commencing day a young, daring apprentice turner, Michael Athokhamien Ominus Imoudu, read the notice and removed it from the notice board. At the close of work he summoned a general meeting of the workers and told them that the hourly system was a device by the management to get cheap labour. He went on: 'The per hour system will be started tomorrow according to the notice. We cannot write now; the only thing is to stop work tomorrow and interview the Chief Mechanical Engineer.'[3] The crowd yelled approval, and the following day the strike began. A delegation interviewed the CME and was assured that the new system would not bring about a reduction in the workers' pay packets. On the basis of this assurance the workers agreed to return to work.

To their surprise, when they received their pay at the end of the month, the workers' experience was contrary to this assurance. The disappointment led them to resolve to found a Railway Workers' Association, which later became the Railway Workers' Union. The principal officers of the Association were Babington A. Macaulay, President, and E. T. Z. Macaulay, Secretary.

Both the leaders and members of the RWU at the time appear to have completely misunderstood the reasons for the Government's economic measures. Participants in its early activities give the impression that the Union was founded as a weapon to fight William Glassford Walker Wilson, the works manager, who they believed was responsible for all the ills of the manual workers of the Nigerian Railway. Wilson was a slim Scotsman, and a bully. He entered the service of the Nigerian Railway on November 28, 1923, and by sheer industry and drive worked himself to the coveted position of Chief Mechanical Engineer on September 23, 1937. He was not altogether the bad character he was always portrayed to be, but he was a very strict supervisor and disciplinarian, and lacked that human touch without which even the best of human beings can be thrown aside as a nuisance. He was not a good mixer, and applied his iron hand and foul tongue almost evenly on his European colleagues and his African subordinates.

Railway workers believed, on the whole erroneously, that he wanted to make money for the Nigerian Railway at their expense, a charge apparently built on the fact that practically all the economy measures introduced during the depression were introduced during Wilson's tenure. Whether he initiated them or merely executed the decisions of his superiors is a moot question, but the workers believed religiously that he initiated them. Even if he had initiated them, it does not appear that he acted without the approval of his superiors. Indeed proof that the economy measures had official backing is furnished in Sir Donald Cameron's address to the Legislative Council on February 8, 1932. Speaking on the measures taken by the administration to effect economy Sir Donald said:

> When I met representatives of the Association of European Civil Servants in July last at my request, I understood them – but not at my prompting – to accept the situation that some retrenchment was inevitable. I gathered the same impression from the delegates of the two African Associations (the Nigerian Civil Service Union and the Association of Railway Servants) whom I received a week earlier.

Referring to the situation in the Railway Workshop, Sir Donald went on:

> The number of daily paid employees in all departments has been reduced and wages have generally been lowered by five per cent to ten per cent. In the Engineering Department, no work is done on Saturday, with a saving of one day's wages per week, except in the case of men employed on the track, where a full day is now worked on Saturdays, and this had enabled a reduction of the total number employed. In the Transport Department the staff employed in Running Sheds and elsewhere had been divided into two shifts, each shift working four days a week, and in the workshops artisans are laid off for varying periods without pay, depending upon the amount of work available during the week.[4]

Table 1 shows the revenue and expenditure of the Railway for the period 1929–34, and illustrates vividly its precarious financial position. As will be observed, the Department operated on a deficit throughout the period, save once.

Table 1

NIGERIAN RAILWAY AND COLLIERY REVENUE AND EXPENDITURE 1929–34[5]

	1929–30 £	*1930–31* £	*1931–32* £	*1932–33* £	*1933–34* £
Gross receipts	2,732,837	2,195,198	1,869,519	1,889,000	1,885,600
Total working costs	1,367,062	1,342,384	1,191,446	1,111,126	1,086,126
Contributions to renewals	322,682	—	—	—	—
Interest on capital	963,063	987,220	1,000,022	1,041,825	1,046,202
Surplus	75,030	—	—	—	—
Deficit	—	134,406	321,949	253,901	246,668

Up till 1938, and even beyond, the financial position of the Nigerian Railway showed little improvement. The situation was worsened by the trade recession of that year. The Government blamed the recurring deficits on alleged unfair competition from motor transporters and, in an attempt to improve the situation, amended the traffic regulations so that lorries plying between areas from which the Railway got some of its traffic would be compelled to pay double the licence fee imposed on other lorries. The double licence fee provoked sharp reactions from transporters, and led to the 'transporters' strike' of January 1937, in which Obafemi Awolowo, who later became Federal President of the Action Group, played a leading role. Although broken by police action, the strike achieved its purpose, for the double licence fee was abolished the following year.

Opposition to the hourly system had been going on since 1931, but in 1938 it was dovetailed in a new agitation for improved conditions of employment. Meetings were held at the Railway compound in furtherance of this agitation. On one occasion the police rushed to the scene, and beat up and dispersed the workers. Public opinion condemned the police action, particularly as there was no breach of the peace and no threat to the security of Railway property. To many people, and particularly to the workers concerned, the incident was a sign of things to come. It did not kill the agitation; rather it made the workers think that before they could proceed further they had better seek advice and guidance. They approached Sir William Neville Geary, Bart, a British lawyer, who petitioned the Secretary of State demanding free medical facilities, paid annual leave, free transport to and from leave, retiring benefits, overtime pay on

Sundays and public holidays and wage calculations based on the daily as against the hourly system. Before doing so he interviewed the General Manager of the Railways, who not only rejected the demands but called the workers agitators.

When forwarding Sir William's petition, Governor Bourdillon said that in the present state of Railway finances it was impossible to contemplate any improvements involving heavy expenditure. He said the conditions of employment of the manual workers were identical with those of other Railway and Government employees and these conditions were recognised as fair and reasonable.[6]

But were conditions identical on the Railways? Table 2 shows improvements in wages granted by Governor Bourdillon himself to certain Railway workers in January 1938, with effect from August 1, 1937. It was this one-sided concession, made to ward off a strike planned by Railway station staff, that forced the manual workers to agitate.

Table 2

WAGE INCREASES GRANTED TO RAILWAY EMPLOYEES, JAN. 1938

	Old Scale	*New Scale*
Station Staff	£48×6 – £60	£48×6 – £78
Mechanical Department		
Engine crews	£60×5 – £80	£72×8 – £128
Workshop	£55×5 – £80	£55×5 – £80
Civil Engineering Department		
Gangers Grade 2	£72×8 – £112	£72×8 – £128

Whether Sir William's petition was responsible for the enactment in December 1938 of the Trade Union Ordnance is not easy to say with accuracy. It is probable that, coupled with the incident in the Railway compound and with public indignation, these activities went a long way in forcing the Government to act. Saying this, however, is not necessarily saying that the Government had not been thinking about a law to legalise trade unions. As early as 1930 this question had been engaging the Government's attention. And it followed a directive issued on September 17, 1930, by Lord Passfield (formerly Sidney Webb), Secretary of State for the Colonies, urging all colonial governments to take appropriate measures to encourage the existence of trade unions. Lord Passfield said: 'I regard the formation of such associations in the Colonial Dependencies as a natural and legitimate consequence of social and industrial progress, but I recognise that there is a danger that, without sympathetic supervision and guidance, organisations of labourers, without experience of combination for any social or economic progress, may fall under the domination of disaffected persons, by which their activities may be diverted to improper and mischievous ends. I accordingly feel that it is the duty of Colonial Governments to take such steps as may be possible to smooth the passage of such organisations, as they emerge, into constitutional channels. As a step in this direction it is in my opinion desirable that legislation on the lines of Sections 2 and 3 of the Trade Union Act 1871 should be enacted in all Dependencies, where it does not already exist, declaring that trade unions are not criminal, or unlawful for civil purposes, and also providing for the compulsory registration of trade unions.'

The Trade Unions Ordinance came into effect on April 1, 1939. Under the Ordinance a union could not engage in collective bargaining with an employer or take industrial action without first being registered. The Railway Workers' Union had not done this, when its representatives met Wilson in 1939 to discuss the Union's demands for a reversion to the daily pay system and for the inclusion of Saturday in the working week. Wilson refused to discuss with them on this technical ground. The rebuff forced the Union to apply for registration.

In the meantime, things moved pretty fast. Seeing that the Union was gaining strength rapidly, the Railway management tried to break it. Babington was transferred to Zaria, and E. T. Z. Macaulay to Kafanchan. Babington died after a brief spell, and was succeeded by Okpayemi, who held out until the annual conference of 1940, when Imoudu was elected President.

In January 1940 the RWU received its certificate of registration. The certificate gave it added vigour to press its demands, which had been approved by the 1940 conference. The Union addressed a memorandum to the Railway management, which later made representations to the Government. In a letter dated May 6, 1941, the Chief Secretary to the Government informed the General Manager of the Nigerian Railway that Government had accepted his proposals in principle, and directed that the Railway Workers' Union be informed henceforth that:

(i) their claim regarding Saturday pay will be adjusted and the loss occasioned to those men whose earnings were reduced as a result of the conversion in 1931 from daily to hourly rates of pay will be made good;

(ii) skilled workers in trades to which an apprenticeship is required to be served will in future be appointed to graded posts, which will be added to the fixed establishment of the

Railway. These posts will be added to Schedule to the Provident Fund Ordinance. All qualified skilled workers at present in the service of the Mechanical Engineering Department will be so appointed to the establishment in due course, not later than October 1, 1941;

(iii) those appointed to the establishment will enjoy the leave privileges provided under General Orders. All other workmen will, in future, be granted full pay for public holidays;

(iv) the privileges of free transport by rail for the purpose of spending leave at the men's homes or native places will be granted to those appointed to the establishment;

(v) those appointed to the establishment will enjoy the privileges provided under General Orders regarding pay during absence from duty owing to illness;

(vi) the question whether a case exists for granting assistance to certain classes of government employees towards increased cost of living is receiving the careful consideration of the Governor.[7]

The Union was duly informed, and was told that the management's proposals for giving effect to these concessions would be forwarded to it later. For about four months the Union waited in vain for these proposals. On September 8 it forwarded a resolution to the Chief Mechanical Engineer demanding the release of the proposals. No reply came from the CME. The demand was repeated at a mass meeting on September 16 at which another resolution was adopted. The second resolution accused the Railway management of deliberately delaying the proposals because it was making proposals which were not in the best interest of the workers. The Union threatened to 'speak in the only language understandable' if the proposals fell short of expectation. Commenting on the matter *The West African Pilot* of September 25, 1941, said: 'If the Railway administration means to be fair to the men concerned, then all its actions and conduct should be above suspicion, and if the men demand to know what their fate will be, then it should be willing to let them know. Why all the secrecy about conditions which the men are bound to know sooner or later? We can see no justification for it and do not blame the men for being anxious.'

The Railway management's proposals were released a couple of days later. On seeing the proposals, the Railway Workers' Union requested that their implementation should be suspended until representations could be submitted in respect of certain clauses which the Union considered had been misinterpreted by the Railway authorities. The request seems to have been treated with contempt. On September 26, a joint meeting of the Railway Workers' Union and the African Loco Drivers' Union adopted a resolution reaffirming 'their conviction that the present CME is entirely responsible for the poor economic condition in which their members employed in the Mechanical Department are placed today. That utter lack of sympathy for the condition of employees under his administration has been shown consistently since he became CME as revealed by the disputes after disputes from year to year'.[8] The resolution also accused the CME of preparing 'draft proposals which contained discouraging interpretations of the concessions granted by Government' and finally demanded the removal of Mr. W. G. W. Wilson as Chief Mechanical Engineer in keeping with a similar demand made at the Chief Secretary's Office earlier in the day. The text of the resolution was published by *The West African Pilot* of Monday, September 29.

The publication of the resolution seems to have set somebody working. When the men came to work the following morning they found the gates leading to the Mechanical Workshops locked. It was this lock-out which brought Imoudu to the limelight, for it was he who led about 3,000 railwaymen on a protest demonstration to Government House. Although the lock-out affected only the workers in the Mechanical Workshops yet others in the Carriage and Waggon Section and the Stores joined the demonstration. Loco drivers abandoned their trains and also joined the five-mile trek to the Marina. The demonstrators carried placards some of which read 'W. G. W. Wilson Must Go' and 'Wilson Must Go or Die'. The demonstration was peaceful throughout and won great public sympathy. *The West African Pilot* of September 30, 1941, reported that 'all through the route they were blessed by old women and others whom they passed, whilst the whole route was lined by a cheering and sympathetic crowd'. As the demonstrators came close to Government House [the official residence of the Governor] they were diverted by the Police to the Race Course, where the Governor, Sir Bernard Bourdillon, the Chief Secretary to the Government, the Hon. S. A. Thomas and the Hon. Ernest Ikoli met them and listened to their complaints.

Speaking to them, the Governor said he was sorry that they should have walked so long a distance. He added that a 'silly mistake' had been made, and whoever was responsible for it would be punished. Sir Bernard went on to say that the lock-out was not just a mistake; it was an offence against the Defence Regulations. There was a great deal of misunderstanding about the concessions granted in the

Government letter of May 6, and he promised to come to the loco workshop the following day to explain them to the workers. As a compensation for the great trek, the Governor asked the men to go home and regard that day as a holiday.

The promise to come to the loco workshop the following morning was fulfilled. Addressing the workers, Sir Bernard repeated what he said the previous day about the lock-out and added: 'It is going to be a very expensive mistake for the Railway management because yesterday will be treated as if it was a public holiday. In other words those men who did not work will get full pay, and those men in the Running Shed who did work will get double pay.' Sir Bernard said the Union rejected the proposals because it did not understand them. He had discussed the proposals with the Union's President and some other workers, and they gave him the impression they did not understand them either. He then proceeded to explain the concessions one after the other, and when he finished the men were satisfied. Speaking on the demand that Wilson must go, the Governor announced amidst a thunderous ovation that the man had of his own volition asked for leave and transfer, and the request had been granted.

Wilson's exit marked the end of an age, and the opening of a new chapter in conditions of employment and in labour–management relations in the Railway. From October 1, 1941, the hourly rate was abolished and the losses incurred by the workers as a result were made good with effect from 1931. In the Mechanical Workshops 1,270 and in the Running Shed 530 men were absorbed into the permanent establishment which guaranteed 15 days paid leave in the year with free transport, sick leave, regular annual increments subject to good conduct and efficiency, improved promotion prospects and membership of the Provident Fund. These privileges were innovations hitherto unknown to loco men. On October 1, 1942, railway workers celebrated what they called 'Freedom Day' marking the anniversary of the concessions and Wilson's exit. The celebration was attended by the new CME, who appealed for increased productivity.

REFERENCES

1. *Nigeria: Background to Nationalism*, page 213.
2. *The West African Pilot*, June 20, 1946.
3. *The West African Plot*, June 6, 1945.
4. Address by HE the Governor to the Legislative Council, page 8.
5. Nigerian Railway and Colliery: Annual Report for the Financial Year Ending March 31, 1934. Until 1951 the colliery was part of the Nigerian Railway.
6. Despatch to Secretary of State dated October 19, 1938.
7. *The West African Pilot*, May 7, 1941.
8. *The West African Pilot*, September 29, 1941.

4

THE COLA AGITATION

The enactment of the Trade Unions Ordinance and the experience of the Railway Workers' Union encouraged workers in other Government departments and in industry to form unions and seek registration so as to secure legal authority to engage in collective bargaining with their employers or to seek amelioration of grievances relating to wages or other conditions of employment. By the end of 1940, 14 trade unions representing 4,629[1] workers had been registered. By December 1941 the number of registered unions had increased to 41 with a total membership of 17,521.[2] There had been a general dissatisfaction with the existing wage rates and general conditions of employment, but by 1941 the hardships imposed on the workers by war conditions had become the principal grievance.

In July 1941 a representative meeting held in Lagos and attended by the representatives of the Railway Workers' Union, the Posts & Telegraphs Workers' Union, the Nigerian Marine African Workers' Union and the Public Works Department Workers' Union, founded the African Civil Servants Technical Workers' Union 'to protect the interests of African technical workers and establish better understanding between them and the Nigerian Government'.[3] Its principal officers were L. A. Nkedive, President; M. A. O. Imoudu, Vice-President; and C. Enitan Brown, Secretary. The ACSTWU was not a union as such, but a quasi-federal body acting as a rallying point and spokesman for Government technical and unskilled manual employees in all industrial disputes.

Soon after its inauguration, the ACSTWU in collaboration with the CSU and the Nigerian Union of Railwaymen began to agitate for the grant of a cost of living allowance which was then known as 'war bonus'. The agitation eventually led to the appointment in November of that year of a Committee of Inquiry with the following terms of reference:

> To consider the adequacy or otherwise of the rate of pay of labour and of African Government servants and employees in the Town-

ship of Lagos, having regard to any increase in the cost of living which may have occurred since the outbreak of war, and to make recommendations as follows:

(i) whether a temporary increase by way of bonus or other addition to pay should be made;
(ii) whether any other form or relief is desirable such as, for example,
  (*a*) free meals at work;
  (*b*) provision of cheap meals on purchase;
  (*c*) stricter price control;
  (*d*) rent restriction;
  (*e*) provision of quarters or assisted schemes.[4]

The Committee had as its Chairman A. F. B. Bridges, Senior District Officer, and comprised 18 other members including such prominent trade unionists as J. A. Ojo, President of the CSU, and C. Enitan Brown, Secretary of the ACSTWU. Before its report could be published the need for relief had become such a pressing necessity that on December 5, 1941, the Government was obliged to make an interim award of 3d. per day to all Government employees in Lagos whose annual wages or salaries, inclusive of the cost of living allowance, did not exceed £36. The award was without prejudice to any recommendation of the Bridges Committee. Table 3 shows price trends of a few selected articles taking 1939 as a base year.

Table 3

PRICE TRENDS OF SELECTED ARTICLES (LAGOS)[5]

	1939	*1942*	% *increase*
Beef (per lb.)	3d.	5¾	91
Mutton (without bone) (per lb.)	3½d.	7d.	100
Pepper (per lb.)	1d.	2½d.	150
Salt (per lb.)	½d.	2½d.	400
Pawpaw (ripe)	¼d.	1d.	300
Rice (per cwt. bag imported)	32s.	61s. 9d.	92
Milk (doz. tins)	2s. 6d.–3s. 9d.	4s. 6d.–5s. 8d.	86
Beer (bottle)	1s.–1s. 4d.	1s. 7d.–2s. 5d.	48

The Bridges Committee Report was published in July 1942, and among its recommendations were:

(i) That a scheme for the issue of a daily free meal at work to labour, both Government and non-Government, be considered as early as possible in consultation with the principal commercial employers of labour, accredited representatives of the labouring population and representatives of the market women's societies.

(ii) That the provision of good, cheap meals on purchase for the employees of Government and commercial firms be considered at the same time; such a scheme should not be regarded, however, as an alternative to the provision of daily free meals for labour.

(iii) That the existing organisation for the control of prices generally be strengthened and that closer attention be given to the problem of controlling the prices of local foodstuffs if possible in co-operation with the local societies of market women.

(iv) That the provision of quarters or assisted schemes for tenements for the poorer population be given early consideration.

(v) That commercial employers, who at present, do not register the names of, or keep a record of individual payments to, casual labour be urged to do so in the future.

(vi) That commercial employers be advised to adopt provisions for hours of work, pay for overtime, and sick leave with pay on lines of those observed in respect of Government labour.

(vii) That commercial employers be urged to raise the wages of their labour where they are considerably lower than 2s. per diem.

(viii) That a Labour Advisory Board be established in Lagos, comprising the Heads of the principal Government Departments employing labour, representatives of the commercial employers and representatives of the labouring population for the better co-ordination of conditions of employment and for concerted action in the removal of legitimate grievances.

Table 4 shows the cost of living allowances awarded to Government employees throughout the country based on the recommendations of the Bridges Committee and the Provincial Wage Committees. A Government statement announcing the awards on July 25, 1941, said that the awards 'may be varied upwards or downwards as the cost of living increases or decreases'. Later that day Governor Bourdillon reaffirmed the undertaking to review the COLA award when he said in a broadcast: 'When I use the words "final decision"

I do not, of course, mean that the living allowance which is being awarded today will necessarily remain the same figures for the duration of the war; it will be subject to constant review and will be revised whenever a rise or fall in the cost of living appears to make such revision necessary.'[6]

Table 4

COST OF LIVING ALLOWANCE, 1942: DAILY RATED EMPLOYEES

Area	*Grade*	*Basic rate of pay Sept. 1941*	*Oct. 1941*	*Cost of living allowance*	*New daily rate*
		s. d.	s. d.	s. d.	s. d.
Lagos Township	A	1 0	1 0	1 0	2 0
Lagos Colony	B	9	9	4	1 1
NORTHERN PROVINCE					
Ilorin: Province	C	6	6	2	8
Niger: Minna	B	4	4	4	8
Kabba: Lokoja	B	5	5	4	9
Benue: Makurdi	B	3	4	4	8
Jos, Bukuru, etc.	A3	5	5	5	10
Adamawa: Province	C	4	4	2	6
Bauchi: Province	C	5	5	2	7
Bornu: Province	C	4	5	2	7
Zaria: Kaduna and Zaria	A3	5	6	5	11
Kano: Township	A3	6	7	5	1 0
Katsina: Province	C	5	5	2	7
Sokoto	C	4	5	2	7
WESTERN PROVINCE					
Abeokuta: Town	B	9	11	4½	1 3½
Benin: City	B	6	9	4	1 1
Ondo: Province	C	8	9	2	11
Oyo: Ibadan Town	B	9	10	4	1 2
Warri: Town	A2	8	9	6	1 3
Warri: Sapele	A3	8	9	5	1 2
Ijebu: Province	B	8	9	4	1 1
EASTERN PROVINCE					
Port Harcourt, Aba, Calabar, Enugu	A1	8	9	9	1 6
Owerri Province, Calabar Province, Victoria, Buea, Kumba Township	B	6d.–8d.	9	4	1 1
Cameroons, Onitsha, Ogajo Provinces, except places separately named	C1	3d.–5d.	9	—	9

B*

SALARIED EMPLOYEES: SELECTED GRADES

	Lagos Township		*Port Harcourt, Aba, Calabar, etc.*		*Kaduna, Jos, Enugu, etc.*		*Benin City, Onitsha, etc.*	
Basic Rate Oct. 1941	COLA	*New Rate*	COLA	*New Rate*	COLA	*New Rate*	COLA	*New Rate*
£1 10s.	£1 6s.	£2 16s.	19s. 6d.	£2 9s. 6d.	15s.	£2 5s.	12s.	£2 2s.
£2	£1 6s.	£3 6s.	£1	£3	£1	£3	16s.	£2 16s.
£3	£1 10s.	£4 10s.	£1 10s.	£4 10s.	£1 10s.	£4 10s.	£1 4s.	£4 4s.
£4	£2	£6	£2	£6	£2	£6	£1 12s.	£5 15s.
Exceeding £48 p.a. but not exceeding £72	£2		£2		£2		£1 12s.	
Exceeding £72 p.a. but not exceeding £96	£1 10s.		£1 10s.		£1 10s.		£1 4s.	
Exceeding £96 p.a. but not exceeding £128	£1		£1		£1		16s.	
Exceeding £128 p.a. but not exceeding £180	15s.		15s.		15s.		12s.	
Exceeding £180 p.a. but not exceeding £220	10s.		10s.		10s.		10s.	

The COLA awards were a temporary palliative. Although the Government statement had indicated willingness to revise the rates upwards or downwards depending on the trends in the cost of living index, any hope of a downward revision would have been unrealistic. The cost of living was bound to increase for a number of reasons. The war was still on, and local foodstuffs and imported goods were getting scarcer and scarcer. The resources of the country were still very much directed towards the war effort. Indeed, increase in the cost of living had been noted a few months after the payment of the COLA awards. It has been a common experience in Nigeria that, whenever there is a general increase in wages, importers of manufactured goods, retail traders in local foodstuffs and landlords of dwelling houses combine to benefit and sometimes to cheat. Prices of imported goods and local foodstuffs and rentals for bare, sometimes ill-kept rooms suddenly go up, not because of any appreciable increase in the cost of production, but because some people want to take undue advantage of small additions to the pay packet. Thus the workers tend always to be worse off in every general increase in wages, for although they enjoy greater purchasing power in terms of money wages, their real wages continue to fall because of the fall in the value of money.

Table 5

COST OF LIVING INDEX, LAGOS, SHOWING COMPARATIVE INDEX FIGURES WITH DETAILS OF FIVE MAIN HEADS OF EXPENDITURE[7]

Items	*Sept. 1939*	*April 1942*	*Oct. 1942*	*April 1943*	*Oct. 1943*	*April 1944*	*Oct. 1944*
Food	100	153	159	169	185	160	165
Rent	100	103	106	106	106	106	106
Clothing	100	167	178	181	211	215	221
Fuel, light, etc.	100	159	154	160	160	160	166
Other items	100	132	144	147	154	157	159
Index figure	100	147	154	159	174	161	165

Table 5 shows the cost of living index figures for five items in Lagos, and illustrates the changes that had taken place, particularlv in food and clothing, between October 1942 and October 1943. These and the resultant hardships forced the workers to begin a fresh agitation for wage increase. On June 28, 1943, the ACSTWU submitted a memorandum to the Government demanding a 'drastic revision of salaries, wages and other conditions of service'. The organisation had, by this time, gained considerable influence and prestige, and it was hoped that the new agitation would be carried out with the same spirit as had been employed in the COLA agitation. It took as much as fourteen months to get a reply to that letter. In its letter dated August 31, 1944, Government said: 'A general review of emoluments and other conditions of service of Government servants will, it is proposed, be undertaken as soon as possible after the war.'[8]

The reply was disappointing, but it was an undertaking. However, the workers could not wait for the war to end before seeking relief from the hardships imposed by rising prices. For this reason, and considering the 1942 undertaking, the ACSTWU changed the demand for a comprehensive salary review to 'a review of the COLA awards'. Accordingly it addressed a letter to the Government. No reply was received to this letter. In October 1944 the demand was repeated, but still no reply came. The Government's attitude gave rise to the feeling that it was neither prepared to honour its pledge nor was it prepared to take steps to remove an important grievance. This feeling brought a realignment of forces.

Hitherto, the Posts and Telegraphs Inspectors' Union, the Railway Station Staff Union, the Nigeria Union of Nurses and the Railway Typographical Society had not been members of the ACSTWU. The levity with which Government treated correspondence on the COLA revision demand forced the unaffiliated unions to agree to work together with the ACSTWU. At a representative meeting held on February 10, 1945, a Joint Executive of the ACSTWU and the co-operating unions was set up to prosecute the new COLA demand. The emergence of the Joint Executive marked a turning-point in the struggle. What followed thereafter is discussed in Chapter 7.

REFERENCES

1 & 2. *Department of Labour Annual Reports* 1940 and 1941.

3. *The West African Pilot*, July 2, 1941.

4. *Report of the Cost of Living Committee*, Lagos, 1942, page 5.

5. *Report of the Enquiry into the Cost of Living and Control of the Cost of Living in the Colony and Protectorate of Nigeria* by W. Tudor-Davies.

6. *Department of Labour Annual Report 1942*, pages 16 and 17.

7. *Department of Labour Annual Report, 1944*, page 24.

8. *The General Strike; Background Review* by T. A. Bankhole (unpublished manuscript).

5

IMOUDU THE MARTYR

We have seen that the Trade Unions Ordinance of 1938 legalised trade unions and gave them the right to engage in collective bargaining. It follows that any union wishing to take advantage of its provisions must first satisfy the condition of registering according to law. The Railway Workers' Union led by Michael Imoudu was the first to do so, and Imoudu's claim to be 'Labour Leader No. 1', though a creation of *The West African Pilot*, is not unconnected with this coincidence.

Born of a humble family in Ora-Oke in Afemai Division, Benin Province, on November 20, 1906, Michael Athokhamien Ominus Imoudu attended several schools before finishing his elementary education at Agbor Government School in 1927. In 1928, he came to Lagos and joined the Posts and Telegraphs Department as a lineman. He resigned his appointment in 1929, and entered the Nigerian Railway first as a labourer and later as an apprentice turner.

His leadership of the Railway Workers' Union is due, in the main, to the daring role he played in founding the Union, and the leading part he played in the historic demonstration march of railway workers to Government House in 1941. Although bold and fearless the success of that demonstration appears to have made him infatuated, and from then thenceforth he seems to have shown no scruples in fighting whatever and whoever he considered to be the evil forces in the Nigerian Railway.

The troubles which eventually threw him out of the services of the Nigerian Railway are many and varied, and began after the protest demonstration. Imoudu had constant clashes with European officials, some of whom he insulted in and out of season. It has been said that he did so because he took exception to certain things of preferential treatment meted out to Europeans, which was denied to Africans. At that time, for example, all technical and manual workers in the Railway Workshops were expected to return to their work immediately after their breakfast in the mess. Violation was punishable by disciplinary action. It was common knowledge that the rule was strictly applied in violations by Africans, and greatly relaxed when Europeans were involved. Europeans would finish their breakfast and chat for five or ten minutes without suffering any reprisals: a similar violation by an African would earn a warning and sometimes a graded warning. In those days it was a code of ethics for an African to answer a European 'Sir' for almost every word he uttered, and to stand to attention when he spoke to him. Failure to observe this code was treated as misconduct, and many Africans had had their careers ruined by standing against this piece of 'hat-in-hand Uncle Tomism'.

The Europeans whom Imoudu insulted took umbrage, and those who watched him perform were dismayed by his audacity. They reported him to their superior officers, who took appropriate action. Between 1941 and 1943 queries were his constant companion, and he earned the necessary warnings in keeping with existing disciplinary procedure. Matters came to a head on January 23, 1943, when he was summarily dismissed for alleged misconduct and insubordination. Later that day he was served with a detention order under the Nigeria General Defence Regulations, 1941, and removed to Benin Province. The detention order issued by Governor Bourdillon says: 'I am satisfied that it is necessary to prevent you, Michael Athokhamien Ominus Imoudu, acting in a manner prejudicial to public safety or defence.'

But in order to understand what happened and why it happened it is important to bear in mind the following facts:

(i) that the Nigerian Railway was the largest single employer of labour of all the Government departments. In 1940 it employed 18,162 workers, a figure which must have been increased greatly in 1943 because of the war;

(ii) that because of the strength of the Railway Workers' Union and the potential strength of railway workers in general, the attitude taken in an industrial dispute by railway unions is likely to influence the action of other unions, particularly unions of public employees;

(iii) that after the highly successful protest demonstration of 1941, railway workers, particularly those working in loco workshops, believed almost fanatically that the best and most effective method of prosecuting trade union demands is coercion, with railway workers in the vanguard;

(iv) that the success of that demonstration made Imoudu a hero; the feeling then grew, particularly among railway workers, that this hero should always direct activities in industrial disputes requiring coercive action which would force the Government to yield;

(v) that because of the vital role which the railway was playing in the war effort, any rumour that railway services were likely to be impaired by strike action in furtherance of union demands would readily receive credence from a suspecting administration, particularly if the rumour alleged that the spirit was behind the move was the leader of a previous protest demonstration.

For some time before Imoudu's arrest and detention, the Railway Workers' Union had not been having an easy time in the ACSTWU. There had been constant disagreements between its leaders and the leaders of other unions over objectives and strategy, disagreements that dated back to the early days of the COLA agitation in 1941. The awards made in 1942 were accepted under protest, and with mixed feelings. Certain union leaders felt that the workers had had a raw deal because the leadership of the ACSTWU was not as dynamic as they expected. They felt, therefore, that any future agitation must be directed by a more dynamic leader.

Before the end of 1942, complaints were rife that the cost of living had risen considerably. The complaints set many union leaders thinking. Rumours spread that railway workers under the powerful influence of Imoudu were planning to begin a new agitation for wage increase. The rumours did not just stop there: they went further. It was alleged that in the proposed agitation they planned to put the ACSTWU in the shade, and were determined to pursue their demands with methods bordering on sabotage. Rumours of plans to derail trains and remove vital railway stores if the demands were not granted leaked into official quarters, and the administration suspected Imoudu to be the spirit behind these plans. The Government's reaction was swift and decisive: a detention order was issued against him. It was a strange coincidence, for the detention order was served a few hours after his dismissal from service. He was taken into a black car and he disappeared. No one, save the police, seemed to know where he was going, and it was some days before his family and his union knew his whereabouts.

Imoudu thus became a martyr. The workers, particularly his followers at the loco workshops, took it that he was being punished for championing their cause. The more fanatical among them claimed that he had been persecuted because he refused to make a deal with officialdom and thus compromise the workers' demands – an argument implying that union leaders, who would not pursue union demands in the characteristic Imoudu fashion, had made deals with employers. This type of propaganda later developed and became an effective instrument for destroying able and level-headed leadership in Nigerian trade unions, throwing off the 'missionary' and enthroning the 'mercenary', substituting senseless and fruitless rivalry and idolatory for fruitful co-operation, informed, loyal but critical followership and implanting chaos for order and discipline. Nigerian labour history had reached a turning-point.

Soon after Imoudu's arrest and detention, desperate efforts were made by trade unions and politicians to secure his release. On January 24, E. T. Z. Macaulay, General Secretary of the RWU, addressed a letter to the Chief Mechanical Engineer of the Nigerian Railway seeking an interview to discuss Imoudu's dismissal from service and his subsequent arrest and detention. The CME replied that 'the dismissal of Chargeman Imoudu is not a matter which permits of discussion, but I am willing to tell you the reasons why he was dismissed. With regard to the question of alleged arrest I know nothing about this.' Imoudu's case echoed at the Budget Session of the Legislative Council in 1943. On March 17 the Chief Secretary to the Government said in reply to a question by Ernest Ikoli, Third Member for Lagos, that 'Mr. Imoudu was detained under the provisions of the Defence Regulations because it was necessary to prevent him acting in a manner prejudicial to public safety or defence. The Detention Order has now been replaced by a Restriction Order requiring him to reside in a certain area and to report to the Police Station, Auchi, twice a week.'

On March 31, 1943, the RWU forwarded a resolution to Government demanding reasons for the detention of their President, and how long the detention would last. Government reply merely repeated the Chief Secretary's answer to the question in the Legislative Council and added that 'the Restriction Order will remain in force until such a time as the competent authorities shall revoke it'. The efforts of the RWU were supplemented by those of the ACSTWU, the TUC and its President, Timothy A. Bankole, who was also President of the ACSTWU. It is one of the ironies of Nigerian labour history that the same Bankole should have fallen by the wayside as a result of the activities of the man he did his best to get out of restriction. The ACSTWU protested as soon as Imoudu's arrest was known and pleaded with the Government for his release, without avail. Later it appointed a committee to investigate the circumstances leading to his arrest and detention. The committee consisted of T. A. Bankole, C. Enitan Brown, I. S. M. O. Shoenekan and E. T. Z. Macaulay.

Hitherto the ACSTWU took the view that Imoudu's arrest and detention were acts of victimisation of a militant trade unionist, no matter how much they disagreed with him. The evidence which appeared before the Committee showed that the Government's suspicion had not been altogether unfounded.[1]

For obvious reasons, the ACSTWU did not disclose this fact. In the first place such a disclosure would have strengthened Government in its measures against Imoudu, and secondly it could have been interpreted as a betrayal of a worthy colleague, whatever his shortcomings. The ACSTWU pretended to have known nothing, and stuck to its original interpretation of the Government action as an act of victimisation. It frequently appealed to the Government to release Imoudu, or to tell the public what he had done to warrant restriction. For equally obvious reasons the Government did not accept the challenge to tell the public what Imoudu had done. Thus the interpretation given by the ACSTWU stuck with the workers and the general public. Imoudu's martyrdom was confirmed.

In the meantime the ACSTWU held a meeting and considered what further action it should take on the matter. Since pleas for his release had not yielded any good result, it was decided to pray the Government to pay him subsistence allowance for the period of restriction. The request was granted after several appeals, and Imoudu was placed on a subsistence allowance of £128 per annum.

Although the Government would not entertain any request for Imoudu's release, nevertheless the campaign continued. In the vanguard was the ACSTWU and its President, T. A. Bankole. Everywhere was his platform, at home and abroad. While attending the World Trade Union Conference in February 1945, he declared in London that 'the continued restriction of the personal liberty of Mr. M. A. O. Imoudu, President of the Railway Workers' Union, is regarded as a specimen of the exercise of arbitrary power by the Government. No tangible reason has been given to justify the rather uncompromising attitude being maintained by the Government in this matter.'[2]

The campaign for Imoudu's release took a turn for the better on May 14, 1945. On that day *The West African Pilot* published a leading story with a streamer headline captioned '76 Main Sections of Defence Regulations Are Repealed: Mr. M. A. O. Imoudu May Be Released'. Among the sections repealed were numbers 57 and 63 relating to the control of suspected and potentially dangerous persons, under which Imoudu had been arrested and detained. It was apparently after having read the story that Bankole redoubled his efforts for Imoudu's release, but in his enthusiasm to achieve his objective he said something which discretion or second thought would have blushed to own. Such a statement as 'I advised him (J. M. Osindero) to use his influence to prevent his union members, in their own interest, from indiscriminately recalling Mr. Imoudu to active leadership after his return',[3] though sound and probably genuinely motivated, could serve its purpose only where people can hear much and talk little, and regard discretion as the better part of valour. In the prevailing situation at the loco workshops none of these things existed. Wise counsel was regarded as one of those attempts by some trade unionists to compromise the workers' demands. Discretion was a valueless asset because the only language which the loco men knew and which impressed them was force or a demonstration of force.

It is, of course, doubtful whether Imoudu ever heard the advice given to Osindero, and even more doubtful whether the advice given, apparently in strict confidence, leaked from Osindero's quarters. It is possible that Imoudu had some knowledge of this advice, which was sufficient to annoy him and make him more determined to fight Bankole and his colleagues so ruthlessly as he eventually did.

No reply had been received to a series of letters addressed to the Government concerning Imoudu's release, but the publication of the repeal of certain sections of the Defence Regulations provided an opportunity to raise the matter again. Bankole took the initiative and addressed another letter to the Government. No reply came, but he received an oral invitation by telephone to come for an interview. At the interview he was asked whether he could give a guarantee that Imoudu would not 'cause trouble' if released. Bankole did not hesitate to give the assurance, and the interview ended. He returned, and immediately called Osindero, who was then the General Secretary of the RWU, and reported on the interview. It was at this juncture that he gave the advice referred to earlier, and went on: 'I told him I relied on him to see that railwaymen did not cause trouble. He gave me an assurance that nothing would happen, and indeed, nothing happened.'[4]

That was the end of a hard-fought battle. Imoudu was released from restriction, and he returned to Lagos on June 2, 1945, amidst the cheers and jubilation of the workers. Early that day, S. I. Bosah, Acting President of the RWU, urged railwaymen as follows: 'More production today in the name of President Imoudu.' A budding poet, Moses S. Ekpeyong, greeted Imoudu with a poem published in *The Daily Comet* of June 2. Part of the poem runs thus:

In the midst of our woes
Thou didst receive our blows;
Powers assailing;
Re the award of cost of living
'Twas better to die' . . . as the saying goes.
Man took you away to suffer,
God has brought you back to prosper;
Two and half years in exile,
We're sure you're now more virile
To fight the cause of the worker.

A crowd estimated at about 50,000 welcomed Imoudu at the Oko-Awo playgrounds. Addressing the crowd, the veteran politician Herbert Heelas Macaulay said the people wholeheartedly welcomed Imoudu and wished he could carry on his service to the country. Nnamdi Azikiwe, who spoke next, said that Imoudu had paid the penalty of leadership; he had borne the cross, was crucified and he had resurrected and returned full-blooded. He concluded by charging Imoudu as follows:

Courage brother, do not stumble.
Though the path be dark as night;
There's a star to guide the humble,
Trust in God and do the right.

REFERENCES

1. Interview with T. A. Bankhole, February 27, 1963.
2. *The Voice of Coloured Labour*, page 2.
3. *1945 General Strike: A Review of the Background* by T.A. Bankole.
4. Interview with Bankole on February 27, 1963.

6

THE TRADES UNION CONGRESS

The COLA agitation of 1941 showed the strength and influence of organised labour, but it also underscored the need for an organisation representing all sections of labour in Nigeria. The ACSTWU, the Civil Service Union and the Nigerian Union of Railwaymen represented a considerable number of workers, but they suffered from the fact that they represented only public employees in the central Government. The large army of public employees in the local authorities were not represented by any of them, and were not even organised. The need for an organisation that would speak for all sections of organised labour inspired the leaders of the ACSTWU to organise a meeting in Lagos in November 1942, which inaugurated the Federated Trades Unions of Nigeria. What quickened action in this direction was a Government proposal to introduce an essential works order, which the workers suspected would be heavily weighted in favour of employers and against workers.

Soon after its inauguration, the FTU published a manifesto stating 'the ends to which it would use its good offices and defining tersely its method of approach in furthering the cause of Nigerian labour movement. . . . It further pledged itself to be loyal to and co-operate with the Government so long as the latter acted in the best interest of the people.'[1] In April 1943 the FTU published the maiden issue of its official organ, *The Nigerian Worker*. The maiden issue contained brilliant articles and an inspiring editorial captioned 'We Must Unite'. In July of the same year the organisation organised a conference, which adopted a resolution changing the name of the FTU to the Trades Union Congress of Nigeria. The aim and objects of the TUC as entrenched in its constitution were:

(i) to unite all trade unions into one organised body;
(ii) to deal with the general labour problems affecting workers in the whole country;
(iii) to protect the legal status and rights of trade union organisations;

(iv) to see to the proper organisation of trade unions;
(v) to organise annually a congress of all trade unions;
(vi) to establish a workers' newspaper;
(vii) to establish a trade union secretariat;
(viii) to establish a Nigerian Labour College;
(ix) to promote scholarships for trade unionists to study abroad.

The conference adopted many other resolutions 'dealing with such matters as the industrialisation of Nigeria and post-war reconstruction, workers' education and the regrouping of unions according to trade or craft'.[2] Two resolutions called on the Government to nationalise all mining industries, and demanded workers' representation on the Legislative Council. One resolution sought that October 6 to 12, 1943, be proclaimed Workers' Day during which union leaders would undertake a house-to-house collection of funds to finance a workers' secretariat.[3] The conference elected the following officers: T. A. Bankole, President; Chief A. Soyemi Coker, Vice-President; M. A. Tokunboh, Secretary-General; I. S. M. O. Shonekan, Kofi Austin and F. O. Ogunbajo, Under-Secretaries; P. S. Taiwo, Treasurer; and Obafemi Awolowo, Secretary/Editor of *The Nigerian Worker*.

The TUC was accorded official recognition soon after its formation. In furtherance of that recognition the Labour Department instituted a system of monthly consultative meetings with its representatives at which current labour problems were discussed. The TUC also assisted in resolving many industrial disputes. Indeed TUC assistance in this respect has been eloquently acknowledged by the Labour Department itself. In its Annual Report for 1943 the Department says the TUC 'has rendered considerable assistance to the Department of Labour in settlement of disputes and the general application of labour standards'.

The TUC held another conference in August 1944. That conference is remarkable for its representative character, the high quality of its debates and the wide range of subjects discussed. For the first time in central labour affairs, delegates from the Eastern and Northern Provinces attended. In his presidential address Bankole announced that the circulation of *The Nigerian Worker* had reached the impressive figure of 10,000 copies. The report on activities showed, among other things, that officialdom had become so worried about the impact of *The Nigerian Worker* that it decided to place the magazine under official censorship with effect from July 1, 1944. An official statement announcing the censorship said that the magazine had 'contained incorrect statements or allegations of fact and has repeatedly contained unfair and unjustified comments . . . and that such statements, allegations and criticisms are likely to excite disaffection and create or encourage discontent against the Government of Nigeria'.

The conference adopted resolutions relating to (i) the resettlement and rehabilitation of ex-servicemen; (ii) scholarships for training Nigerians for responsible positions in the public service and industry; (iii) social security schemes; (iv) labour participation in schemes for achieving good industrial relations; (v) revision of wages and salaries; (vi) the introduction of a minimum wage of 2s. 6d. per day; (vii) slum clearance; (viii) provision of adequate dwelling houses for workers; (ix) effective rent control; and (x) amendment of the Workmen's Compensation Ordinance to provide improved rates of compensation for industrial and occupational accidents and to cover cases of industrial and occupational diseases, which were then outside the scope of the existing Workmen's Compensation Ordinance.

The TUC influenced labour legislation. An indication of its influence is seen in the Labour Department Annual Report for 1944. The relevant portion reads: 'It was proposed to introduce legislation in 1943 increasing the powers of the Registrar to ensure the proper and punctual rendition of returns. Enactment of the legislation was postponed at the request of the TUC, which asked for time to put things right.' Thus, but for the timely intervention of the TUC, things might have been made more difficult or uncomfortable for the unions, many of them lacking personnel with accounting experience. In a previous report it was stated that 'after careful enquiry and consideration, it was decided to pursue educative rather than punitive policy and thus give growing unions time to secure more efficiency in the conduct of their affairs'. It is a sad fact that this liberal policy has failed, even today, to achieve its purpose.

The TUC showed an intense interest in workers' education. The cordial relationship between the Congress and the Labour Department paved the way for the first trade union education classes ever held in Nigeria. Known as the Summer School for Trade Unionists, the classes opened on January 6 and ended on January 10, 1947. It was a joint venture of the TUC and the Labour Department, and 46 trade unionists from various parts of the country attended. Lectures were given on trade union organisation, collective bargaining, trade union accounts, the wage question and the trade unions, trade unionism and the employer and the functions of the TUC and the Labour Department. In the same year the British Trades Union Congress offered the TUC a scholarship tenable at Ruskin College,

Oxford. This enabled the TUC General Secretary, A. A. Adio-Moses, to proceed to the United Kingdom later that year.

In 1945 the TUC held another conference, which was attended by observer delegates from Sierra Leone and the Gold Coast (now Ghana). After the conference, TUC representatives and the fraternal delegations from Ghana and Sierra Leone discussed the need for a West African Trade Union Federation.[4] A preliminary discussion had taken place earlier in the year, when delegates from Nigeria, Sierra Leone and Ghana were attending the World Trade Union Conference, which paved the way for the founding of the World Federation of Trade Unions. Reporting on the progress made at that discussion, George Padmore, the veteran West Indian journalist, says: 'Imbued by the spirit of unity, the West African delegates have already issued a statement declaring that the time is fully ripe for the formation of a West African Trade Union Federation, and that this should be an immediate objective aiming at co-ordinating the advance of the territory of West Africa as a whole. As a preliminary step they propose the formation of a West African Trade Union Advisory Council, on the approval of the respective West African trade union congresses or their equivalents, which shall consist of the present heads of congresses or their accredited representatives, and which shall meet at any early date in one of the British West African colonies for the purpose of formulating the basis of the proposed federation.'[5]

These and other praiseworthy activities of the TUC later gave way to the schism, which arose out of conflicting views on strategy for prosecuting the 1945 General Strike, an event of tremendous significance in Nigerian labour history. How it began, why it was organised, who was the spirit behind it and what was the outcome, are premises to be covered in the next chapter.

REFERENCES

1. 'The Nigerian Labour Movement: Brief Historical Sketch' by T. A. Bankole (unpublished manuscript).
2. Address by J. M. Johnson to TUCN Conference on April 20, 1960.
3. *The West African Pilot*, August 2, 1943.
4. *Labour Department Annual Report, 1945.*
5. *The Voice of Coloured Labour*, page 5.

7

THE 1945 GENERAL STRIKE

The General Strike of 1945 is one of the most important events in Nigerian labour history. With the exception of the Iva Valley shooting incident of 1949, and the General Strike of 1964, no industrial dispute has so thoroughly shaken the foundations of the Nigerian nation as the tremendous event which began throughout the country at midnight on June 21, 1945. In Lagos, the strike lasted for 44 days, but in the provinces (now Regions) it dragged on for as long as 52 days. Estimates of the total number of workers involved in the strike vary. Coleman puts it at 30,000; Padmore quotes the figure as 150,000. Labour Department figures appear to be more reliable. According to its Annual Report for 1945, the total number of workers involved was 42,951. Of this figure 41,165 were public employees, who were directly involved; the rest were employees of commercial and construction companies, who came out in sympathy.

With the exception of essential services like electricity and the hospitals, the strike hit practically all the technical and industrial establishments of the Government. Even office workers joined in the struggle. Railway and port services were paralysed; telegraph keys and telephones were dead. Never had Nigerian workers demonstrated such impregnable solidarity. Never had they been more united in opposition to bad faith and the injustices of colonial administration.

The immediate cause of this epoch-making event was the unwillingness of the régime to honour its pledges. We have already seen that the Government supplemented the wages and salaries of its employees in 1942 with the grant of a cost of living allowance, and in making that grant promised to review the allowances according to trends in the cost of living index. That undertaking was given by Sir Bernard Bourdillon, who retired as Governor of Nigeria in 1943, to be succeeded by Sir Arthur Frederick Richards (now Lord Milverton of Clifton). If Sir Bernard was the shrewd diplomat, having a temperament and disposition that earned respect and admiration, his successor was precisely the opposite. Sir Arthur seemed to look upon every desire for improvement or reform with a jaundiced eye as unnecessary political agitation, which must be crushed at all costs. This weakness soon became an obsession, and was largely responsible for the strained relationship between him and leading political figures in the country throughout his tenure of office.

The COLA award was made in July 1942, and by early 1943 there were indications of a sharp rise in the cost of living. Table 5 shows that in April 1943 the cost of living was 159 as against 147[1] in July 1942. By October 1943, the index had risen to 174. On the basis of the promise made by Sir Bernard Bourdillon in 1942, the index figure in October 1943 clearly justified a review of the COLA awards. Indeed, if the Government had kept its promise there might have been no general strike in 1945. The tragedy was due to the different characters who happened to be at the helm of affairs in 1942 and in 1945. If promises were bonds to Sir Bernard, they were piecrust to Sir Arthur and his administration.

On March 22, 1945, the Joint Executive of the Government technical workers, set up at the representative meeting of February 10, addressed a letter to the Government demanding a minimum wage of 2s. 6d. for labourers and a 50 per cent increase on the existing COLA with effect from April 1, 1944, 'the date on which His Excellency found it expedient to extend relief by way of a Local Allowance to officials in the Intermediate and Superior Grades of the Civil Service'. The letter painted a lucid picture of the plight of the workers, and reminded the Government 'that most technical workers are "essential workers" under the Defence Regulations and have not only to do a fair day's job but must not refuse to work overtime until they have done 77 hours in the week on pain of imprisonment'. It examined the machinery for determining the cost of living index and said: 'The official barometer known as the Cost of Living Index impresses this Committee as a mysterious jumble of metaphysical figures. We are unable at any rate to realise how these figures can be related to the actual running of African homes often composed of large families. Our representatives on this scientific committee do not seem to know half again as much as ourselves how these mysterious figures are arrived at.' Finally the letter demanded increased COLA 'in order to minimise the tide of fast approaching national disintegration in health and stamina and in order to reduce further sapping of vitality amongst the workers'.

In a letter dated May 2, 1945, the Government admitted that the cost of living had risen because 'certain essential commodities are in short supply, and difficult to obtain'. At the same time it argued that 'there is no evidence that there is any "fast approaching national disintegration in health and stamina" or "sapping of vitality amongst workers", and consequently "His Excellency is not prepared to revise the rate of pay or cost of living allowance" '. The letter blamed rising prices on the unwillingness of the public to co-operate with the Government by 'indicating as suitable for price control commodities of which the price has been forced up by the manipulation of profiteers. Nor does the public assist in enforcing price control of such articles as have been included in price control regulations.' The letter went on: 'Unless the public is willing to do without or reduce the consumption of commodities which are scarce, or to substitute other commodities for them, instead of taking the least line of resistance and buying (regardless of value and price control) in the black market, no benefit will result from increasing cost of living allowance'.[2]

Was the Government fair to its employees in the manner in which it was treating the COLA revision demand, and were the arguments adduced in the letter of May 2 an objective approach to the problem? Answering these questions involves a brief résumé of the experiences gained since the outbreak of war in September 1939. On January 19, 1940, the first price control regulations were made under the Emergency Powers (Defence) Act, 1939. These were subsequently replaced by the Food Control Regulations, Part 6, Section F, of the Nigeria General Defence (Control of Prices) Regulations, 1943, which set up special markets in Lagos island and the mainland, including Apapa, popularly known as 'Pullen Markets'. The Pullen Markets (named after Captain Pullen, Acting Commissioner of the Colony, who was appointed Controller of the Lagos Market Scheme) sold local foodstuffs at controlled prices, which were considerably lower than prevailing prices in the ordinary markets. The purpose of establishing them is stated in the Labour Department Report for 1943: the markets were not intended 'to feed the whole of Lagos, but to provide enough food that could act as a stabiliser by forcing other traders to lower their prices in order to compete with the Government retailers'. Against this background, therefore, the Government argument about buying from the Pullen Markets has to be considered.

The original intention might have been achieved, given two conditions: first, that there was enough food supply available; secondly, that the Pullen Markets had the capacity to serve the population of Lagos. In its Annual Report for 1945 the Labour Department says that 'in May 1945, some of the principal foodstuffs were completely absent from the markets, and the Lagos community had to rely on Pullen Markets'. These markets served only 4,000 people per day out of an estimated population of 200,000.[3] The number of people in wage-earning employment in Lagos at the time was about 45,000, of which number more than half, both bachelors and married men, were not living with their families because of the housing shortage in the city. These people were always at work, when the Pullen Markets were open, and therefore could not buy from them and enjoy the benefit of the low prices. They lived at the mercy of profiteers.

The fact that a large number of the population could not buy from the Pullen Markets encouraged those who could to take undue advantage of the situation. Families who had unemployed relatives living with them devised a means of increasing the family income by getting the unemployed persons to join housewives to go and buy from the Pullen Markets. By so doing they doubled and sometimes trebled the quota of foodstuffs they were entitled to buy at a particular time. The increased quota was sold to those unable to take advantage of the Pullen scheme at prices ranging from 100 to 300 per cent above the purchase prices. The lust for making easy money, and the opportunity for doing so thus created, accounted for the great disorders which were a regular feature of the Pullen Markets. Those disorders invariably frightened away some people, particularly pregnant women, who would have wished to buy from them. These unfortunate women and their families joined the ranks of the victims of profiteers.

The Government argument about the Pullen Markets implies that the great rise in the cost of living was confined to Lagos. Indeed, the findings of the Provincial Wage Committees set up about the same time as the Bridges Committee show that this was not the case. Thus, if the Pullen Markets had been the magic wand for solving the problem in Lagos, something had still to be done to meet the situation in the Provinces. The tragedy of the official attitude was that the wiseacres of the Nigerian Secretariat took the COLA demand as a Lagos agitation and not a Nigerian problem.

If the Government's refusal to grant relief by way of increased COLA was applied to all its employees its stand might have been understandable, although the reasonableness of such a stand in the face of the realities of the situation would have been in doubt. But it went out of the way to give special relief to Europeans, and thus strengthened, if not created, the accusation that its refusal to concede the demand was based on racial discrimination and not on ability to pay. In May 1942, the Government introduced the payment of 'separation allowance' to Europeans, whose wives were not living together with them in Nigeria. Under this dispensation an officer on a salary of £400 per annum was paid £128. In November 1943 it was 'decided to increase the amount of separation allowance and to make it payable for other dependents as well as for wives'.[4] The new concession enabled those who received £128 to be paid £160 with effect from December 1, 1943. In August 1944 the payment of 'local allowance' was introduced with effect from April 1, 1944. This gave officers on £400 per annum, whose wives were living with them in Nigeria, an extra £84 per annum. For the first time it was decided to extend the payments to Africans holding what were then known as 'superior posts'. But, although Africans were to receive local allowances, they were to be paid only three-quarters of the amount that a European received. The reason for this discriminatory treatment is given in Circular No. 45/1944 as follows:

> An African Officer in a superior post will be treated in accordance with the present practice that a quarter of a European officer's emoluments is expatriation pay; he will draw 75% of the European allowance.[5]

In 1945 local allowance rates were revised, and the revision brought Europeans receiving £84 to £96; Africans receiving £63 got £72 with effect from January 1, 1945. In contrast, the wages and salaries of Nigerian workers, whose claim for 2s. 6d. minimum daily wage and 50 per cent increase in the existing COLA was so strenuously resisted, were:

DAILY RATED UNSKILLED LABOURERS (PRINCIPAL TOWNS)

Lagos	2s.
Port Harcourt	1s. 6d.
Kaduna, Jos, etc.	10d.
Ibadan, Abeokuta, etc.	8d.

MONTHLY SALARIED EMPLOYEES

Artisans	£3 19s.
Skilled craftsmen and Clerical grades	£7
Chargemen and Assistant Chief Clerks	£8–£14
Foremen and Chief Clerks	£15–£18

On May 19 a mass meeting was held at the Glover Memorial Hall under the auspicies of the Joint Executive. The meeting, which was attended by representatives of the seventeen co-operating unions representing a cross-section of technical and manual workers in Government industrial establishments, resolved among other things:

(i) that we strongly deplore the callous attitude of Government to the sufferings of the masses of African workers, mostly with large families, as set out in a previous memorandum issued by the African Civil Servants Technical Workers' Union (Nigeria) and followed by a reminder on the dates respectively December 14, 1944, and March 22, 1945;

(ii) that we deprecate and view with disaffection the class discrimination introduced, as between African and African, by the extension of local allowances to Africans holding so called European posts, whereby an official of that class enjoying a salary of £300 per annum is eligible for an allowance of £72, as against COLA of 10s. per mensum payable to a member of the African staff also enjoying a salary of £300 per annum;

(iii) that the Chief Secretary to the Government be informed in distinct terms that the situation can no longer be sustained;

(iv) that in the name of equity we demand immediate revocation of this discriminatory award hereinafter described;

(v) and further that, failing to grant in full (repeat in full) with effect from April 1, 1944, the extremely modest demand contained in the letter No. ACSTWU/6/91 of May 22, 1945, to wit:

Labour: Minimum daily wage to be 2s. 6d.
Subordinate Grade between Labour and Standard Grades: 50 per cent increase on the existing COLA.

Standard scale:

£48–£128	£3 COLA per month
£136–£220	£2 10s. COLA per month
£240–£300	£2 COLA per month
£310–£400	£1 10s. COLA per month

Super scale:

£420–£600	£1 COLA per month

within one calendar month hence, i.e. not later than Thursday, June 21, 1945, the workers of Nigeria shall proceed to seek their own remedy with due regard to law and order on the one hand and starvation on the other.

This resolution was transmitted to the Government on May 21. On May 30, a four-man delegation of the Joint Executive interviewed the Acting Chief Secretary to the Government, G. F. T. Colby, on the resolution of May 19. The delegation consisted of T. A. Bankole, J. M. Osindero, J. O. Erinle and A. Abosede. The delegation stressed the need for relief of the hardships imposed on the workers by war conditions, and the determination of the workers to go on strike if their claims were not met before the deadline. The Acting Chief Secretary promised to present their views to the Governor and to advise them of the Government's decision in due course.

In the meantime, things were happening behind the scene. Imoudu, who had just returned from restriction, had been holding discussions with some workers and some union leaders. On June 6 he visited Bankole, and both leaders discussed the COLA and the minimum wage claim. Bankole says of that visit: 'After exchanging cordial greetings with me, Mr. Imoudu himself initiated discussion over the COLA dispute, revealed that rumours had prevailed that the workers would eventually strike if not granted their just demands, but finally unequivocally expressed preference for all possible constitutional measures to a general strike. For once since our trade union connection, Mr. Imoudu's views apparently harmonised with mine; for our ideas over local policies on all previous occasions had always been poles apart. Mr. Imoudu, accompanied by me at his request, then made for Mr. Osindero's somewhere along Glover Street, Ebute Metta, where, in the presence of the latter, he confirmed the views he had expressed to me on the COLA issue. Happily, Mr. Osindero was agreeable to these views, particularly as the members of his union had expressed themselves not in a position to strike.'[6]

On June 7 a representative meeting of all the unions concerned met again at St. John's School Hall, Aroloya, to consider what further action should be taken, since the Government's final attitude was unknown. The meeting marked another turning point in the history of the COLA demand, for it witnessed the first signs of schism over strategy. Nine unions, including the Railway Workers' Union and the African Loco Drivers' Union, signified their intention to abide by the resolution of May 19 if the demands were not met within the deadline; six unions, including the Nigerian Marine African Workers' Union, the Lands and Survey African Technical Workers' Union and the Lagos Town Council Workers' Union, favoured an extension of the deadline in the hope that the Government might signify its intention to negotiate before the deadline, a belief apparently built on the trends of the discussions between the Acting Chief Secretary and the Joint Executive delegation on May 30. The Nigerian Union of Nurses appeared to be the only union which had not yet made up its mind. In view of the conflicting views expressed, it was agreed that the executive committee of each union should consult with its rank and file and indicate their reaction to strike action if the Government failed to concede the demands before June 21, or authorise the Joint Executive to proceed if the Government offered to negotiate.

On June 11, the Government replied to the resolution of May 19. The reply not only rejected the workers' demands, but introduced a new argument, which the Supreme Council of Nigerian Workers later described as an 'inflation bogey'. The letter said: 'To accede to a request for increased COLA would result in the present circumstances in adding materially to the circulation of currency at a time when the objects on which the increase could be spent are remaining static or even decreasing in volume. The result would be inevitable. A higher pressure of purchasing power would be applied to the same quantity of goods with the result that prices would rise still further and the wage earners would be no better off. . . . In the circumstances and in the sincere conviction that an increase in COLA would operate to the detriment of the wage earners themselves and of the general situation, His Excellency regrets that he is unable to accede to the request that the cost of living allowance and daily rates should be increased.'

Commenting on this letter, *The Daily Comet* of June 15 said: 'We have read Government reply with care, and as far as we can see it is based on the assumption that if prices of rice, gari and palm oil can be forced down, the African workers' wages may safely be frozen where they now stand. We are afraid we cannot subscribe to this view because it is a faulty belief that one or two cheap foodstuffs can cause any material improvement.' The editorial suggested that the cost of all foodstuffs and the imported articles, house rents, school fees, agricultural tools, books and everything which affected the life of the African worker should be frozen to the December 1942 prices. After freezing all those it was possible to freeze, earnest efforts should be made to find out the rise in the cost of living index caused by increased prices of those items which it was impossible to freeze, and to adjust wages accordingly.

The Government's letter of June 11 was the last straw. The workers felt that their appeal to reason had failed, and with its failure came contempt for any union leader preaching the gospel of sanity in a confused situation. The African Loco Drivers' Union set the ball rolling in a frenzy of notices of strike action, which followed the publication of the Government's letter in the press two days later. On June 14 the union notified the General Manager of the Nigerian Railway that it would call out its members on strike at midnight of June 21 if the workers' demands were not granted to loco drivers before that day. A delegation of the Railway Workers' Union, led by Acting President S. I. Bosah, later met the General Manager and gave a similar notice.

A mass meeting of about 8,000 irate workers considered the Government's letter on June 16. The meeting was attended by representatives of the seventeen unions involved, including those of the Nigerian Civil Service Union, the Federal Union of Native Administration Staff, registered in 1943, and the Nigerian Union of Railwaymen. The meeting reaffirmed the resolution of May 19, but decided to leave the door open for negotiation should the Government offer to negotiate before the deadline. The meeting also endorsed the decision of the Joint Executive to set up a Workers' Security Fund (a sort of strike fund). Bankole reports that 'an aggregate of over £1,000 had been collected up to that date'. On his suggestion, 'the meeting finally decided not to take over the component amounts from the different unions until a custodian and board of management had been appointed'. Unfortunately this noble scheme could not be continued because the schism took a turn for the worse.

On June 18, the TUC held its usual consultative meeting with the Labour Department. The Commissioner of Labour took the opportunity of that meeting to point out an anomaly in the actions of the Joint Executive which violated the Defence Regulations. Section 156 of the Regulations provides that 'an employer shall not declare or take part in a lockout, and a workman shall not take part in a strike in connection with any trade dispute unless the trade dispute has been formally reported to the Governor and the Governor has not within 21 days of the receipt of the report directed that the dispute shall be determined in accordance with the provisions of this Part'. Violation was punishable with a fine of £20 or two months imprisonment or both fine and imprisonment. After reading the relevant section of the Regulations the Commissioner assured the TUC representatives that he would be prepared to intervene if only the Joint Executive could follow the procedure laid down by law.

The TUC Working Committee met later that day, and decided to contact the leaders of the Joint Executive and persuade them to follow the course suggested by the Commissioner. Its leaders volunteered to make the necessary contacts. That evening they met the General Secretary of the Joint Executive, J. Marcus Osindero, and the President of the African Loco Drivers' Union, and convinced both of them. They later met the Executive Committee of the RWU, holding a meeting which was presided over by its President, M. A. O. Imoudu. The men also convinced the RWU Executive. Railway workers, particularly members of the Railway Workers Union, were generally a difficult lot, and to secure their co-operation in any general industrial dispute was to secure the support of the most volatile trade unionists in the country.

Having thus secured the co-operation of the RWU, the TUC leaders, some of whom were also the leading officers of the Joint Executive, addressed a letter on behalf of the Joint Executive notifying the Commissioner of the existence of a trade dispute. The Commissioner said he was unable to accept the letter as a notification of dispute since the letter conveyed 'a definite action already agreed upon by one of the parties, thus rendering the procedure laid down in the Regulations unworkable'. At 7 p.m. that day, Sir Gerald Whitley, Officer Administering the Government, broadcast to the nation. Referring to the workers' decision to go on strike, he said that such a strike would be illegal, and if they took the action they should be prepared to face the consequences. 'It is my duty' Sir Gerald said, 'to see that the law is upheld and it is my duty to see that essential services are maintained. I shall do my duty as I have always tried to do it, without fear or favour, and my friendship with the workers is not going to make me fail in my duty.'[8]

The Commissioner's letter and Sir Gerald's broadcast were considered by a representative meeting which was held later that night, attended by about 300 delegates. The choice before the meeting was either to comply with the Commissioner's requirements, which meant postponing the strike, or to carry out the strike threat and damn the consequences. The choice produced two schools of thought, the moderates and the extremists. The moderates, headed by the leaders of the Joint Executive, favoured a postponement of the strike so as to afford the Government and the workers an opportunity to negotiate, and when negotiation failed to call out the workers on strike. The extremists, led by persons who held no positions in the Joint Executive, felt that postponing the strike was a sign of weakness and a capitulation to official threats. Indeed, F. Modupe Alade, President of the African Loco Drivers' Union, emphasised the point when he called upon Bankole to resign his position of Chairman of the Joint Executive if he felt unable to lead the strike – a suggestion which was greeted with an admixture of shouts of approval and rejection. In the teeth of stern opposition, the meeting decided to call on every union to prevail upon its members to be calm and await the outcome of negotiation, which it believed would soon begin. In accordance with this decision, the Joint Executive issued a release on June 20 informing the workers that the proposed strike had been postponed for 14 days with effect from June 19. The release was signed by J. O. Erinle, Secretary of the ACSTWU, and J. Marcus Osindero, Secretary of the Joint Executive.

Another turning-point had been reached in the struggle. It is one thing for people to take a decision, and quite a different thing for them to get their followers to abide by it. This is particularly so when there is a powerful under-current at work. The experience gained at the Loco Workshop the following day is a case in point. A mass meeting of the RWU was held on June 20, and was attended by leading officers of the Joint Executive who, having heard of the explosive situation in the Railway Workshops, wanted to explain to the workers the decision of the previous day and the reasons for that decision. The meeting was first addressed by Imoudu, who least expected the officers of the Joint Executive to be present. Dressed like a juju priest and brandishing his horse tail fan, which his followers and admirers believed to be the secret of his power and iron will, Imoudu tried to create an impression that negotiation would serve no useful purpose, and that anybody advocating negotiation was a traitor to the workers' cause.

Bankole reports what transpired thereafter as follows: 'I then mounted the rostrum and, after successfully silencing the men, reminded them of part (*d*) of the resolution passed four days previously (to which they were privy), and in a quarter of an hour explained the position to the minutest detail. My conviction, based on their previous sober reaction, is that the men – if left completely alone – would have preferred negotiation to an immediate strike. Without allowing some moments for reflection, Mr. Imoudu, apparently bewildered by the prevailing quiet, overtook me upon the rostrum, and with a stentorian voice, counteracted the effect of my reasoned appeal in the following terms:

> ' "I am the President and owner of the Railway Workers' Union throughout Nigeria, and I am going to speak for you. Am I not going to speak for you? [Shouts of 'Yes, yes'.] Negotiation has failed. We are going on strike on 22nd." '

'After re-echoing the last sentence of Mr. Imoudu's declaration the men sprang frantically upon their feet and staring at me shouted thief, thief, you have been bribed; the Government has bribed you.'[9]

Opposition to the decision of the representative meeting of June 19 was not limited to the loco workshops. Similar signs of disapproval were also noted at the Marine Dockyard, Apapa. By 4 p.m. the situation at the dockyard had so deteriorated that three leaders of the Nigerian Marine African Workers' Union were compelled to come to Bankole at the close of work to seek advice. While the men were discussing with him, four leading trade unionists from the Railway came in. They were M. A. O. Imoudu, S. P. Wilhem, E. T. Z. Macaulay and Odugbesan. According to Bankole they 'came purposely to discuss the possibility of disposing of the mess so wantonly made by Imoudu that afternoon'. The discussion ended with agreement that Imoudu and Macaulay should use their influence to dissuade railway workers from going on strike on June 22.

In the belief that a rapprochement had been reached, and that all the parties to the discussion would be faithful to their pledge, permission was obtained for the release of some leaders of the Joint Executive and the TUC to undertake a 'persuasion' mission to Government industrial establishments with a view to paving the way for securing approval for negotiation, which was to be discussed at a mass meeting in the evening of June 21. The 'persuasion' mission split itself into three teams. Team 1, consisting of J. O. Erinle and A. Abosede, took the Government Printing Department, the Public Works Department and the General Post Office. The situation in these places was fairly well in hand, so the team easily secured the workers' support for negotiation. Team 2, consisting of I. S. M. O. Shonekan and P. S. Taiwo, took the Loco Workshops and the Marine Department. The situation in both these places was explosive; the emissaries were chased out with stones. Apparently little or nothing had been done by the union leaders on the lines agreed to at the meeting of the previous night. Team 3, consisting of T. A. Bankole, E. A. Songonuga and A. A. Adio-Moses, took the Posts and Telegraphs Workshop, the P. & T. Technical School and the Lagos Town Council. In these places the situation was also well in hand and the team secured the same support as Team 1.

Teams 1 and 3 later attended a meeting at the Iga Idungaran, convened by His Highness Oba Fabolu of Lagos, to consider the crisis with leading trade unionists. The meeting agreed that the Oba should send some of his chiefs to attend the mass meeting and speak to the workers. From the Oba's Palace the combined team proceeded to the PWD Sawmill at Ijora, where the battle was thickest. Imoudu had visited there earlier, and had worked up the minds of the workers in favour of strike action. Thus when the team arrived they were chased out, and only the timely intervention of the works manager, R. C. S. Fowler, saved them from being beaten up. The team visited two other places and later returned to Lagos island to find that Imoudu's campaign had completely turned the table.

That was the end. The members of the Joint Executive consulted among themselves and resigned en masse 'in view of the fact that the mass of the workers has misconstrued the good intention of their leaders in advising peaceful negotiation'.[10] Their joint letter of resignation was published in the press the following day.

The resignation of the members of the Joint Executive had far-reaching consequences. First, it strengthened the allegation, which however was absolutely unfounded, that those campaigning for negotiation had made a deal with the Government, an unfortunate accusation worsened by the fact that, having resigned, the leaders failed to turn up at the mass meeting which they themselves had arranged. The thousands of irate workers who attended the meeting believed the allegation to be true. If it were not, they argued, why did Bankole and his colleagues not attend the meeting and explain their stand to the workers? Secondly, it showed Imoudu for the second time as the workers' champion, and an incorruptible one at that. Imoudu thus rose from a departmental to a national hero of the working class. Thirdly, it made it impossible for the Government to arrest and prosecute any strike leader for organising an illegal strike. Undoubtedly the Government would have liked to do so, but the doubt and confusion, created by the unexpected resignation of the Joint Executive who were known to be organising the strike, made the possibility of a successful case rather remote.

Perhaps it was the search for a scapegoat which led the Administration to ban from July 8 to August 15 *The West African Pilot* and *The Daily Comet*, two leading national daily newspapers of the Zik Group, which gave the workers wholehearted support. In order to effect the ban, wide powers were given to the Governor under Emergency Powers (Defence) Act, 1939 and 1940 (Regulation No. 19/45), to prohibit any publications in Nigeria and to penalise every editor, manager or director connected with such publication. In answer to these powers *The West African Pilot* of July 7 published the immortal words of James Russell Lowell

They are slaves who fear to speak
For the fallen and the weak;
They are slaves who will not choose
Hatred, scoffing and abuse;
Rather than in silence think,
From the truth they needs must shrink;
They are slaves who dare not be
In the right with two or three.

On its front page in the same issue, the *Pilot* reminded the Administration that

> A free press is the most watchful of the state. A 'yes' press is fatal to good Government.

Truth crushed to earth shall rise again;
Th'eternal years of God are hers;
But errors, wounded writhes in pain,
And dies among his worshippers.

The General Strike began as planned. But were the workers justified in going on strike in the manner that they did? Did Bankole and his colleagues betray the workers by leading them to the brink of battle and 'deserting' them? Did Imoudu, in his efforts to ensure that the strike was not postponed, act with the responsibility expected of a union leader? Obviously these are questions on which opinions are bound to differ. If the workers must be rebuked for not honouring their pledge, having at a previous meeting agreed to respond if the Government offered to negotiate, the Government itself stands condemned for deliberately provoking an unfortunate situation. Apart from its unwillingness to fulfil its own promise, there is no indication that it was ever prepared to negotiate, let alone reach an agreement. The technicalities raised by the Commissioner of Labour can hardly be an objective approach to an explosive and rapidly deteriorating situation. It is little wonder that Imoudu should have concluded that negotiation would not serve any useful purpose, since all indications pointed to the obvious unwillingness of the Government to yield ground. Bankole and his colleagues might have had good reasons to be hopeful that the Government was willing to negotiate, but the whole drama points out the futility of being a gentleman in an encounter with a rascal.

Be that as it may, credit must go to Bankole and his colleagues for not offering to lead a strike they considered to be ill-timed. For one thing they might not have made a success of it. There is little doubt that but for Imoudu's activities there might have been no General Strike on June 22. It might still have taken place but not on that day. If these activities were intended to help the workers win some concessions, as apparently they were, then their reasonableness or otherwise can be measured from the fact that no concessions were granted until the end of the negotiations, which began on August 24, twenty days after the strike had been called off. Thus what was achieved by strike action might still have been achieved through collective bargaining. This would have saved the workers and the nation the untold hardships and losses that followed.

The strike was called off on Saturday, August 4. As Monday was a Bank Holiday, normal business life did not return in Lagos until August 7. In the Provinces the strike dragged on till the 14th, mainly because the workers did not believe that the numerous

'Strike Called Off' telegrams sent from Lagos were authentic. Delegations of workers' leaders had to undertake, at Government expense, a tour of the Provinces to assure the workers that the strike had in fact been called off.

The General Strike received profound sympathy inside and outside the country. Throughout the country people took it as a justified struggle by the workers for a better standard of living, and they also felt they were witnessing a calculated act of persecution against Nnamdi Azikiwe and his newspapers on the part of the Government. Coleman claims that 'Azikiwe emerged from that event with enhanced prestige and a reputation as the champion of labour'. Anthony Enahoro, who was the Editor of *The Daily Comet* during the strike, claims that 'the consensus of opinion in the Provinces was, and still is, that Nnamdi Azikiwe engineered and inspired the strike'.[11] In the United Kingdom, meetings organised jointly by the West African Students' Union and the International African Service Bureau in London, Manchester and Liverpool raised a total of £225 to support the strikers.[12] The London meeting deplored the refusal to grant the workers' demands, the 'fascist methods' adopted to stifle public opinion by the banning of the *Pilot* and the *Comet*, the alleged threat to deport Zik and the deliberate policy of racial discrimination in the public service pursued by the Government of Nigeria.

REFERENCES

1. *Labour Department Annual Report, 1943.*
2. *Report of the Enquiry into the Cost of Living and the Control of the Cost of Living in the Colony and Protectorate of Nigeria*, by W. Tudor-Davies, page 69.
3. *Labour Department Report, 1945.*
4. Tudor Davies Report, page 214.
5. Tudor Davies Report, page 217.
6. T. A. Bankole, *The 1945 General Strike: Background Review.*
7. T. A. Bankole, *The 1945 General Strike: Background Review.*
8. *The West African Pilot*, June 20, 1945.
9. Ibid.
10. *The Daily Comet*, June 22, 1945.
11. *Nnamdi Azikiwe: Saint or Sinner*, page 16.
12. *The Voice of Coloured Labour*, page 45.

8

THE TUDOR DAVIES COMMISSION

The negotiations, which started after the General Strike had been called off, ran into difficulty on August 29. On that day the Government made an offer of a 3d. increase on the existing COLA for Lagos and promised to increase the COLA for the workers in the Provinces by 20 per cent. The offers were rejected on the ground that they were too small. The Chief Secretary to the Government, G. Beresford Stooke, appealed to the workers' representatives (F. O. Coker of the Postal Workers' Union; G. U. Umeanya of the P. & T. Linemen Union; J. M. Osindero of the Railway Workers' Union, S. A. Olukoya of the PWD Workers' Union; M. K. Antonio of the Railway Station Staff Union; E. A. Oyetoro of the Railway Typographical Society; E. O. Smith of the Marine Workers' Union; T. U. Udoh of the Postal Workers' Union; Luke M. E. Emejulu of the Railway. Workers' Union; T. O. E. Okparake of the RWU, Enugu, and H. O. Oluwole, Northern Provinces Representative) to consider the offer carefully and make a statement at a resumed meeting scheduled for September 4. He warned, however, that if the offers were rejected the alternative would be to appoint a commission of enquiry, which would take some time. If the men opted for an enquiry, the Government would withdraw its offer and wait for the recommendations of the commission.

At the resumed meeting on September 4, the workers' representatives reaffirmed their rejection of the Government offers and accepted the alternative of a commission of enquiry. In keeping with this request, the Secretary of State for the Colonies appointed a commission of enquiry in October 1945, with the following terms of reference:

> To consider the representations made by the Nigerian Government and Native Authority employees concerning an increase in the cost of living allowance and, having regard to the present cost of living and other relevant factors, to make recommendations as to whether any action should be taken by the Nigerian Government,

whether by variation of the cost of living allowance or by controlling the cost of living, or in any other way; and to make recommendations as to the future compilation and computation of the cost of living in Nigeria.

The commission consisted of W. Tudor Davies, Commissioner; and F. W. Dalley and G. P. W. Lamb, Assessors. The commission started work late in November, and continued till March 1946, during which time it toured various parts of the country taking evidence and receiving memoranda from several organisations and individuals. Among them were representatives of Government and of the Supreme Council of Nigerian Workers – an *ad hoc* organisation set up to present the workers' case to the commission; the Government Press Technical Workers' Union; the Land and Survey African Technical Workers' Union; and the Trades Union Congress of Nigeria representing fifty-six affiliated unions.

In its fearless 225-page report covering special problems of Nigeria, the development of trade unionism and industrial relations, the Tudor Davies Commission said that 'from the evidence submitted by the trade unions and the Government it is clear that Sir Bernard Bourdillon, in his broadcast speech of July 24, 1942, made a definite promise, and the trade unions are fully justified in expecting implementation of that promise'. The Commission rejected the Government argument about inflation, arguing that while too much money in the hands of the *entire* population chasing too few goods might cause inflation, nevertheless it could not 'agree that cost of living allowances, paid for not by means of bank credits or the printing of extra paper money but by means of taxation or diversion of existing Government expenditure, and paid not to the entire population or to a large part of it but only to Government employees, could involve the country in the widespread inflation, which the Government seems to fear'.

The commission described as irrelevant the Government's argument that it could find the money with which to pay the increased cost of living allowance only by means of increased taxation, or by means of postponing essential social and development work. Maintaining that inability to pay had not been established, the commission pointed out that Government estimates of revenue and expenditure and the memoranda on them indicated considerable increases in proposed taxation without any reference to the cost of living allowance. The report declared: 'The Commission does not feel that the purposes on which it is proposed to spend the proceeds of that taxation are invariably more necessary than increasing the cost of living of the African civil servants.'

The commission said it was unable to attach any significance to the memoranda submitted by the General Manager of the Nigerian Railway, the Director of Public Works and the Commissioner of Labour, to support the Government's case. Regarding the first two, the commission pointed out that 'many factors enter into efficiency of output besides those which the General Manager and the Director of Public Works took into consideration: problems of industrial efficiency are economic problems of which technical matters are only a small part'. It said that many of the figures about comparable wage-rates submitted by the Commissioner of Labour were figures within ranges too wide for proper deductions to be made.

Turning to allowances paid to European civil servants, the commission said it was unable to accept the Government contention that they were not within its terms of reference. Whether the Government could rightly pay allowances to Europeans and whether that payment involved the danger of inflation were, in the commission's judgement, relevant factors when the Government put forward as part of its argument against increasing the cost of living of African employees the contention that such increases would be illegitimate or inflationary. It was the commission's considered opinion that the capacity to pay argument and the inflation argument apply as much to allowances paid to Europeans and to Africans.

The Commission dealt at length with the price level and the Government offer, and said that since 1939 the price level had doubled. On the basis of that fact the Government offer of a 20 per cent increase with effect from August 1, 1945, was too small. Consequently it recommended that:

(i) the cost of living allowance existing in July 1945 be increased by 50 per cent with effect from the various dates on which work was resumed after the General Strike;

(ii) the 50 per cent award should apply not only to Africans earning £220 per annum or less but also to the special allowances paid since October 1944 to African employees, whose salaries were over £220, except for those receiving local allowances because they held superior posts;

(iii) although the future cost of living allowances payable under (i) and (ii) would be payable together with the future wages in the normal way, the retrospective cost of living allowances, which were also payable under (i) and (ii), should be paid to the African civil servants by being credited to them in Post

C*

Office Savings Accounts or in Bank Accounts, or in the various Treasuries from which they drew their pay;

(iv) the award should remain in force until a new wage structure was set up by a team of statistical officers and nutritionists, which should be set up within two years from the date of the report.

The commission then examined the machinery for determining the cost of living indices, and said that the basis of computation in the Bridges Committee Report was unsatisfactory. It congratulated the authors of the report for the enthusiasm with which they carried out their task and the tenacity with which one of them defended the report, when it was under fire. But, the commission remarked, their zeal outran their judgement, for the report was defective on four grounds. First, it endeavoured to apply a technique of analysis which had doubtful application even to the problems of the United Kingdom, let alone the more intricate problems of Nigeria. Secondly, it was based on far too cursory an investigation of the facts: for example, to base a cost of living index affecting the incomes of thousands of workers on the expenditure pattern of 256 households. Thirdly, it was based on statements which, the commission pointed out, were not facts. Fourthly, in view of the purposes for which the committee was set up and for which the index figure was required, the report was too complex. In the circumstances 'the commission feels much sympathy with the trade union leaders, who referred to the 1942 report as a mysterious jumble of metaphysical figures'.

As an alternative to the cost of living surveys of the Lagos type, the commission recommended that the Government, in consultation with the representatives of the African civil servants, should compile properly thought-out statements in terms of a small number of essential items of expenditure, of what in fact the cost of living was if people spent their money wisely: these compilations should be both a record of movements of the cost of living and an indication of the best expenditure patterns. Thirty-five items of expenditure in Lagos and other towns and twenty-five items in the rural areas would give quite as accurate a result as would many more items. It was important, the commission went on, that the indices thus prepared should be based on a reasonable assumption regarding the size of the normal family: for example, on the assumption that the normal family comprised husband, wife, one other adult, and five children, and that the total of eight persons considered together were equivalent to five adults. By this means the indices would be studies not only in the movement of the cost of living but also of the essential minimum expenditure and the essential minimum wage.

The commission then reviewed the development of trade unionism in Nigeria and observed that quite a number of workers' organisations registered as trade unions were mere 'house associations', which would not be recognised as trade unions by either the British TUC or the international trade union movement. The development of the unions had been allowed by law. The object of those who framed the Trade Unions Ordinance and the Arbitration and Conciliation Ordinances was clearly not to regulate the activities of unions but to help them develop 'a responsible character'. Unfortunately the Ordinances were loosely drawn and were too much on the British legal model, without sufficient recognition of local circumstances. Referring to the role of the Labour Department in advising unions, the commission said that advice by a Government department, no matter how disinterested, particularly to unions catering for Government employees, was bound to be viewed with suspicion. Moreover, Government advisers themselves were not fully aware of the importance of establishing appropriate organisations or even of the principle of trade unionism – a fact acknowledged by no less a personage than Sir Arthur Richards, the Governor, when addressing the Legislative Council on December 10, 1945. Said Sir Arthur: 'This Government is also to some extent to blame, for it is more than probable that wise advice at the time when unions were in their infancy would have guided workers into recognition of the main principles of trade unionism, but unfortunately trade unions were allowed to develop on the lines of a family council or friendly society composed of all the employees of one firm or person, and in some instances the employer himself became the president of the union.'

The commission said that the difficulties confronting trade union leaders in the country were many and varied. If the unions were to get over their 'teething troubles' they needed not only sympathetic encouragement but the sort of help given to the British working class in the nineteenth century by prominent humanists.

On industrial relations, the commission observed that a Labour Advisory Board was set up in January 1944 to advise the Government on all labour questions, but the Board had no executive powers; furthermore, there was little operation of conciliation machinery with regard to wages and conditions of employment. In the commission's opinion the establishment of the Labour Advisory Board seemed to be putting the cart before the horse, in that it meant superimposing on the industrial structure powers which ought only to be implemented after conciliation had been tried and failed. The commission recommended that the Board be reconstituted under a new name – 'Labour, Wages and Conditions of Employment Commission' – and its primary function should be to examine the scope and the application of wages and conditions of employment in any industry and, having examined the industry thoroughly, to make concrete suggestions concerning the establishment of a Wage Council. The Commission then made a general recommendation as follows:

(i) that a new Registrar of Trade Unions be appointed forthwith, who should be a qualified solicitor or barrister, possessing trade union and administrative experience;
(ii) that Labour officers be recruited more frequently from the ranks of trade unionists in Britain;
(iii) that every labour officer, whether from the ranks of the Administration in Nigeria or a new appointee, should have six months' training in the Industrial Relations Department of the United Kingdom Ministry of Labour before proceeding to take any responsibility in the Labour Department. In addition, every labour officer should spend twelve months in a British labour exchange;
(iv) that a special ad hoc committee, to be named 'National Negotiating Committee', be set up consisting of representatives of the various Government departments and representatives of the trade unions associated with Government work, and providing a machinery for settlement of disputes by Arbitration;
(v) that the law regarding trade union accounts be more rigidly enforced with a view to strengthening the reality of trade unions both to union officials and members
(vi) that the General Council of the British Trades Union Congress be requested to send a delegation, including a representative or representatives of the civil service organisations, to Nigeria to give advice and assistance to the trade unions;
(vii) that a law be enacted giving the Rent Assessment Board powers to fix rents, irrespective of those obtaining at any given time. In this connection, it was further recommended that rents should be fixed on a percentage basis of the capital value of new houses and of the replacement value of standing houses, with a steep reduction where the house is dilapidated or not in good condition.

Finally, the commission expressed the belief that labour, be it black or white, should be adequately paid in accordance with the standard of efficiency and results of work performed, and that, with the monetary results of that labour, the consumer goods available would be purchaseable.

9

FROM HARRAGIN TO BROOKE

(i) THE HARRAGIN COMMISSION

In this chapter I propose to discuss certain events that occurred between 1946 and 1949 – events of varying importance but which, nevertheless, left their marks on the development of trade unions and industrial relations in the country. The first is the commission on the civil services of British West Africa, popularly known as the Harragin Commission. The promise to review the salaries and general conditions of employment of civil servants was fulfilled three months after the General Strike. In November 1945 the Secretary of State for the Colonies appointed Sir Walter Harragin, then Chief Justice of the Gold Coast, to:

> Review and make recommendations upon the structure and remunerations of the Civil Services (with the exception of unestablished and daily paid staff) of the four West African Colonies, with special reference to the following points:
>
> (i) the general standards of remuneration and superannuation payments;
>
> (ii) the relationship of the salaries and conditions of service of locally recruited and externally recruited officers;
>
> (iii) the machinery for adjusting remuneration to variations in the cost of living;
>
> (iv) the provision of suitable arrangements for consultation between Governments and organisations representing the interests of the staff on matters relating to salaries and conditions of service;
>
> (v) the provision, by means of Public Service Commissions or otherwise, of suitable machinery, where this is not already in existence, for regulating the selection and promotion of candidates for posts, the filling of which is not subject to the approval of the Secretary of State.

The Harragin Commission began work in Nigeria early in 1946. Indeed it and the Tudor Davies Commission were taking evidence at about the same time. This coincidence would appear to explain why very few unions catering for civil servants gave evidence or submitted memoranda to the Commission. All attention was concentrated on the Tudor Davies Commission, which showed some promise of producing a quick return. Union leaders and their followers held high hopes that the Tudor Davies Commission report would be published with despatch, particularly when the Supreme Council of Nigeria Workers advised the workers to accept the interim COLA award offered by the Government. In offering the advice the Council promised to influence the Government to release the report as quickly as possible, but unfortunately the publication of the report was unduly delayed. Once again, delay led to frustration, which sparked off recriminations among union leaders. For some time rival union leaders tried to outmanoeuvre one another in attempts to force out the report. They did this for two reasons. First, since workers were anxious about the report and were hopeful that its recommendations would favour them, whoever could force out the report would definitely be a hero. In the desperate struggle for leadership that had been going on since the eve of the General Strike, there could have been no better qualification for any aspirant than ability to help the workers get what they wanted. Secondly, ability to force out the report would put powerful ammunition into the hands of anybody who succeeded, for he would use it to demonstrate his dynamism and discredit his opponents.

Francis Olu Coker, President of the splinter All-Nigerian Technical and General Workers' Federation, set the ball rolling. On September 16 he held an interview with officials of the Nigerian Secretariat and secured an assurance that the report would soon be published. Four days later the representatives of the Supreme Council of Nigerian Workers – the principal spokesman of Nigerian workers during the enquiry – held a similar interview with Government officials. After the interview the Government issued a release announcing that the Supreme Council representatives had held a discussion with them on the release of the Tudor Davies Commission report. Coker's reaction was swift and bitter. He accused the Supreme Council of indolence, and said that the Government statement was a calculated attempt to steal the credit for the release of the report from his Federation. His accusation was quickly supported by the Railway Workers' Union, which objected to the Government having any further dealings with the Supreme Council. The Union wanted the Government to deal with the unions concerned and not with 'a body of clerks who, during the battle for existence by the workers, did not show their faces but who, now enjoying the benefits of the labour of the workers, decide on dictating to them'.[1] The Tudor Davies Commission report was released a few weeks after this dialogue.

A new problem arose when the report was to be discussed with trade unions. The All-Nigeria Technical and General Workers Federation claimed to represent and speak for Government technical workers. The ACSTWU (from which the Federation's members had broken off) made a similar claim. To resolve these claims, unions affiliated to both organisations were asked to declare their stand. The result of these declarations made the Government decide not to recognise the Federation for the purpose of discussing the report. The Government decision caused hard feelings among some sections of Government technical employees, and the disunity in the labour camp became deeper.

In an attempt to find a solution the Trades Union Congress set up a special commission to:

> Look into the trouble now in the Nigerian labour circle, examining the structural and functional relations of the existing organisations, namely the TUC, the African Civil Servants Technical Workers' Union and the All-Nigerian Technical and General Workers' Federation;
>
> [and] look into any issues considered by the Commission to be germane to the cause and interest of the movement with a view to finding out the cause or causes of the trouble in the movement, and recommend to the TUC of Nigeria remedial measures considered capable of removing the cause or causes of trouble and bringing about harmonious and friendly relations in the movement.[2]

The members of the commission were Archdeacon L. A. Lennon, Dr. E. Udo Udoma and K. Soluade. Little is known of the work of this Commission or of its findings.

(ii) THE SECRET DOCUMENT CASE

Towards the end of 1946 Coker's trade union activities had become such a problem to the Posts and Telegraphs authorities and to the Government that it was decided to relieve him of his job in the P. & T. He lost the rewards of over ten years of meritorous service. On December 5, 1946, the police searched his home and the home of S. A. Olukoya, Secretary of the PWD Technical and General Workers' Union, and also Secretary of the All-Nigeria Technical and General Workers' Federation. As a result of the search both men were arrested. Olukoya was later released, but Coker was charged with receiving an official secret document.

When the case opened at St. Anna Court No. 1 on December 6, the Acting Solicitor-General, C. W. Reece, made an application that the case be tried *in camera*. He said he was making the application in the interest of public policy regarding the content of the document. The application was granted, and the trial Magistrate ordered everybody out, save those connected with the case. When asked to quit, however, irate workers and sympathisers not only disturbed the Court but some threw stones and others made themselves a nuisance.

The case continued on December 18 at the Lagos Assizes. Defending Coker were J. I. C. Taylor, Magnus Williams and F. O. B. Blaize. Before the trial opened that day, Magnus Williams appealed to workers to behave. He said: 'Coker's trial begins today, and the workers are warned to go about their work. A repetition of last week's show will not be doing their cause any good. There is no earthly need for demonstration. No self-respecting Nigerian would tolerate lawlessness.' Coker himself joined in the appeal. He asked 'all persons interested in me and in my trial taking place in the Supreme Court of Nigeria in connection with an alleged receipt of official secret document today at 9.00 a.m. to be cool and calm, while the trial is going on'. He added: 'It is well known that the British Court has traditional sense of justice, fairplay and frankness which you all and sundry respect. Those of you who will not be permitted to leave your seats at work I specially appeal to be patient, calm and cool, trusting that justice will ge done. Those of you who will come to witness the trial, I do ask to please take the instructions of the Police Officers and be gentle wherever you may be.'[3]

In all, seven witnesses gave evidence for the prosecution, among them H. F. P. Marshall, Principal Assistant Secretary (Political Section) in the Nigerian Secretariat, and S. A. Olukoya. Marshall said he had prepared the document of which 270 copies were produced and circulated to heads of departments and District Officers. The remaining copies were kept in a secret safe. Olukoya said Coker came to his home on December 4 and told him he had been fasting for 40 days. He was happy and thanked God because that morning he came across a document, which proved conclusively that the Government was responsible for the disunity in the trade union movement. Coker, he went on, said he found the document on the door-step of his office. The witness said that Coker gave him the document to read, and after he had read it he requested that his wife be permitted to read it also. After both of them had read the document, he asked Coker not to attach any significance to the document, as it bore nobody's signature, but to treat it as anonymous, and suggested that copies be made and distributed to other union leaders so that they could settle their differences and present a united front. Coker acted on this suggestion and the following day handed him his own copy.

In his judgement Mr. Justice Charles Abbott said there was no doubt that Coker came into possession of a document belonging to the Government, and no doubt also that he made copies. Everybody in official circles knew the document to be secret. The Judge found Coker guilty. Before binding him over to keep the peace for five years and ordering him to pay £10 for the cost of prosecution, the Judge advised Coker to maintain high integrity if he wanted to be a good union leader. Coker's conviction was later quashed by the West African Court of Appeal.

The Secret Document Case had two important effects. First, it earned Coker the nickname Secret Document Coker by which he was popularly known in Nigerian labour circles. Secondly, it made him a hero, a go-getter and a popular leader with indomitable courage to fight for the cause of the workers.

(iii) THE HARRAGIN RECOMMENDATIONS

The Harragin Commission report was published in 1947. Among its recommendations were substantial wage increases for Government employees, and a higher entry point of salary for African technical staff. The Commission also recommended the introduction of 'expatriation pay' for European officers recruited outside Nigeria and the other African colonies. Another important recommendation was that advisory councils modelled on the lines of the Whitley Councils in the United Kingdom to be set up to advise the Government on all matters of general interest concerning the salaries and conditions of employment of civil servants.

For various reasons many of the Harragin recommendations were rejected by the Nigerian Civil Service Union, the Association of Nigerian Railway Civil Servants, the All-Nigeria Technical and General Workers' Federation and the PWD Technical and General Workers' Union. The NCSU and the ANRCS were particularly opposed to higher entry points for African technical staff, their contention being that it was unfair to discriminate in entry points for persons possessing the same educational qualification. Under the Harragin dispensation a School Certificate holder entered the public service in the standard technical grades on £96 per annum, while his counterpart entered the standard clerical grades on £84 per annum. Sir Walter offered a justification for his recommendation when he said: 'As a class of public servants, technicians are to be encouraged in view of the many development schemes that Governments have in hand and the apparent unpopularity of working with the hands as compared with clerical work.'[4]

(iv) THE COWAN ENQUIRY

Pursuant to the Harragin recommendations, the Government in 1948 appointed T. M. Cowan of the UK Ministry of Labour and National Service to investigate and report on the methods of negotiation between the Government and Government employees on questions affecting conditions of service in Government industrial establishments. His report published the same year sums up all the problems that have bedevilled industrial relations in Nigeria. It stressed the need for improving industrial relations, and pointed out that future improvement depended on two complementary factors: first, improving the organisation of trade unions, continuity of leadership and, most important of all, the need for discipline and education of the workers in sound trade union principles; and secondly, developing a refreshed attitude of mind on the part of many officers in the Departments to the conduct of labour relations.

The report examined the quality of union leadership and said: 'I have been very favourably impressed by the ability of many of the individual trade union representatives I have met. In the main they are well-informed and keenly interested in their task, and ready to receive guidance in the problems which beset them. They expressed themselves as fully appreciative of the difficulties of management sides of the Departments and of the wisdom of moderation and compromise. . . . The main union problem, as I see it, is one of how these able officers can keep the confidence of their members without resort to undue aggressive tactics and unreasonable demands in which they personally may not believe.'[5]

About departmental management the report observed: 'On the other side of the account, however, there are some who exhibit ill-concealed impatience in these matters. They show a tendency and a peremptory decision mentality. They stress the all too obvious shortcomings of the unions, whilst they themselves make no effort to foster better relations and, unfortunately, the resentment and ill-feeling created by this minority extends beyond their own spheres of influence. I would suggest to this minority that in a free society these unions have come to stay, and that a duty falls upon everyone close to such problems to contribute what he can to a better understanding.'

The report enumerated the fourfold duties of Government to meet the situation as follows:

(i) the enactment of legislation giving scope for union development (this first duty had already been discharged by the passage of the Trade Unions Ordinance);

(ii) the Government as the largest and most influential employer should improve its side of labour–management relations by employing personnel officers in some of the principal industrial departments;

(iii) the provision of independent assistance to the growing trade union movement;

(iv) the need for adequate facilities for consultation and negotiation between the Government, its Departmental representatives and the unions.

Labour Officers (Trade Unions) were appointed after the publication of the Cowan report to advise and give guidance to the unions and also to conduct elementary trade union education classes. Whitley Councils were also set up. Their functions included the determination of the general principles governing conditions of service like recruitment, hours of work, promotions, discipline, tenure, remunerations and superannuation. Decisions were taken by agreement and not by vote, but such decisions were subject to approval by the Governor. Two of the most important Whitley Councils (Junior Whitley Council (A) for the clerical and other office employees and Junior Whitley Council (B) for industrial workers) ran into difficulties in 1949 because of the lack of a proper attitude from the official side. How it happened is what we shall consider presently.

(v) THE BURUTU SHOOTING INCIDENT

Exactly two years after official bungling had provoked the General Strike, which in turn caused a good deal of hard feeling against British administration, another incident occurred in Warri Province which increased resentment against colonial rule. It was the brutal shooting by the police on June 21, 1947, of defenceless UAC employees in Burutu, who went on strike in furtherance of a wage demand. Panic swept through the whole labour movement. Politicians and nationalists found a new justification for their demand for an early termination of British rule in Nigeria. The TUC protested to the Government alleging that 'many are now at the point of death',[6] and demanded a commission of enquiry into the cause of the shooting. Addressing a mass meeting on the incident, TUC President N. A. Cole said that 'Government was using all means, fair and foul, to dwarf the growth of trade unionism in the country'.[7] The Congress sent A. A. Adio-Moses to investigate and report. Unfortunately his investigation was cut short as he was recalled by the General Council to take over from M. A. Tokunboh, the TUC General Secretary who was leaving for the United Kingdom for further studies.

Beyond the official version very little is known of the real cause of the shooting. In the House of Commons, replying to a question by William Gallacher, a Communist MP, the Colonial Secretary, Arthur Creech-Jones, said that 'on June 21 a large crowd [of strikers] formed and adopted a menacing attitude. Four employees of the company were set upon and severely beaten after the crowd had refused to disperse in spite of repeated warnings, and an unsuccessful attempt was made to break up without the use of firearms, and the order to fire was only given after the Police had been attacked with large stones and other missiles. Only two rounds were fired, as a result of which two men were wounded in the legs.'[8]

A dialogue ensued after the Colonial Secretary's reply. The questioner wanted to know whether any statements were obtained from the strikers. In reply Creech-Jones said: 'I have the completest confidence in the Governor [Lord Milverton] and I have taken my reports from the Government of Nigeria and from various sources which are open to me. I am completely satisfied with regard to the facts.' Another MP, James Carmichael, asked: 'Will the right honourable gentleman state whether, in making this impartial enquiry, he did not know full well that the answer he has been given about the strikers provoking the trouble has been a familiar story in this country for the last half century.' Gallacher recalled a similar incident in the United Kingdom, when he and David Kirkwood, MP for Dumbarton Burghs, were accused of stone-throwing, an accusation that he said was false.

Against this background of officialdom ever trying to find a justification for a reprehensible act, the official version of the circumstances of the shooting incident has to be judged. It is common knowledge that employers often invite the police in times of strikes. In doing so they claim that their property is in danger, and that they therefore want protection for such property; what they want, in fact, is police assistance to enable them to admit strike breakers. Most disturbances during strikes owe their origin to strikers' resistance to employers' attempts, aided by the police, to admit strike breakers. Undoubtedly this was what happened in the Burutu episode. This conclusion is reinforced by the findings of Mr. Justice Eric Hallianan, who enquired into the incident. The Commissioner found that 'the Police should have given protection to the clerks on June 21 rather than wait until they were attacked before defending them'.[9] It was the duty of the police, the Commissioner declared, to disperse a crowd of workers if the crowd was unlawful or became riotous, and the police should go beyond that duty. As to the reason for the strike, the Commissioner found that 'it was the Union's suspicion that the management were playing with them' which made them go on strike.

(vi) THE RISE OF THE UNAMAG

Until 1946 trade unions in mercantile establishments were not organised on a national basis. A few unions existed, but these were little house organisations which drew their membership from the employees of the particular establishment. If a company had branches in Lagos island, Ebute Metta, Yaba and Apapa the employees of each branch would organise a union of their own, register it, and remain autonomous, having no relationship with its counterpart in the other branches of the same firm. Thus, for example, there were five UAC workers' unions in Lagos before the General Strike. There are at least three important reasons for this development.

First, employers were very reluctant to accept trade unionism in their establishments. Most of them were ardent believers in the theory of the 'divine rights of management', which unions want to curtail, if not abolish completely. Those who were persuaded to tolerate unions laid down certain conditions which the unions had to fulfil before they could be recognised and dealt with. One of these conditions was that union membership be drawn exclusively from the employees of the establishment and the union's representatives and spokesmen must be persons on the employer's payroll.

The Barclays Bank DCO African Staff Union is a case in point. For over five years, the union had a full-time salaried general secretary who could not be recognised by Barclays Bank and he could not participate in collective bargaining with management because the Bank wanted, as one employer put it, 'someone who understands the economics of the industry'. Nat Pepple, the Secretary of the Barclays Bank DCO African Staff Union, carried out his union negotiations by writing lengthy briefs and rehearsing bargaining techniques with other union leaders on the employer's payroll. As late as 1954 employers were still insisting on determining the jurisdiction of unions. For example, one of the conditions imposed by the Railway Administration before recognising the Railway Technical Staff Association was that 'the Union will not widen its sphere of influence by representation of workmen in other employment than that of the Railway Administration and accept that, if it sought to do so, the Administration would reconsider its recognition of the Association.'[10]

The second reason is that union development in Nigeria did not follow the traditional craft structure. Except for one, none of the existing unions in the country could be called a craft union. From their inception the unions adopted an industrial character by grouping workers irrespective of their skill or trade. But that industrial character suffered from one ailment – that the union's jurisdiction did not extend to other establishments engaged in the same trade or industry. This limitation of union jurisdiction to the employees of one establishment played into the hands of employers afraid of union power who, in an attempt to discourage mighty unionism, mounted the propaganda, sometimes spread with relish by uninformed union members, that it is basically wrong for workers in one establishment to join hands with others in another establishment because their interests are not the same. This propaganda is still being carried on today, and is largely responsible for the break-up of amalgamations that have taken place in recent years in the oil and construction industries.

Thirdly, none of the existing trade union leaders was determined to build a truly industrial or general workers' union. Although they talked passionately about the need for bigger organisations, there was neither the spirit nor the drive to achieve that objective. The few who seemed to be determined were ultimately bogged down by consideration of what positions they were likely to occupy in the new organisation. When the positions to which they aspired could not be easily assured they let sleeping dogs lie, and preferred, as a UK trade unionist has described it, to be 'big fishes in small ponds, rather than be small fishes in big ponds'.

In 1946 the employees of the United Africa Company decided to change the pattern of union organisation in the mercantile establishments. They amalgamated the five UAC workers' unions into one union called the Amalgamated Union of UAC African Workers (popularly known as UNAMAG), and to be organised on a country-wide basis. The spirit behind this achievement was A. A. Adio-Moses, himself a founder and secretary of one of the unions. Adio-Moses joined the UAC in 1940 as manager-in-training in the Kingsway Stores. A few months later he organised the workers into a union, and this earned him the wrath of the management. It was understandable for a low-grade worker, living on a starvation wage, to summon his colleagues and persuade them to join a union to further their economic interests; but such a thing was unthinkable of a management trainee, whether now or in 1941. That was the feeling of the UAC management about Adio-Moses: to them he was a terrible disappointment, in spite of the promise he showed in his work. In 1942 he was dismissed for trying to buy sugar with a customer's pass book. He was later recalled, but resigned in 1946 to take up the General Secretaryship of the TUC.

Although he had cleared the ground for the building of a great national union of UAC workers, the realisation of that objective was not to be his responsibility, but that of Nduka Eze, a dedicated Zikist. On Adio-Moses's recommendation he was employed as General Secretary. The Union also accepted Adio-Moses' recommendation that UNAMAG's secretariat be sited in the same building as the TUC secretariat so that the new inexperienced General Secretary might be shown the ropes.

Nduka Eze learned fast, and proved to be a competent organiser, On April 17, 1947, he led a delegation on a tour of the country, to organise branches and collect mandates from such branches to present a memorandum to the UAC for a wage increase and for improved conditions of employment. In most of the places visited the workers told incredible stories about their wages and conditions of employment. One address of welcome cried aloud. It said 'For so many years the United Africa Company Limited has applied instrument of transforming the total African employees here in the Plateau Region into perpetual slaves, without the least regard for our comfort, without provision for us when we are old or incapacitated. Notwithstanding our personal grievances against the UAC, whose continued existence constitutes a very grave danger in this country, we vehemently deplore the role which has been ours – hewers of wood and drawers of water. In the face of all these things we hereby resolve that as from today's date we not only form ourselves as a branch of the Amalgamated Union of UAC African Workers of Nigeria but hereby mandate the said UNAMAG to fight the cause of all UAC workers including ourselves so that the lot of European servants of the company could be realised by us, other things being equal.'[11] Another address of welcome alleged that after twenty-five years' service some UAC employees in the north were still being paid 25s. per month.

Between April 17 and August 26, 1947, the delegation inaugurated twenty-seven branches. Armed with the mandates from these branches and a few from the branches in Lagos, the UNAMAG in September 1947 forwarded a memorandum to the UAC demanding the following:

(i) minimum salary of £6 per month for sub-clerical grades;

(ii) minimum salary of £10 per month for standard clerical grades;
(iii) minimum salary of 3s. 6d. per day for general labour;
(iv) provision of free medical service;
(v) sick leave of 28 days with pay and thereafter half pay for a maximum of six months;
(vi) non-contributary pension scheme;
(vii) vacation leave of 60 days in two years with free transport;
(viii) standard grades and salary scales for artisans, technical workers, professional staff, special and general labour, tailors, telephone operators, store keepers and salesmen, messengers and shop assistants.

Subsequent demands were made for conversion of the plantation minimum wage to the township minimum, and for the adjustment of salaries of permanent staff, arising out of the revision of salaries in June 1947, which a Director of the Company's London office had admitted was wrongly calculated. Other demands were for the reinstatement of 1,000 employees dismissed as a result of union activities, and security of tenure for union officers. The memorandum asked that concessions arising from these demands be made retroactive from January 1, 1946.

Although, in acknowledging the receipt of the memorandum, the Company admitted that the Union's demands were 'reasoned, constitutional, and moderate',[12] no steps were taken for over eighteen months to concede them or invite the Union for negotiation. The Union's agitation led to the appointment of a conciliator. At the conciliation meeting the Company representative walked out. The reason for the walk-out is not clear, but the Union claimed in a release published by *The West African Pilot* on May 4, 1949, that the 'Company representative walked out without regard and respect for the conciliator just because he is a colonial Nigerian'.

The Union planned a country-wide strike with effect from May 2. In order to prevent the strike the Company offered a wage increase as follows: ungraded staff and labour 5s. increase per month or 2d. per day if daily paid, the increase to be effective from January 1, 1950. During the union's agitation, *The Daily Service* for very strange reasons published a number of stories which union leaders described as false. The stories forced the Union to adopt a resolution at a mass meeting on May 13, 1949, to boycott the paper. An uneasy peace prevailed in labour–management relations in the UAC until the 1950 strike of which more is to be said later. The emergence of the UNAMAG had a tremendous impact on union development in the other mercantile establishments, and from then onwards sporadic efforts were made to organise existing unions on a national basis even though they remained essentially house organisations.

(vii) 'WHITLEY COUNCIL CLAP-TRAP'

There was a general dissatisfaction among government clerical employees with Sir Walter Harragin's recommendation that technical staff should enjoy a higher entry point of salary than they did on entering the public service. Early in 1949 the Civil Service Union and the Association of Nigerian Railway Civil Servants jointly presented a claim for uniform entry points for standard clerical and technical grades. The matter was included in the agenda of the Whitley Council meeting of August 18, 1949.

When the matter came up for discussion the official side showed no willingness to negotiate. Their spokesman just read a typewritten statement rejecting the demand of the staff side. In protest the staff side walked out and immediately announced their determination never to return to the Council again unless there was a change of attitude from the official side. T. O. Songonuga, President of the ANRCS, declared: 'Constitutional approach has no meaning to the Nigerian Government. We reserve the right to take any further action we consider justifiable.'[13] Both the NCSU and the ANRCS set up a joint executive to press their demand. The joint executive demanded 'an independent, impartial commission composed of persons wholly untainted by local prejudices or influences or vested commercial interests'.[14] Later the joint executive organised a one-day sit-down strike in which many civil servants participated. Disciplinary action was taken against the strikers. The joint executive then declared a formal dispute, which was later referred to an arbitrator.

At the arbitration hearing both unions told arbitrator T. D. Shiels that a uniform entry point for clerical and technical grades was the only thing that could restore peace and harmony in the clerical service. They argued that Sir Walter's emphasis on the important role which technicians would play in the country's development ignored the fact that paper-work performed by clerical employees would increase with the increase of technical work. Secondly, that the efficiency of the clerk increases over the period of years (a point made by Sir Walter himself in his report) but that of the technician does not. Thirdly, that the physical strain of clerical work was far greater than that of technical work.

The arbitrator denied an award in respect of the general claim of the unions. Nevertheless he made an award with the effect that, as from March 1, 1950, new entrants to the clerical grades, who had satisfactorily completed the course of training at the Clerical Training School at Oshogbo, or at any other similar institution recognised by Government, should enter Scale F at £96, which was two increments above the standard entry point.

About three months after the breakdown in Junior Whitley Council A, another breakdown occurred in Junior Whitley Council B. The staff side walked out of the Council meeting on November 3 and accused the official side of non-co-operation. Whether the accusation was fair or not could be judged from the composition of the official side. Under the constitution of the Council, the official side consisted of heads of departments. Individual unions were to negotiate with the heads of departments and, when they disagreed on any matter, that matter would be brought to the Whitley Council B by the Federation of Government and Municipal Non-Clerical Workers' Unions. In effect this meant that heads of departments who had rejected claims presented at departmental negotiation meetings would sit again in judgement over previous decisions. The staff side considered this situation anomalous and not conducive to effective collective bargaining. They demanded a change in the composition of the official side.

Commenting on the breakdown in Junior Whitley Council B, *The West African Pilot* in an editorial entitled 'Whitley Council Clap-Trap' said: 'At a time when the trade unions are being accused of disregarding the machinery for settling trade disputes, it helps towards a better understanding of the particular circumstances of such machinery or aspects of it that the case of the Whitley Council should come to the notice of the public. As in any other meeting whose purpose is to arrive at the settlement of a dispute, attendance at the Whitley Council necessarily implies a willingness and readiness to give and take. So that refusal to consider the point of view of an opposing party, and attendance at such meeting with ready-made proposals to be offered as Hobson's choice, are a complete negation of the spirit and purport of the Whitley Council. . . . If the Whitley Council is not merely a clap-trap and window dressing that ought to be scrapped in the interest of sincerity and industrial peace, then a revision of its composition and its official attitude is overdue for serious consideration.'[15]

In August 1951, F. Carruthers, President of the Association of Officers of the British Ministry of Labour and National Services, was appointed to investigate the cause of failure of the Junior Whitley Councils and make recommendations. His report led to many changes in the Whitley Council machinery. Carruthers stayed in the country until the first meeting of the reconstituted Whitley Council in order to advise on the practical working of the procedure.

(viii) THE MACDONALD ARBITRATION

In 1948 three disputes were settled by arbitration. They involved two unions and the Railway administration and the Nigerian Mercantile Shipping Workers' Union and the United Africa Company. The disputes between the Railway unions and the Railway administration are particularly important because they throw light on industrial relations practice in the Railways and illustrate the different attitudes of Railway unions to arbitration awards.

The dispute between the Railway Workers' Union and the Railway management followed a demand for wage increase for craftsmen, chargemen and supervisors. Williams Gorman, KC, who arbitrated in the dispute, made the following awards:

(i) With effect from January 1, 1946, daily paid artisans on 2s.–2s. 5d. be graded Artisan Grade II and paid 4s. 6d. per day.
(ii) Anti-mosquito inspectors, helpers, tube cleaners, auto truck drivers, scalers, lighters-up (shops), beltmen and oilers, brick arch builders, fitters, furnacemen, head cleaners, assistant drivers (ice plant), drivers (stationery engine), head coalmen, brickmakers and stores issuers were awarded £60 per annum.
(iii) An award was denied in the case of firemen, lorry checkers, shunters, cranemen, drivers (yard shunters), overseers (sanitation), gangers, pump drivers, chainmen grades I and II, tally issuers, strikers, rivetters, chargemen and supervisors.

The arbitrator paid tribute to all who gave evidence, particularly to A. W. L. Savage, Financial Secretary to the Government, and Luke Emejulu, the Union's General Secretary, and added that he was 'tremendously impressed by the indications of goodwill between the two parties'.[16]

The dispute between the Railway Station Staff Union and the Railway management also concerned wage claims. Claim 1 sought a wage increase for level-crossing keepers, porters and head porters. At arbitration the Union claimed that the Railway management had actually agreed to the regarding of level-crossing keepers as Special Labour Grade II with effect from January 1, 1943, but this agreement was not implemented. An award was made in favour of the level-crossing keepers and denied in respect of the others.

Claim 2 was also for a wage increase for pointsmen, shunters and signalmen Grades I and II, and for the abolition of the post of assistant shunter. Award was denied.

Claim 3 sought an increase in the salary of yard foremen. The arbitrator argued that while the duties and responsibilities of yard foremen were similar to those of assistant yard master or chargeman in other Departments of the Railway, yet the qualifications required of a yard foreman were not as high as those of the occupants of the other posts, and therefore denied award.

Claim 4 sought an alteration in the conversion point of station staff halted on the old promotion bars of £60, £78 and £104 per annum, who converted to £170 per annum. The Union wanted the men placed on special scale GIB (£180 × 10 – £250) with effect from January 1, 1946, on the ground that they had suffered hardship in the past. The arbitrator made awards as follows:

(i) Qualified second-class station staff who had less than seven year's service on a salary of £128 per annum, who converted to £170 per annum on Scale GI on January 1, 1946, should be regraded to £180 per annum in Special Grade I with effect from January 1, 1946, to proceed to £190 per annum with effect from January 1, 1947.

(ii) Qualified second-class station staff with seven years' service or more on £128 per annum and who converted to £170 per annum in Scale GI on January 1, 1946, should be regraded to £190 per annum with effect from January 1, 1946.

(iii) No person should advance beyond £190 per annum under (i) and (ii).

By universal practice, arbitration or the industrial Court is the final step in the settlement of industrial disputes, unless the law of the particular country provides otherwise. When both parties to a dispute submit themselves to an arbitration they usually accept its award, even though the award may not favour one of them, and the law of the country may not compel them to do so. This is the practice in the United Kingdom, the North American sub-continent and many other countries where arbitration is voluntary. As a British dependency, whose institutions had been nurtured on British traditions and practices, it was expected that the UK practice would be followed in Nigeria; at least, the Railway management expected this. But the Railway Station Staff Union thought otherwise. Depending on the *letter* and not the *spirit* of the law, they felt they could reject the awards of Arbitrator I. W. MacDonald, published in October 1948.

On June 12, 1949, the Union addressed a letter to the Railway management seeking an interview. At the interview held the following day, the Union expressed dissatisfaction with the MacDonald awards, and put forward nine claims similar to those rejected by the arbitrator. The Railway management refused to consider the claims on the grounds that they had been settled by arbitration a few months earlier. At a resumed meeting on June 15 the Union submitted additional claims. The meeting was to be continued the following day, but 'the Union's annual delegates' conference then in session decided against further negotiation and preferred to press its claims by means of resolutions and a 30-day ultimatum'.[17]

The Commissioner of Labour appointed an enquiry into the dispute, but the Union refused to co-operate with the officer conducting it. On July 17 the Union called its members out on strike. The Government reacted by issuing a statement warning all station staff that they would be liable to dismissal if they did not return to work by midnight of July 20. The strike was called off, and negotiations were resumed.

About the same time trouble was also brewing in the Eastern District of the Railway Administration. On June 10 the Makurdi Engineering Branch of the Railway Workers' Union passed a resolution giving the Railway management 21 days' ultimatum to remove the engineer in charge of the District, against whom several complaints had been lodged. A meeting held on July 4 to resolve the matter failed to achieve its purpose, and another meeting was arranged with the General Manager. That meeting was yet to be held when the Union's members at Enugu and Makurdi began a 'go slow' strike. A three-man delegation of the Union, accompanied by a representative of the Railway management and the Deputy Commissioner of Labour, went to Makurdi and Enugu to resolve the matter. Discussions were still going on, though very little progress had been made, when the management issued notices warning the strikers that they would render themselves liable to dismissal if the 'go slow' should continue. The warning ruined the negotiations. Union negotiators withdrew and refused to continue.

(ix) THE BROOKE COMMISSION

The breakdown in the negotiations led to the appointment of a commission 'to investigate the causes and circumstances of the existing unsatisfactory labour situation in the Railway and review the existing machinery for the settlement of trade disputes and for the removal of grievances and to report on both matters'. The commission consisted of Mr. Justice N. J. Brooke, Chairman; H. F. Pallant, Mallam Belo Kano, S. I. Kale and L. P. Ojukwu.

The Nigerian Union of Railwaymen (Federated) welcomed the commission, but requested that Dr. Nnamdi Azikiwe and H. O.

Davies be accepted as substitutes for S. I. Kale and L. P. Ojukwu. The Union argued that Kale and Ojukwu had not sufficient experience in public affairs and were therefore ill-equipped to undertake the task of the commission. The request was rejected by Government on the ground that Dr. Azikiwe and H. O. Davies were actively engaged in politics. The NUR appealed to the Government to reconsider its decision, arguing that the Government excuse 'is not a sufficient reason to reject the services of the two pillars of society in whom the workers have implicit confidence'.[18] The Government stuck to its guns.

The Union sent a deputation to interview H. M. Foot, the Chief Secretary to the Government; again the Government refused to budge. Foot tried to assure the Union representatives of the integrity of members of the commission, and argued in a letter dated August 13, 1949, that 'in arbitration each side appoints its own assessor, but in a commission of enquiry there is no question of appointment or nomination by anyone other than the Officer Administering the Government. . . .' – another instance of undue reliance on the letter and not the spirit of the law. The Union representatives argued that 'the rejection of barely two alternatives on a commission of five in spite of cogent submissions, cannot be appreciated as a sincere offer of co-operation by the Government'. In the evening of August 13, the NUR decided at a mass rally to boycott the Brooke Commission.

In keeping with their decision none of the Railway unions appeared before the Commission to give evidence or submit a memorandum. To break the boycott the Railway management began a mass transfer of their objection to the inclusion of Kale and Ojukwu and to the tactics of the Railway administration, the NUR organised a lightning strike which, although intended for the Lagos area only, spread quickly to other areas and paralysed railway services throughout the country. All African employees, from the highest to the lowest, joined. The strike affected the work of the commission, whose sessions were adjourned for a few days. When the enquiry resumed, the unions refused to co-operate and the Commission concluded its work without taking evidence from them.

In its report published on November 17, 1949, the Brooke Commission said that 'some of the causes leading up to the present position are failure by the Railway unions, and on occasions by the Railway management, to use the negotiating machinery and to adhere strictly to the procedure relating thereto; refusal by the unions to accept awards and also the failure in some cases of the bargaining agent with whom the management have been dealing to enforce the decisions reached.' The Commission recommended an additional step in the negotiating machinery, to be followed only after disagreement had been reached at the third step, and before step was to be known as Railway Staff Council, and its membership was to consist of equal numbers of representatives appointed by the unions and the management respectively. Its chairman would be an independent person whose integrity was beyond doubt, to be selected by agreement between the Railway management and the NUR, failing which the Government should make the selection. The functions of the Council were to deal with collective issues. In the event of disagreement on any issue the matter should be referred to independent referees, who might be British railway union leaders and staff department experts of British Railways. Before reference was made, however, both sides must sign a written undertaking to abide by the referees' decision.

The Commission also recommended that management representation at each step of the negotiating machinery be increased by one responsible labour officer, possibly an African. It said it was making the recommendation in the belief that industrial relations in the Railway were likely to be improved by the inclusion of officers with a better understanding of local conditions. Other recommendations included the enactment of legislation that unresolved disputes be referred to arbitration; that legislation be enacted to vest in a Government appointee powers to take steps to establish the bona fides of applicants before a union could be registered; and that the Government should provide tutors to educate and train union leaders.

REFERENCES

1. *The West African Pilot*, September 30, 1946.
2. *The West African Pilot*, November 18, 1946.
3. *The West African Pilot*, December 18, 1946.
4. *Report of the Commission on the Civil Services of British West Africa, 1945–1946*, page 20.
5. Report on Methods of Negotiation between Government and Government Employees on Questions affecting Conditions of Service in the Industrial Departments, page 71.
6. *The West African Pilot*, June 26, 1947.
7. Op. cit., August 11, 1947.
8. Reported in *The West African Pilot*, July 23, 1947.
9. *The West African Pilot*, September 2, 1948.
10. General Secretary's Annual Report to the First Annual Delegates' Conference of the RTSA April 22–24, 1955.
11. *The West African Pilot*, June 30, 1947.
12. *The West African Pilot*, May 4, 1949.

13. *The West African Pilot*, August 19, 1949.
14. Ibid.
15. *The West African Pilot*, November 19, 1949.
16. *The West African Pilot*, March 3, 1948.
17. *Department of Labour Annual Report, 1949–50.*
18. *The West African Pilot*, August 13, 1949.

10

LABOUR IN POLITICS

Until 1946, the trade unions were not involved in politics. There are two main reasons for this aloofness. First, the Colonial Government was vehemently opposed to the idea. It was feared that trade unions might 'fall under the domination of disaffected persons by which their activities may be diverted to improper and mischievous ends'. Secondly, few politicians or political parties then existing had given serious thought to the immense power of organised labour in the nationalist struggles, let alone to the idea of going all out to utilise that power. The arrival of Sir Arthur Richards as Governor turned the scale. Sir Arthur is perhaps the most controversial governor Nigeria ever had, and many people attribute the great political consciousness of most Nigerians to his doggedness in pushing through unpopular measures, which he believed to be right or expedient. For precisely the same reason he was disliked, if not hated, by leading politicians and nationalists.

Sir Arthur first stamped himself on the Nigerian mind by his swift action in dealing with the strike of King's College students in 1944. The students had been complaining about bad food and unhealthy accommodation brought about partly by mismanagement and partly by war conditions. When it appeared to them that their complaints had been falling on deaf ears, they decided to go on 'strike' by refusing to eat their meals and to attend classes. Students' protest strikes are normal occurrences in educational institutions, and when they occur school authorities usually try to restore normal relations by listening to the students' grievances and making earnest efforts to ameliorate them. This is not what happened in the King's College strike. Rather than consider the students' complaints with sympathy, the Governor ordered the ringleaders of the strike to be conscripted into the army and others to be prosecuted for conduct likely to cause a breach of the peace. One of the conscripted boys died a few days later.

Sir Arthur's action on the King's College strike outraged the country. For the first time in contemporary events, leaders of the various political parties forgot their differences and found a common ground for united action. The Nigerian Bar came all out in defence of the boys by sending its leading members to defend those standing trial, who were eventually bound over to keep the peace.

The results of the King's College strike determined a group of former students of the College and the leaders of the Nigerian Union of Students to organise a conference of all organisations, to found a body which would unite the people and give leadership to the country. The conference was held at the Glover Memorial Hall on August 26, 1944, and resolved to found the Nigerian National Council, which later became the National Council of Nigeria and the Cameroons. The TUC was represented at this inaugural conference. The Congress later applied for formal affiliation and the application was accepted.[1]

If the aftermath of the King's College strike was a bitter pill to many Nigerians, what followed a few months later drove them mad. In March 1945 Sir Arthur laid on the table of the Legislative Council his proposals for constitutional reform, which nationalists of all shades of political opinion had been demanding. It was the first indication to the country that a new constitution was in the offing; no attempt had been made to discuss the proposals with political parties and the people's chosen representatives. Before his retirement in 1943 the former Governor, Sir Bernard Bourdillon, had announced that after the war Nigerians would be given an ample opportunity to discuss the draft of their future constitution. Yet in spite of that promise, Sir Arthur urged a quick approval of his proposals so that they could be considered by the British Parliament before the June 1945 general elections, which brought into power the first all-Labour government in Britain. The members of the Legislative Council were true to type, and the constitutional proposals were passed into law with slight amendments.

Apart from the cavalier treatment thus meted out to the people and their leaders, there were several features of the new constitution which nationalists opposed. The first was the concept of regionalism, which introduced a tripartite division of the country. The leaders of the Nigerian Youth Movement accepted regionalism as a working basis, but the NCNC leaders rejected it as a divide-and-rule instrument. The second objectionable feature was its introduction of unofficial majorities in the legislature. Under the new constitution regional assemblies were to be established at Enugu, Ibadan and Kaduna. These assemblies would merely discuss proposed legislation and make recommendations; but they had the right to pass their own budgets. Most unofficial members of the regional assemblies were to be elected by native authorities, which were themselves created as executive organs of government. Each regional assembly was to have a ratio of official to unofficial members as follows: North 19:20, West 14:15 and East 13:14. In the Legislative Council the ratio was to be 20:29. Among the unofficial members of the regional assemblies were to be four or more persons (Europeans or Africans), who were to be appointed by the Governor to represent special interests. In the Legislative Council, 10 of the 29 unofficial members were to be chiefs or Europeans also nominated by the Governor. Thus, while ostensibly the intention was to give unofficial members majority representation, the composition of that majority was such as to guarantee an official majority at all times, since persons nominated by the Governor could hardly be expected to vote against Government measures.

The inclusion of Chiefs and Emirs as unofficial members was a third objectionable feature. Nationalists argued, and with some justification, that these dignitaries were part and parcel of the official framework, since they owed their position to the Government. Indeed, a statement credited to the Oni of Ife on the functions of chiefs is proof positive. On November 4, 1946, in *The Daily Service*, the Oni was reported as saying that 'we [Chiefs] are part and parcel of the Government, and we must support the Government as well as serve our people'. Furthermore, nationalists argued that assembling natural rulers to discuss on the same platform with their subjects was derogatory to their traditional position.

The property franchise was another objectionable feature. Indeed, it was this provision, more than anything else, which forced Obafemi Awolowo, then a law student in the United Kingdom, to remark in his *Path to Nigerian Freedom* that 'the new constitution retains some of the objectionable features of the old, contains unsavoury characteristics of its own, and falls short of expectation'. Under the constitution, only persons with an income or property valued at £100 per annum in Lagos and Calabar could elect four representatives to the Legislative Council. The vast majority of the people of Nigeria were denied the right to vote – a situation which dates back to the first constitution of 1923. Nationalists attacked the denial of universal franchise as a calculated attempt to exclude all those who were 'sufficiently conscious of their rights' from playing an effective role in the country's affairs.

Apart from the Richards constitution, four Ordinances passed by the Legislative Council in its Budget Session of 1945 – the so-called 'obnoxious bills' – also annoyed the nationalists. Coleman describes three of them (the Minerals Ordinance, the Public Lands

Acquisition Ordinance, and the Crown Land (Amendment) Ordinance) as giving the impression that 'the British administration was seeking to arrogate to the Crown (by implication the British people) the title to Nigerian minerals and lands'. Indeed, this was also precisely the impression created in the public mind by articles and editorial opinions in the nationalist press. Press opinion seem to have been built on the categorical statement in one of the Ordinances that 'the entire property in and control of all minerals and mineral oils, in, under or upon any lands in Nigeria, and of all rivers, streams and water-courses throughout Nigeria, is and shall be vested in, the Crown'. Since 'the Crown' was understood to mean the British sovereign, the interpretation given in the press stuck with the people. The challenge before them was, therefore, whether they should sit unconcerned and allow their lands and mineral resources to be expropritated by foreigners, or fight to retain what was theirs.

The fourth of the 'obnoxious bills' empowered the Governor to appoint and depose chiefs. Strictly speaking it was not a new law, but an attempt to consolidate existing legislations. But because the relationship between the Governor and the nationalists was strained and his actions were therefore suspect, the law was interpreted as empowering the Governor to impose any person he liked as a chief on the people, and to remove out of hand anybody he did not like and who would not do his bidding.

Both the NCNC and the NYM were opposed to the Richards constitution and the obnoxious bills, but they differed in their strategy to fight them. The NYM felt that the constitution and the obnoxious bills could be effectively fought at home, while the NCNC felt that salvation could be found by sending a delegation to London. Sending a delegation to London would not come of mere wishful thinking: money must be found to finance the journey. In April 1946, the NCNC announced its intention of sending a delegation to tour Nigeria to educate the people on the Richards constitution and the obnoxious bills. The delegation was also to collect funds and a mandate with which a Pan-Nigeria to London Delegation was to be sent. The delegation was composed of the National President, Herbert Heelas Macaulay; the General Secretary, Nnamdi Azikiwe, and three others. One of these three was M. A. O. Imoudu. The delegation toured the country from April to December except for a brief period, when the tour was suspended because of Macaulay's death.

Imoudu's selection as one of the delegates brought organised labour into the vanguard of nationalist struggles for independence. Two months earlier, individual union leaders and members had, in their own little way, identified themselves with politics through their membership of the Zikist Movement, a mass youth organisation which became the militant wing of the NCNC. The Zikist Movement spread rapidly throughout the country, and did a good job in preparing the ground for the rousing receptions and handsome donations made to the Pan-Nigeria to London Delegation Fund.

Imoudu's selection was apt and in keeping with Zik's desire that organised labour should be closely identified with the struggles for independence, despite official opposition. If it were to be so identified, and could submit to party discipline, then its immense power could be gainfully employed to hasten the dawn of independence. For the NCNC, working in close collaboration with labour meant at least having a popular labour leader as an associate. By many considerations no other labour leader at the time was better qualified than Imoudu. For over twelve months, Zik's Group of Newspapers had been parading him as 'Labour Leader No. 1', and the impression had been entrenched in the public mind that he was indeed Labour Leader No. 1 in name and in substance. His arrest and detention made him a hero, and the leading role he played in the General Strike showed him to be an undisputed champion of the working class.

The Pan-Nigeria to London Delegation left Lagos in June, 1947 and on August 13 held its historic meeting with Arthur Creech-Jones, the Secretary of State for the Colonies. Apart from demanding a radical change in the Richards constitution, the delegation submitted a memorandum containing many grievances which it wanted ameliorated. Replying, the Colonial Secretary assured the delegation that it was British policy to work for self-government for Nigeria, and the Richards constitution provided a basis for achieving that objective. The constitution was not a static instrument; it would be subject to revision depending on experiences gained concerning its shortcomings. The Colonial Secretary added that the constitution would not be amended or repealed without first giving it a fair trial, and concluded by urging the delegation to return home and co-operate in trying it.

The outcome of the interview was given a wide publicity in the British and Nigerian press. 'Go Home and Co-operate', read a banner headline in one British newspaper, and this was echoed with avidity and relish by *The Daily Service* and *The Nigerian Daily Times*, which represented an opposite line of political thinking. The alleged failure of the Pan-Nigeria to London Delegation provided powerful ammunition in the hands of the Nigerian Youth Movement and its leaders with which to ridicule the NCNC and its leadership. In this campaign of denigration, the zeal of *The Daily Service* sometimes outran its judgment as a responsible public organ; in an attempt to play down the NCNC and its supporters it frequently published false and misleading stories, which provoked bitter controversy and cost it a sizeable readership.

In official quarters there was great rejoicing that the inveterate opponents of the régime and of the new constitution had been beaten hollow. The impression had been created in the Colonial Office that the NCNC represented a vocal minority in Lagos which could not, therefore, speak for the whole country. Partly in order to prove officialdom wrong, and partly in order to demonstrate its continued opposition to the Richards Constitution, the NCNC launched a big membership drive aimed at winning almost all organised bodies in the country. A representative meeting was organised shortly after the return of the Pan-Nigeria to London Delegation to enable the NCNC to report to the nation and appeal for support in meeting the challenges of the future. Invitations were issued to affiliated and unaffiliated organisations. The TUC was represented at this meeting by two delegates.

The delegates later reported to the TUC General Council. Their report raised again the question whether the TUC should or should not affiliate to a political party. The annual delegates' conference held at Ibadan the previous year had decided against affiliation, but for some unexplained reason that decision was not implemented. A probable reason is that the decision was unpopular with the rank and file membership of the various unions affiliated to the TUC; this conclusion is supported by H. P. Adebola in an article published in *The West African Pilot* of December 9, 1947. Adebola said in defence of affiliation that 'before the General Council meeting of November 29, most of the member unions had decided to secede from the TUC if the Congress should sever its connection with the NCNC. The provincial members refused to attend and, as in the case of the Dakar Conference delegation incident,[2] the text of telegrams had been prepared ready for despatch to the Congress Secretariat and the press. It was only left to the TUC to decide whether to sever connection with the NCNC and lose an overwhelming majority of the member unions or to remain in the NCNC and retain its member unions.'

There might have been little dissension in the intervening period between 1946 and 1947 had two things not happened. In an effort to advertise its strength, the NCNC continued to claim the TUC as a member, having not received a formal letter of resignation. On the other hand *The Daily Service* continued to assert that the TUC was not an affiliate. These claims and counter-claims forced the leaders of the TUC to include the question of affiliation in the agenda of the General Council meeting of November 29, 1947. The Council decided by 11 votes to 7 in favour of affiliation. A TUC release announcing the decision said that 'having made a thorough and impartial examination of previous discussions on the relation of the TUC and the NCNC in the light of facts available in the Congress Secretariat, the General Council resolved by a majority of votes that the TUC has been within the NCNC and that it should continue as such until the formation of its proposed Labour Party'.[3]

The affiliation decision raised a storm in labour and political circles. Behind the storm was the political rivalry between the NCNC and the Nigerian Youth Movement. To the NCNC the decision was a major political victory; to the NYM it was a humiliating defeat, which was not taken in a good spirit. In a desperate attempt to find a scapegoat, *The Daily Service*, the NYM's official organ, blamed the Ibos in the TUC. It attacked the decision and poured venom on the Ibos. 'Down with Ibos in the TUC', 'TUC in Distress' and 'They that have turned the world upside-down have come hither unto us' – these were some of the slogans that it published with relish. But were the Ibos really responsible for the decision? *The West African Pilot* examined the accusation and reported that Ibos were 'numerically an inconsequential minority'[5] in the General Council when the decision was taken.

Two incidents would appear to explain other developments. On June 17, 1948, Charles Daddy Onyeama, an Ibo lawyer and member of the Legislative Council, predicted that 'Ibo domination of Nigeria is a matter of time'. That unfortunate statement provoked the Ibo–Yoruba feud of 1948, which had a disastrous effect on many trade unions. To ensure that Onyeama's prediction did not come to pass, members of the newly formed Egbe Omo Oduduwa, a cultural organisation catering for Yoruba hogemony, infiltrated many unions and contrived arrangements to remove Ibos holding key positions and replace them with Yoruba men. Efforts were concentrated on important unions like the Railway Workers Union and the Amalgamated Union of UAC African Workers. Thus for the first time tribalism was introduced into the labour movement.

About this time Adeleke Adedoyin and Ibuyinka Olorun-Nimbe were expelled from the NCNC for alleged subversive activities. Attempts by both men to split the NCNC-Democratic Party Alliance, which had a predominantly Yoruba membership, failed, and proved the futility of trying to build a mass movement by playing one tribe against another. To members of the Egbe the experiences of Adedoyin and Olorun-Nimbe in trying to split the NCNC-Democratic Party Alliance made plain the amount of work that would be required to dislodge the NCNC. While NCNC supporters in the trade unions retired to rejoice at their victory, members of the Egbe set to work. They worked silently and tirelessly, and succeeded in getting the question of affiliation included in the agenda of the Sixth Annual Delegates' Conference of the TUC, which opened at the CMS Grammar School, Lagos, on December 27, 1948.

When the matter came up for consideration, anti-affiliation elements led by O. Olatunde, Secretary of the Public Utility, Technical and General Workers' Union, said they were not just opposed to affiliation to the NCNC, they were opposed to affiliation to *any* political party. Olatunde suggested that the matter be deferred until the workers had formed a Labour Party which, like the TUC, would show an identical interest in the workers and the welfare of the country.

Nduka Eze, Secretary of the Amalgamated Union of UAC African Workers, leading the pro-affiliation group, said that four distinct changes had taken place since the TUC reaffirmed its affiliation to the NCNC in 1947. These changes were:

(i) more applications for membership of the Congress;
(ii) the co-operative attitude towards the Congress of the once apathetic Railway Workers' Union;
(iii) more funds coming into the coffers of the TUC through affiliation fees and dues, as revealed in the report on activities; and
(iv) greater recognition of the TUC and the cause of the working-class movement.

He pointed out that the union that was proposing disaffiliation from the NCNC (the Federal Union of Local Authority Staff) was in default of its dues payment and was indebted to the Congress to the tune of over £140 and asked: 'Why do we worry with the vituperations of a debtor union whose balances in the ledger book of the Congress are anything but enviable?'

Michael Imoudu, another affiliation supporter, asked the advocates of a workers' party whether the NCNC had prevented the TUC from organising a Labour Party. O. A. Fagbenro-Beyioku, supporting disaffiliation, said that politics and trade unionism could not go together. Political leaders were capitalists, whom the TUC was out to fight. The TUC should found its own political organisation because politicians were using the workers as instruments to further their political ambitions. Eze then moved a formal motion for continued affiliation, which read:

> Whereas in the ideals of the NCNC, as contained in their Freedom Charter and Constitution, the right of a Nigerian worker to a free labour association, decent wages and economic and social security is guaranteed;
>
> And whereas in the realisation of these ideals the NCNC set out on a country-wide tour of Nigeria and the Cameroons in 1946 in preparation for a Pan-Nigeria to London Delegation;
>
> And whereas the said NCNC in their memorandum to His Britannic Majesty's Secretary of State for the Colonies did state all those things that would normally guarantee to the average worker all the good things of life;
>
> And whereas there is a semblance of unity in diversity in the said NCNC which makes possible the union of the many conglomerations of tribes, trades, and associations in Nigeria for the purpose of a united forward march to freedom;
>
> And whereas the workers of Nigeria share the same common suffering – political serfdom and national humiliations at the hands of the British Government – with the farmers, the traders, the middle-class people, the businessmen, the professionals, the peasants and the general public who have found hope in the God-sent national canopy called the NCNC;
>
> And whereas the voice of the NCNC is world-famed; its organisation most exemplary and representative and its leadership locally and internationally accepted;
>
> And whereas the NCNC today reveals itself to be the harbinger of Nigerian freedom and the spearhead of a movement that will unlock the iron gate of Africa's might in international relations; Now therefore I move that the bogey of 'unholy wedlock' of the TUC with the NCNC be not countenanced;
>
> That the TUC now throws its full weight into the NCNC because the Nigerian proletariat and masses desire the continued affiliation of the TUC with the NCNC.[6]

The motion was voted upon and defeated. Commenting on the defeat of the motion, *The West African Pilot* of January 12, 1949, recalled how opponents of the NCNC had been trying to get the TUC to withdraw from the NCNC. It recalled the campaigns of *The Daily Service* and its tirades against the Ibos and declared: 'The TUC depends on the working masses for bare existence to pursue its plans. It cannot browbeat the whole of them, however righteous it may consider its cause to be, and hope still to exist with their support.

This is the view not of trade union academicians but of practical realities in a material world. The TUC certainly needs even bare existence in order to practicalise its ideals, however noble the latter. Let time tell who is correct.'

Replying, the TUC said expressions like 'Ibos in the TUC' quoted in the editorial were repugnant and repulsive to the ideals of the TUC and could never come from it. The TUC could *rightly claim* that it had never pursued a tribal policy. The statement appealed to 'all responsible men and all men of goodwill with a sincere wish for the good of this country and the working class not to sow this baneful seed of tribalism in our movement'. Explaining the reason for disaffiliation, the statement said that withdrawal of membership did not necessarily mean withdrawal of support or co-operation. Affiliation had considerably weakened the TUC. As an organisation grouping people with diverse political sympathies, the Congress felt it should maintain a stand independent of all political or tribal groups in order to avoid an obvious clash of interests. The statement expressed the hope that 'you would, as a responsible organ, see the sanity of this policy . . . and true to your motto you would show the light for the people to find the way'.

The effect of disaffiliation was felt three days after. The Domestic Workers' Union resigned from the TUC and was followed in quick succession by the Public Utility Technical and General Workers' Union. The Nigerian Union of Nurses gave their General Secretary, N. A. Cole, who was the President of the TUC, an ultimatum to choose between leaving the TUC and retaining his job or remaining in the TUC and losing it. He chose the former. The Elder Dempster Lines African Workers' Union followed and urged all other unions to emulate the examples of others who had withdrawn.

On January 20 the Amalgamated Union of UAC African Workers, one of the largest unions in the TUC, left the organisation. Seven days later, Imoudu and 'Secret Document' Coker organised a mass meeting at which a resolution was adopted urging the complete overhaul of the TUC or its liquidation. Twelve leading trade unionists, among them M. A. O. Imoudu, F. O. Coker, Nduka Eze, P. O. Balonwu, Ralph Aniedobe and Richard Aghedo, constituted themselves into a Committee of Trade Unionists and began to prepare the ground for launching a new national centre. The stage was therefore set for the first split in the central labour organisation.

At the inaugural meeting of the Nigerian National Federation of Labour (NNFL) in March 1949, speaker after speaker levelled charges against the TUC. They said that since the 'questionable displacement' of 'Secret Document' Coker as President of the TUC the Congress had fallen into the hands of weak and repudiated union leaders. Since 1945 it had been living only in name. From its inception the Congress had been controlled and directed by the Government and Government agencies thereby undermining the interests of the workers. Big and powerful unions in the country no longer had confidence in it as was evident in the mass resignations which followed its disaffiliation from the NCNC. They said that the TUC had failed to interpret the aspirations of the workers and therefore must be supplanted by a more dynamic organisation.

The meeting elected the following officers: M. A. O. Imoudu, President; Nduka Eze, General Secretary; P. O. Balonwu, Assistant Secretary; R. Aghedo, Treasurer; F. A. Olatokuboh, Permanent Under-Secretary; and K. O. K. Onyioba, Field Secretary. The aims and objects of the new organisation were:

(i) to assist by practical efforts the attainment of the objects of member unions in the Federation;
(ii) to foster a spirit of working-class consciousness among all the workers of Nigeria and the Cameroons;
(iii) to fight for the realisation of the social and economic security of workers and to advance their educational and political aspirations by imparting political knowledge to the workers;
(iv) to press for the socialisation of important industries in the country with a view to realising a socialist government where the identity of the working class would not be lost;
(v) to co-operate with all democratic federations of trade unions the world over in order to make possible the clarion call of 'Workers of the world, unite' for the triumphant emergence of a World Parliament of the working class.

Efforts were made without avail to reconcile the TUC and the NNFL. The main differences between the two organisations lay in their objectives and strategy. These differences were complicated by the split which took place in December 1949 in the international trade union movement. Long before then, and particularly after the General Strike, the almost limitless flow of Marxist literature into the country had created a good deal of communist orientation in the leadership of some trade unions. Thus when the split in the international trade union movement took place, it was not what should be done to further the economic interests of the workers that dominated the thinking of union leaders in the NNFL, but whether the young trade union movement should identify itself with ICFTU or WFTU.

Since the philosophy of the WFTU seemed more in tune with some of the aims and objects of the NNFL, the leaders of the latter organisation were easily attracted to the WFTU, and they received financial and material aid as a result of their connections. In February 1950, the NNFL began publication of a weekly newspaper, *The Labour Champion. The Labour Champion* was registered in the name of the Amalgamated Union of UAC African Workers whose General Secretary was also the General Secretary of the NNFL. The paper's motto was 'Towards the Creation of the Socialist Republic'. *The Champion* showed an intense interest in politics and especially in communism, and carried on for some weeks without carrying advertisements. The owners eventually became bankrupt because of a breakdown in plant, and incurred a fine of £265 for contempt.

REFERENCES

1. H. P. Adebola in an article captioned 'Affiliation of the TUC to the NCNC' published in *The West African Pilot*, December 18, 1947.

2. In 1947, the WFTU organised a West African trade union conference in Dakar. Some union leaders were selected to attend that conference as Nigerian workers' representatives. Those opposing the decision drafted telegrams advising the TUC of their union's decision to disaffiliate in protest. As a result of this threat the decision was not implemented.

3. *The West African Pilot*, December 8, 1947.

4. *The West African Pilot*, January 12, 1949.

5. Ibid.

6. *The West African Pilot*, January 10, 1949.

11

THE ENUGU BLOOD BATH AND AFTER

What would have happened if striking miners in a British Colony had been shot down under the Baldwin or Chamberlain Governments? An explosion from the National Union of Mineworkers, a protest from the TUC General Council, and some parliamentary fireworks from the Labour front benches. But this is not the 1930s. Our Government is not Tory. The rulers of Britain and the Colonies are the leaders of Democratic Socialism, defenders of Western civilisation, upholders of human rights. So when all the hypocritical phrase-mongering dissolved in the cordite smoke of the Nigerian volleys, not even a whisper is forthcoming at top level in the labour movement here. – *The Daily Worker* editorial entitled 'Shoot 'Em Down' published on November 29, 1949.

This was how *The Daily Worker* rebuked the British trade union movement for its silence during the Iva Valley shooting incident of November 18, 1949. This was how the paper saw the shifting reactions of the British trade union movement and the Labour Party to colonial questions. The shooting incident is perhaps the most significant episode in Nigerian labour history. In terms of the losses sustained, the emotion it excited and the grief it created in the public mind, no industrial dispute in Nigeria can be matched with it. Crowds rioted at Aba, Port Harcourt, Onitsha and Calabar in protest against the police killing of twenty-one defenceless miners on strike and the wounding of fifty-one others. The criminal elements in these places took advantage of the situation and looted the shops of European trading firms. Later, innocent members of the public were called upon to pay for damage done in the riots.

The circumstances leading to this tragic incident make an epic story and date back to 1944. The relationship between the workers and the Colliery management had long been strained, partly because of the poor human relations existing between the European officers and their Nigerian subordinates, and partly because of the management's opposition to the existence of a militant trade union in the Colliery. There had been a spineless Colliery Surface Improvement

Union, whose membership comprised only time keepers. Its ineffectiveness and very limited jurisdiction led to the founding in 1940 of the Colliery Workers' Union, which represented the underground men, who were the majority of Colliery employees.

Up till 1950 the Enugu Colliery was administered as an integral part of the Nigerian Railway. Because of this relationship European officials in the Colliery, particularly the underground men, developed the habit of handling their African subordinates with the same iron hand as did their counterparts in the Nigerian Railway. Matters came to a head on September 2, 1945, when T. Yates, a European overman, slapped Okwudili Ojiyi, a mine improver, who was then Secretary of the Colliery Workers' Union. Ojiyi reported the assault to the police, who eventually prosecuted Yates, who was fined ten guineas.

The Yates assault case brought two things in its train. First, it checked some of the excesses of white officials, who frequently insulted and assaulted the miners; secondly, it made Ojiyi a hero in the eyes of the workers. He had bearded the lion, which was an unprecedented event in the Colliery, but even so he suspected that he might be victimised. In spite of an assurance to the contrary given by the Resident of Onitsha Province, Ojiyi resigned his post. In May 1946 he became a full-time salaried Secretary of the Colliery Workers' Union.

On February 3, 1944, 280 miners stopped work in protest against some new departmental instructions issued by the Colliery management. The men remained on strike for four days. Instead of looking into their grievances, the Colliery had thirteen of their leaders prosecuted for violating the Defence Regulations. Later the men and seven others were dismissed.

In September the Colliery Workers' Union and the Colliery Surface Improvement Union declared a dispute over claims for a wage increase and the payment of daily allowance for hewers. Attempts to settle the dispute by conciliation failed, so the matter was referred to arbitration. Harold W. Long, who arbitrated in the dispute, recommended, among other things, the introduction of the piece rate system of wage payment as a solution to the agonising problem of declining productivity. Table 6 shows the number of employees and output from 1938 to 1949. According to the report of the Fitzgerald Commission of Enquiry the cost per ton of producing coal increased steadily from roughly 8s. 4d. in 1941–42 to 23s. 5d. in 1948–49, while the sale price per ton was 8s. in 1941–42 and 21s. in 1948–49. For the eight years ending 1948–49 there was a net loss of £465–247.

Table 6

ENUGU COLLIERY:
WORKFORCE AND OUTPUT 1938–9 TO 1948–9

Years	No. of Hewers	Others Underground	Ordinary Surface	Total Daily Paid	Output (Tons)
1938–9	564	1,640	589	2,793	323,266
1939–40	537	1,503	547	2,587	300,090
1940–1	461	1,365	418	2,244	318,593
1941–2	503	1,461	413	2,377	402,639
1942–3	658	1,822	448	2,928	463,978
1943–4	920	2,470	680	4,070	528,421
1944–5	1,046	2,986	843	4,875	668,158
1945–6	931	2,766	1,385	5,082	506,040
1946–7	955	2,940	1,471	5,366	634,527
1947–8	1,187	3,465	1,408	6,060	554,681
1948–9	1,355	3,442	1,206	6,003	610,197

The piece rate system, which might have helped to increase the workers' income, was opposed by them mainly out of ignorance. Because of the poor relationship existing between the workers and their employers, the Colliery management made no effort to explain the system to the men. As far as the management was concerned, the miners were to accept the new system and keep their jobs or reject it and be shown the door. This tough line only incensed the workers into greater resistance. In April 1945, all those workers who refused to work on piece rate were dismissed, and new hands were employed to replace them. The new system failed mainly as the result of the method which was used for its implementation. Productivity did not increase as expected. The failure of the scheme forced the management to climb down; the dismissed workers were re-engaged, and the time-rate system was reintroduced following an agreement between the management and a committee of representatives of the workers appointed at the instance of the management. The Colliery Workers' Union and the Colliery Surface Improvement Union, which were suggested in the appointment of the Long Arbitration, were not a party to the agreement, nor had they even been invited to participate in the negotiation.

In 1947 the Colliery Workers' Union made a claim for a wage increase following the recommendations of the Miller Committee, which enquired into the wages and working conditions of Government unestablished labour. The claim was rejected by the Colliery management on the grounds that the Union was not recognised. The Union threatened to call out its members on strike, and the management replied by issuing a warning notice that workers participating in the strike would be summarily dismissed. It was precisely a similar warning that had deterred the Colliery Workers' Union from joining the General Strike of 1945. Secretary Okwudili Ojiyi describes that notice as a 'great challenge to me': in an attempt to answer that challenge and at the same time save the miners from losing their jobs, he taught them 'go slow' tactics, which he interpreted into Igbo as '*welu nwayo*'. He went into the mines and demonstrated '*welu nwayo*'. After three weeks of intensive practice the men were ready to do his bidding.

The Government had asked the Colliery management to make recommendations as to how Colliery workers could be fitted into the various scales recommended in the Miller Committee Report. The scales proposed by the management were arrived at without any consultation with the unions in the Colliery, not even the Colliery Surface Improvement Union that was recognised by the management. When the scales were published, the miners reacted sharply by 'going slow'. So effective was the 'go slow' that the management was compelled to invite its puppet Committee of Representatives, who confessed they could do nothing to stop the strike because they had no control over the workers. Attempts to get village heads and Udi Clan Councillors[2] to influence the men failed. Finally the Colliery manager, Russell Bracegirdle, approached the Colliery Workers' Union, which called off the 'go slow' on condition that a conciliator would be appointed.

One of the claims in dispute was payment of mine allowance provided for in the Coal Mine Ordinance. At that time the allowance was paid to white officials only, and each received 2s. a day. As a result of the conciliation, an agreement was reached on December 22, 1947, providing for the payment of some arrears to mine workers with effect from January 1, 1946. The arrears amounted to about £150,000, and payment was made in March 1948. After the payment, the Colliery Workers' Union submitted another claim on behalf of certain groups of workers alleged to have been paid incorrect amounts. Management refused to entertain the claim on the ground that it was based on a wrong interpretation of the agreement of December 22, 1947.

On December 8, 1948, the miners started another 'go slow' in furtherance of their claim. A conciliator was appointed. After a three-day meeting, an agreement was entered into on December 16. Under the agreement certain arrears were due to screen and haulage men, screen foremen, token collectors, token hangers, token shouters and token clerks, and payment was to be made not later than March

1949. A similar deadline was agreed upon in respect of arrears for overtime payment retroactive from January 1, 1946. The agreement covered several other matters including a provision for recognition of the Colliery Workers' Union as the sole representative and collective bargaining agent of the workers. According to the Fitzgerald Commission Report, the management recognised that, by that agreement (Para. 14) and the agreement of December 22, 1947, all claims regarding payment of arrears arising from the application of the Harragin and Miller Reports had been met and the machinery for joint consultation set out in the December 16, 1948, agreement should be used in settling any other individual cases that might arise.

A Whitley Council, as recommended in the Harragin Report, was set up in the coal mining industry early in 1949. On February 22 it held its first meeting and adopted its constitution. A second meeting held on April 13 discussed briefly claims put forward by the Staff Side, and decided to continue discussion of the matter when the Staff Side had submitted briefs in keeping with the procedure laid down in the constitution. The next meeting of the Council was scheduled for July 11 and 12. Before the date of the meeting, however, the workers began another 'go slow', for which nobody seemed to know the reason, not even the Secretary of the Colliery Workers' Union, Okwudili Ojiyi. It is possible that they were protesting against the new procedure for disposal of grievances which was slow and cumbersome. Briefly the procedure was as follows:

Step 1: A fortnightly meeting would be held between the personnel manager and the representatives of the Colliery Workers' Union.

Step 2: Matters which could not be settled at Step 1 would be referred to another meeting, which a labour officer could attend and help in bringing about a settlement.

Step 3: If agreement could not be reached at Step 2 the matter would then be referred to the Colliery manager.

Step 4: Failing agreement at Step 3 the matter would then be referred to the Whitley Council or to a conciliator.

Against these cumbersome arrangements involving tremendous delay stood the speedy action taken by management following the 'go slow' strikes of 1947 and 1948. The promptitude of the interventions and the concessions resulting from them must have convinced the workers that the 'go slow' was a quicker and more effective instrument for securing amelioration of grievances.

The 'go slow' was called off after three days, and only after the management had abandoned its threats of disciplinary action against the workers. At the third meeting of the Whitley Council held on

July 11 and 12, the Staff Side submitted twenty-one claims. Agreement was reached on nine claims only: disagreement was recorded on most items relating to up-grading. Whether the Official Side's doggedness in resisting the claims was mere bluff or due to the unsoundness of the claims is a matter for conjecture. The statement made by Ojiyi when opening the case of the Staff Side suggests a combination of both. Ojiyi said that 'the principal reason why the Staff Side wishes to press claims for a general upgrading of practically all categories of Colliery workers was because of a recent deterioration in relations between the Colliery Workers' Union and the Colliery Management'.[3] He alleged that anti-union elements were responsible for management's rejection of the Union's claims; these elements had sent a document to local chiefs informing them that a sum of £2 million was available for improving the lot of Colliery workers provided they got rid of 'the wizard' Ojiyi. He also alleged that the document had been handed to the Colliery manager, who failed to return it.

Another 'go slow' began on November 7, 1949. According to the Fitzgerald Commission report the reasons for it 'were at least not related to anything which had been done or left undone by the Colliery Board'. There has been general discontent among the workers following the outcome of the July meeting of the Whitley Council. Contrary to their expectation, that meeting agreed on upgrading and the payment of arrears to only certain classes of workers. Those particularly disappointed by its outcome were the hewers, who staged several protest demonstrations. On September 13, 1949, they made a formal demand for seniority pay and pressed their claim through the Executive of the Colliery Workers' Union. The claim for seniority pay for all underground workers was one of the items considered by the July meeting of the Whitley Council. When the matter came up for consideration, the official side opposed it, pointing out that a mistake had been made in the case of the hewers (who were then receiving it), and argued that there was no good reason for repeating that mistake. After discussion it was agreed that 'a legitimate claim for all underground workers, who were in receipt of seniority pay at January 1, 1946, to be in enjoyment of that pay as it had already been approved for hewers in addition to the other benefits they derived as a result of the 1947 memorandum of agreement'.[4]

At a meeting with the assistant personnel manager on September 13 it was explained that hewers had already received their seniority pay and that other underground workers were receiving theirs. That explanation did not impress the hewers or their leaders. They had seen other underground men being paid arrears, and felt that they too were entitled to arrears. After the meeting with the Assistant Personnel Manager the agitation for seniority pay entered a confused stage. On October 25 a group of hewers demonstrated outside the offices of the Colliery manager and the chief accountant. The following day a large group repeated the performance at the assistant personnel manager's office, and booed the Colliery manager when he entered the office. Attempts by the Union Secretary to control the men were of no avail.

Another meeting was held on November 1, and was attended by the assistant personnel manager, representatives of the Colliery Workers' Union and representatives of the hewers. Once again the claim for arrears of seniority pay for hewers was made, together with another claim for payment of arrears for rostering. Both claims were rejected by the management on the ground that they were baseless. On November 7 the Hewer's Executive (a militant pressure group set up by the hewers to prosecute this demand) ordered a 'go slow'. The following day they informed the assistant personnel manager that the strike was in furtherance of their claim for payment of arrears for rostering in 1946 and 1947. A couple of days later they added more claims, one of which was for upgrading of hewers to artisans' grade and another was for the payment of travelling and housing allowances. As the 'go slow' proceeded, more and more claims were made.

On November 8, L. P. Ojukwu and L. N. Obiora, two Nigerian members of the newly created Colliery Board, held a meeting with representatives of the Colliery Workers' Union and the Hewers' Executive. After discussions which lasted for about sixteen hours, Ojukwu and his colleague advised the miners to call off the strike and press their claims through the Whitley Council. Ojukwu himself promised that, if normal production were resumed, he would go into the mines with the leaders of the Union to inspect conditions so that he could be in a better position to represent the men's case to the Board.

Ojiyi and Agu, two top officers of the Colliery Workers' Union, tried the following morning to persuade the men to call off the strike. Up till 11 o'clock they had made no significant progress, and reported their failure to Ojukwu. At 1 p.m. the Colliery management posted notices warning the hewers that 'severe disciplinary action which may result in dismissal' would be taken if the strike should continue. The following day, November 10, notices of summary dismissal were served on fifty hewers. Similar notices were served on others on the 11th and 12th.

In the meantime, the events in the Colliery were hitting the headlines of leading newspapers in the country. Sympathy for the workers' claim gained momentum after *The New Africa*, an Enugu daily, had published a news item that £80,000 was due to the miners, but the money was being withheld by management for no just cause. Tension mounted as more and more of the leaders who were pressing the demand were relieved of their positions. On November 15, H. J. Honey, Senior Labour Officer, Enugu, offered to mediate in the dispute. His offer was discussed at a meeting which the Chief Commissioner of Eastern Provinces held the following day with senior Government officials. The meeting was attended by the Chairman of the Colliery Board and the general manager, both of whom advised against accepting Honey's offer on the ground that the workers would regard it as a sign of weakness; their views were supported by the Civil Secretary. As a result, the services of an experienced officer in industrial relations were thrown overboard. From then onward the Administration took the Colliery dispute as a political agitation.

A few days earlier, and following the summary dismissal of many hewers, miners' wives demonstrated against the treatment being meted out to their men. The demonstration got out of hand and led to some damage being done to property, but it was quickly brought under control.

On November 17 the Chief Commissioner held another meeting with Senior Government officials. That meeting decided that explosives be removed from Obwetti and Iva Valley Mines. The operation was planned for the following morning, and detailed arrangements were left with the Assistant Commissioner of Police and the Colliery manager.

Why did the Administration see a purely industrial dispute as a political agitation, and why did it decide, as the Fitzgerald Commission emphasised, that explosives must be removed 'at all costs'? The evidence given before the Fitzgerald Commission by J. O. Field, Senior Assistant Secretary in charge of Defence and Security, provides an answer. Field said that since 1948 it had been apparent that certain elements had been trying to acquire arms and explosives. Although there was no evidence that these elements had had any dealings with the miners, the fact remained that several thefts had been committed, involving the loss of thirty cases of explosives in the Colliery magazine. Early in 1949 instructions were given on the necessity to safeguard explosives.

Apparently it was the suspicion (even though unsupported by evidence) that some sort of alliance existed between the miners and

1. Struggle between police and miners before the shooting. According to the Fitzgerald Commission Report 'the reason why the miners objected to the explosives was because they feared that once the explosives were removed nothing stood in the way of the management closing the mine and thus effecting a lock-out. . . . Not one policeman was injured, not one missile was thrown at them. . . . Yet this was one of the main contributory factors which decided Mr. Philip to open fire.' Drawing by Aninkwu Jones.

the so-called political agitators that convinced the Chief Commissioner and his advisers that the events in the Colliery were no longer an industrial dispute. This belief soon became an obsession, and was undoubtedly responsible for the rejection of the services of a mediator, and for the rather rash decision that explosives should be removed at all costs. The decision was of doubtful propriety and liable to various interpretations. If the intention was to prevent explosives falling into the hands of subversive elements, the same purpose could have equally well been achieved by posting adequate sentries to guard the magazine stores. The hewers, who depend on explosives for production, were not likely to take kindly to the removal. Indeed, as the Fitzgerald Commission pointed out, 'the reason why the miners objected to the removal of the explosives was because they feared that once the explosives were removed nothing stood in the way of the management closing the mine and thus effecting a lock-out'. The Commission went on: 'There seems little doubt that the miners would have resented the removal of explosives by agitators as strenuously as their removal by Government. There was no reason to believe that the miners would not have agreed to the explosives being removed if they had been convinced that the removal of the explosives did not prejudice their case on the question of the lock-out.'[5]

At 8 a.m. on Friday, November 18, the Assistant Commissioner of Police received information about the quantity of explosives to be removed and detailed three parties of armed policemen under the command of three assistant superintendents of police, to proceed to Obwetti and Iva Valley to carry out the assignment. The Obwetti party completed their assignment and left before noon. The Iva Valley party could not make the same progress for three reasons. First, the quantity of explosives available for removal was much greater than had been reported; secondly, the means of conveyance was inadequate, and could not be taken close to the magazine stores where the explosives were kept; thirdly, attempts to get the miners to assist in removing the explosives were of no avail. Alternative arrangements had to be made, and at about 1 p.m. a locomotive engine and a coach arrived.

Two out of three stores were easily evacuated. On his return to Enugu, Assistant Superintendent of Police H. J. W. Watkins, who was in charge of the operation, reported to the Assistant Commissioner that he had some difficulties in getting out, and in his opinion the situation at Iva Valley was deteriorating. The Assistant Commissioner detailed F. S. Phillip, Senior Superintendent of Police, two other senior police officers and seventy-five riflemen to reinforce the Iva Valley party. When the party arrived, Phillip, who had assumed overall command of all the parties, decided that the explosives should not be removed immediately but that his forces should be disposed in such a way as to keep them out of contact with about 1,500 miners, who had gathered, some of them armed with sticks. One of the senior police officials was detailed to lead the policemen in a single line across a narrow foot-bridge and 'post them on the high ground beyond the stream where they could be remote from the crowd'. While the policemen marched across the foot-bridge, the miners sang war-songs. Seventy out of the 105 policemen had crossed when a struggle ensued between three policemen and some of the miners. The incident put Phillip out of gear. He said: 'I will have to fire.' But he did not just fire a warning shot, which might have been appropriate in the circumstance. 'Firing also took place from the ranks all along the line and on the hill as well, and when the cease-fire was given it was only the prompt action, which we commend, of Mr. Brown, in going along the ranks and knocking up the rifles of the individual policemen that caused them

Table 7

MINERS KILLED AT IVA VALLEY NOV. 18, 1949

No.	*Name*	*Tally No.*	*Occupation*	*Town/Village*	*Province*
1.	Sunday	1,396	Hewer	Obazu Mbieri	Owerri
2.	Ani	1,671	Hewer	Ajukwu Ebe. Udi	Onitsha
3.	Andrew	1,682	Hewer	Owa. Udi	Onitsha
4.	Augustine	1,879	Hewer	Owa. Udi	Onitsha
5.	Onoh	11,051	Tubman	Enugwu Ngwo	Onitsha
6.	Ngwu	10,078	Tubman	Ngwo	Onitsha
7.	Nduaguba	11,773	Tubman	Owa	Onitsha
8.	Okafor	11,550	Tubman	Umuabi Udi	Onitsha
9.	Levinus	24,039	Mach. man	Ohi Owerri	Owerri
10.	Jonathan	3,190	Railman	Uboji Ngwo	Onitsha
11.	Moses	2,307	Mach. man	Umuohoho Amaimo	Owerri
12.	Chukwu	24,137	Mach. man	Amorie Agbani	Onitsha
13.	Simon	24,267	Mach. man	Ubaha Mbutu	Owerri
14.	Agu	2,165	Mach. man	Enugwu Ngwo	Onitsha
15.	Ogbonnia	2,015	Mach. man	Ihe Agwu	Onitsha
16.	Nnaji	4,598	Screen Labr	Ndembara Amaimo	Owerri
17.	Nwahu	4,017	Engine Driver	Amuzi Bende	Owerri
18.	James	4,364	Clip Operator	Amauwani Ukana-Udi	Onitsha
19.	Felix	S.671	Apprentice Electrician	Akpugo Agbani	Onitsha
20.	Ani	1,669	Hewer	Amankwo Ngwo	Onitsha
21.	Thomas	24,163	Mach. man	Mbaha Okigwi	Owerri

to cease fire and thus prevent what might have been an even more lamentable loss of life.'[6]

News of the shooting incident spread like wildfire. The country was outraged. An indication has already been given of what happened in Eastern Nigeria. In Lagos the press and leading political figures were unanimous in condemning the shooting and demanding a commission of enquiry. On Sunday, November 20, eighteen leading Nigerians from various walks of life gathered at 2 Garbar Square, the residence of Dr. Akinola Maja, and founded the National Emergency Committee. They were Dr. Akinola Maja, S. O. Gbadamosi, F. R. A. Williams, K. O. Mbadiwe, F. U. Anyiam, the Odemo of Ishara, Oba Samuel Akisanya, O. A. Thomas, Oged Macaulay, G. B. Okeke, P. O. Balonwu, M. A. Ogun, A. A. Adio-Moses, A. K. Blankson, Mokwugo Okoye, H. O. Davies, N. Okoro, Mbonu Ojike and Dr. I. Olorun-Nimbe. The aim of the NEC was to tackle immediately the problems arising out of the shooting incident and explore the possibilities of forming a permanent National Emergency Council. Dr. Maja was elected chairman and Mbonu Ojike secretary.

In the labour camp a National Labour Committee, comprising leaders of the Trades Union Congress and the Nigerian National Federation of Labour, was set up to tackle the problems of the shooting and see that justice was done. The NEC sent a three-man delegation consisting of H. O. Davies, Bode Thomas and K. O. Mbadiwe to investigate and report on the incident. The decision to send an investigation team followed a Government statement that 'the Police were surrounded by a large number of miners armed with crowbars, picks, matchets and spears, who rushed at the Police and attempted to disarm them and obtain possession of the explosive store. The officer in-charge of the Police endeavoured to reason with the miners, without success. In spite of repeated warnings the situation became so dangerous that the police were compelled to open fire in self-defence.'[7]

The findings of the NEC investigation team appeared to disprove the Government account of the shooting. In their report the team said it was untrue that the miners were armed and attempted to disarm the police. It was a matter for regret that such a false publication, which was likely to prejudice the public mind against the miners, had been made by the Government. The report revealed that the Government was trying to coerce people in an effort to find a justification for the killings. It recommended a commission of enquiry and declared, with reference to coercion, that 'this statement is made with full responsibility'. Emphasising the need for an enquiry with full powers the report said:

> Unless the Commission of Enquiry is given the fullest facilities to establish the truth, the whole truth and nothing but the truth, about the loss of 21 lives and the wounding of 55 men, relations between the Government and the people of this country would have suffered an irreparable damage.[8]

The Iva Valley shooting incident found an echo in the House of Commons when seventeen MP's harrassed the Colonial Secretary, Arthur Creech-Jones, with a barrage of questions. They wanted to know how unarmed miners could have rioted against armed policemen. A *West African Pilot* correspondent, who covered the debate, reported that:

> In spite of very cold weather Mr. Creech-Jones sweated profusely as his department was subjected to a constant barrage of embarrassing questions not only from Opposition MP's but also from the Labour MP's.[9]

Against the commendable role of British MP's over the Enugu blood bath stood the despicable role of Nigerian legislators. It is to their eternal shame and discredit that no member of the Legislative Council raised the question during the December 1949 session. Their silence became an additional justification for demanding not only a representative Government based on direct elections, but also for self-government. At a mass meeting of the NEC held at Enugu on December 8, Dr. Maja announced that from thenceforth the slogan of Nigerian nationalists would be 'Self-government for Nigeria Now' – SGNN.

Mounting pressures from the National Emergency Committee, the National Council of Nigeria and the Cameroons and the Nigerian Youth Movement forced an unwilling administration to yield. On December 28, the Governor appointed a four-man Commission 'to enquire into and report on the recent disorders in Nigeria with special reference to the recent labour troubles at Enugu Colliery and the events which followed'. The Commission consisted of W. J. Fitzgerald, Chairman; S. O. Quashie-Idun, A. A. Ademola and R. W. Williams. The NEC and NLC rallied round and secured some of the best legal brains in the country to represent the miners. Among them were H. O. Davies, F. R. A. Williams, H. U. Kaine, Jaja Wachuku, G. C. Nonyelu, M. O. Ajegbo, G. C. Nkemena, G. C. M. Onyiuke, C. D. Onyeama and M. O. Ibeziako. The Commission sat from December 12, 1949, to January 5, 1950, and took evidence from eighty-two witnesses.

In its 60-page report published in June 1950, the Fitzgerald

Commission blamed both the Government and the trade union leaders for the unfortunate incident at Iva Valley. Referring to the development of trade unionism in the country the Commission accepted the point made in evidence by A. A. Adio-Moses, Secretary of the Trades Union Congress, that 'although all the necessary laws were placed on the statute book, there was no spirit behind them'. The result had been that unscrupulous individuals had taken undue advantage of the situation and, 'under the guise of workers' leaders, have exploited them and prostituted the movement for their own subversive ends'.

The report dealt at length with industrial relations in the Colliery and declared that, while union leadership was weak and inefficient, management could not be absolved of responsibility for exacerbating troubles in the industry. It referred to the circumstances leading to the 'go slow' of November 1949, and pointed out that what 'was agitating the miners was this industrial issue whether £80,000 was

2. Some of the miners shot dead at Iva Valley Coal Mine, November 18, 1949. 'We feel bound to state that the report made by the Police to the Chief Commissioner and later published that the Police were attacked by a lot of armed miners was not substantiated by evidence.'—Fitzgerald Commission Report. Drawn by Aninkwu Jones.

due to them and whether they were being locked out'. It blamed 'the worthless Secretary Ojiyi' and *The New Africa* for creating the false impression that £80,000 was due to the hewers and was being withheld by the Colliery Management without just cause.

The report then dealt with Ojiyi's role in the miners' claim for upgrading and declared: 'We have considered the significance of the attitude of Ojiyi in this matter and we are satisfied that, faced as he was with a challenge from the workers, who had commenced proceedings in connection with the accounts of the Union, he sought to discredit them to his advantage in the eyes of the members of the Union. He therefore did all he could to bring about a deterioration in the industrial relationship at the Colliery and sought to fix the responsibility for that deterioration on his rivals. . . . We consider that Ojiyi's behaviour in this matter has been utterly unscrupulous.'

On the role played by the Chief Commissioner and his advisers, the report emphasised the need for drawing a distinction between industrial disputes and political agitations. Although political agitators might stand poised ready to strike, yet that did not convert an industrial dispute into a political agitation. Indeed, to treat such a dispute as a political agitation very often played into the hands of agitators. The dispute at the Colliery was a purely industrial one; and had arisen because the miners were led to believe that some money was due to them. The men were induced to this belief by Ojiyi and by 'the lie – we cannot avoid the conclusion that it was a deliberate lie – published in the newspaper *The New Africa* to the effect that £80,000 was due to the miners and was being purposely withheld from them.'

The report examined in detail the circumstances leading to the shooting incident and said that Superintendent Phillip committed an error of judgment in ordering the shooting. It pointed out that the miners could not have prevented the police from completing their movement across the bridge on the hill, but they would have opposed any attempt to remove the explosives. Although evidence was given to the effect that some miners were armed with matchets, it was significant that the crowd had been assembled there for some hours and yet made no attempt whatsoever to use force against the police. 'Not one policeman was injured, not one missile was thrown at them. At the lower ground level near the magazine door there were three policemen completely cut off; there were others on top of the magazine who were also at the mercy of overwhelming superior numbers. It is true that there is some evidence that they were struggling, but if the crowd were bent on using force against the police nothing could have saved these policemen from grave injury, whereas in fact they were not injured at all. Yet this was one of the main contributory factors which decided Mr. Phillip to open fire.' The report went on: 'We feel bound to state that the report made by the Police to the Chief Commissioner and later published that the Police were attacked by a lot of armed miners was not substantiated by evidence.'[10]

The report also dealt with the need for a system of conciliation independent of Government. It stressed the grave consequences likely to arise in industrial relation when the 'go slow' was being used by the workers on the one hand and large numbers of summary dismissals were being used by management on the other. Pinpointing the lack of a system of conciliation independent of Government as an outstanding deficiency that had been revealed in the incidents at the Colliery, the report remarked that the Industrial Boards and Whitley Councils which had been recently set up by the Government were steps in the right direction, but were not enough. It observed that the workers of Nigeria were not imbued with the spirit of discipline which is so essential to progress, but added that it would be unreasonable to expect them to acquire in a few years what it had taken their counterparts in Britain a century to attain.

The report suggested the setting up of Statutory Boards to manage Government industrial establishments like the Colliery, the Railway and Electricity Undertakings. It remarked that one of the most disturbing features of the industrial situation was the growing hostility between employers and workers, and it was essential that this hostility be eliminated. To this end it recommended the establishment of 'not only a Ministry of Labour enjoying the necessary status and authority but a system of conciliation whereunder industrial disputes would be finally disposed of by an authority which would command the respect and support of all parties'. It further recommended the establishment in Government industrial undertakings and large private firms like the UAC of Conciliation Boards similar to that of the National Coal Board in Britain. These Boards, it said, should operate in two stages. The first stage should be the Joint Negotiating Committee, and the second the National Reference Tribunal. The Conciliation Boards should consider any question raised by the employer or unions: if disagreement was reached at the Board meeting, the matter should be referred to the National Reference Tribunal for settlement.

Following the recommendations of the Fitzgerald Commission, the Secretary of State for the Colonies appointed a group of experts in trade union organisation and labour relations to visit Nigeria and study the problem of industrial relations not only in the Colliery but in the country as a whole. The experts were to assist both sides of industry work out the details and put into effect the recommendations of the Commission, and consisted of E. Cain, Secretary of the Wheatley Hill, Durban Branch of the National Union of Mineworkers; A. Dalgleish of the British TUC; E. Parry, Assistant Labour Adviser to the Secretary of State for the Colonies; Col. C. E. Ponsonby, of the British Employers' Confederation; and P. G. Weekes, Manager of Oakdale Colliery, South Wales. They remained in the country from June to September 1950. Cain and Weekes devoted their attention to the Colliery, with particular reference to joint consultation on day-to-day working conditions. Parry conducted a special enquiry into the situation existing in the Colliery with a view to making recommendations for achieving an improved industrial relation.

His recommendations formed the basis of a draft legislation entitled the 'Nigerian Coal Corporation Industrial Council Bill', published in the *Nigeria Gazette* later in the year. The Bill provided for a Council composed of an independent chairman and an equal number of representatives of the workers and the Colliery management, appointed by the Governor after due consultation. The Council was to have powers to make orders fixing wages and conditions of employment, and such orders were to have the force of law. The Bill was to be enacted into law at the Budget Session of the Legislative Council in March 1951, but its enactment was delayed because of the opposition of the fledgling Nigerian Coal Miners' Union, an unregistered organisation which had arisen in place of the discredited Colliery Workers' Union. It was clear from its agitation that the Bill and the purpose of introducing it were misunderstood by the Union. Explaining the reasons for delaying the Bill, the Commissioner of Labour said at the Budget Session of the Legislative Council in 1951:

> The aims [i.e. of the Bill] are such that we are confident that no one would question their desirability. But if the Joint Council we have proposed is to succeed in achieving these aims, it is essential that it should itself be fully understood and fully endorsed by every one concerned with it. It has appeared to us recently that the essential measure of full understanding has not yet been reached. We do not wish the successful achievement of ends, which in themselves are beyond reproach, to be prejudiced by suspicion born of misunderstanding of the means. Consequently it has been decided that we shall not proceed with the enactment of the Bill during the present session of the House.[11]

The decision to suspend enactment of the Joint Industrial Council

Bill meant that there was no effective or regular means of joint consultation between the Coal Corporation and its employees except the District and Surface Consultative Committees which met monthly. These Committees were concerned with safety, health, welfare, production and related technical matters; wages and other conditions of employment which are subjects for collective bargaining between employers and trade unions were specifically left out of their terms of reference.

The Nigerian Coal Miners' Union was registered in April 1951. While trying to establish good relations with the Corporation management, it adopted towards the Consultative Committees a hostile attitude, which arose out of the Union's suspicion that management would take them as substitute for a trade union. This suspicion, when considered together with a provision in the proposed Joint Industrial Council Bill, by which the Governor-in-Council was to appoint the representatives of the Staff Side of the Council, meant, in the Union's view, that those likely to be appointed were management nominees who, in all probability, would be *personae non gratae* as far as the Union was concerned. Because of the general misunderstanding it was decided that more efforts should be made, with the active participation of the Union, to explain to the rank and file the value of joint consultation. The task was carried out by labour officers. Their efforts were reinforced by literature in simple English distributed to the literate members of the Executive Council of the Union. In June 1951 the Union expressed its willingness to accept joint consultation. The Nigerian Coal Corporation also indicated its willingness to accept.

The Commissioner of Labour then suggested, and the suggestion was accepted by both sides, that if and when it became clear that the Union could be regarded as reasonably representative of the workers, the scheme of joint consultation and the Joint Industrial Council could be set up. Shortly afterwards, the Union claimed a membership of 3,962 out of a total labour force of 6,425. It was not possible to verify this claim, but there was no doubt that, by the end of June 1951, the union had gained considerable ground. Labour Officers, who were in regular contact with the Union, were of the opinion that it could now be regarded as 'reasonably representative'. Unfortunately this view was not shared by management.

At the end of June the Labour Department forwarded copies of a draft agreement on joint consultation to the management and the Union. Negotiations opened a few days later under the chairmanship of the Commissioner of Labour. The negotiations were concluded on July 30 and an agreement was signed.

On August 1, shift workers began a sit-down strike in protest against undue delay in payment of wages, a matter which had been the cause of constant agitation. That strike was a severe test on the Union's influence over the men. Although it was soon contained, the events which followed showed clearly that the Union had very little influence over them. The Corporation and the Union began discussions on a new system of wage payment shortly after the strike was called off. As the discussions proceeded, the Union's influence over the workers weakened because of differences among the various groups. On August 6, the underground men began a 'go slow'. The reason for that strike is not clear. Early attempts to resolve the 'go slow' failed because the union was not as representative as it was believed to be. The strike was called off when the Union agreed to accept the suggestion of labour officers mediating in the dispute that the Executive be enlarged to accommodate representatives of the underground men. An *ad hoc* committee consisting of eight union men and eight men representing the underground men was set up. On August 10, the Corporation and the *Ad Hoc* Committee reached agreement on the new system of wage payment.

The emergence of the *Ad Hoc* Committee clearly showed that the Union had little influence over the workers, and was therefore incapable of discharging one of its obligations in the agreement of July 30, which says:

> The Union undertakes to use its endeavours to ensure that the terms of every agreement (i.e. agreement under the scheme if joint consultation) shall be observed by all workers or class of workers intended to be affected thereby, whether or not they be members of the Union, and also to ensure that, until the procedure of the scheme has been exhausted, there shall be no stoppage of work of either a partial or general character.

The Union, realising its weak position, continued to work with the *Ad Hoc* Committee while at the same time trying to increase its membership by systematic organising of the underground men. By October its membership had come to include a large number of underground men, and this strengthened its claim as sole representative and collective bargaining agent. Behind this happy augury, however, lay the problem of correcting the imbalance in the union leadership position.

Hitherto almost all the key offices in the Union were held by clerical men from the Corporation's head office, who were an infinitesimal minority of the employees. This anomaly arose from the fact that office workers were the founders of the Union and were in the vanguard of the struggles against Ojiyi. When Ojiyi and his associates were convicted and sentenced to various terms of imprisonment for conspiring to embezzle the funds of the Colliery Workers' Union, all those who gave evidence leading to their conviction gathered themselves together, set up a rival organisation and installed themselves in office. Manual workers were not interested in the new organisation for two reasons: first, they had little confidence that a union that was led by clerks could be effective in championing their cause; and secondly, although he was thoroughly discredited by the findings of the Fitzgerald Commission and his subsequent imprisonment, Ojiyi still commanded considerable support among the miners who, since the Yates incident, regarded him as a hero. The tide turned in favour of the Union when the new organisation succeeded in enrolling a popular mine clerk, J. A. Diewait, as a member.

In July 1951 the first conference of the Nigerian Coal Miners' Union elected Diewait President of the Union. Four months later, he (his real surname was Onwuchekwa, but he adopted Diewait, which is the literary rendering in English of his Igbo surname) was removed from office by the Union's Executive Council. The reason for his removal is obscure, but his constituents, the underground men, believed that he was a victim of intrigue, and accused the Union's General Secretary, C. P. Morris, with whom he had not been pulling well, of being the brain behind it. At a mass meeting held shortly after his removal, Diewait told a cheering crowd that he was removed because he could not subscribe to being a management stooge, which he claimed his opponents in the Executive were. The meeting rejected Diewait's removal and expelled Morris and other members of the Executive.

From then for the next three months, the leadership of the Nigerian Coal Miners' Union became a disputed issue. The Coal Corporation management accepted Diewait's removal as legal and valid, and refused to recognise or deal with him as the workers' representative. They preferred to deal with Morris and his colleagues. The Corporation's preference for a group of men who were clearly *personae non gratae* caused much hard feeling among the miners and bedevilled relations in the industry for some time.

On January 29, 1952, the workers staged a peaceful demonstration before the Lieutenant-Governor demanding the removal of the Corporation's Chief Accountant, Major Allan William Dickes, whom they accused of being the spirit behind the bad industrial relations in the industry. The demonstrators also demanded that Diewait be recognised as President and spokesman of the Union.

E

Two days later the *Nigerian Daily Record,* a daily newspaper published at Enugu, suggested the holding of a plebiscite as an answer to the disputed leadership question. The paper argued that such a plebiscite would throw some light on who really commanded the confidence of the workers. On February 1 the miners on first shift at Asata Mines went on strike for two hours in protest against the continued recognition of Morris as the leader of the Union. The strike was called off on the condition that a plebiscite would be held to determine the leadership question.

The plebiscite, the first of its kind in Nigerian labour history, was held on February 3 and 4, 1952, under the supervision of H. C. Alder, Senior Labour Officer; R. Curry, Labour Officer (Trade Unions); N. O. Akinyemi, Labour Officer (Conciliation); J. C. Jones, Agent, Nigerian Coal Corporation; J. N. Moran, Colliery Manager, Obwetti; S. T. Saint, Personnel Manager; and T. Cox, Underground Manager. The results were:

	Votes Cast[12]
ASATA	
J. A. Diewait	2,494
C.P. Morris	1
	2,494
IVA VALLEY	
J. A. Diewait	1,400
C. P. Morris	Nil
	1,400
TOTAL (BOTH MINES)	
J. A. Diewait	3,894
C. P. Morris	1
	3,895

The result of the plebiscite disappointed the Coal Corporation and the Labour Department, as is clear from the subtle manner with which they tried to play down the result. The Corporation said: 'The Executive Committee appeared to have boycotted the voting.'[13] The Labour Department claimed: 'it appeared to some observers that some, perhaps many, of the workers taking part in this affair had very little idea of what they were about.'[14]

The plebiscite did not completely resolve the dispute as, for three weeks afterwards, the struggle centred around how to get the Union's books and other property from Morris and his colleagues. A suggestion that the Executive should resign as a means of resolving the dispute was discountenanced, the Executive arguing that:

(i) they had always acted constitutionally and had done nothing wrong;
(ii) many men still supported them in principle but were temporarily deceived or overwhelmed by trouble makers;
(iii) they had to prepare the annual statement of accounts for the Registrar of Trade Unions;
(iv) they could not easily divest themselves of responsibility for the safe custody of the Union's property;
(v) they still believed it was possible that a solution could be found by way of agreement.[15]

Diewait and his supporters appealed to the Labour Department to intervene. When this failed to achieve the desired result a series of work stoppages began, which forced the Coal Corporation to withdraw recognition of the Executive. On February 29, Morris and his colleagues resigned and handed over the Union's property.

Morris's fall from power marked a turning-point in industrial relations in the Corporation, but it was a short-lived peace. In the intervening period the Corporation set to work to destroy the Union. By a systematic campaign, they got some workers to express lack of confidence in the Union's leadership, and this became a justification to apply the sledge-hammer. On October 7 the Corporation withdrew recognition of the Union on the ground that it no longer represented or exercised control over a majority of its employees. Although an undertaking was given on October 20 that recognition would be restored as soon as the Enugu Council of Labour, the Union's solicitor and the Labour Department could certify that the Union was 'reasonably representative', that undertaking was never kept. Rather, all persons who worked to achieve the objective were systematically relieved of their positions in the Corporation.

REFERENCES

1. *Report of the Commission of Enquiry into the Disorders in the Eastern Provinces of Nigeria*, November 1949, page 57.
2. Members of the local authority council of a clan in Enugu Province (previously under Onitsha Provincial Administration).
3. *Report of Commission of Enquiry into the Disorders in the Eastern Province of Nigeria*, November 1949, page 26.
4. Ibid., page 23. 5. Ibid., page 36. 6. Ibid., page 39.
7. *The West African Pilot*, November 21, 1949.
8. Ibid., November 24, 1949. 9. Ibid., December 7, 1949.
10. Ibid., page 40. 11. Proceedings of the Legislative Council.
12. *Nigerian Daily Record*, February 3 and 4, 1952.
13. *Nigerian Daily Record*, February 11, 1952.
14. Labour Department Annual Report, 1951–52, page 24.
15. Ibid., page 24.

12

THE MERCANTILE WORKERS' STRIKE

Throughout 1949, efforts were made to reconcile the Trades Union Congress of Nigeria and the Nigerian National Federation of Labour, but without avail. By early 1950 it was clear that both organisations had become spent forces and were ready to consider unity talks. Preliminary talks began in March, and in April the representatives of both bodies and the Federation of Government and Municipal Non-Clerical Workers' Union met and agreed to dissolve the three organisations and set up a new central labour organisation. A Caretaker Committee was appointed to prepare the ground for an inaugural conference where the constitution of the new organisation would be considered and officers elected. The officers of the Caretaker Committee were F. O. Coker, President; N. A. Cole and T. O. E. Okpareke, Vice-Presidents; E. O. Effiom, Secretary; and R. Aghedo, Treasurer. The Caretaker Committee organised a conference on May 26, which inaugurated the Nigerian Labour Congress. Its principal officers were M. A. O. Imoudu, President; F. O. Coker, Deputy President; Nduka Eze, General Secretary; T. O. E. Okpareke, Treasurer; and N. A. Cole, Information and Publicity Secretary. A few weeks after the inaugural conference, the NLC announced its affiliation to the World Federation of Trade Unions.

The NLC planned extensive organising and educational activities, and divided its secretariat into seven departments, each headed by a Secretary and with a committee. The departments and their Secretaries were: A. A. Adio-Moses, Secretary to the Department of Education and Research; A. Nehru Ikoro, Secretary to the Department of Public Relations and Foreign Affairs; S. M. U. Asemota, Secretary to the Department of Finance and Economics; J. Ola Oduleye, Secretary to the Department of Government and Municipal Workers; P. O. Balonwu, Secretary to the Department of Mercantile and Private Concerns; and L. U. Agonsi, Secretary to the Department of Welfare and Co-operatives.

The organising and education activities of the Congress were frustrated by lack of funds, brought about partly by the refusal of two of the contracting parties to the fusion to transfer their assets and liabilities to the new organisation, and partly by the failure of the affiliated unions to pay their affiliation dues. It had been agreed by both the Caretaker Committee and the inaugural conference that the TUC, the NNFL and the Federation of Government and Municipal Non-Clerical Workers' Union should transfer their assets and liabilities to the Congress. For unknown reasons the TUC and the Federation refused to comply. The Council had to rely on the lean resources of the NNFL for its operations.

The new organisation engaged in much political activity, which seemed to be the ultimate ambition of its leaders. At the Lagos municipal elections of November 1950, four of its leaders were returned in a landslide victory of the Nigerian National Democratic Party. Among them was Nduka Eze, the NLC General Secretary. The political gains made at the municipal elections were quickly destroyed the following month by the intemperate strike of mercantile workers organised by the NLC. The mercantile workers' strike was an attempt by the NLC to extend a dispute in one establishment to all establishments in the retail and distributive trades. The dispute was between the United Africa Company and the Amalgamated Union of UAC African Workers.

At its conference in 1948, the UNAMAG decided to declare a dispute with the UAC over several matters concerning conditions of employment. An enquiry was set up by the Labour Department, and the officer succeeded in getting both parties to agree to negotiate, but negotiation was hampered by personal discord between the management representative and the Union's General Secretary following threats of strike action. Eventually the negotiation was concluded and agreement reached on all but five of the points in dispute. Having won several concessions the union decided to suspend its request for arbitration and to endeavour to maintain good relations with the UAC. That was in May, 1949.

Early in 1950 the union renewed its strike threat because of what it termed the failure of the conciliation of May 1949. The UAC refused to reopen negotiation on matters it regarded as closed. In June the Union announced the existence of a trade dispute and claimed that 'the annual conference of the Union had authorised the Central Executive Council to pursue the matter of settling the remaining points in dispute up to the point of strike'.[1] Because of the strained relationship existing between the Union and the Company it soon became clear that there was little hope of settling the matter by direct negotiation between them or by conciliation. The matters were therefore referred to arbitration, and the Union was advised accordingly on July 28, 1950.

On August 1 the Union said it wanted six other points included in the terms of reference. Among them was the demand for payment of 12½ per cent cost of living allowance, which had been granted to Government servants in April. Announcing the award in the Legislative Council, the Financial Secretary had expressed the hope that private employers would follow the Government's example since there had been no general revision of salaries and wages since the Harragin awards of 1946. The Financial Secretary's statement was given wide publicity by the press and radio. Immediately Unions catering for workers in industry and commercial firms interpreted the Financial Secretary's statement as an order to employers to grant similar wage increases. Employers, who might have granted wage increases before then were pressed to pay the 12½ per cent COLA. The UAC was one of these employers.

When the UNAMAG requested that six additional points be included in the terms of reference of the arbitration tribunal the UAC pointed out that payment of cost of living allowance was a new issue and five of the six items had been settled in May 1949. The Company's answer infuriated the Union, which called a strike that hit most UAC establishments in the country. It was called off when the company agreed to the inclusion of the six points, but not until there had been a considerable violence resulting in damage to property, and assaults on strike breakers. That same day Mr. Justice V. R. Bairamain, a Judge of the High Court, was appointed sole arbitrator.

The Bairamain arbitration made four awards out of the eleven points in dispute, one of which was the payment of 12½ per cent cost of living allowance. Payment of the new wage rates was delayed because of differences in interpretation of the effective date. The UNAMAG claimed the effective date was April 1, 1950, but the UAC argued that it was November 10. Since the parties could not agree on the date, the arbitrator himself was asked to give the correct interpretation. He interpreted the effective date as November 10, 1950, and immediately 'the Union shifted its ground and stated that the whole award was unjust and unacceptable'.[2]

A strike threat followed, and on December 14 the Union called out its members on strike. Compared with the massive response in August, the December strike was a failure. From the first day, only a minority of the workers went on strike, after which support weakened, and on December 26 the strike was called off.

The Nigerian Labour Congress, whose Secretary was also the General Secretary of the UNAMAG, began a campaign in November urging all mercantile workers who had not been paid 12½ per cent cost of living allowance with effect from April to make demands for it, and to be prepared to go on strike on December 14 – the deadline of the proposed UNAMAG strike – if their demands were not met. Soon afterwards the Amalgamated Union of Clerical and Allied Workers, an industrial union of employees of various mercantile establishments and an affiliate of the NLC, asked for official intervention in the matter. The Deputy Commissioner of Labour was assigned to preside over negotiation meetings with each of the fourteen firms against which a general dispute had been declared. Effective intervention was possible in only one firm. Five companies argued that there was no dispute existing between them and their employees; six held negotiations with representatives of their employees; while in the remaining two firms negotiation meetings were cancelled because the workers' representatives failed to turn up.

In spite of these remarkable developments the NLC pursued its policy of calling out the workers on strike. The strike, involving 29,860 workers and a loss of 239,663 man-days, began on December 14. Like the UAC workers' strike, it proved a failure. Before it, many employers warned their employees that participants would be dismissed. Those who defied the warning and went on strike were dismissed out of hand.

The mercantile workers' strike had the same effect on the NLC as the 1945 strike had had on the TUC. But while the Tudor Davies awards alleviated the effects of the 1945 strike, the colossal failure of the mercantile workers' strike dealt a severe blow to the NLC. By the end of 1950, the majority of the unions had left the organisation. The Congress came into public limelight again in March, 1951, when it expressed opposition to an ICFTU delegation to Nigeria. The delegation (consisting of F. A. Bailey, W. L. White, M. Grant, H. Snell and W. Wood) was part of a big ICFTU mission which visited West Africa between January and March 1951. NLC officials came to Ikeja airport with a motley crowd to tell the delegation 'Go Home'. To demonstrate their opposition the crowd clashed with those who claimed to support the TUC. The scene left a poor impression of the NLC among the workers and an even poorer impression of the Nigerian labour movement in the minds of the visitors. The impression undoubtedly influenced the mission to recommend Accra instead of Lagos as the ICFTU base for initial operations in West Africa.

Some labour leaders in Nigeria often recall the Ikeja airport fracas as one of the underhand tricks of the labour movement of a sister African state to deprive the country of contacts likely to benefit the workers of Nigeria. This explains why the Nigerian labour movement was never carried away by Ghanaian propaganda during President Nkrumah's régime that ICFTU is an imperialist agent working against the interests of African workers.

Before the arrival of the ICFTU mission, a leading Ghanaian trade unionist, visited Nigeria and held meetings with several trade union leaders in Lagos; he urged them not to welcome the delegation. His message was given a cold reception in some labour quarters and hailed in others. Supporters of free trade unionism took exception to a foreigner coming to Nigeria and virtually handing down an order as to what Nigerians should do in their country. Apart from the fact that outside interference is repulsive to Nigerians, the suggestion that they should turn their backs on visitors was one to which no Nigerian with respect for his traditions would take kindly. Other labour leaders, particularly members of the fledging Marxist Group, among them some NLC leaders, accepted Mettle-Nunoo's suggestion with gusto, and proceeded to do his bidding.

The visiting mission eventually left for Accra, where they were accorded a warm reception. They held discussions with leaders of the Gold Coast Trades Union Congress, which eventually decided to affiliate to the ICFTU. A few months later, Accra became the base of ICFTU operations in West Africa. As a result of that affiliation, the Gold Coast trade union movement received invaluable services and financial assistance, which even the former leaders of the Ghana TUC still acknowledge.

In September 1951 the Nigerian Labour Congress announced its disaffiliation from the World Federation of Trade Unions. One national newspaper said of the announcement that 'the NLC is dead and buried'. From then until the emergence of a new central labour organisation in 1953, the Congress was a façade existing on letter-heads and on the pages of certain newspapers.

REFERENCES

1. *Labour Department Annual Report, 1950–51*, page 53.
2. Ibid. page 33.

13

THE DEVELOPMENT OF REGIONAL UNIONISM

Considerable damage was done to the development of big unions in Nigeria by the Macpherson Constitution of 1951, which introduced a tripartite division of the country, and created Regional Governments with exclusive responsibilities for certain subjects. The effect on the trade union movement was tragic. Borrowing a leaf from the actions of the politicians, employees of the Regional Governments and the agencies they created began to think of their interests in terms of Regions and not of the nation as a whole. The spirit of oneness, which a unitary system of government had fostered, was shattered, and a process of proliferation began. The district organisations of some national unions of public employees severed connections with their parent bodies and constituted themselves into Regional Unions, whose memberships were limited either to a department or a section of a department of public employees of that region. They were encouraged in this behaviour by two things. One of these was that there were many outstanding grievances needing amelioration. These grievances, particularly the wage question, were to be resolved by negotiations through appropriate machinery set up by the state for that purpose. In the case of the public services, the machinery was to be the Whitley Councils.

The Junior Whitley Councils ran into difficulties in 1949. Up till 1951 they had not been properly reconstituted. Moreover, the constitutional changes of 1951 meant that the Junior Whitley Councils could not determine wage claims and conditions of employment on a national basis, since there were many authorities instead of one to deal with. This difficulty might have been avoided by drawing the membership of the Official Side from representatives of the various Regional Governments and the Central Government, and by so doing achieve a uniform policy in staff matters. Unfortunately, no such foresight existed. The emergence of Regional Governments engendered healthy rivalries and sometimes senseless ones also. Not infrequently the various governments tended to substitute regional for national interests. The need for co-ordination and uniformity was appreciated only when it became clear that some, if not, all of the governments were likely to be ruined by the consequences of their own actions.

The 1951 constitutional changes meant that grievances like pay claims should either wait for the creation of appropriate machinery in each Region, or must be dealt with by the Governments and their employees without necessarily waiting for the creation of this machinery. The Governments and the workers chose the latter to avert a major industrial upheaval.

Another reason for the breakaway movement would appear to have been the thorough disgust of the district organisations with some of the performance of their unions' headquarters or of their principal officers. A case in point was the experience of delegates to the sixth Annual Delegates' Conference of the Nigerian Union of Local Authority Staff in 1951. Delegates had come all the way from the North, East and West to attend the conference at Ibadan. Apart from the fact that no arrangement was made to receive them and no accommodation was reserved for them, they waited for several hours at Mapo Hall, where the conference was scheduled to take place, without seeing the Secretary, who had convened the conference. Where was he? He was attending an executive meeting of a political party. In other words, the party meeting was more important to him than the conference of the union from which he earned a living. It was no wonder, therefore, that a few months later the Eastern District organisation of the Union and the Eastern District of the Township Workers' Union, Eastern and Western Provinces, severed connections with their counterparts in the West and formed a new union known as the Nigerian Association of Local Government Employees. In spite of its name, the NALGE, which was deregistered in 1966 for violation of the Trade Union Act, was not a national organisation: it was a regional body. Its constitution specifically limited membership of the Association to local government employees in Eastern Nigeria. The spirits behind the merger were Job Whemekwa Wamuo, now a county council secretary, and M. A. Ohuonu, at present an Administrative Officer in the Eastern Nigeria Public Service.

The emergence of the NALGE meant that the NULAS had become more or less a Western regional organisation since it had a little following in the North. In 1957, native authority employees in the North followed the example of their colleagues in the East in founding the Northern Native Administration Staff Association. Their action seems, however, to have been motivated by political consideration rather than by a desire to get a more serviceable organisation, which was the basic consideration in founding the NALGE.

After the promulgation in 1954 of the Northernisation policy by the Government of Northern Nigeria, a consistent effort was made by the ruling party and other influences in Northern Nigeria to create a 'Northern brand' of every organised group. The Northern brand is isolated from Southern influence and exists by preaching hatred against the southerners, particularly the Ibos of Eastern Nigeria. By the middle 1960s, there are such organisations as the Northern Teachers' Association, Northern Civil Service Union, Northern PWD Workers' Union, Northern Mine Workers' Union and Northern Federation of Labour. A report in 1965 on the trade union situation in Northern Nigeria says: 'The Government directly or indirectly has employed all sorts of means to see that the ULC in particular in the North does not exist. The Northern Federation of Labour are given financial support which makes them very active and mobile, they are able to go from town to town in the North preaching to workers that Southerners are trying to dominate the North and that unless workers stage war against the Southerners there will be nothing good for Northerners.'[1]

The organisation of the Northern Mine Workers' Union began much earlier, and was both a manifestation of extreme tribalism and the desire of the ruling party to get a union in the mining area that it could control and dominate. In the early 1950's when the experiment of representative government was begun, Sir Ahmadu Bello, Sardauna of Sokoto, then Leader of Government Business in the Northern House of Assembly, expressed concern that the leadership of the two unions – the Nigerian Mine Workers' Union and the Amalgamated Tin Mines of Nigeria African Workers Union – was in the hands of Southerners, particularly the Ibos of the East.[2] The tin mining industry is the key industry in the region. Having the leadership of the unions in the hands of the Ibos held out little prospect of the NPC realising one of its main political objectives in the mines, which was to capture the votes of the mine workers during election times. That objective could be achieved in one of two ways. Either the union leaders were to be convinced or 'bought' to toe the NPC party line and retain their memberships intact, or the solidarity of the mine workers was to be broken by setting up a rival organisation.

The first alternative could not be considered, for three reasons. First, the NPC was pursuing policies detrimental to most members of both the Nigerian Mine Workers' Union and the ATMN African Mine Workers' Union. In the circumstances no union leader worth his salt could support the NPC. Secondly, Partick Okoye and Emmanuel Okei-Achamba, General Secretaries respectively of the two unions, were well-known Ibos. The impression had been created among most Northerners and among people of other tribes in the country that the Ibos could never have any other political affiliation than to the NCNC because of their loyalty to their tribe and to Dr. Azikiwe. Thirdly, Okoye and Okei-Achamba were also well-known Zikists. Okei-Achamba had earlier been jailed at Minna because of his activities in the Zikist Movement. Because of these considerations a panacea was found in founding the Northern Mine Workers' Union registered in August 1954.

In promoting the Northern Mine Workers' Union, the NPC had taken certain precautions. They saw to it that Alhaji Isa Haruna, a mine contractor and therefore an employer of labour, became President, while Alhaji Audu Danladi, a welfare officer of the Bisichi Tin Mining Company became Secretary. It goes without saying that, on many grounds, neither of these men ought to have been a member of the union, let alone becoming its principal officer. The fact that he was not an employee disqualified Alhaji Haruna for membership; by the same token Danladi did not qualify for membership being in a managerial position in the Bisichi Tin Mining Company. Clearly, therefore, the main consideration for their membership and the key positions they held was their NPC political soundness and their ability to get the union members to do the bidding of the party.

If politicians should be condemned for their role in this game, the role of the managements of the various mining companies was not without blemish. Not only did they acquiesce, but some of them gave unqualified support and encouragement. The performance of the management of the Amalgamated Tin Mines of Nigeria, Ltd., is a case in point. In 1952, the employees of the ATMN withdrew from the Nigerian Mine Workers' Union and set up their own organisation. The withdrawal was occasioned by bitter experiences in collective bargaining. This probably was one of the few cases where fragmentation might have been justified for economic reasons. Since after the 1945 general strike collective bargaining in the minesfield had been carried out on industry-wide basis. Claims, particularly wage claims, were invariably settled not on the basis of the ability to pay of the individual company concerned but on the capacity to pay of the mining industry as a whole. As a rule this was not determined from the profit margins of the big companies, but from the fortunes of small companies or marginal operators. The situation meant that workers from big mining companies like the ATMN, which produced about 70 per cent of the country's tin products and could afford to pay wages about 300 per cent higher than the existing rates, did not always get a fair share of the tremendous profits they helped to create. Attempts to revise the prevailing method of wage determination failed, and this decided the union members from the ATMN to sever connections with the NAMU and set up their own organisation to negotiate directly with the ATMN. ATMN management was not favourably disposed towards the new union; they refused to recognise it, and for several months would have nothing to do with it. Recognition was eventually granted rather reluctantly following bitter struggles and many interventions by the labour Department.

A new day dawned in labour–management relations in the mines when the Minesfield Joint Industrial Council was formed following the Abbott Commission of Enquiry into industrial unrests in the mines. Its first meeting fixed wages and general working conditions which increased labour costs. Apparently to reduce costs and retain their huge profit, the employers had recourse to sub-contracting. The result was that the labour force employed by the companies was considerably reduced. Persons employed by mining contractors suffer from many disabilities: they normally do not get the minimum wage paid by companies operating in the mines; they work longer hours and receive no overtime, and are not issued with any protective clothing. Vacation leave is out of the question, as also is any free medical facility. It is said that, before the wide use of subcontracting, the mines employed about 100,000 workers. At the time of writing, less than half of that number are in regular employment; the rest eke a living by contract labour. Within the last five years one of the main preoccupations of the Nigeria African Mine Workers' Union which, since 1962, has been amalgamated with the ATMN African Mine Workers' Union, has been to abolish or minimise sub-contracting in the mines. In spite of considerable efforts no remarkable progress has been made. The companies resolutely resist the attempt of the Union to interfere, maintaining that sub-contracting is a management prerogative.

Something happened in 1952 which led to the founding of another regional union in Eastern Nigeria. An expatriate officer slapped his Nigerian subordinate because, he claimed, the latter did not do his job well. The incident was at the Eastern Nigeria Development Corporation Pioneer Oil Mill at Ihie, nine miles from Aba on the Aba-Port Harcourt Road. Another worker who could not brook such an affront felt called upon to accept a challenge. He not only retaliated on behalf of his helpless colleague but also gave the assailant a good hiding. For this Anthus Erondu Nwachi, an ex-serviceman, who had had a notable career with 82 Division of the Royal West African Frontier Force during the Second World War, was suspended from duty. Later he was reinstated after a thorough investigation into the matter, and on resuming duty summoned a meeting of his fellow workers. The meeting decided to petition the management of the Pioneer Oil Mill Scheme about conditions of service. On submitting the petition the management asked the workers' representatives to produce their certificate of registration as a union before discussing with them. This led Nwachi and a few enthusiasts to found the Pioneer Oil Mills African Workers' Union, which later became the Eastern Nigeria Development Corporation and Allied Workers' Union.

The important thing about the Morgan–Igbudu assault case was not that an expatriate slapped a Nigerian worker. At the time of the incident this would not have been news in Nigeria Labour history. Three considerations would appear to have moved Nwachi into action. The first was the reason for the assault; the second, the comparative age of both men *vis-à-vis* the Nigerian tradition of respect for age; and the third was the comparative experience of both men in the operation of the oil mills. John Igbudu was old enough to be Morgan's father. A few months earlier, when Morgan was just a new recruit, Igbudu was showing him the ropes about mill operations and the necessary records required to be kept and the method of keeping them. It is perhaps one of those ironies of fate and of colonial administration that the 'recruit' should turn boss after a brief period, and reward his 'teacher' with a slap.

The ENDC and Allied Workers' Union has been growing in strength since 1953, and is acknowledged as one of the best organised and ably led unions in the country. From a modest membership of 526 in 1955, it had reached, by the end of 1965, the impressive figure of 14,000 with a total annual income of £12,000. Among its many achievements is the improvement of the minimum wage from 2s. 6d. to 6s. 3d. a day.

Regional unionism also developed in Western Nigeria. A move in this direction started in 1952, when certain employees of the Western Region Production Development Board met agricultural workers at a palm wine shed in Moor Plantation at Ibadan and told pathetic stories about their plight. Mechanics worked several hours overtime and were not paid for it; drivers went on long-distance tours and received no allowances. Moreover, nobody seemed to care about how many hours a day a driver worked. At the time of the fateful meeting, Moor Plantation workers had been organised, and their union had won for them several concessions including those about which their friend was complaining. After listening to their story one of the agricultural workers made a statement which later became food for thought. He said: 'My friends, the answer is simple. We had similar, if not worse, problems; and we did something which I will now recommend to you. We formed a union; all of us joined and supported it. That union helped us to solve our problems, and has been helping us ever since. Go and do the same thing, and you will see the result.'[3]

The words formed the propelling force behind the formation of what was then known as the Western Region Production Development Board African Workers' Union registered in October 1956. It was not easy to form the union; the initial difficulties almost killed the morale of the pioneers. Thanks to the iron will and indomitable spirit of its President, Alfred Williamson Adeniran, and his lieutenants, after a four years' struggle the union was registered. Even after its registration the management of WNDC refused to recognise it. It took a costly strike in 1961 involving 10,000 workers to gain recognition. Before the strike the Union successfully fought a test case. Two employees, who complained of malpractices against a plantation manager, had had their belongings removed from their homes and thrown away, when they went to Ibadan to report, on the orders of the plantation manager. As a result of the Union's struggles the WNDC paid £500 damages.

Trade unionists and students of Nigerian labour history often refer to the early history of what has come to be known as the Western Nigeria Development Corporation and Allied Industries Workers' Union as one of the dark spots on the pages of the glorious history of the Action Group. That the Action group – which appeared to be sympathetic to workers' claims, as demonstrated in the 5s. minimum wage issue, the 10 per cent interim wage award of 1959, and the promises of workers' welfare contained in its various election manifestos – should have been in control of a public corporation that refused for so long to recognise workers' organisation and to deal with it, sounds stranger than fiction.

It is perhaps necessary to examine other causes of union proliferation. Within the past two decades several unions have been split and members driven into mutually hostile, irreconcilable camps – either because of alleged lack of interest in the aspirations of some members or because of irresponsible talk, or a combination of both. A few case histories will help to illustrate this point. There might have been one or two unions in the Nigerian Ports Authority but for a sad incident which happened in 1943. Engine-room ratings broke off from the Nigerian Marine African Workers' Union because the majority of union leaders from the other sections of the Nigerian Marine would not show any interest in the aspiration of the ratings that Africans be appointed as foremen as had been done in other departments and in some sections of the Marine. They formed the Engine Room Ratings African Workers' Union, Nigerian Marine, which was not registered. In 1947 deck staff comprising river masters, boatswains, quartermasters, able-seamen, signalmen, radio operators, berthingmen and boatmen, also broke away from the union and joined the engine-room ratings to form the Engine Room and Deck Ratings African Workers' Union, Nigerian Marine, registered on November 25, 1948, and which later became the Marine Floating Staff Union.

The Union existed as one body until 1955, when it demanded that quartermasters and engine drivers be placed on the same scale of salary. At that time quartermasters were on 'J' Scale and had £26 higher than the minimum of marine drivers, then on 'E' Scale, but who enjoyed £26 higher maximum. The Union succeeded in its case on behalf of drivers. Just before negotiation on the quartermasters' case began, the driver members of the negotiating team withdrew from the meeting. Their reason: they could not live to see quartermasters earn the same salary as they earned. In a fit of anger they ran to the Union's office, and removed the certificate of registration. The splinters formed their own union known as the Marine Engineering Assistants' and Allied Workers' Union. Its principal officers were J. Ola Coker, President; and E. E. Dadson, Secretary. The splinters originally planned to operate with the certificate of the Marine Floating Staff Union, believing that whoever held the certificate of a union could legally operate. When it became clear that this was not possible they decided to apply for registration and were duly registered in January 1957.

However, unity within their ranks was short-lived. In 1958 a split occurred. The firemen and greasers decamped, and formed the Nigerian Ports Authority Firemen, Greasers, Technical and General Workers' Union. They claimed that engineering assistants felt themselves superior to others, and did not want other workers to be given training opportunities or converted to their trade.

The Nigerian Marine became a statutory corporation in 1955, and was split into three: the Navy, the Inland Waterways and the Nigerian Ports Authority. As a result, the functions and staff of the Marine Department were divided among the three. The NPA offered the inducement of a 10 per cent wage increase with effect from April 1, 1955, to those staff of the Marine Department who were seconded to its service. Members of the Marine Floating Staff Union in the Inland Waterways Department were disappointed that this inducement was not extended to them and the Union appeared incapable of helping them to win the concession. They also broke away and set up the Deck Staff Union, Inland Waterways Department, which was registered in February 1959.

Union proliferation also occurred in the Railway. In 1949, track construction and track maintenance men broke away from the Railway Workers' Union and set up the Permanent Way Workers' Union. This was the climax of a series of complaints about the RWU's alleged lack of interest in the affairs of track construction and maintenance men. Although they had constituted the majority of the Union's membership, their men were in the minority in the Executive: the majority were workshopmen, who seemed to care very little about their lot and their aspirations, and who often joked about their jobs calling them by the nick-name 'beater, beater'. Matters came to a head at the 1949 conference of the Union, when a track maintenance delegate was speaking on one of the items on the agenda and made reference to the plight of permanent way workers. Shouts of 'Sit down, sit down, you beater, beater' filled the air. Much of the heckling was a joke, but some of the delegates did not take it as such, but rather as further evidence of the Unions' lack of interest in their affairs. When the conference adjourned, F. O. Njoku initiated a move, which culminated in the founding of the Railway Permanent Way Workers' Union registered in April 1950.

The 1949 conference is remarkable for two other incidents. The General Secretary, Luke Emejulu, reported that tribalism had made a serious inroad into the Union. The situation had become so serious that there was even the stupid talk of founding an Ibo Railway Workers' Union.[4] The development of tribalism in the trade unions was not a spontaneous growth: it followed similar trends in the political arena, triggered off by *The Daily Service* Ibo domination scare of April 1948, and compounded by C. D. Onyeama's irresponsible utterance of June 17, 1949 that 'Ibo domination of Nigeria is a matter of time'.[5]

As a result of a sharp disgreement between the President, Imoudu, and the General Secretary, Emejulu, the conference decided that the Union's secretariat be under the entire control of the General Secretary. Imoudu opposed the decision and offered one of the following alternatives: 'that he be retired on his present salary; that he be paid 10 years' salary; that he be returned to the Railway Workshop; or that he be transferred to either Zaria or Enugu

District for six months observation.' The conference accepted the fourth proposal and he was to shift to Enugu, and submit a report of his work to the 1950 conference.[6]

In 1953 there was a further break-up of the Railway Workers' Union. What led to it makes an epic story in itself. In 1925 the Nigerian Railway established the Railway Technical School, which was a training school for supervisors. Although supervisors were being trained, there was no training scheme for craftsmen. A training scheme for craftsmen began only in the late 1940s, and its first products brought to the fore the problems of many years of neglect. Alongside the problems thus revealed came the feeling among craftsmen that they deserved improved pay. A former General Secretary of the Railway Technical Staff Association explains the reasons for this feeling as follows:

> Craftsmen wanted a higher maximum for many reasons. When under apprenticeship, they undergo an all-round training in their jobs, both theoretical and practical.
>
> They know not only how to do the job, but also the history of the job. They come in and take a work order, and proceed without supervision. They can make alterations to the job when needed and can make suggestions for improvement of a particular job. The untrained cannot do these things. They have learned to do their jobs by watching trained craftsmen perform. They don't know the history of their jobs, and whenever an alteration is made in the work schedule they are ill-equipped to deal with it. Training craftsmen reduces supervision and increase productivity.[7]

During the Second World War, the great demand for labour to undertake engine and wagon repairs led to the employment of a class of unskilled labour known as 'helpers'. As their name implies helpers help craftsmen do their jobs by cleaning dirty equipment and doing other minor jobs assigned to them by the men they helped. Eventually the helpers learned to do the jobs of craftsmen and in some cases did them efficiently. The Railway administration tried to encourage them by paying them the same wage as trained craftsmen. Because of the exigencies of war and their extremely weak position, the craftsmen did not take steps to protect their trades from 'invasion'. The existence of a large number of helpers and lack of pressure from trained men encouraged the Railway administration to relegate training to the background. As a result efficiency and productivity fell, and more supervisors than should have been necessary were employed.

In 1946 the trained craftsmen became very sensitive to the dangers of helpers, and rushed to the Railway administration with a request that the helper grade be abolished. They were too late. Employing helpers had become a tradition. An arbitrator was appointed in 1947, but he made no award altering the *status quo*. The trained craftsmen made up their minds to fight on. To achieve their objective they struggled to get trained craftsmen elected as officers on the branch level. By 1950 they had achieved their objective, and the Executive Council of the Railway Workers' Union was dominated by them. Using their majority they got the Executive Council to demand a separate scale for craftsmen. The negotiation which followed was rewarding, and trained craftsmen were raised from £36–£170 to £48–£180 with effect from May 1951. When the new scale was announced the untrained artisans reacted unfavourably. They wanted the concession to be extended to them or the agreement terminated, arguing that they performed the same duties as trained craftsmen. Imoudu sympathised with the aspirations of the craftsmen, being himself one of them, but since the majority of union members were untrained and supported the demand for termination of the agreement, he decided to back the majority.

Having failed to persuade the Railway administration to grant their request, the artisans made up their minds to terminate the 1951 agreement at all costs. To achieve this objective they used every means, fair and foul. They organised a massive purge. Using their majority in all branches they saw to it that craftsmen were removed as office-bearers. Until the 1951 agreement, the Executive Council members had been elected from among branch officers. Having got a majority against the 1951 agreement they worked to get the matter on the agenda of the annual delegates conference held in 1953. Before the conference opened, craftsmen made a desperate effort to persuade the delegates not to terminate the agreement, pointing out that it was a violation of trade union principle to seek to lose a concession won. In spite of this plea the conference adopted the following resolutions:

> Whereas this Union [Railway Workers' Union of Nigeria] still believes in the principle of equal pay for equal work and equal responsibility;
>
> And whereas a discrimination in the salary scales of apprenticed and unapprenticed workers will split the Railway Workers Union of Nigeria from head to toe, since the unapprenticed workmen are by far in the majority in all the departments, e.g. Mechanical, Operating and Engineering Departments;
>
> Be it resolved that the Union stands firm and insists on equal pay for both the apprenticed and unapprenticed workmen.

Before the adoption of the resolution, President Imoudu made a statement which has been described as 'the last straw that broke the camel's back'.[8] He said: 'The untrained train the trained', implying that, regardless of their five years' intensive apprenticeship, craftsmen still learned their trade from artisans, who had never undergone any recognised apprenticeship. To put it mildly, that was saying too much. Craftsmen who hitherto had made up their minds to remain in the Union and fight from within saw it as more than a specious argument; to them it was proof positive of the extent to which Imoudu could go to sacrifice truth on the altar of cheap popularity. Craftsmen like P. S. Thomas, T. O. Taylor, Nwafor Oti, B. A. Omoyeye, V. A. Odusote, B. A. Bakare, Gabriel Okigbo, T. T. Adesubokan, N. A. Otsumah and J. M. Odoh, took the statement as a challenge, and went all-out to organise the Railway Trained Staff Association which was later renamed Railway Technical Staff Association.

President P. B. Thomas later explained the reasons for the break-away. He said: 'People mistakenly call us a break-away union, but any group of workers who were in our position would have taken exactly the very action we took. When we were openly told that fighting out our case would split the Railway Workers' Union from head to toe because the unapprenticed workers, who were in majority, would desert the Union, we rightly considered that the best we could do was to give way to the "majority". One other important reason why we decided to stand on our own was that the policy being pursued by the Union in respect of promoting unskilled employees to skilled jobs was detrimental to our interests and contributed to the cheapening of the work of the craftsman and lower production.'[9]

After the break-away, Imoudu made overtures through a 'Committee of Gentlemen' to effect reconciliation. The Committee failed because the RTSA would not co-operate, and they believed that 'reconciliation was only from the lips and not from the heart'.

In 1954, linesmen and wireless attendants broke from the Union of Posts and Telecommunications Workers and set up the P. & T. Engineering Workers' Union. They had been complaining that the Union as a whole and the Secretary in particular had not shown sufficient interest in their case, particularly their demand for upgrading from artisan to technician grade. They had begun agitating for recognition as technicians as far back as 1949, when the issue was first raised at the annual delegates' conference. The linesmen and wireless attendants argued that their jobs were of a technical nature and that they should therefore be recognised as technicians and paid as such. Postal clerks and telegraphists, who dominated the Union's executive council, felt that the claim was unjustified because the men had low educational qualifications and had not undergone any recognised apprenticeship scheme. Put to vote the matter was defeated.

The rejection of the demand did not kill the agitation. It had angered the men and created an unfortunate feeling – the 'minority feeling'. Up till that time, and even five years later, the linesmen and wireless attendants were a minority of the Union membership, though they were a majority of P. & T. employees. This minority feeling soon became an obsession and led to the constant charge that the Union was not interested in their affairs. The case of the linesmen echoed at successive conferences, and was always rejected because postal clerks and telegraphists seemed more interested in arguing in favour of management instead of ministering to the cravings of their own members. They not only stressed the low educational qualifications of the men but played down the importance of their jobs by calling them 'wiremen'. Matters came to a head at the 1954 conference when a linesman delegate raised the issue again and received a hostile reception. This man and other linesmen delegates walked out of the conference and set up their own union. Their claim for recognition as technicians was conceded following the recommendations of the Lydbury Commission of enquiry.

In 1956 the telephonists accused the Union of Posts and Telecommunications Workers of not presenting their cases properly to management, and sometimes not presenting them at all, and broke away, setting up the Posts and Telegraphs Telephonists' Union. One of those who organised the break-away claims that postal clerks and telegraphists often played down their complaints. When out of sheer pressure the Union agreed to take some of their grievances their case would be so poorly prepared that management would always beat them at negotiations. More than that postal clerks and telegraphists ridiculed them by nicknaming them the 'hello boys and girls' who should be satisfied with their existing conditions and not to attempt to seek equality in pay and conditions of employment with their superiors. This was very similar to the experience of the linesmen.

In recent years a number of unions have contracted amalgamations, only for some of the parties to opt out of it soon afterwards. In 1961 four dock workers' unions formed the Nigerian Dockers Transport and General Workers' Union. The Biney Workers' Union withdrew from the amalgamation because it could not abide by the decision of the founding conference to elect E. A. Okon General Secretary of the new organisation. In 1963 six unions in the construction industry founded the Amalgamated Union of Building and Woodworkers of Nigeria. Twelve months later the African Timber and Plywood Workers' Union contracted out of the amalgamation because of alleged 'unsatisfactory administration'.[10] The same year four unions in the petroleum industry formed the Nigerian Oil, Chemical and Allied Workers' Union. Dissensions among members of the Shell-BP and Allied Workers' Union, one of the parties to the amalgamation, led a powerful dissident group to oppose it. Encouraged by an influence outside the trade union movement and outside Nigeria seeking to control the unions in the oil industry, the dissidents challenged the decision of the Shell-BP and Allied Workers' Union to join the amalgamation. The Port Harcourt High Court ruled in favour of the NOCAWU. The court ruling forced the dissidents to change tactics. They went to the office of the Registrar of Trade Unions and, taking advantage of the Registrar's absence during his annual vacation, managed to obtain the duplicate copy of the certificate of registration of the Shell-BP and Allied Workers' Union. The possession of this document strengthened their campaign among the workers, and with massive support they successfully pressed the Shell-BP management to agree to conduct a plebiscite to determine the comparative strength of NOCAWU and the resuscitated union in Shell-BP. NOCAWU announced that it was boycotting the plebiscite, and did so; but its refusal to co-operate did not stop the plebiscite which was conducted on June 3, 1966. The result showed 1,682 votes to 21 in favour of the resuscitated union. NOCAWU later challenged the decision of the Acting Registrar of Trade Unions to issue a duplicate certificate of registration to the dissident group. Before the case came up for hearing at the Port Harcourt High Court, the Registrar of Trade Unions authorised to administer the Trade Unions Act wrote as follows:

(i) I refer to your letter No. HO/RTU/A.20 of the May 31, 1966, and have to inform you that my stand on this matter is, and has always been, that when two or more registered trade unions become amalgamated together as one trade union *with dissolution of funds* the constituent unions stand dissolved as the logical sequence. Otherwise, the absurd situation would arise where many registered live trade unions exist and operate within a single registered trade union separately as autonomous unions and jointly as a single entity.

(ii) Because the constituent unions are regarded as dissolved, the Shell-BP and Allied Workers' Union ceased to perform all the statutory obligations which the Trade Unions Act imposed on all registered trade unions, with effect from the date of registration of the amalgamation.

(iii) It is also on the basis of this principle, that I attempted unsuccessfully to recover the so-called certified copy of certificate, issued by my relief, for cancellation, to enable me to finalise action on the fresh application for registration submitted by Mr. Igwe.

(iv) My relief apparently acted on his own interpretation of the law, which omitted to take cognisance of the existing principle and practice on the subject, but I am nevertheless fortified in my interpretation by the decision of the Port Harcourt High Court, which remains the only local authority on the matter until reversed or overruled by the Federal Supreme Court.[11]

The remarkable thing about union proliferation in Nigeria is that the splinter unions have often won concessions which members could not win when the union was intact. For example, the emergence of the Railway Technical Staff Association led to improvements in pay and service conditions of trained craftsmen in the Railway. Linesmen, wireless attendants and telephone operators might never have been recognised at the time they were and paid as technicians if there had been no P. & T. Engineering Workers' Union or P. & T. Telephonists' Union. Similarly the great improvements in pay and service conditions of the employees of the Nigerian Ports Authority might never have been made at the time they were, had all the workers been in the NPA Workers' Union or any union of transport workers.

Are these successes therefore, a case for, or against, union proliferation? The successes are examples of what workers can do, assuming there is the will and the determination to do it. If Nigerian workers could join hands together in bigger units, and work with the same determination, sense of mission, industry and drive, they could achieve much more for themselves, the nation and posterity.

REFERENCES

1. Letter dated December 14 1965 from Yinusa Kaltungu, Northern District of ULC to General Secretary ULC, Lagos.

2. Interview with Dozie Igwe-Onu, former General Secretary of Nigerian Mine Workers' Union, May 24, 1966.

3. Interview with G. Kola Balogun, General Secretary, WNDC and Allied Industries Workers' Union, on June 15, 1966.

4. *The West African Pilot*, January 8, 1949.

5. *The Daily Service*, June 23, 1948.

6. *The West African Pilot*, January 13, 1949.

7 and 8. Interview with N. A. Oti on June 21, 1965.

9. Presidential Address to the First Annual conference of RTSA, April 1955.

10. *History of African Timber and Plywood Workers of Nigeria*, page 17.

11. Letter No. TU. 1353/110 of June 3, 1966, addressed to the General Secretary of the Nigerian Oil, Chemical and Allied Workers' Union.

INTERNATIONAL CONFEDERATION OF FREE TRADE UNIONS
24 rue du Lombard, Brussels, Belgium

13th December 1957

APPLICATION FOR AFFILIATION

We, the ALL-NIGERIA TRADE UNION FEDERATION

of 26, KING GEORGE AVENUE, YABA ESTATE, LAGOS, NIGERIA
(Address)

declare that we are a bona fide, free and democratic trade union organisation. We have read the Constitution of the I.C.F.T.U. and we accept the aims set out there.

WE HEREBY APPLY TO THE INTERNATION CONFEDERATION OF FREE TRADE UNIONS FOR AFFILIATION. We note that our membership is conditional upon fulfilment of the obligations laid down in the Constitution of the I.C.F.T.U.

We agree to accept the responsibilities of an affiliated organisation, and in particular to:

(i) Keep the ICFTU informed of major developments in our country:
(ii) Keep our constituent bodies informed of the work and progress of the ICFTU;
(iii) advise the ICFTU regulary of the dates of our Congresses, the decisions reached there and the composition of our Executive Committee.

We note that in accordance with Article VII (a) of the Constitution, affiliation fees are payable on the following scale:

Up to 5,000,000 members	£3-15/- sterling per annum per thousand members or part thereof
For additional members over	£2-10/- Sterling per annum per thousand members or part thereof

The membership of our organisation as at 29th November 1957 is 89,239 eighty-nine thousand two hundred and thirty-nine)

We therefore enclose a bankers' draft or cheque for the sum of .... being payment of one quarter's affiliation fees in advance. (PLEASE ADVICE US).

We also attach hereto the replies to your detailed questionnaire on membership and other matters together with a copy of our Constitution. We will arrange for you to receive three copies of all our publications in the following languages ENGLISH ....

We desire to receive the official publications of the ICFTU in the following language: English.

Signed on behalf of the ..ALL.NIGERIA.TRADE.UNION.FEDERATION.... ....
(Organisation)

President ~~or Chairman~~ General Secretary or Other responsible officer

Application by the ANTUF for affiliation to ICFTU (see page 152).

14

ANTUF AND NCTUN

From March 1951 until August 1953, there was virtually no national trade union centre in Nigeria. Attempts to revive interest in the Nigerian Labour Congress through the Federal Whitley Council (Staff Side) failed because of lack of confidence in its leadership.

In July 1953, Lewis Uwaezuoke Agonsi, Acting General Secretary of the Railway Workers' Union, convened a meeting of trade union leaders to explore the possibilities of founding a new central labour organisation. Forty-eight trade union leaders from the main trade unions in the country attended the meeting, which set up a committee to prepare the ground for a founding conference. The committee consisted of M. A. O. Imoudu, Chairman; L. U. Agonsi, Secretary; Ayo Ogunsheye, H. P. Adebola, N. A. Cole, Gogo Chu Nzeribe, M. I. Ijegbor, O. Egwunwoke and E. U. Ijeh.

In August 1953 the Committee convened a conference, which inaugurated the All-Nigeria Trade Union Federation. Its principal officers were M. A. O. Imoudu, President, and Gogo Chu Nzeribe, General Secretary. The aims and objects of the new organisation were:

(i) to improve the position and living conditions of the workers of Nigeria and to unite them in the realisation of all objectives common to the interests of the working class;
(ii) to organise and unite the trade unions of Nigeria irrespective of creed, nationality, region, sex and political conception;
(iii) to encourage the spirit of oneness and collective security among all working peoples, and establish Trades Councils all over the country;
(iv) to lead the struggle of trade unions against influences which oppose their democratic rights and liberties by striving to obtain for them social and economic security;
(v) to secure improvements in wages and service conditions, to obtain full employment, to encourage the introduction of, and watch developments in labour and social legislations;

(vi) to plan and provide for the education of trade union members and to awaken them to realise their real functions in the state;

(vii) to seek for the state ownership of major industries in the country;

(viii) to co-operate with democratic federations of trade unions or other organisations whose aims are acceptable to the Federation;

(ix) to undertake or participate in the printing and publishing of newspapers and other literature in the interest of the Federation and of trade unionism generally;

(x) to establish and support the political wing of the workers' movement (political party) with a view to realising a socialist government.

A dispute arose at the inaugural conference following an attempt to unseat certain persons as delegates. F. O. Porbeni, General Secretary of the Public Utility, Technical and General Workers' Union, had challenged the credentials of Nduka Eze, S. G. Ikoku, and E. A. Cowan on the ground that they were not *bona fide* trade unionists. Considering the fact that three years before Eze had been the undisputed General Secretary of one of the most powerful unions in the country, and was also Secretary of the Nigerian Labour Congress, the suggestion that he was not a *bona fide* trade unionist might sound arrant nonsense. The crux of the matter, however, was whether at the material time he and his two colleagues were connected with any registered trade union in Nigeria either as members in good standing or duly appointed officials, and whether they were accredited to the conference by any registered trade union in the country. The facts were that Eze's powerful UNAMAG had been destroyed by the intemperate strike of 1950 and had been deregistered before the inaugural conference. The Nigerian Labour Congress was also dead as a result of that strike. Most of the 200 delegates who attended the conference knew these facts and knew also that to ignore them would make a poor start for the new organisation.

When the debate on the matter opened it was explained that Ikoku was acting as economic adviser to Eze and Cowan. Some delegates who were championing the cause of the three men made a poor impression by the way they presented their case. A case in point was Emmanuel Okei-Achamba of the Mine Workers' Union, who threatened to set up a splinter group and form a labour congress in Northern Nigeria if the three men were excluded. The conference eventually decided to exclude them, and the chairman asked them to withdraw. Immediately after the chairman's ruling, representatives of the two unions backing their admission announced their decision to withdraw as well. Later the three men and their supporters announced the formation of another Committee of Trade Unionists. The committee tried to discredit the ANTUF and question its representativeness.

It is doubtful whether this drama could have been staged had it not been for the activities of members of the Marxist Group, a communist front organisation founded in the early 1940s. Eze, like other young trade unionists, was a member of the Group, which comprised budding intellectuals, professionals, teachers and journalists. Before the conference took place, Eze had been discredited not only by the abortive strike of mercantile workers in 1950 but by the whispering campaigns alleging abuse of office in deals connected with the founding of *The Labour Champion*. Moreover, his attacks on Zik, which culminated in his expulsion from the Executive Council of the NCNC, added to his unpopularity. Dedicated Marxists in the labour movement felt that, by giving cause for allegations against him of abuse of office, Eze had betrayed the Marxist cause, and therefore was not a fit and proper person to hold a position in the labour movement 'to carry out the communist assignment'. But they did not want to block his chances and leave it at that; they wanted another member of the Group to step into his shoes, and they succeeded. Gogo Chu Nzeribe, hitherto an unknown figure in the trade union movement, was elected General Secretary, a position to which Eze aspired and had been almost certain of winning by his personal charm and powerful oratory. The background was as follows:

Before the conference, the Marxist Group held a meeting and decided that members must infiltrate important organisations, among them political parties and trade unions. Some members were already well placed in unions, and efforts were to be made to place others. Just before the ANTUF founding congress, members of the Group likely to attend the congress met to plan strategy. Discussion centred around how to capture the post of General Secretary, and how to diminish ICFTU influence in Nigeria, which had gained momentum as a result of the activities of the West African Educational and Advisory Centre in Accra. There was general agreement on the need for a member of the Group to capture the post of General Secretary, but there was no unanimity on who that person should be. To frustrate Eze's ambition a small but influential group made deals with other trade union leaders whom they had always regarded as reactionaries. Members spoke frankly and objectively about the growing ICFTU influence and popularity, saying that the organisation's aims and objectives were in general accord with the aspirations of Nigerian workers, but that, since it was an anti-communist organisation, they regarded it as an enemy. To fight the enemy, however, one had to be realistic. Colonial policy and the general political climate were not conducive to an easy flow of Marxist philosophy. Since the majority of the workers were oriented to the West, pre-ICFTU sentiments could be whittled away by advancing the argument that the most important problem facing Nigerian workers was how to achieve unity. The workers were not interested in the cold war between the East and the West, and as a demonstration of disinterestedness, the new national centre should not be affiliated to any international trade union organisation. That was the origin of the gospel of non-affiliation, sometimes referred to as non-alignment or positive neutrality. It was the reason for one of the recommendations of the Preparatory Committee on which more is to be said presently.

The ANTUF was accorded official recognition after a month of its existence, and soon began to hold monthly meetings with the Ministry of Labour on current labour problems and policies – a tradition established by the first Trades Union Congress. A surprise came, however, on February 27, 1954, when the Commissioner of Labour informed the Federation in a letter that he had been instructed by the Minister not to continue policy discussions with them. The letter informed the Federation that the Committee of Trade Unionists had challenged its representativeness and asked it to submit signed declarations from its affiliates. Declarations from twenty-seven unions representing 63,000 workers were submitted. The failure of the Committee of Trade Unionists to submit declarations from its own supporters, even after many months of grace, helped to restore ANTUF's recognition. But this did not happen until after seven months.

Why did the Government treat the ANTUF in this manner? Two probable reasons could be given. Recognition was accorded by Dr. E. M. L. Endeley and withdrawn by his successor M. T. Mbu. Perhaps Mbu did not feel bound to accept expert advice as some ministers were wont to do before and during the First Republic, or wanted to oblige his friends in the Committee of Trade Unionists. The episode illustrates the utter futility of disturbing cordial relationships with organised labour – a tendency which has become a tradition with succeeding governments.

The inaugural conference adopted a number of resolutions for example, on political independence for Nigeria, labour representation on public boards and corporations, housing schemes for workers and the creation of a Ministry of Housing and Town Planning, payment of children's allowance to all workers in Nigeria, the high cost of living and foreign trade, freedom of association and civil rights, factories ordinance, the condition of workers in the Plateau mining industry, uniform wage rates for local government employees in the country and the fight against bribery and corruption in Nigeria. It also adopted the recommendation of the Preparatory Committee that 'the new central organisation should join neither the WFTU nor the ICFTU as such a step would introduce a disruptive factor into the Nigerian trade union movement'.[1]

The ANTUF held its second congress in 1954. An event that took place before that congress led to the break-up of the Marxist Group. A two-day meeting was held at Abeokuta, attended by many members of the Group and a guest from the British Communist Party. Discussion centred around the stumbling-block which leading and wealthy nationalists constituted to proletarian revolution. The chief theoretician at the meeting and ideological director of the Group later became General Secretary of one of the leading political parties in the country. The first day of the meeting went through smoothly with general agreement on objectives but there was a difference of opinion on strategy. The following day the communist guest attended and addressed the meeting. He advocated the use of force to eliminate the so-called stumbling-blocks and quoted extensively from history to support his argument. As in every controversial issue, there were supporters and opposers of the proposal. The supporters saw in it the only way to hasten the achievement of independence and the introduction of a new social order in Nigeria. Those who would not subscribe to it called the proposal a British plot to annihilate Nigerian nationalists. They argued that, if it was not, the advocate and his fellow communists in Britain would have first eliminated men like Churchill and other Tory leaders to demonstrate their sincerity. So outraged were they that some did not disguise their feeling that if plotting to kill fellow Nigerians was the objective of the Marxist Group, then they had reached a parting of the ways.

The meeting broke up in confusion, and sharp exchanges followed among members. Among those engaged in these exchanges were trade unionists. On leaving the meeting place each of them seemed to have resolved that the next stage of the battle was in the trade union movement. A few months later, a police swoop led to the arrest of several members of the Marxist Group, who were subsequently prosecuted for being in unlawful possession of seditious literature. Some of those arrested suspected that they had been betrayed by their colleagues with whom they had not been able to see eye to eye at the historic Abeokuta meeting. This feeling of mutual distrust persists even today, and explains why certain trade union leaders cannot feel comfortable in the company of some of their colleagues. The break-up of the Marxist Group can be said, therefore, to have been largely responsible for the perennial disunity in the Nigerian labour movement. Against this background subsequent events must be judged.

The 1954 ANTUF congress introduced an innovation in the structure of the Federation and created a precedent in the structural organisation of national centres in the country. Realising Imoudu's limitations in carrying out the responsibilities of President of a national centre, particularly in the conduct of meetings, the conference created the office of chairman in addition to the existing office of President. The President was to be a sort of ceremonial figure-head, while the chairman presided over meetings and assisted in the proper administration of the congress. N. A. Cole, General Secretary of the Nigerian Union of Nurses (as it was then called) was elected chairman, while Imoudu retained the position of President.

The 1954 congress also considered many other matters, including a 9s. minimum wage, and £200 p.a. as the point of entry into standard clerical grade. These claims were later presented in a memorandum to the Gorsuch Commission of Enquiry into the structure and remuneration of the public services of Nigeria. The Commission recommended £150 per annum for standard clerical grades. Unestablished labour were later offered daily rates varying from 5s. in Western Nigeria to 2s. 2d. in the North. Other matters discussed included the problem of mushroom unions, the formation of a labour party, industrial relations, and the functions of the Ministry of Labour in indistrial disputes, particularly in disputes involving the Government.

In 1955 the ANTUF Secretary attended the 38th conference of the International Labour Organisation as workers' representative on the Nigerian delegation. That conference provided an excellent opportunity to make contacts. Shortly after his return, rumours began to spread that the ANTUF secretariat was making contacts with trade unions in Eastern Europe. It was also alleged that some Nigerian trade union leaders were writing fantastic stories about the difficulties placed in the way of the workers wishing to organise. These stories, supported sometimes with photographs of specially staged incidents, were invariably sent to organisations in the Eastern bloc with solicitations for funds to enable the workers to organise.

In the spirit of international solidarity, these organisations sent money. But the contributions were neither reported to properly constituted meetings of workers or workers' representatives, nor were they used for the purpose intended. Until certain trade union leaders were being tried in 1958 for submitting false declarations to the Registrar of Trade Unions, very few people in the country knew that some trade union leaders had in fact been trading with the name of Nigerian workers, It was partly to check this fraud and partly to end its policy of isolationism that the fourth annual congress of the ANTUF, held in 1956, discussed again the controversial issue of international affiliation. Although the President and Secretary were opposed to it, international affiliation was popular among certain unions, particularly those whose leaders had since 1953 been attending trade union courses held at Accra by the West African Educational and Advisory Centre. In April, 1956, these unions formed the Committee of ICFTU-Affiliated Trade Unions through which they maintained contact with the ICFTU.

International affiliation was discussed in two stages. In stage one the conference considered a motion 'that congress-in-session suspends its previous decision of non-affiliation with an international trade union organisation'. Speaker after speaker supported international affiliation as being in tune with Karl Marx's clarion call, 'workers of the world, unite'. Because of this popular feeling, international affiliation was accepted unanimously. In stage two the conference considered to which particular international trade union organisation the ANTUF should affiliate. Six unions (Nigerian Civil Service Union, Nigerian Ports Authority Workers' Union, Railway Technical Staff Association, Nigerian Transport Clerical Staff Union, Railway and Ports Transport Staff Union and Public Utility Technical and General Workers' Union) had sponsored a motion 'that this congress decides to affiliate the All-Nigeria Trade Union Federation with the International Confederation of Free Trade Unions'. The motion provoked acrimonious debate. Some of the delegates, who had supported international affiliation in principle, came all-out against affiliation to ICFTU. Strangely enough they did not advocate affiliation either to the World Federation of Trade Unions or the International Federation of Christian Trade Unions. Pro-ICFTU delegates accused them of wanting to drag the Nigerian labour movement to the WFTU through the back door. When eventually the question was put, it was defeated by 46 to 45 votes.

The fourth annual conference was, by many considerations, one of the best conferences ever organised by national centres in Nigeria. Its organisation was excellent. Working papers were prepared on such matters like trade union rights, the national political situation, wages and Nigerianisation, financial problems of the labour movement, and increasing job opportunities. The main points in the papers may be summarized as follows:

(i) *Trade Union Rights.* The paper examined ILO Conventions 87 and 98 and the report of the committee of experts on Freedom of Employers' and Workers' Organisation to organise *vis-à-vis* the attitude of employers like the United Africa Company, John Holt & Co., A. G. Leventis, A. & N. Zarpas & Co., and Barclays Bank to trade unionism and trade unions in the country, and declared 'to what extent the Government has fulfilled its obligations under the general provisions of these Conventions and the specific cases of employers' attitude above will now demand the attention of the movement . . . we must take a firm and rigid stand in defence of the established sanctity of right we now possess over decisions upon whom we are to appoint as our officers at all levels of our trade union organisation'.

(ii) *National Political Situation.* 'From the Nile to Cape Town, from East to West of this vast continent of Africa, the name Nigeria has given hope and promise to the indigenous Africans of Africa. Trade unionists from Kenya, Uganda, Rhodesia, Tanganyika and Nyasaland have in repeated chorus chanted this Hope and this Promise. "Must we Nigerians fail these hopes and betray so sacred a trust?" – is the question. To accelerate the pace of advancement to national independence, the various governments of the Federation should give immediate consideration to the following:

(*a*) Nigeria should seek associate membership of the UN and all its specialised agencies;
(*b*) A State Bank with full powers to mint Nigerian coins and currency notes;
(*c*) Vigorous training of Nigerians for foreign service;
(*d*) A Nigerian Army, Navy and Air Force must now be established;
(*e*) University and other professional training must not be limited to the United Kingdom alone; immediate steps should be taken to secure training facilities in other countries;
(*f*) The number of faculties in the University College at Ibadan should be increased and further expanded;

(*g*) All Nigerians entering the University College at Ibadan should be awarded full scholarships;
(*h*) Extensive mass education scheme;
(*i*) Set up ministries of Housing and Town Planning;
(*j*) Set up iron and steel industries to bolster industrialisation of the country.

(iii) *Wages And Nigerianisation.* Although the wage rates of the average Nigerian worker had risen by over 200 per cent within the past ten years, the significant thing was that it had not meant an increase in purchasing power. 'Our immediate objective', the paper added, 'will therefore be to demand the introduction of the industrial wage pattern in a comprehensive system and also take effective action to obtain an adequate industrial minimum wage for each specific industry in the country. This also involves the re-organisation of existing machinery for wage negotiation, remodelling them on the lines of industry and the early introduction of statutory wage regulations for the "sweated trades".' The paper recommended the adoption of job evaluation as a means of wage fixation and cited the experiment made at the Soap Company, Apapa, as an example. On Nigerianisation the paper demanded that 'emphasis in all sectors of industry must be shifted from mere academic certificates (which have been responsible for quite a substantial number of the present wrong placings) to consideration of training, experience and ability in the particular field of labour. Only by this can it be ensured that the proper person gets into the right job, and therefore able to understudy and advance rapidly to the top.'

(iv) *Financial Problems of the Trade Union Movement.* The greatest obstacle to the development and furtherance of the over-all functions of our trade union movement is the very limited financial resources available to the movement. The position is so precarious that virtual 'liquidation' seems to suggest itself as the only possible next step. Despite the fact that the singular efforts of the trade union movement over the past decade have won for the wage-earner quite substantial sums as a reward, including in addition a number of social benefits, the unions find so much difficulty in getting out dues from the members. The voluntary will to pay is not there, and the movement has to strain every nerve to be able to get out the meagre rates of contribution from the membership.' The paper saw a panacea in the check-off of union dues and said that every member of the movement looked forward to the introduction of check-off as the 'magic wand' expected to solve the present financial miseries of the movement.

Other recommendations were:

(*a*) Rate of monthly subscriptions to be 6d. in the £ with effect from November 1957;

(*b*) Rate of affiliation dues should be 1d. per member per month, and unions with less than 240 members should pay £1 per month;

(*c*) ANTUF affiliation fee should be raised to £15 15s. with effect from November 1957;

(*d*) Congress recommends to unions to treat with more serious concern the question of adequate salaries and attractive terms for full-time officials, calls for substantial increases in the rates, and appeals for regular reviews aimed at further improvement of salaries and conditions of full-time men;

(*e*) Congress calls on unions to improve their taste in the choice of office accommodation, materials and general outlook.

(v) *Increasing Employment Opportunities.* According to a report on wage-earning employment published by the ILO in September 1956, Nigeria appeared to be the most backward in tropical Africa in providing opportunities for wage-earning employment. 'The whole question of the early extension of wage-earning employment in Nigeria is material to us in the trade union movement because the expansion of the country will depend on its numerical size and therefore influence.' The paper advocated large-scale industrialisation with emphasis on heavy industries.

The fears expressed by many delegates during the debate on affiliation to ICFTU soon became justified. General Secretary Gogo Chu Nzeribe told a meeting of the Executive Council, held after the conference, that since the conference had adopted a resolution in favour of international affiliation, and having defeated the motion on affiliation to ICFTU, it meant that the conference had approved affiliation to the World Federation of Trade Unions. This interpretation annoyed people like Lawrence Leo Borha, who parted company with the Marxist Group after the Abeokuta meeting, and H. A. P. Nwana, General Secretary of the Association of Locomotive Drivers, Firemen and Allied Workers of Nigeria. In co-operation with other union leaders, they organised a massive withdrawal of unions from the ANTUF. By March 1957, the ANTUF had become little more than a façade. In April the unions which had withdrawn set up the National Council of Trade Unions of Nigeria. Its principal officers were N. A. Cole, President; H. P. Adebola, F. W. Miriki, E. C. Okei-Achamba and Franco Olugbake, Vice-Presidents; Lawrence L. Borha, General Secretary; L. U. Agonsi, R. O. Gbadamasi, N. Anunobi, Assistant General Secretaries; and O. Egwunwoke, Treasurer. Its aims and objects which underscore the difference between the depleted ANTUF and the NCTUN, were:

(i) to provide a powerful and effective central trade union body independent of any ideological influences, and pledged to the task of promoting the interests of working people in the country and of enhancing the dignity of labour;
(ii) to encourage the organising of workers in free and democratic trade unions; to unite them towards their common objectives regardless of sex, tribe and differences of political views, and to afford them a free and democratic platform for consultation and collaboration in furtherance of their genuine interests;
(iii) to aid the establishment and maintenance of trade unions in all industries in the country;
(iv) to seek the full recognition and application of rights of the trade union movement;
(v) to promote and support activities designed to secure the improvement in wages and working conditions and the raising of the standard of living of workers;
(vi) to advocate and seek the expeditious industrialisation of this country, with a view to raising the general level of prosperity and standard of living, and realising an increased and properly planned national economy.
(vii) to seek for state ownership of major industries in the country;
(viii) to represent the trade union movement in all national agencies or statutory bodies which exist or may be set up to perform functions affecting the social and economic conditions of working people;
(ix) to promote and foster legislation in the interest of the working class;
(x) to engage or participate in educational and publicity work with the object of:
    (*a*) increasing the people's knowledge and understanding of national and international problems, so as to enable them to make their struggles more effective;

(*b*) furthering the aims of the Council and of trade unionism generally;

(xi) to establish a political committee to promote political action in support of the above aims and objectives;

(xii) to co-operate, in whatever manner it is deemed fit, with free and democratic international trade union federations, whose aims are acceptable to the Council.

The ANTUF and the NCTUN engaged in identical press warfare as did the TUC and the NNFL, the ANTUF calling its rival an imperialist stooge, while the NCTUN consistently charged the ANTUF with being a communist front organisation. Communism had no popular support in the country, and was generally understood by the common people as a godless ideology out to subvert and destroy the Nigerian way of life.

In order to improve their public image and make people believe they had shed themselves thoroughly of communist connections, the ANTUF applied to the ICFTU for affiliation in 1957. Dated December 13, 1957, the application was made on behalf of the organisation by the President, M. A. O. Imoudu, and the General Secretary, S. U. Bassey. Before then, however, the NCTUN had made a similar application. In keeping with its policy of accepting only one affiliate from a country (unless circumstances necessitated a variation of that policy) the ICFTU sent a mission to explore the possibilities of reconciling the ANTUF and NCTUN. That mission failed to achieve its objective because of the allegedly unco-operative attitude of ANTUF leaders.

In March 1958, NCTUN's application was accepted by the ICFTU Executive Board. News of the affiliation was published in the local press, and at once a new press war began. ANTUF attacked the affiliation as a disservice to the workers, and said it wanted a labour movement that would not be committed to any international trade union organisation. For obvious reasons it did not disclose that it had also applied for affiliation. NCTUN replied that the affiliation was being attacked because ANTUF wanted to drag the labour movement to WFTU without the consent of the workers, and by so doing sustain the practice of unscrupulous individuals who used such a connection to collect huge sums of money to line their pockets. For unknown reasons they too failed to disclose that ANTUF had applied for affiliation. The ICFTU itself did not help its affiliate by supplying them with a photostat copy of the ANTUF application (Fig. 3). Had it been supplied and published, the great anti-ICFTU campaigns which followed would have had no effect on the workers and the people of Nigeria. The photostat was supplied and published four years later when former ANTUF leaders were again making capital out of international affiliation.

It is of course debatable whether the anti-ICFTU campaigns, which gained momentum after the affiliation of the NCTUN, could have been prevented by accepting ANTUF's application in preference to NCTUN's, or whether the problem could have been contained by accepting the applications of both organisations. On this point two schools of thought have emerged. The feeling of one is that ANTUF's attack on affiliation was a manifestation of injured pride, and that, had ANTUF's application been accepted, its leaders could not have promoted anti-ICFTU campaigns as they did. This conclusion must be considered against the bakcground of the past performances of ANTUF leaders. Their record had been one of consistent opposition to ICFTU, based on the ideological orientation of the ANTUF leadership. ANTUF's application for affiliation was not born out of any genuine belief in the principles and policies of the ICFTU: its leaders were pressed to the wall by constant charges of communist leanings, and wanted a cover for their operations, and to leave the workers and the people of Nigeria in a false sense of security. In such a situation it would have been unfair to proven friends if NCTUN's application had been rejected and that of an inveterate opponent accepted.

Another school of thought argues that, since ANTUF had changed its mind about the ICFTU, and had even gone to the extent of seeking affiliation, their application ought to have been received with more sympathy, and treated as one of those special cases where two affiliations could be accepted from one country. They quote the AFL and CIO in the United States of America as an example to strengthen their case. This school believes that it would have been possible in the long run to achieve unity through this process. It points out, and perhaps with some justification, that at that time both the ANTUF and the NCTUN were engaged in some sort of prestige battle, and in such a situation it was indiscreet to take a decision that would have the effect of making one of the contending parties lose face. These arguments may be cogent. What must be considered, however, and perhaps was considered by the ICFTU Executive Board, is whether there was a genuine change of heart. The reported attitude of ANTUF leaders during the conciliation talks in 1957 did not inspire confidence. The analogy with AFL and CIO does not fit in the groove. There was no disagreement between the AFL and CIO on international relations, particularly as far as the ICFTU was concerned. In Nigeria one of the perennial causes of difference has been the conflicting views of union leaders on international relations. One school of thought believes in international affiliation, which another believes in dencouncing while all its activities are ordered and directed by external agencies.

The rivalry between the ANTUF and the NCTUN continued till late in 1958, when a group of union leaders founded the National Labour Peace Committee charged with the task of effecting a lasting unity in the trade union movement. Its principal officers were Ayodele Adeleke, Chairman of the Enugu Council of Labour, Chairman; and Adolphus U. D. Mba, General Secretary of the Shell-BP Workers' Union, Secretary. The Committee held meetings in Lagos and Ibadan, and after protracted negotiations an anxious Nigeria was informed on January 21, 1959, that unity had been achieved on the following terms:

(i) that the two organisations (ANTUF and NCTUN) agreed to merge and have a new name and a new constitution;
(ii) that the affiliated unions of both organisations should become *bona fide* members of the new body;
(iii) that a joint merger conference of the two organisations should be held at Enugu on March 7 and 8, 1959,
(iv) that, while recognising the right of the individual to believe in any brand of political ideology, cognisance was nevertheless taken of the events which had led to disunity in the past, and it was therefore agreed that, in the interest of permanent unity, communism, fascism, and national political partisanship should not be projected in the Nigerian labour movement;
(v) that the two organisations agreed to set up a Joint Committee – consisting of six members from each side – to meet the National Labour Peace Committee at Ibadan on January 31, 1959;
(vi) that the two bodies should submit proposals for the merger conference to the NLPC;
(vii) that the assets and liabilities of the two organisations, including the existing international affiliation of either ANTUF or NCTUN, be taken over by the new organisation.

What followed this announcement we shall consider in Chapter 16.

REFERENCE

1. General Secretary's Report to the first General Council Meeting of the All-Nigeria Trade Union Federation.

15

'EMERSON MUST GO'

Two important protest demonstrations were staged in 1959. They are important in the general context of Nigerian labour history because of what happened in the process, and because of their results. In January, the Airways Workers' Union organised a strike in furtherance of a wage claim and improved conditions of employment. To beat the strike the management of the West African Airways Corporation (Nigeria) Limited offered and actually paid £10 to each worker who failed to join the strike. It was the first payment of its kind ever made in Nigeria, and sparked off unpleasant reactions.

The WAAC loyalty bonus was discussed at the inaugural congress of the second Trades Union Congress of Nigeria, founded in March 1959. The congress not only condemned it but directed the Central Working Committee 'to mobilise full support for the Airways Workers' Union in their protest action'.[1] The demonstrations eventually organised by the TUC(N) in important towns and cities were aimed at securing:

(i) a deterrent to future occurrences of loyalty bonus to strike-breakers;
(ii) removal of the official or officials responsible for the scandal; and
(iii) the reconstitution of the Airlines into a Statutory Corporation.[2]

Although all the objectives could not be realised, yet striking successes were achieved in some of them. For example, the management admitted that the payment of a loyalty bonus was an indefensible action, and denied that it was made with their authority. Whether the denial could be taken seriously was, of course, quite a different matter. It is significant, however, that the appointment of the official who authorised the payment was eventually terminated. Moreover, the 'unequivocal condemnation of the loyalty bonus both by the Governments and leaders of this country, no doubt inspired by our protest action gives cause for the trade union movement to hope, even if it cannot be accepted as a firm guarantee, that no employer in this country would be likely to take a similar action in the future'.[3]

The demonstration of railway workers on December 10 was in protest against bad faith, maladministration and organised corruption. It was the spontaneous outburst of a smouldering fire, which had been building up for a huge conflagration over the years. Since its inception, the Nigerian Railway has hardly paid its way. The intention of making it a paying concern motivated its conversion from a Government Department to a public corporation. Chief Bode Thomas, Nigeria's first Minister of Transport, made the case for a railway corporation in August 1952, when he said: 'It is the Government's view that a public utility of this kind is better operated on quasi-commercial lines by a statutory corporation than by a Government Department. The rigidity of control and the established formalism, which are proper and necessary in the operation of a Government Department, are not suited to a public utility, which should not only provide the service required by the public but should do so on sound financial basis.'[4]

Unfortunately the purpose was not achieved. For almost five years after becoming a public corporation, the Railway continued to be what it had been from the outset – a big waste-pipe. For this there were several reasons. On its becoming a statutory corporation, many new posts with fabulous salaries and allowances were created, and filled mostly by expatriates. The Nigerian Union of Railwaymen (Federated), grouping the nine registered trade unions in the railway industry, claimed that many of these posts were redundant. The salaries and allowances of the top executive posts were increased out of all proportion. For example, the Assistant General Manager (Works) got a salary increase of £1,975; the Chief Engineer, Chief Superintendent and Chief Mechanical Engineer £815; the Chief Accountant £975; the Controller of Stores £750; the Electrical Engineer £700; and the Principal Accountant £625.

In May 1959 there were 163 expatriate officers on contract, receiving between 20 and 25 per cent of their salaries as contract addition. The NUR estimates that the total amount paid as contract addition was about £50,100 per annum. By contrast, the wage increase for Nigerians in the junior segment of the railway service varied from one to three pounds a month.

If much-needed money was squandered in fantastic salaries and allowances, the railway revenue was equally reduced by organised corruption in the Corporation. A committee set up by the NUR in 1959 to examine the causes of the fall in revenue found that corruption in the Railway was no secret. Officers aided and abetted it, and its opponents were victimised. It cited a police constable, who investigated allegations of corruption and recommended the prosecution of certain officers, as a case in point. Not only were the officers not prosecuted, but the police constable who made the recommendation was forced to resign his appointment.

Railway management often complained that their fall in revenue was due to road competition. The Committee found that several good customers of the railway boycotted its services and took to vehicular transport because of what it called the 'wagon racket'. A customer could not get a wagon unless he paid a £5 bribe. Although the Corporation had priority registers for allocation of wagons, these registers turned out to be valueless, as people not in the list could get wagons and very often got them at the expense of those in the list.

The Committee examined the problem of nepotism and found 'the whole administration of the Railways is in a complete muddle as far as promotions are concerned. Efficiency means nothing. Educational qualifications have no value, experience and length of service count very little. The only qualification to earn you promotion if you are an African in the Railway is that you must have a senior officer as a relative in the Railway Headquarters or District Headquarters. As an alternative to your having a relative you must have a clannish connection or a "father", usually a white man, in the office or you must offer heavy sums of money as bribes. If you are successful in all these, all your warnings (starting from grade I to grade IV) mean nothing. You should not associate yourself openly with a trade union for you will be taken as a spy who is ready to expose the welded cord of corruption.'

Other matters examined by the Committee included industrial relations and the responsibility of the Railway Corporation as a public carrier. The Committee found that the Railway Corporation had no personnel officers with the right type of training. The Elias Commission arrived at a similar conclusion. As a result, most disputes were allowed to develop into industrial conflicts. Unions had had to organise strikes in season and out of season. The Committee also found that poultry dealers often complained that frequent increases in freight charges were not being matched with corresponding good services. They were being cheated. For example, they would pay high rates in the hope that their goods would be carried by passenger or parcel trains, whereas the Railway carried them in cattle trains. As a result poultry died, and the traders lost many other perishable goods.

The Committee also found that Nigerianisation was moving very slowly and that, in promotions to senior posts, Nigerians with requisite qualifications were always at a disadvantage in relation to their expatriate colleagues at interviews before Selection Boards. It asked: 'Why training Railway Staff in Britain and wasting money when such training cannot qualify them for officers' grades?' It quoted figures to show, for example, that, apart from contract addition, it cost £1,300 more to employ an expatriate traffic inspector than his Nigerian counterpart.

In 1959 the Railway Board discussed the deteriorating state of Railway finances and directed the General Manager to appoint an inquiry into the causes of the fall in revenue, and to recommend ways of overcoming them.

On September 25, 1959, the General Manager held a consultative meeting with representatives of the Nigerian Union of Railwaymen (Federated) and informed them of the state of Railway finances. He also informed them that a special committee would be set up to investigate the situation and make recommendations. This would not be a retrenchment committee, and its members would be instructed that retrenchment was to be the last thought in their minds. The union representatives were assured that should management resort to retrenchment the unions concerned would be duly consulted before action could be taken.

The men thanked the General Manager and pointed out that the unhealthy financial situation was not due to road competition as alleged by management but to many redundant posts and different kinds of unnecessary allowances paid to expatriates. The General Manager said he would welcome constructive suggestions for improving Railway finances.

The NUR hoped to meet the General Manager's expectation by having one of their representatives as a member of the committee of inquiry. The committee eventually appointed did not include any NUR nominee. Its members were top departmental heads whom the Union were accusing of being responsible for most of the anomalies in the Railway. The Union had no confidence in the (Crawford-Astley-Phillips) Committee and believed its members would do all in their power to cover up their alleged iniquities.

On October 19, 1959, the NUR addressed a memorandum to the Minister of Transport and sent a copy to the Railway management. It outlined the evils in the Railway and suggested possible remedies. It complained that, in spite of assurances to the contrary, the Railway management had terminated the appointments of about 1,000 daily paid workers without consultation with the unions concerned. Moreover, 3,000 more had been retrenched as a result of dieselisation.

On December 3, 1959, the NUR addressed a letter to the Railway management asking for a meeting to discuss Nigerianisation in the Corporation. Another letter of the same date asked the management not to discuss matters relating to the effects of dieselisation and the fall in revenue with individual unions but with the NUR. A meeting was subsequently fixed for December 11 at 4 p.m. In the interval the NUR held a meeting to discuss strategy and nominate its representatives. Two schools of thought emerged at the meeting. One, the moderates led by President H. P. Adebola, felt that more positive action should be taken after the meeting of the 11th, depending on the outcome of that meeting. The other, the militants led by Imoudu, felt that a demonstration should be organised to give positive expression to the workers' feelings against Railway policies. The militants carried the day, and it was agreed that a demonstration be staged before the General Manager's office on December 10, at 10 a.m.

The news leaked. The Railway management quickly issued notices warning the workers that anyone absenting himself or leaving or refusing to carry out his duties would break his service and render himself liable to disciplinary action. No payment would be made for time lost. The notice quoted General Rule 2(*b*) in support, which says 'No Railway servant shall absent himself from duty or leave his place or station without permission. Any servant who does so may be summarily dismissed.' The workers defied the warning and staged the demonstration. From loco workshops and running sheds, Railway workers carrying placards marched to the General Manager's office, Ebute-Metta. Some of the placards read 'Emerson Must Go'. It was a peaceful demonstration all the way until it reached General Manager's Office. Here the more militant leaders rushed into the office, dragged out and sometimes assaulted clerks who were unwilling to join. The assault soon turned into a riot, which brought in the police. They charged the demonstrators. Unable to disperse them by this method they used tear gas. The men took to their heels. The police pursued them, beating with reckless abandon any person they came across. Even pregnant women, who were not among the demonstrators, were beaten up. By the time it was over, 168 persons had been arrested. Most of them were later released, but seven were prosecuted for conduct likely to cause a breach of the peace. Those prosecuted were H. P. Adebola, NUR President; S. O. Oduleye, NUR Secretary/Treasurer; M. A. O. Imoudu, President of the Railway Workers Union; P. B. Thomas, President of the Railway Technical

Staff Association; Nwafor N. Oti, RTSA General Secretary; E. C. Okei-Achamba, General Secretary of the Permanent Way Workers' Union; and Peter Otu. Adebola was acquited; Imoudu was sentenced to three months imprisonment; Oduleye, Oti and Okei-Achamba each got one month; Thomas and Otu were fined £10 and £5 respectively.

Adebola's acquittal soon became a blessing and a sorrow. It was a blessing in that it enabled him to rally round Railway workers and prepare the NUR's case, which was presented to the Elias Commission of Enquiry. It was a sorrow in that it played into the hands of his opponents and he lost the Presidency of the NUR as a result. At the NUR conference in 1962, his detractors exploited his acquittal without scruples; they claimed he had been discharged because he betrayed his colleagues. The lie stuck with those who heard it, not because it was true but because of other grouses which many of his colleagues had against him. For one reason or another, Adebola's popularity among railwaymen had been waning. The main consideration for electing him President of the TUC(N) in 1960 was that he showed promise of being the man most capable of meeting Imoudu's challenges in the Railway. At that time the TUC(N) had seven of the nine trade unions in the Railway as affiliates. Six years later the United Labour Congress, its successor, could boast of only one affiliate in the Railway, namely Adebola's Railway and Ports Transport Staff Union, which had left the NUR; at that time some leaders of the Railway trade unions told the writer that, as long as Adebola remained President of the ULC, their unions would not return into its fold.

The 'Emerson Must Go' demonstration led to the appointment of a commission of Inquiry into the administration, economics and industrial relations of the Nigerian Railway Corporation. Its members were Dr. T. O. Elias, Chairman; Dr. P. N. C. Okigbo and Sir Arthur Kirby. In their report published in 1960, the Elias Commission said the Railway management was 'vested with too much power to take action on major issues without reference to the Corporation'. The Commissioners felt that a number of changes in the existing power structure would improve the general tone of Railway administration. They criticised section 13 of the Railway Ordinance, which required the Chairman to notify the Minister within 10 days of any decision affecting the public interest and to suspend the carrying out of such a decision until the Minister's directions were known. Section 13 also provided that, if all members were present when such a decision was taken, the chairman might suspend action for one month during which he would reconvene a meeting of the Railway Board to reconsider the matter. 'In the first place,' said the Commissioners, 'although the Ordinance is silent on the point, we consider it strange that the Chairman with such wide powers should have been based in London or that Sir Ralf Emerson, for all his good intentions and undoubted professional competence in his office as the General Manager of the Nigerian Government Railways, should have accepted office as Chairman of the Corporation on relinquishing his post as General Manager.'[5]

The Commissioners found that Sir Ralf took certain high-handed actions during his tenure of office as Chairman. For example, he by-passed other senior officers and appointed the Corporation's Secretary as Acting General Manager, when the General Manager was away on leave – an action which infuriated the officers and the unions and which, according to the NUR, was one of the remote causes of the 'Emerson Must Go' demonstration. Sir Ralf also appointed Dr. Rishworth both as a member of the interviewing and recruiting panel in the London Office and as a medical officer certifying the fitness of persons selected for appointment. The unions felt it was unfair and hardly above board for one man to combine both offices. As if these appointments had not passed the bounds of propriety, Sir Ralf also authorised the payment of gratuities to certain secretary-typists, who were dismissed after a short term of service. The Commissioners found that 'neither the Standard Conditions of Service of 1956 nor the Ordinance itself gave Sir Ralf Emerson any authority for these payments'. They went on: 'We need draw attention to only one more incident – the Darvell Agreement about air and sea passages between Nigeria and London for Railway staff. Whilst the Agreement is in itself apparently innocuous, we feel that the stipulation that Mr. Irving (son of the Irving of the well-known law firm of Irving and Bonar practising in Lagos) should be appointed as a Director of the newly-formed Company, to which Dr. Rishworth was also appointed as a member, was bound to lend colour to the charge of nepotism.' The commissioners suggested changes in the Ordinance and recommended that 'it would be eminently desirable at this stage of Nigeria's political advance that the next chairman of the Nigerian Railway Corporation to succeed Sir Ralf Emerson should be a suitably qualified Nigerian. In this connection, the existing Ordinance requirement for the Chairman of the Corporation to have had previous Railway experience should be dispensed with, the two main requisites being appropriate administrative experience and good industrial management on the part of the candidate for the office.'[6] The Commissioners examined the promotion procedures in the Railway and found anomalies which 'seem to confirm the allegation by the Nigerian Union of Railwaymen (Federated) that educational qualifications have no value.' With regard to Nigerianisation the Commissioners found the management's argument that the number of Nigerians in the senior segment of the service had risen from 17 per cent in 1948 to 43 per cent in 1959 as fallacious. 'Nigerianisation', they pointed out, 'does not simply mean that the number of Nigerians in the service will rise, because this is in any case inevitable; it means that duly qualified Nigerians will have preference over other nationals when first appointments are made, and that, as a matter of policy, they will even be promoted, often prematurely, to supersede other nationals.'

Dealing with corruption, the Commissioners said it was 'worthy of note that much the greater number of the instances quoted before us by the Union concerned the irregularities and frauds committed and being committed by their own union members and, on that account, we consider that the Union was in this matter genuinely anxious to be helpful to the management. But we feel that not enough encouragement is being given to their efforts to spotlight cases of corruption in many aspects of Railway operation.' The Commissioners found that one specific case of corruption was proved against an expatriate permanent way inspector, who consumed ninety-nine bottles of beer from twenty-three subordinates promising to recommend them for promotion. Although management knew of the case, no action was taken against him, except that he was asked to return the total number of bottles he collected from each person together with 50 per cent of the cost of each bottle.

Like the NUR investigation Committee, the Commissioners found that poultry dealers often paid high rates in the hope that their goods would be carried by passenger trains when in fact the Railway Corporation carried them by cattle trains. When, owing to trains running late or not running at all for several days, poultry and other perishable goods died or were destroyed, the Railway management would refuse to pay compensation or at best paid little, taking shelter under the cloak that the goods were accepted for transit 'at owner's risk'.

The Commissioners then examined the problem of industrial relations and declared: 'The Corporation would do well to come from their Olympian heights and attempt seriously to grapple with the social and commercial problems incident to the operation of the Railway. That Sir Ralf Emerson himself should deny in cross-examination that the Corporation's public relations were bad is a symptom of the extent to which the management needs to take off its blinkers'. It also examined the machinery for settlement of industrial disputes and said: 'We need say no more than that we believe that the existing machinery is adequate but that the will to negotiate is not always there.' It was not the machinery itself that was ineffective but the implementation of agreements reached that sometimes proved to be unsatisfactory. In such a case the fault lay in industrial relations officers, who should be carefully trained and oriented towards the promotion of industrial peace. Theirs was to present official views to the unions in a friendly and understanding manner, and at the same time acquaint management with the unions' point of view in respect of the day-to-day problems of the administration.

The Commissioners emphasised that if industrial relations officers were to possess the qualities of patience, tact and understanding in dealing with unions, then their superiors who instruct them in their dealings with unions must also possess these and other qualities. In particular management should make an earnest effort to bridge the gulf existing between them and the unions – a gulf which arose out of suspicion and truculence. With regard to allegations of breaches of agreement the Commissioners said: 'We consider it a matter for regret that the management should have seen fit to retrench staff with such long periods as 20 to 30 years continuous service with the Railway, even though these men might have been engaged on capital works that had now been completed. Quite apart from any question of failure on the part of the management to consult the Union, the management should certainly have reviewed the whole policy of retrenchment which made it necessary to terminate the careers of Corporation employees with such long and apparently unblemished service.'

The Commissioners drew attention to another evidence of lack of imagination in handling staff matters. After the demonstration of December 10, the Railway management wrote to the Minister of Transport and Aviation saying it proposed to retrench 1,127 redundant employees. The Minister ruled that the action be suspended pending the report of the Commission which was about to be set up. Yet in spite of the Minister's ruling, no less than 235 employees were dismissed or suspended. Retrenchment of employees continued even when the Commission was sitting in Lagos. Some Railway union leaders claim that the Railway management defied the ruling of the Minister because Sir Ralf Emerson had no regard for him. He believed he held his office at the pleasure of the Prime Minister who, it was claimed, appointed him when he was Minister of Transport.

The Commissioners themselves tried to find out why the Minister's ruling was defied and reported as follows: 'When we asked the management why it has been found necessary to continue to retrench staff even as our commission was sitting in Lagos, we were informed that the Minister's letter asking them to hold over all further retrenchment of staff did not in their view apply to non-established employees of the Corporation, whom alone they were retrenching. Such a legalistic approach might be technically correct and the retrenchment might have been inevitable, but we doubt the wisdom either of the policy or of its timing. If anything it is likely to promote industrial disharmony and needless irritation between the management and the Union. It could even be interpreted as dictated by a motive to victimise as well as intimidate the workers. We also consider it rather unfair that those who had been tried and discharged from accusations of involvement in the disturbances should still be harried by the management in the way both sides described to us at the Inquiry.' They went on: 'A mood of self-righteous indignation is hardly suited to the formulation of an enlightened policy of staff reduction, however justifiable on pure economic grounds. It seems to us that what is needed is that the management should get back to the basic agreement concerning the procedures dealing with redundancy, and that the entire staff position should be reviewed in full and friendly consultation with the representatives of the Nigerian Union of Railwaymen (Federated) round a conference table.'

The Commissioners then made 24 main recommendations. Among them were:

(i) that the posts of General Manager and Secretary to the Corporation be Nigerianised within two years of the publication of their report;

(ii) that a scheme be established for the rapid advancement of Nigerians in the service of the Corporation with a view to their becoming substantive Heads of Departments in three years;

(iii) that changes be introduced into the existing statutory provisions relating to the Corporation's delegation of functions to the General Manager and the General Manager's delegation of functions to others, so that their exercise may be subject to effective Parliamentary scrutiny through the Minister of Transport either before, or as soon as possible after, their operative dates;

(iv) that, as a means of ensuring true accountability to Parliament of the Nigerian Railway Corporation, as also of the

Coal Corporation, the Electricity Corporation and similar public corporations, the Federal House of Representatives be strongly advised to set up a Committee on Statutory Instruments, made up entirely of Members and charged with the duty of subjecting all forms of subordinate law-making to detailed and expert scrutiny, and of reporting their findings to the House from time to time. To this end, a set of provisions similar to the Statutory Instruments Act, 1946, for the United Kingdom be drawn up by the Law Officers of the Federal Government to regulate the principles and procedures of the Committee and of the House in relation to it;

(v) that the whole of the Nigerian Railway Corporation Ordinance be referred to the law officers for a comprehensive review and possible redrafting;

(vi) that a Nigerianisation Officer be appointed solely for the carrying out of the Nigerianisation proposals recommended;

(vii) that the Railway Corporation should establish as part of the General Manager's Office a Public Relations Section charged with the preparation and dissemination of handbills, notices, advertisements and other similar literature designed to make known as widely as possible the more important day-to-day activities of the Corporation; the education of the general public and the Railway's customers as to their rights and entitlements to certain specific services rendered to or for them by all categories of Railway officers and servants, in an all-out attempt to eliminate bribery and peculation; the publicising through all legitimate means of the Corporation, and the publication of a well-produced quarterly or even monthly magazine for the benefit of both staff and the public;

(viii) that an All-Nigeria Transport Authority be set up comprising representatives of the Corporation, the Federal and Regional Governments, important road transport operators and the Nigerian Ports Authority to co-ordinate policies relating to fixing of rates, and freight and other charges, to the mutual advantage of all concerned;

(ix) that the method of operating selection boards for promotion purposes be improved so that the criteria could be more uniformly defined and applied throughout the Railway system;

(x) that as part of the over-all economy measures needed to make the Corporation a viable organisation, the London office run at a cost of £14,000 in 1958–59 and estimated to cost £20,000 in 1959–60 be abolished and its functions taken over by the Nigerian High Commission in London. Similarly the services of the Corporation's medical officer in London be dispensed with;

(xi) that, as a means of discouraging corruption among Railway Traffic staff in their dealings with the public, the operations of the 'raiding squad' disbanded early in 1960, be restored. In addition to this an Anti-Corruption Committee consisting of two representatives each of the management and the NUR be established to eradicate all internal traces of corruption among Railway staff;

(xii) that management and the unions should make the existing machinery for the settlement of disputes work more effectively by showing a greater willingness to negotiate. Management should come down from their Olympian heights and take the staff into their confidence by sincere and well-directed efforts to explain and discuss, and not command in negotiable matters;

(xiii) that the contemplated retrenchment of 1,127 workers be not proceeded with. The machinery for prior consultation with the unions be complied with so that, if a genuine case of redundancy were made out, the unions would appreciate the need for reduction of staff. Moreover, management must not give the impression that the only victims of retrenchment were to be members of the junior service;

(xiv) that all future vacancies required to be advertised in the United Kingdom must also be advertised in Nigeria, and the policy should be to endeavour to fill as many vacancies as possible from within the Corporation's service;

(xv) that all mileage, travelling, abnormal and inconvenience allowances be carefully reviewed and tightened up so as to cut fraudulent claims on the part of certain members of both the junior and senior services of the Corporation.

The Elias Commission Report was hailed throughout the country both for its recommendations and for its forthrightness. In a state-statement, the Federal Government said it welcomed the report 'as a constructive and realistic attempt to diagnose the causes of the Corporation's weaknesses and to prescribe remedies for their cure'. The outcome of the commission was dramatic. Sir Ralf Emerson was soon succeeded by a Nigerian, Dr. Okechukwu Ikejiani. In less than two years another Nigerian, J. C. Egbuna, became General

Manager of the Corporation. Many other Nigerians also assumed positions of responsibility. So the sweat and tears of December 10, 1959, the privations in the dingy rooms of Broad Street Prison, and the broken heads and fractured limbs of Railway workers had yielded rich dividends – not only to those who endured the ordeal but to many of those who had called them irresponsible rascals.

But that was not all. The hopes of a better future which the workers had pinned on the change-over from white to black men did not cure the ills in the Railway, Again, four years later, Railway workers were stageing another demonstration. This time it was for the removal of Dr. Ikejiani. With their characteristic forensic skill, Railway union leaders successfully organised the overthrow of the man they had once hailed as a redeemer.

REFERENCES

1. Report of the Central Working Committee to the National Executive Committee of the TUC(N) on August 22, 1959.
2. Ibid.
3. Ibid.
4. *Report of the Elias Commission of Enquiry into the Administration Economic and Industrial Relations of the Nigerian Railway Corporation 1960*, page 16.
5. Elias Commission Report, page 17. Sir Ralf Emerson, formerly an official of the Indian Railways, was also Chairman of the Nigerian Railways Board.
6. Ibid.

16

THE SECOND TRADES UNION CONGRESS

Although an attempt to achieve unity, the Enugu merger conference was in fact a trial of strength between the long established All-Nigeria Trade Union Federation and the comparatively young National Council of Trade Unions of Nigeria. Long before the conference, ANTUF activists had been in the field trying to get their affiliates and uncommitted unions to vote on all issues according to ANTUF dictates. They seemed to have succeeded pretty well in Lagos and Western Nigeria; their headache was Eastern Nigeria. Eastern unions took the position that they would not commit themselves in advance to any body and on any issue; they would judge every issue according to its merits, and vote accordingly.

The conference opened according to schedule at the Dayspring Hotel, Enugu, on March 7, 1959. It was presided over by Ayodele Adeleke, Chairman of the National Labour Peace Committee. More than 300 delegates from Lagos and Eastern and Western Nigeria attended, many representing unions not affiliated to either the ANTUF or the NCTUN. The notable absentees were delegates from Northern Nigeria. At that time there were very few unions in the North, the largest of them being the Tin Mine Workers' Unions, which had been decimated by internal dissensions. The others were, in the main, inconsequential house organisations, which no national centre had tried to contact, and which did not seem to care anyway about central labour organisations in the country.

Fraternal greetings were received from the various Governments of the Federation and from friendly organisations overseas. The conference received with applause the chairman's opening address in which he said that the conference had been convened to achieve unity in the labour movement and to forget the past. After the chairman's speech, leaders of the ANTUF and the NCTUN made speeches welcoming the return of unity and pledging their co-operation to ensure a lasting unity in the labour movement. From the pious statements thus made, it seemed the conference had started on a good footing. In this spirit of good will and co-operation it unanimously ratified the merger instrument signed on January 21, 1959, on behalf of the All-Nigeria Trade Union Federation by M. A. O. Imoudu, President, and Samuel U. Bassey, Secretary; and on behalf of the National Council of Trade Unions of Nigeria by N. A. Cole, President, and Lawrence L. Borha, Secretary.

The conference then went on to consider the constitution of the new organisation – Trades Union Congress (Nigeria). In many respects the aims and objects of the new organisation as outlined in the draft constitution were identical to those of the NCTUN, the only exception being the clause prohibiting the projection of communism or fascism in the labour movement. A major disagreement arose when the conference was debating the headquarters of the organisation. Certain delegates blamed the perennial splits in the labour movement on the inordinate ambitions of Lagos trade union leaders and felt that a panacea to that problem lay in having the headquarters of the organisation outside the Federal territory of Lagos. That suggestion divided the conference into two camps, which some delegates called the Federalist and the Regionalist Groups.

The Federalist Group argued that the shortcomings of individual unionists should not blind the conference to the advisability of siting the headquarters in the country's capital. To support their contention they pointed out that a national centre would be dealing constantly with the Federal Government, and its capacity to do so effectively would be hampered if its head office were outside the seat of the Federal Government. The main argument of the Regionalist Group was that siting the Head Office outside Lagos would kill the lust for office, which had been responsible for splits in the past.

Another matter which generated much heat was Patrick Okoye's attempt to reverse the decision of the conference on international affiliation. Clause 7 of the merger instrument, unanimously ratified by the conference, provided that: 'We agree that the assets and liabilities of the two organisations including existing international affiliation of either ANTUF or NCTUN be taken over by the new organisation.' At the time of signing that agreement, and up till the merger conference, the only international affiliation known to have existed was the affiliation of the NCTUN to the ICFTU. By ratifying the merger instrument the conference had in effect voted for the affiliation of the TUC(N) to the ICFTU. It would appear that the implication was not well known to some ANTUF leaders when they were voting for the ratification of the merger instrument. The full implications seem to have been known the following day, which would explain what happened thereafter.

Attempts have often been made by anti-ICFTU elements in Nigeria to give a garbled account of the proceedings of the Enugu merger conference, particularly its decision on the controversial issue of international affiliation. These accounts have created considerable doubts in the public mind as to what the conference actually decided on international affiliation. These doubts would continue as long as the proceedings of that conference remain unpublished. It is even doubtful if they would ever be published, and if published it is still more doubtful that they would command respect, for each of the contending parties would want its own account of the proceedings to be accepted as the truth of what transpired. The conference stenographer was a prominent member of one of the unions in the ANTUF, which had always been opposed to ICFTU. It is said that he left the country for Moscow soon after the conference, and did not hand over the minutes to anyone. Efforts to get him to produce the minutes or hand over his notes were of no avail.

There is probably one way of establishing the truth about the conference decision on international affiliation, and that is to get an account of what happened from delegates from the uncommitted unions. Being affiliates of neither the ANTUF nor the NCTUN, these unions had no stake at that time in international affiliation.

The writer happens to be one such delegate, and can say emphatically that the account given by the TUC(N) in their memorandum to the Labour Reconciliation Committee in 1961 is true and accurate. The relevant portion of that memorandum reads: 'Our friends, in an attempt to justify their breakaway, have stated that the Enugu conference decided against affiliation. This is not correct. The facts are that, after the conference had ratified the merger instrument signed by the NCTUN and the ANTUF, Mr. Patrick Okoye, now a leading member of the NTUC, moved a motion suggesting that the TUC(N) should not affiliate to any international organisation in the interim. The motion was ruled out of order by the conference chairman on the contention that it sought to reverse the decision of the conference.'[1] There is, however, one missing link in the TUC(N) memorandum which must be stated to complete the story. It is that the chairman's ruling was not made immediately after the motion had been moved. If it had, then there might not have been the stampede that followed. The chairman allowed a debate to take place, during which some ANTUF leaders tried to break the conference and blame it on foreign interference. His ruling followed a point of order raised nearly forty minutes after the commencement of the debate.

Some delegates who attended the merger conference have often wondered why Okoye moved that motion. Some think that Bassey and Imoudu did not receive the blessing of the ANTUF Executive before concluding the merger agreement. Others feel that the Executive was split over the terms. The dissidents decided therefore to fight the issue in the conference. Some others believe that Imoudu and Bassey planned the move to save themselves from the indignation of their supporters, some of whom were well-known agents of anti-ICFTU organisations in Europe. This conclusion may not be an unfair judgment on both men since neither of them came out in defence of the instrument when one of its clauses was being attacked by Okoye.

The conference adopted a number of resolutions. One authorised the TUC(N) Executive to demand wage increases of 50 and 30 per cent for unestablished and junior service employees of the public services of Nigeria. The resolution also empowered the TUC(N) to negotiate wage demands on behalf of the workers with the various Governments of the Federation. Another important resolution considered by the conference was one demanding the amendment of the Labour Code to permit the introduction of check-off of union dues. Until November 1960 check-off was illegal. For almost a decade the trade unions had fought in vain for its introduction, and in 1953 the matter was raised in the House of Representatives. Replying to a question on the matter a Government spokesman said it was Government 'policy to encourage the voluntary regulation of industrial regulations, and unions and employers are subject to protective provisions of the Labour Code Ordinance regulating deduction from wages, free to negotiate on this matter if they so desired.' It was, in fact, these 'protective provisions' that were the rub.

But by far the most important decision of the conference related to the election of officers. And it was here, more than in anything else, that the test of strength was conducted. No prior agreement had been reached on this between the ANTUF and the NCTUN. Both sides took the view that it was basically wrong to impose leaders on the workers; that the leaders of the new organisation must be elected by the workers purely on the basis of their own choosing and without recommendation from interested parties; that, in view of the claims and counter-claims of popularity often made by union leaders, any attempt to reach agreement on the matter would install into office persons who ought not to be there. Whether these arguments were cogent and could ensure lasting unity is a different matter. They seem, however, to underscore the determination of each party to capture the whole positions without yielding an inch to the other. Under these circumstances the conference proceeded to elect the officers and members of the Central Working Committee of the TUC(N).

Two persons (M. A. O. Imoudu and N. A. Cole) were nominated for the office of President. Imoudu won by an overwhelming majority. His victory immediately created the impression that ANTUF nominees were going to dominate the offices of the TUC(N), but the impression was false. What followed showed beyond doubt that Imoudu won purely on his personal merit and not on the ticket of the ANTUF. Successive elections of Deputy President and Vice-Presidents did not arouse much enthusiasm, so NCTUN nominees won an easy victory. However, it was not in these positions that ANTUF activists were interested. As some of them confessed later, they did not attach importance to those posts, and would easily have conceded them to the NCTUN if there had been a prior negotiation on office-bearers. Their whole interest centred around the office of General Secretary, and they were interested in that position because they believed that through it they could manipulate the labour movement to suit their ideological orientation, and reverse the will of the majority. It was precisely to forestall this conspiracy that NCTUN leaders were equally interested in the office. The nominations which followed were a straight fight between the ANTUF General Secretary, S. U. Bassey, and Lawrence Borha, General Secretary of the NCTUN. Borha won a landslide victory.

Immediately after hearing the result of the election, ANTUF leaders disappeared from the conference hall. Most of them were out when the members of the Central Working Committee were elected. The election showed a sweeping victory for NCTUN nominees, although a few ANTUF leaders were included. It is said that ANTUF leaders who left the conference hall after the result of the election of General Secretary held a little caucus at the Dayspring Hotel, and pledged themselves to make things impossible for the new organisation. How they translated this decision into action may be summarised as follows:

(i) *Non-Co-Operation*. The TUC(N) began its existence under very trying circumstances. Although unity had been achieved at Enugu, that unity was short-lived for one important reason. The necessary spirit to back the hope-raising pledges of unity and co-operation was lacking. It would appear that some of those pledges were made in the hope that certain persons would be elected to office. When, through the unfettered will of workers' representatives, it became a forlorn hope, the disgruntled elements banded themselves together in a concerted action of non-co-operation and sabotage.

The first evidence of non-co-operation was the attitude of ANTUF leaders to the merger instrument provision on assets and liabilities of the ANTUF and the NCTUN. It should be remembered that the instrument provided that the assets and liabilities of the two organisations would be taken over by the TUC(N). Attempts to get ANTUF leaders to co-operate in implementing that decision were of no avail. The usual excuse given by the ANTUF was that its trustees (M. A. O. Imoudu, S. U. Bassey and Richard Aghedo) could not be assembled together to take a decision.

Perhaps the most important evidence of non-co-operation was the failure of some affiliated unions, particularly those from which the dissident elements were drawn, to pay their dues to the Congress. On the surface it would appear that the weak financial position of Nigerian trade unions was responsible, but a closer examination of the problem shows that much more than this was involved. In most of the big unions, default in dues payment was not due to financial weakness: it was a deliberate act of union Secretaries to starve the Congress of funds and thus make it impossible for it to operate. Having thus rendered it inactive, the persons responsible would then accuse the Congress leaders of failing in their responsibilities. This was part of the master-plan to make things impossible for the Congress. Frequently the dissidents argued that their unions would not pay dues because they did not see what the TUC(N) was doing, but they did not just stop at that. Rumours filled the air, particularly after August 1959, that certain union leaders were going from union to union urging the leaders not to pay subscriptions to the TUC(N). It has been reported that the campaigners even went to the extent of offering bribes in the form of money, or Moscow, Peking, East German and other Eastern European scholarships, to certain union leaders and their children to get them to withdraw financial and moral support from the TUC(N). Whether the charge of inactivity is fair can be judged from TUC(N) activities during the first nine months of its existence. In thus judging, it must be appreciated that no organisation can function effectively without money. A few pounds were raised at the Enugu unity conference, and this constituted the funds with which the Congress was to operate for a considerable length of time. Subscriptions from affiliated unions were slow, and sometimes did not come in at all for the reasons already given. The situation might have been corrected if the President and other leaders had given a lead. Rather than do this they allowed the subscriptions of their own unions to fall heavily in arrears. Defaulting member unions therefore saw no need to pay. Moreover, the general trade union situation could not encourage the TUC(N) to insist that dues be paid or defaulting affiliates lose either their membership or certain rights. Because of its financial position, the Congress could not rent an office or employ staff. For the first couple of months it operated on the little money raised at Enugu and the scanty assets of the NCTUN. Thereafter it depended entirely on the kindly disposition of the Association of Locomotive Drivers, Firemen and Allied Workers of Nigeria, whose General Secretary was also the General Secretary of the TUC(N). It was this pathetic inability of the Congress to maintain itself and its heavy dependence on the Association that provoked the dissensions which eventually forced Borha to resign his position in the Association.

(ii) *Sabotage:* The TUC(N) Central Working Committee held its first meeting on March 26, 1959, and considered among other things the Congress' programme of work for the year. In pursuance of the decisions of that meeting, Regional Working Committees were established in April in the Eastern and Western Regions as 'organic parts of the administrative and Executive machinery of the Congress'.[2] About the same time the Congress organised protest demonstrations in Lagos and various parts of the country against the decision of the WAAC management to pay a loyalty bonus to strike-breakers during the strike of Airways workers in January 1949. The dissidents tried to sabotage the demonstrations by concealing from their members circulars sent to affiliated unions. The result was that many unions complained of being left out of an important activity that was in furtherance of trade union rights.

(iii) *Unjustified Attacks.* In June the TUC(N) addressed a memorandum to all the Governments of the Federation on the demand for revision of wages and salaries. A similar memorandum was forwarded to the Nigerian Employers Consultative Association. It demanded an interim wage increase of 30 per cent in the salaries of established junior staff and a 50 per cent increase in the wages of unestablished labour. The memorandum said that the demands were justified because of the rise in the cost of living, the need to improve the living standards of the workers and because both the Governments of the Federation and employers in the private sector had the capacity to pay. A series of discussions followed as to whether the Congress could be accepted as a bargaining representative of the workers of Nigeria. By many considerations the idea was a revolutionary development in industrial relations in the country. The existing practice had been for the various unions catering for public employees to set up an *Ad hoc* Committee to press their claims and probably force the setting up of a Commission of Enquiry to which the national centre submitted memoranda and sometimes gave evidence.

The various Governments and the NECA opposed this seeming break with tradition. Happily two good things came out of the discussions and strengthened the workers' case. First, the Federal Government admitted that there had been a substantial increase in the cost of living since the Gorsuch awards of 1954 ,and secondly, it became clear that the Federal Government and the Regional Governments were considering the appointment of a Commission of Enquiry to determine the extent to which the cost of living had risen and make recommendations on wage increase.

While these discussions were in progress, a former ANTUF leader, and one of the prominent members of the dissident group, accused the TUC(N) of failing to win wage increases for the workers as demanded by the inaugural Congress.

In August 1959, the TUC(N) held the first meeting of the National Executive Committee. That meeting adopted a resolution giving the Governments of the Federation a thirty-day ultimatum to concede the demand for a wage increase, otherwise to take a general strike on November 1, 1959. The decision was well-timed and given wide publicity by the press and the Nigerian Broadcasting Corporation. 1959 was an election year. At the time of the meeting the various political parties were busy in the field wooing the electorate for a mandate to lead Nigeria to independence. Partly in order to avoid the threatening cataclysm and partly in order to score a political point and get itself into the warm embrace of the workers, the Action Group, then the ruling power in Western Nigeria, announced a 10 per cent interim wage award to all junior employees of the Western Regional Government and all local government bodies in the Region. The shock announcement forced the other Governments to grant a similar concession.

The 10 per cent interim award was followed by an announcement of the appointment by the Federal, Eastern, Western and Southern Cameroons Governments of the Mbanefo Commission of Enquiry to review the wages and salaries of junior civil servants. The Western Nigeria Government also announced the appointment of the Morgan Commission, and explained that it had opted out of the Commission appointed by the other governments because its terms of reference were circumscribed.

The 10 per cent interim award was hailed by the workers and their leaders as a welcome relief from the hardships of rising prices. The only person who held a contrary view, and expressed it through the press, was M. A. O. Imoudu, President of the TUC(N). On his arrival home from his first trip to Moscow, he condemned the interim award and accused the other officers of the TUC(N) of betraying the workers of Nigeria by accepting the award. He had been away from the country when the struggle for the interim award was going on, and had travelled without the consent and approval of the TUC(N) Central Working Committee. At the first meeting of the National Executive in August many delegates asked his whereabouts. The General Secretary, Lawrence Borha, reported that Imoudu had told him he was sick and was travelling to his home town for treatment. But he did not go to Ora-Oke; he went to Moscow. It soon became an open secret that his former colleagues in the ANTUF who, at the August meeting, persistently asked for his whereabouts, were the very persons who had arranged the trip. He had been in constant touch with them ever since the Enugu unity conference, had been holding secret meetings with them, and had been deeply involved in the master-plan to make things impossible for the TUC(N). At one of these meetings the trip to Moscow was discussed. He was selected to go because of the key position he occupied in the trade union movement.

(iv) *Violation of the Constitution.* While in the Soviet Union, Imoudu was reported to have given a talk over Moscow Radio in which he praised communism as a system and promised to commend it to the workers and people of Nigeria. On his return he proved faithful to his pledge. Addressing a conference of the Electrical Workers' Union at Yaba, President Imoudu said he had been to the land of communism, had seen communism at work, and had come to the conclusion that it was the best system for the workers and people of Nigeria to follow.[3] He made a similar remark at a meeting organised by the Nigerian Union of Railwaymen (Federated) at Enugu and was hooted down by his own men.[4] Clearly these uterances were a violation of Article 2(*k*) of the TUC(N) constitution, which ought to have been protected by the President. Article 2(*k*) provides that one of the aims and objects of the Congress is 'to safeguard against the projection of communism or fascism in the Nigerian labour movement, but without prejudice, however, to the right of individuals to believe in any brand of political ideology'.[5] In Moscow, Yaba, and Enugu, Imoudu did not speak as an individual, or President of the Railway Workers' Union; he spoke as President of the Trades Union Congress of Nigeria. The Central Working Committee repeatedly pointed out this fact to him, and tried, without avail, to get him to retract. We shall presently consider what followed.

(v) *Alliance with the Ghana TUC.* After the All-African People's Conference in Accra in 1958, the thought of Pan-African unity gained momentum. Inspired by this feeling and the thought of

West African labour unity, which had begun in 1945, the TUC(N) in August 1959 addressed a letter to the Ghana Trades Union Congress suggesting a meeting between the two organisations to consider a joint protest action against the proposal of the French Government to test its first nuclear device in the Sahara. Many governments in the world, including those of most African states, had pleaded with France to reconsider her decision in view of the likely effect of radio-active fall-out on the peoples of Africa. The joint protest action was intended to support world opinion on the matter.

In reply, the Ghana TUC welcomed the idea, and suggested a meeting about the end of August. The TUC(N) had not yet indicated whether the time suggested would be suitable when a cable was received that the meeting could take place earlier. An emissary came and discussed the matter with the leaders of the Congress and an agreement was reached that the meeting would take place on August 22.

The Ghana TUC delegation, led by its General Secretary, John K. Tettegah, arrived Lagos on August 21. It consisted of 22 persons, 13 of whom represented that number out of the 16 trade unions in the reconstituted trade union movement in Ghana. The other 8 were GTUC officials, who were advisers to the delegation. Almost every one of the visitors came in a brand-new car, and showed no restraint in advertising the wealth and influence of the new unionsim in Ghana. The delegation held a meeting with representatives of the TUC(N). Discussion centred not only on the proposed French atomic test but also on the possibility of founding a West African Trade Union Federation. The writer was fortunate to act as joint Secretary for the Nigerian side at that meeting, at the end of which two joint communiqués were issued, signed on behalf of the two organisations by Lawrence Borha and John Tettegah. The texts are as follows:

COMMUNIQUÉ ON THE PROPOSED ATOMIC TEST IN THE SAHARA

(i) This joint conference, fully aware of the repercussions and consequences of atomic tests wherever they have been carried out and which have been proved by eminent scientists to be dangerous to mankind, on behalf of all working peoples of Nigeria and Ghana vehemently condemns this inhuman intention of the French Government to carry out the projected atom test in the Sahara.

(ii) This joint conference fully supports the protest made by countries in Africa and other organisations outside Africa against the proposed test.

(iii) The conference hereby further protests against the test and calls upon all working peoples of Africa to join in this protest; we appeal to all workers of the world to use their influence to prevent the test from being carried out.

(iv) This joint conference urges the various African Governments to continue their efforts to persuade France to abandon the proposed test in the Sahara.

(v) In the interest of the defenceless people of Africa this joint conference directs that this declaration be sent to all governments and organisations of the world interested in peace.

COMMUNIQUÉ ON FUTURE TRADE UNION CO-OPERATION

The delegation of the Trades Union Congress of Ghana and the Nigerian Trades Union Congress have held a two-day discussion in Lagos on matters of future co-operation.

The two delegations

INSPIRED by the present surge and the

AWARENESS of African unity have

RESOLVED to pursue for the future a common policy on matters of mutual interest. The two delegations are in complete agreement over the formation of a West African Federation of Trade Unions to cover the English-, French- and Portuguese-speaking areas of West Africa and

CONSIDER the present joint meeting the nucleus of the future Federation, and mandate the Secretary General of the Ghana TUC to undertake preparatory talks with the other national centres for a future meeting.

The two delegations fully

SUPPORT the declaration on African trade union unity made by the All-African People's Conference December 1958, at Accra and

ACCEPT to work within the framework of any future All-African Trade Union Federation.

Later the representatives of both delegations discussed the second African Regional Conference of ICFTU scheduled for early November, for which Lagos was being considered as a likely venue. The Ghana delegation agreed to send representatives. A similar conference, the first of its kind, had been held at Accra in 1957, and opened by Dr. Kwame Nkrumah, at that time Prime Minister of Ghana. Eight Nigerian trade union leaders (H. P. Adebola, Lewis U. Agonsi, M. A. Labinjo, N. Anunobi, Mathias M. Ebokoba, R. O. Gbadamosi, J. A. Madika and E. U. Ijeh) attended, representing the Committee of ICFTU Affiliated Trade Unions.

The Ghana TUC delegation left Nigeria on August 24 and 25. According to the TUC(N) it was expected, at least as a matter of courtesy, that they would write to express their pleasure or displeasure at the way the Nigerian trade union leaders received them.[6] Moreover the Congress expected to hear from its Ghana counterpart the progress made in contacting other national centres on the question of founding the proposed West African Federation of Trade Unions, and when another meeting might be convened. None of these expectations was fulfilled.

On November 1, 1959, John N. Eburay, Director of Education of the Ghana TUC, came to Lagos and called at the TUC(N) Secretariat. According to the TUC(N) he came to consult with them on the conference of the Preparatory Committee of the All-African Trade Union Federation (AATUF). He did not notify the TUC(N) in advance of his visit, any more than he informed them of its purpose. Later developments showed that he had informed the dissidents in the Nigerian labour movement that he was coming, and why. Eburay held discussions with O. Zudonu, Vice-President of the TUC(N); L. L. Borha, General Secretary and N. Chukwura, Assistant General Secretary. A transcript of the discussions reports Eburay as saying that he had come to discuss the possibility of the TUC(N) sending a delegation to a conference of the Preparatory Committee of the All-African Trade Union Federation due to be held at Accra on November 4–8, 1959 – the very time when the second Regional Conference of the ICFTU was scheduled to take place in Lagos. Ghana TUC had sent an invitation earlier, and discovered rather late that it was understamped and consequently was returned to the TUC after a long delay at Accra Post Office. Ghana, unfortunately, would not be represented at the second Regional Conference of the ICFTU. Borha quickly replied, saying that it was significant that of all the invitations sent to national centres the only one understamped was the TUC(N)'s. He drew the attention of the visitor, himself a member of the Ghana TUC delegation in August, to the terms of agreement reached at the August conference, and the undertaking given by the Ghana delegation about the ICFTU conference, and wondered why the Ghana TUC did not live up to that agreement. He also pointed out the difficulties likely to arise because of the late notice and reminded the visitor that Nigeria was not a province of

Ghana; any Nigerian travelling to Ghana must satisfy the requirements of international travel. He wondered how this could be done within the next three days, which included a week-end. Nevertheless, he assured the visitor of the willingness of the TUC(N) to participate in the work of the Preparatory Committee, but added that the matter would, of course, be considered against the fact that the TUC(N) had already accepted the honour of playing host to trade union leaders from various parts of Africa. In conclusion Borha said it would enhance the realisation of an All-African Trade Union Federation if the GTUC could reconsider their decision and send a delegation to the Lagos conference.

Eburay said that reconsideration of their attitude was out of the question, because the Ghana Government had just restated its policy of neutrality and non-alignment, and it would not be in the interest of the Ghana labour movement to antagonise that policy. The discussion ended, and Eburay retired to his hotel. The TUC(N) leaders later consulted, and elected two officers – Nwafor A. Oti, Assistant General Secretary; and Emmanuel U. Ijeh, Secretary of the Western Working Committee – to represent the TUC(N) at the Accra conference. In the meantime something had been going on behind the scenes. Eburay had been busy contacting the dissidents in the labour movement. At 10.30 a.m. the following morning, Borha and one other member of the TUC(N) Central Working Committee made a courtesy call on Eburay in his hotel, where they found him in conference with most of the leading members of the dissident group. Those present were Gogo Chu Nzeribe, Sidi Khayam, Amaefule Ikoro, Patrick Okoye, Richard Aghedo, Robert Onyia, M. O. Ewuzie, G. I. Igbokwe, W. O. Goodluck and Egbuna Ifedira.[7] On seeing the two TUC(N) leaders the meeting suddenly broke up.

What happened at Accra three days later throws light on the significance of the Sunday morning meeting. The Preparatory Committee of the All-African Trade Union Federation began its meeting on November 4 as scheduled. From the outset the meeting decided that only accredited representatives of the national centres of the various countries would be admitted and allowed to participate in the work of the conference. Shortly after the TUC(N) representatives had left for Accra, rumours spread in Nigeria that Ghana TUC had nominated three delegates to represent Nigeria from among the dissident group and had in fact sent return air tickets for their travel. The first day of the conference passed smoothly. The second day's session was interrupted by a sudden announcement that the Prime Minister of Ghana had invited the delegates to a cocktail party. In actual fact the party had been arranged to enable the host country to lobby and get the delegates to reverse the conference decision about representation to enable the men nominated for Nigeria by the Ghana TUC to attend.

When the conference resumed the following day, it adopted the recommendation of a special committee that the new delegation from Nigeria, consisting of W. O. Goodluck, S. O. Oduleye and Egbuna Ifedira, be admitted. TUC(N) delegates made a statement objecting to the decision and withdrew from the conference. Radio Ghana and the official party newspaper reported the withdrawal with a twist. They denounced the TUC(N) delegation as imperialist stooges and described the Lagos conference as imperialist-organised and inspired.

(vi) *Falsifying History*. The Accra episode was just a sign of things to come. Shortly after that incident the President and the Secretary of the Ghana TUC paid a secret visit to Lagos. It has been alleged that they gave £1,800 to the dissidents to work for a take-over of the leadership of the TUC(N), or force a split.[8] Armed with this handsome amount, the dissidents strengthened their denigration campaigns against the TUC(N). They published a booklet *The Case for Overhaul of the TUC* in which they made several libellous statements against the officers of the Congress and urged their overthrow. In this despicable role they found a ready ally – President Imoudu. It has been said that after his Moscow trip he seemed ready to do anything in violation of the TUC(N) constitution, particularly those things which suited the designs of the dissidents.

The dissidents later demanded an emergency conference, claiming they had secured the support of one-third of the 112 affiliates of the Congress. In actual fact only four unions were in support of that demand, and the four were unions of which two members of the dissident group were Secretaries, and each was Secretary of two unions. Because the demand lacked popular support it could not be entertained, and the Central Working Committee proceeded to prepare for the Annual Delegates Conference scheduled for April 1960. Immediately the notice for the conference was issued, the dissidents planned a country-wide tour. One of their quarrels with TUC(N) leaders was affiliation to ICFTU. They accused the officers of affiliating the TUC(N) to ICFTU for their own personal ends and without the authority of the competent organs of the organisation.

The facts, however, were that, conscious of the tension which arose from Patrick Okoye's motion at Enugu, the Working Committee did not consider it advisable, in the interests of unity, to proceed immediately with the implementation of that clause of the merger instrument dealing with international affiliation. However, at the National Executive meeting in August 1959, the Railway Technical Staff Association gave notice of a motion urging the TUC(N) to affiliate to the ICFTU. Unfortunately this and other motions could not be debated, as the whole of the meeting time had been taken by debate on the wage issue. It was agreed that the matter be referred to the Central Working Committee, who were fully authorised to take a decision and act on behalf of the National Executive. When considering the matter the Central Working Committee consulted with the Regional Working Committees, which unanimously supported the application for affiliation. As a result of that affiliation the ICFTU made a grant of £4,200 and donated one Opel car for organisational purposes. The car and the cheque for £4,200 were presented at a ceremony on November 22, 1959.

For the first time in the history of central labour organisations in Nigeria, workers' representatives saw aids given in the name of Nigerian workers being disclosed and in the open. It was in striking contrast to previous experiences, and showed the difference between the old and the new leadership. A great part of the money thus received was later used to purchase Volkswagen cars assigned to each of the three Regional Working Committees.

(vii) *Fomenting Division.* The country-wide tour of the dissidents did not produce the result they expected. Its fortunes took a turn for the worse when Imoudu was denounced at Enugu by his own Railwaymen. At the end of the tour the members of the teams assembled in Lagos with their advisers – a Hungarian official of the WFTU and three East German trade unionists – to evaluate their work and strategy and assess their chances of success at the coming conference of the TUC(N). It was clear to most of them that on the merits of their own case they could not carry the majority of the delegates with them. On the contrary it seemed clear that they would earn the wrath and condemnation of the conference. 'The choice before them, therefore, was either to go to the Congress and be defeated again, or refuse to go, set up a splinter organisation and there and then cause a split. It was not surprising that they chose the latter.'[9]

Before this development, President Imoudu, who had god-fathered the dissidents, added yet another thing to his unenviable record. He came out in defence of the Ghana TUC in all they did to humiliate his own organisation at an international conference. About this time a Nigerian delegation comprising representatives of the major political parties and the TUC(N) to the All-African People's Conference in Tunis returned to the country, and unanimously condemned Ghana for its role against Nigeria at the Tunis conference. This condemnation, coupled with his all-out defence of Ghana and the Ghana TUC and various breaches of the TUC(N) constitution, set in motion a series of agitations for Imoudu's removal from office.

On March 5, 1960, the TUC(N) addressed a letter to Imoudu preferring charges against him for gross violation of the constitution and conduct unworthy of an officer of the Congress. He was asked to attend a meeting of the Working Committee to defend himself. He did not attend that meeting. A second meeting was convened, which again he failed to attend on the excuse that it was not convenient for him. On the third occasion President Imoudu was requested to suggest a suitable date and time. He suggested March 29, 1960, and the meeting was convened accordingly. In the morning of the date of the meeting Imoudu came to the Secretariat and told the General Secretary that he had just received a message that his sister was seriously sick at Ibadan, and he was therefore going to Ibadan to see her. For that reason he would not be attending the meeting which he himself had fixed for that evening.

However, the truth about Imoudu's sister's ill-health became known a few hours later. A delegation of the Western Working Committee of the TUC(N) came to the Secretariat and protested against a mass meeting allegedly being organised that evening by the TUC(N) without the consent of the Committee. According to the delegation the meeting was to be addressed by President Imoudu, who had already arrived, and by Gogo Chu Nzeribe, an inveterate opponent of the TUC(N) leadership and leader of the dissident group. The theme of the rally was to be 'The Case for the Overhaul of the TUC', and the dissidents' pamphlet on the matter was being widely distributed at Ibadan. On being assured that no such rally was being organised by the TUC(N), the delegation left and returned to Ibadan. They quickly went into the field and with remarkable effectiveness made things impossible for Imoudu and Gogo. For the first time in his chequered history Imoudu could not speak to workers when he arrived for the meeting at 5 p.m. He was hauled out of the field, and only the timely intervention of the police saved him from being beaten up.

That evening the Central Working Committee of the TUC(N) met and, after considering the charges against Imoudu and his repeated failure to appear to clear himself, decided to suspend him from office. The letter advising him of the suspension said he could appeal to the Annual Congress if he was dissatisfied. Imoudu reacted swiftly and dramatically as soon as he received the letter. On March 31, 1960, he announced that he had dismissed the Central Working Committee and was calling a conference in Lagos of TUC(N) affiliates to elect new officers and a new Working Committee.

REFERENCES

1. *Nigerian Central Labour Movement: The Problems of Unity*, page 7.
2. TUC(N) Constitution, page 15.
3. Charges against Imoudu in letter dated March 5, 1960, from General Secretary, TUC(N), published in *The Daily Telegraph*.
4. Ibid.
5. TUC(N) Constitution, page 3.
6. Report on activities to 1st Annual Delegates conference of TUC(N) April, 1960.
7. Ibid.
8. Ibid.
9. Ibid.

17

'THE GREAT CONSPIRACIES'

There is no provision in the TUC(N) constitution empowering the President to dissolve the Working Committee. Imoudu himself knew this, and knew also that, by announcing he had dissolved the Central Working Committee, he was acting *ultra vires*. The announcement was further evidence of violation of the constitution and of indiscipline, for which the President had become well known, and an attempt to turn a purely disciplinary matter into a power struggle between himself and the rest of the members of the Working Committee. Both sides realised, of course, that the victor would be determined by the number of unions that would be represented at the two conferences proposed for Kano and Lagos. From March 31 to April 20 both sides redoubled their efforts to make their respective conferences as representative as possible.

The Kano Conference organised by the Central Working Committee opened at the International Hotel on April 20, 1960. It was attended by 351 delegates from ninety-eight affiliated unions representing a total membership of 98,000.[1] Fourteen affiliated unions were not represented. The conference received a message of goodwill from the Prime Minister, who expressed regret that the conference was not being attended by all those who had attended the inaugural conference a little over a year before. Nevertheless he hoped that differences in the labour movement would be resolved 'not by keeping apart but by getting together in a democratic manner characteristic of this country'. Later the Hon. O. Oweh, Parliamentary Secretary to the Federal Minister of Labour and Welfare, read his Minister's message of goodwill, which traced the development of national centres in the country and the splits which had occurred. The Minister expressed Government concern that another split was in the offing barely twelve months after unity had been achieved at Enugu. Other messages of goodwill came from the ICFTU headquarters in Brussels, the British TUC and McDonald Moses, ICFTU representative in Nigeria.

The conference then went straight to business. Considering the report on activities it unanimously adopted a motion by Chief A. A. Adegbamigbe, President of the Nigerian Union of Local Authority Staff, that Imoudu be expelled from the TUC(N) forthwith. The conference also unanimously passed a vote of confidence in the General Secretary, Lawrence Borha, who had been the focus of attack by the dissidents. Before it adjourned the conference re-elected Borha General Secretary and elected H. P. Adebola in succession to Imoudu.

The conference convened by Imoudu met in Lagos on April 21, 1960. It is reported to have been attended by delegates from fifty-five unions representing 184,612 workers.[2] The number of unions and the membership claimed are open to doubt for the important reason that some of the unions reported to have attended the conference were themselves represented at the Kano conference. How this came about is not difficult to tell. Disagreement arose in some unions following the TUC(N) decision to suspend Imoudu from office. In those unions where there was a good deal of sentimental attachment to Imoudu, branch officials, who thought he had been unfairly treated, felt that they had an obligation to support him at all costs. They defied their union Executives and attended the Lagos conference.

The Lagos conference was nothing more than a regrouping of the former ANTUF leaders. It decided to set up a splinter organisation known as the 'Nigerian Trade Union Congress', and elected Imoudu and Nzeribe as its President and Secretary. There has been considerable debate in Nigerian trade union circles as to why the splinter group chose to call itself the 'Nigerian Trade Union Congress'. Some people feel that it was deliberately chosen to cause confusion in the trade union movement at home and abroad; others that it was intended to make the workers believe that both organisations were one and the same. Perhaps the latter conclusion is correct, for it was widely reported in 1960–1 that NTUC activists were going from place to place representing themselves as emissaries of 'that TUC formed at Enugu in 1959'.

The emergence of the NTUC reopened old wounds, and set in motion a series of desperate efforts to effect reconciliation. The first attempt was made by three members of Parliament, A. U. D. Ubah, P. E. Ekanem and R. B. K. Okafor, themselves former trade union leaders. The attempt failed because NTUC leaders would not co-operate. Another attempt was made by the Central Executive Committee of the Eastern Nigeria Development Corporation and Allied Workers' Union. In July, 1960, this Committee invited Imoudu and Borha and representatives of the TUC(N) and the NTUC to a peace talk at Aba. Imoudu and Borha accepted the invitation. On the date of the meeting the Aba Council of Labour organised a reception for the leaders. Placards welcoming them were displayed by jubilant workers, who hoped the return of unity was in sight. When the meeting hour came, however, only Borha and two other representatives of the TUC(N) (N. O. Eshiett and N. F. Pepple) turned up.

The third attempt was made by the Labour Solidarity Committee formed in August 'to devise ways and means of solving the rift'. The Committee enlisted the support of His Highness Adeniji Adele II, Oba of Lagos, who agreed to intervene. Two meetings held at the Oba's palace failed to reach agreement again because of the unco-operative attitude of the NTUC delegation. On August 16, 1960, the split was echoed in the House of Representatives. I. A. Brown, Action Group member for Uyo, asked the Minister of Labour what efforts his Ministry had made to reconcile the TUC(N) and the NTUC, and if he would not consider the appointment of a judicial commission to investigate 'the root cause of this unrest and split in Nigeria's labour organisation'. Replying, the Minister said a commission would not be appointed and 'Government takes the view that the factors responsible for the present split in the country's trade union movement are matters that are the concern of the trade union movement itself'.[3]

The fourth attempt was made by the Ministry of Labour itself. The aim this time was not necessarily to resolve the split: it was to secure the agreement of both sides on the selection of workers' representatives on the Nigerian delegation to the first African Regional Conference of the International Labour Organisation. Several meetings were held without reaching any agreement. The NTUC argued that it was the legitimate trades union congress founded by the workers of Nigeria in 1959 and therefore would not discuss workers' representation with any other organisation. They insisted to a breaking-point that the workers' delegate and advisers must be selected from their own nominees. Failure to reach agreement caused the Prime Minister, Sir Abubakar Tafawa Balewa, to intervene.

On December 3, 1960, he held a meeting with representatives of the TUC(N) and the NTUC, which was also attended by the Minister of Labour, the Hon. J. M. Johnson. In the course of that meeting, the Prime Minister is reported to have warned trade union leaders against abandoning the interests of Nigerian workers for specious arguments about Pan-Africanism. Government, he said, was aware that certain Nigerian trade union leaders spent five days of the week in Ghana and two days in Nigeria and drew inspiration for their actions from that country. Government was also aware that the Ghana labour movement was financing certain persons to cause a split in the Nigerian labour movement. He appealed to TUC(N) and NTUC to forget their differences, and in the greater interest of the workers they claimed to represent to try and reach agreement on workers representation on the Nigerian delegation to the ILO conference.

Replying, an NTUC spokesman admitted for the first time that they had received £1,800 from Ghana, but claimed that the money came from the All-African Trade Union Federation – which was yet to be formed. He repeated the familiar NTUC argument for claiming recognition as the only trade union centre representing the workers of Nigeria, and maintained that for that reason the workers' delegate and advisers must be drawn from the NTUC. Since agreement could not be reached, Government felt obliged to select the workers' representatives on the basis of the provisions of the ILO constitution. Borha was appointed the workers' delegate and eleven other nominees of the TUC(N) were appointed advisers.

One thing that happened at the conference became a talking-point throughout. It was the appearance of a strange document captioned *The Great Conspiracy against Africa*. Copies had been smuggled into the pigeon holes of delegates and advisers by unknown persons, most probably leaders of the NTUC. The document, purporting to have been issued by the All-African Trade Union Federation, was said to have been an annex to a British Government Cabinet Paper on policies in Africa.

The Great Conspiracy, as it later became popularly known, appears to explain the hostility of certain African leaders and governments to the ICFTU and the concept of free trade unionism. If, as the British Government representative described it, the document was a forgery, it must have been forged by an expert in the game. The document begins with a narration of the bitter fight in the ICFTU Sixth World Congress of 1959 between the American and British trade union leaders, and explains in general outline the position of the British trade unionists at the Congress. It says, among other things:

> The gradual abdication of direct British and other European rule in favour of measures to establish local independence makes it all the more necessary to maintain our African connections by the development of non-political means. In these conditions the role of trade unionism and therefore the role of ICFTU have acquired a new and vital importance for us. This had been only partially

foreseen as regards Africa when ICFTU was founded. Recent developments there have greatly increased the importance of the unions as an alternative instrument of western influence and especially as a brake on unchecked political and national movements. Since it is difficult to accuse trade unions of serving colonial ends, with their aid it should be possible to establish harmonious relations with the new social and political institutions in Africa now being created and with the administration of industrial and agricultural interests, which we hope to maintain after any political changes. Trade unions will be needed to check irresponsible nationalisation and to maintain control in the key sectors of the economy in the newly-created African states. The principal aim should be the development in Africa of a genuine trade union movement as we know it in Britain and on the Continent. This must be done with our help and under our influence from the start.

The document claims that the US State Department and the American trade unions made no secret in the negotiations which preceded the 1959 Congress that participation of American trade unions in the ICFTU would be used to further the development of US political and economic interests in Africa, and adds: 'We need unfortunately to realise that this American policy has little or nothing in common with our aims in ICFTU, or indeed with our whole policy in Africa. On the contrary the aim seems to be to take advantage of the difficult situation in which the United Kingdom and other European powers find themselves and to replace their influence and interests by direct US penetration in Africa, using the machinery of ICFTU and American contacts that have been built up with African leaders for this purpose.' The document goes beyond that. It denounces prominent erstwhile trade union leaders like Ahmed Tlili of Tunisia and Tom Mboya of Kenya as imperialist stooges just because they believed in the ICFTU and the concept of free trade unionism.

The authenticity of *The Great Conspiracy* has been questioned. As already pointed out, the leader of the British Delegation to the conference denounced it as 'a forgery'. But Gogo Nzeribe, who wrote a foreword to the pamphlet, claimed that its authenticity was beyond doubt. Perhaps the strongest denunciation of the document was made by Borha. Speaking on the matter during the debate on the Report of the Director General, Borha said:

Permit me to refer to a document purported to have been sponsored by the All-African Trade Union Federation that is yet to be inaugurated, and which has been circulated around this august conference. This action, to say the least, is a dangerous conspiracy against the building of an All-African Trade Union Federation. You will see in this document unjustified accusations against some prominent African trade unionists. It is singularly unfortunate that an organisation which seeks to unite African unions should start by stigmatising these honest African trade union leaders simply because they refuse to lend themselves as tools to gratify the leadership hunger of a certain African state.

I am convinced that the great conspiracy against Africa has been carried out by those responsible for the dissemination of that bogus document.

Borha reviewed certain disquieting developments in certain African states, and added:

I am, like most delegates here, concerned that certain governments of independent African states are systematically subjecting the trade union movements of their countries and are making them pliable instruments in the hands of politicians in furtherance of questionable political objectives. We in Nigeria are particularly happy that the freedom and independence of our labour movement are enshrined in our constitution, and it is our hope that the success of the Nigerian experiment on African soil will ultimately provoke similar guarantees in other African states.[4]

Union leaders, particularly the supporters of the TUC(N), also talked about another 'Great Conspiracy'. This concerned the plans of certain persons to introduce 'the dictatorship of the proletariat' after the achievement of independence. The date of Nigerian independence had been announced in 1958 at the end of the constitutional conference of that year. From the date of that announcement almost every activity in the country was planned to meet the challenges of independence, trade union activities being no exception. Those who worked from late 1958 to early 1959 for labour unity were motivated by the feeling that it would be a tragedy for the workers if the country were to achieve independence with a divided, weak and sometimes irresponsible labour movement. Most of the 300 delegates who met at Enugu were of the same feeling.

But independence meant one thing to most people, but quite another thing to a few. To the majority it meant the closing of one chapter in Nigerian history and the opening of another; it meant an opportunity to formulate and direct our own affairs in freedom and democracy, and to plan and direct projects that would bring the greatest good to the greatest number – projects which, for varying considerations, could not be planned or carried out by a British colonial administration. To a few, particularly the few dissidents in the labour movement, the dawn of independence offered an excellent opportunity to exploit the failures of colonial administration to change the Nigerian way of life by force.

It was reported in 1960 that a Nigerian trade union leader had concluded an agreement with a certain foreign power by which the latter was to supply financial and material aids, including arms, to strengthen the struggles of the workers of Nigeria. These struggles were to begin after independence and the 'aids' were to be made available when certain countries had established diplomatic relations with Nigeria and opened embassies in Lagos. These rumours began when Imoudu was away. On his return, rumours of an 'October revolution' began to circulate. At first people discounted them as fabrications of anti-Imoudu elements to discredit the old war-horse. When, however, *The Sunday Times* published a series of articles captioned 'Behind the Iron Curtain', people began to take the allegation seriously. Those articles were written by Theophilus Chukwuemeka Okonkwo, a Nigerian medical student at Moscow State University, who was Secretary of the African Students Union in the Soviet Union for three years. For the greater part of his three-year stay in Moscow, Okonkwo had been a willing tool of the Soviet authorities in denouncing imperialism, colonialism and neo-colonialism. He fell out with them when he realised that all that glittered was not gold. According to him it was with the aid of the American and British embassies in Moscow that he managed to get out of the Soviet Union.

Okonkwo's articles told appalling stories of what happened behind the Iron Curtain, with special reference to the experiences of African students. One of these articles mentioned the visit of a prominent Nigerian trade union leader and a plot to overthrow the Government of Nigeria with the aid of ten Nigerians studying in other communist countries. Okonkwo later undertook a lecture tour of important towns in Nigeria under the auspicies of the Nigerian Society for Public Affairs, a short-lived organisation that emerged in Lagos towards the close of 1960. In lectures he gave in Lagos, Ibadan, Onitsha, Aba, Port Harcourt, Calabar, Enugu, Jos, Kaduna, Kano, Gusau and Sokoto, he repeated his allegation that there was a plot to overthrow the Government of Nigeria; and, referring to the split in the labour movement, asserted that . . .

> the fact that Mr. Imoudu went secretly to deal with the communists without telling his co-workers is responsible for the TUC

> rift, and the fact that he persistently refuses reconciliation in the interest of the unity of the workers of Nigeria suggests that he is otherwise committed. I happen to know there is a plot in which Mr. Imoudu is involved to team up the workers of Nigeria with the communists.[5]

Okonkwo later compiled a summary of his lecture and forwarded it to the Federal Government. No doubt that document and the disclosures in his *Sunday Times* articles influenced the Federal Government in deciding to limit the number of Soviet diplomatic personnel in Nigeria.

As it turned out, there was no October revolution in Nigeria. But it is remarkable that the leader of Nigeria's Opposition should have been arrested twenty-four months later and charged along with thirty-two others with plotting to overthrow the Federal Government. Could it be a coincidence or an irony of fate? Future historians might be in a position to solve this riddle.

Another conspiracy often referred to in Nigerian trade union circles concerns the role of the dissidents in the founding of the All-African Trade Union Federation. At the founding congress in Casablanca, most delegations took exception to the wanton disregard for democratic principles and procedure adopted by the Preparatory Committee and the congress chairman, Mahjoub Ben Seddick of Morocco. Representatives of the NTUC who attended were known to have acquiesced in it. For example, they did not challenge the decision of the Preparatory Committee to accord delegate status to such inconsequential and/or politically-sponsored organisations as the Sudan Workers' Trade Union Federation, the Uganda Federation of Labour, the Kenya TUC, the Mogadishu TUC, the Liberian Labour Congress or the Union of Free Workers of Ethiopia, while treating the *bona fide* trade union centres from those countries as observers. They did not question why national centres from Ghana, Guinea, Mali, the United Arab Republic and Morocco should be represented by six delegates each while organisations like the Trades Union Congress of Nigeria, the Kenya Federation of Labour and the UGTT of Tunisia and a host of powerful national centres from other African countries should either be represented by two delegates or by none at all. It did not appear strange to them that in a trade union congress, the credentials of delegates were not checked; that decisions were to be taken by acclamation and not by vote; that in a meeting of African trade union leaders, and that there should be an army of people from Eastern European countries and communist front organisations 'apparently hired to applaud'.

NTUC leaders played a conspicuous role in the preparatory work before the Casablanca congress. For example, the first draft of the constitution of the AATUF was prepared by Gogo Chu Nzeribe. That draft contained an appendix showing places where the AATUF would establish regional and field offices. Among them were Moscow, Peking, Washington, London and Paris. How would the AATUF get the funds to run these offices and its head office at Accra? The draft constitution provided that contributions from affiliated organisations would be £20 per annum, but donations would be received from independent African states and friendly organisations. Although the draft underwent several amendments, the final constitution adopted by acclamation at the Casablanca congress contained this strange provision. Yet anybody in his right senses, and alive to the operational costs of running trade unions, knows that £20 per annum cannot maintain a branch union let alone an All-African international.

This provision in its constitution exposes AATUF's pretensions that it is a *bona fide* trade union organisation and a free agent of African workers. It was probably provided merely to create the impression that contributions had to be low because of the weak financial position of most African trade unions. Put in its proper perspective, however, many other considerations would appear to have been involved. Why did a trade union organisation which claims to be independent of all other international trade union bodies not try, at least by a provision in its constitution, to be self-supporting? Why should a supposedly free agent of African workers tailor its affairs, by the provisions of its constitution, in a manner that makes it dependent for its existence on the kindly disposition of governments and so-called friendly organisations? Conversely, if a trade union organisation depends for its existence on the sufferance of other bodies, can it be said to be a free agent and a spokesman of the workers of Africa, many of whom have been exploited by those very governments on which it depends? A letter from Ibrahim Zakaria, Director of the International Affairs Department of the World Federation of Trade Unions, to Charles Heyman, Director of the African and International Affairs Department of the Ghana Trades Union Congress, in 1961, provides an answer. It says, in part:

> You know also that we fully agree with our Ghanaian brothers that, for the promotion of our joint political aims, the major part of the All-African Trade Union Federation's financial burden is borne and will be borne by the WFTU. It is however imperative that our financial arrangements should not be exposed to the class

enemy, who would exploit them for hostile propaganda by malicious interpretation. It should therefore be urgently impressed on prospective participants at the congress [WFTU Fifth World Congress] and above all on our African brothers, that the financial implications of our relationship must in no circumstance be disclosed or even hinted at, neither in connection with the Draft Programme of Trade Union Action nor in connection with any part of the agenda. As I told you in March, we are having serious difficulty in getting funds for the Casablanca meeting unless the Ghanaian Trades Union Congress could guarantee that disaffiliation from the ICFTU would be made obligatory for all affiliates of the AATUF. . . . Our primary task is to get the ICFTU out of Africa and destroy its supporters in Africa.[6]

It was in dutiful obedience to this instruction from the WFTU that the Preparatory Committee canvassed for disaffiliation from international trade union organisations before and during the conference. Representation at the conference was arranged purposely to achieve this objective. Debate on the issue lasted the whole day of May 30, 1961, and showed that anti-affiliation delegates were not necessarily opposed to affiliation to any other international, but only to the ICFTU. Pro-affiliation delegates defended the principle of international affiliation and also the affiliation of their organisations to ICFTU. They suggested that the question of affiliation to the ICFTU or to any other international organisation be left with autonomous national centres to decide, and warned against the consequences which forcing the issue would have on African labour unity. Despite that warning, the conference proceeded to adopt by 'consensus' and not by vote that affiliation was incompatible with membership of the AATUF. All national centres who were affiliates of international trade union organisations were given ten months to withdraw from such internationals. The decision was taken after most delegations had left the conference in sheer disgust.

The failure of the Casablanca conference to found a genuine, representative All-African Trade Union Federation, dedicated to the cause of African workers and independent of international trade union organisations, led to another conference of African trade union leaders at Dakar in January 1962, which founded the African Trade Union Confederation. It was attended by representatives of thirty-two organisations from twenty-seven African countries. The emergence of the ATUC meant that the AATUF had become more or less an organisation of the six founding national centres from Ghana, Guinea, Mali, Egypt, Morocco and Algeria. Since 1962 desperate efforts have been made to achieve unity in African trade unionism by the fusion of the AATUF and the ATUC. These efforts have failed because AATUF will not compromise on the question of international affiliation.

REFERENCES

1. Proceedings of 1st Annual Conference of TUC(N), April 1960.
2. Report of the Working Committee to 2nd Congress of NTUC, September 1961.
3. Proceedings of the House of Representatives, August 16, 1960.
4. Proceedings of the ILO First African Regional Conference.
5. Summary of observations made during C. Okonkwo's lecture tour of Nigeria under the auspices of the Nigerian Society for Public Affairs, page 11.
6. *The Voice of Labour*, February 1962.

18

TUC(N) AND NTUC AT WORK

In this chapter I propose to examine some of the important activities of the Trades Union Congress of Nigeria and the Nigeiian Trade Union Congress before the fourth merger conference of Nigerian trade unions in May 1962. At its first Annual Delegates Congress held in Kano in April 1960, the TUC(N) adopted, among others, the following resolution:

> CONVINCED that the fostering of a great and powerful Nigerian labour movement is essential, indeed vital to the building of Nigeria into a truly great and powerful nation;
>
> BELIEVING that the Nigerian labour movement could never attain such a position of strength and responsibility unless it is guaranteed an independent, free and democratic existence and thus able at all times to give adequate protection without let or hindrance to every worker in Nigeria regardless of sex, religion, status or branch of the economy in which he or she is engaged;
>
> CONFIDENT that the independence era will create those conditions favourable to the realisation of the above, the Congress-in-session hereby
>
> WELCOMES with joy, happiness and satisfaction the attainment of Nigeria's independence on the First of October, 1960;
>
> REAFFIRMS its belief in free, democratic trade unionism and its adherence to the principles of liberal democracy;
>
> URGES the Governments and people of independent Nigeria to exert unrelenting resistance to every type of totalitarian or authoritarian rule because such rule leads invariably to the inhibition of free trade union growth, the violation of human dignity and the destruction of man's freedom and the rule of law.

On Oct. 1, 1960, when Nigeria achieved independence, the TUC(N) issued an Independence Manifesto, which it described as 'a clarion call for action and a sacred act of re-dedication'. The manifesto said that workers of Nigeria were 'today architects of an independent Nigeria; tomorrow builders of a better Nigeria'. Dealing with the important question of national reorientation, it said that the motivation of every state and that of every citizen in an independent Nigeria should be unalloyed patriotism in all internal and external matters; it was a matter for regret that most people, including the national leaders, had not shed themselves, in thought or in behaviour in public life, of the influences which the colonial system had established. As a result, Nigeria found herself the inheritor of a chain of misplaced emphasis and priorities not only in the personal living behaviour of the people but also in state planning in the social and economic fields. 'There has been, for instance, a tendency to place emphasis and priority on national projects and pursuits, which satisfy primarily the prestige hunger and showmanship of those at the top as against the basic but essential and urgent needs of the teeming millions of our countrymen and women. The result is that the common people have been robbed of an opportunity of developing a feeling of belonging and of having a stake in the fate and fortune of the country.'

The manifesto expressed concern that the national economy was characterised by any adverse trade balance, a widening of the gap between the prosperity of the few and the degrading poverty of the masses, and growing unemployment worsened by mass retrenchment of workers in the major industrial concerns. The economic policy of independent Nigeria must be to 'seek to eliminate the poverty and misery we see and feel around us'. To this end it called on the Governments of Nigeria to formulate, with the active collaboration of labour and management, a national policy on unemployment and retrenchment and mobilisation of the nation's manpower and other resources, through an organised national effort, with a view to achieving:

(i) Increased food production, the purpose of which should be to satisfy demand at low costs and capable of sustaining a population of seventy million within the next two decades;
(ii) Mechanisation of agriculture and the promotion of large-scale farming projects;
(iii) The immediate launching of a scheme for:

  (*a*) the damming of the River Niger and the Shiroro Gorge;
  (*b*) an iron and steel industry;
  (*c*) the manufacture of finished products of cocoa, rubber and other agricultural products;
  (*d*) a glass and paper industry;

(*e*) vigorous recruiting into the nation's defence forces, and the establishment of a national air force;
(*f*) the building of a second Lagos bridge;
(*g*) more extensive and intensive development of railway, river and road transport and co-ordinated under a national transport commission;
(*h*) co-ordination and expansion of co-operatives.

The manifesto said that the TUC(N) was irrevocably committed to the principle of state ownership of the major means of production. Nevertheless, the Congress recognised the right of the individual citizen to own property insofar as such ownership did not hinder social and economic justice. The manifesto then said that the social policy of an independent Nigeria should guarantee not only the right to the pursuit of a full life, but also the means to its attainment. It should seek to create the conditions which accord with the dignity of responsible citizens. It called on the Governments of the Federation of Nigeria to draw up, in collaboration with labour, a social code for the nation. This code should guarantee adequate housing for workers. To achieve this objective a National Housing Board should be set up with an initial capital of £10 million contributed as follows:

Federal Government		£2,000,000
Regional Governments		
North	£1,000,000	
East	£1,000,000	
West	£1,000,000	
		£3,000,000
Employers in the private sector		£5,000,000
		£10,000,000

The manifesto said that this money should be used to provide houses for workers at cheap rentals or on hire purchase. Existing public housing corporations in the Regions should concentrate on providing houses for the peasantry on hire purchase terms. In this way Nigeria could discourage the prohibitive rents being charged by landlords.

The manifesto examined Nigeria's foreign policy vis-à-vis TUC(N)'s policy on international relations and said:
'The foreign policy of a nation, no less than its domestic policy, has profound influence on and mirrors the characteristics of the citizens of the nation, and is therefore a decisively important aspect of the political functions of the state. The announcement by the

Prime Minister of Nigeria of the nation's foreign policy has quite naturally sparked off many and divided voices. The TUC(N) wishes to take the opportunity of this occasion to make its observation. But first it is necessary to underline a number of self-evident facts:

'(i) that Nigeria will become a full-fledged member of the Commonwealth on attainment of independence – a fact which in itself presupposes the acceptance of certain fundamental concepts;

'(ii) that all the major political parties belong to the Commonwealth Parliamentary Association;

'(iii) that all the Governments of the Federation have made certain sanctions against communism and persons with communist inclinations.

'Against these facts, therefore, must be considered the importance and content of the foreign policy statement of the Prime Minister. There can be no question of any patriotic Nigerian finding fault with a sovereign Nigeria having an independent foreign policy. The point at issue, however, is whether an independent foreign policy is necessarily to be understood as conveying the same import and interpretation as a policy of "neutrality" or "positive neutrality". Clearly, therefore, in spite of any doubt which may seem to be in the statement – a situation which arises from the praiseworthy attempt to reconcile our Government's basic belief and the new gospel of African isolationism – it is a declaration of independence in the discharge and conduct of its external affairs and cannot therefore be interpreted as a positive acceptance of the policy of neutrality. In projecting this interpretation the TUC(N) draws confirmation from the statements of our political leaders, which clearly indicate that Nigeria is committed to being independent in the conduct of its affairs without the routine acceptance of interference by any of the two world power blocs. We cannot add more, except to say that, as loyal citizens, we will co-operate in making a success of this policy – without prejudice, however, to the independence of organised labour in the country.'

The manifesto also dealt with the question of the responsibilities of the trade union movement in Nigeria and reaffirmed TUC(N)'s programme of organising the unorganised, strengthening its affiliates, promoting by persuasion amalgamation of unions on an industrial basis, and engaging in such other activities that would facilitate the rationalisation of the existing trade union structure in the country. It commended Government's policy of permitting international affiliation and advocating a labour movement free of interference or domination of Government, employers or other influences. The TUC(N) recognised the natural desire of Nigerian workers to work together with other African workers for the improvement of their social, economic and political conditions. That was why it reaffirmed its belief in the idea of establishing an All-African Trade Union Federation dedicated to the principles of freedom and democracy. It would be unrealistic and indeed harmful to the effective projection of this ideal if the proposed organisation were to be isolated from the world trade union movement; in keeping with this view and with the basic beliefs enshrined in its constitution, to which an overwhelming majority of Nigerian workers subscribed, the Congress saw no conflict between its affiliation to the ICFTU and the discharge of its responsibilities to the workers of Nigeria. On the contrary it felt stoutly strengthened by this association in the onerous task of building a virile, strong democratic movement of which the country could be proud.

Finally, the manifesto condemned the anomalies in the wage structure and reaffirmed the determination of the TUC(N) to press forward with renewed vigour its demand for removal of these anomalies and the improvement of general conditions of employment in the public services, public corporations and the private sector of industry; the introduction of a national minimum wage; the abolition of large-scale use of the daily wage system as a cheap labour device, and equal pay for work of equal value without discrimination on account of sex.

In pursuance of this declaration, the TUC(N) set up in January 1961 a Committee to 'carry out an investigation into the structure, remuneration and other conditions of service in wage-earning employment in Nigeria, and to make recommendations to the Central Executive Council, having regard to Congress' claim for a general revision of salaries in order to bridge the existing gap between the salary scales of the senior and junior service personnel in the Public Services in Nigeria; for the introduction of a national minimum wage as well as for the orientation of the existing wage policy in a manner consistent with the national economy and the new political status of the country.' Its members were O. Zudonu, Chairman; Wogu Ananaba, Secretary; N. Anunobi, P. O. Ero-Philips, H. O. Coker, A. E. Okon, and Ene Henshaw. The veteran Nigerian economist, Dr. S. A. Aluko, was an adviser to the Committee.

In its 24-page report the Zudonu Committee found that the existing wage structure was the cause of the permanent resentment noticeable among the general labouring, technical and clerical personnel in the junior segment of the public services. This resentment, the Committee pointed out, had been consistently harmful to inter-class labour relationships, caused incessant demands for the review of wages and salaries, caused strikes and demonstrations and loss of many working days with consequent loss of output, thus checking a rapid growth in the national wealth. The inequities in the wage structure and general conditions of employment made those in the lower income groups feel they were not part of the economic system. Consequently they did not bother to increase their productivity or even maintain its existing level.

The history of the present wage structure showed a consistent widening of the gap between the salaries in the senior and in the junior segments of both the public and private sectors. In 1942, when the first attempt was made to review wages and salaries, the entry points into the standard grades in the lower and upper segments of the public service were £36 and £300 per annum respectively. Successive wage revisions only succeeded in widening the gap more and more, as could be seen from the following statistics. Before the Gorsuch Commission, the figures were £124 and £570; that Commission raised the figures to £150 and £624, and the Mbanefo Commission raised them to £174 and £720. Thus the working population had been divided into two classes in which those on top had continued to grow richer and those below to become poorer. Price levels had tended to be determined in the main by the overpaid minority. The danger in such a situation could not be overstressed.

The Committee said that the present wage structure had also been criticised for the multifarious sub-divisions existing in the standard grades. These were said to have been created to accommodate less qualified personnel. A more realistic approach to the problem, it maintained, would have been to abolish sub-scales and sub-divisions and regroup the salary scales in a manner that offered scope for continuous and easy rise to the maximum in the scales. No person should be appointed into a position without first undergoing the requisite training for the job.

The Committee made a strong case for a reconstituted wage-structure. The starting-point, it said, should be to determine a living wage for the lowest class of workers. Thereafter, wages for other grades of workers could be determined by six criteria of wage fixation as follows: the agreeable or disagreeable nature of the employment; the easiness and cheapness or difficulty and expense of learning a trade; the constancy or inconstancy of employment; the degree of responsibility required of the holder of the post; the probability or improbability of success or failure in the post and the output of a given job. A strong case was also made out for a national minimum wage. In determining what it should be the Committee worked out the following monthly budget as representing the expenditure pattern of the average worker in the Federal Territory of Lagos:

	£	s.	d.
Accommodation	4	10	0
Food	5	5	0
Clothing	1	0	0
Transport	1	0	0
Medical	1	0	0
Drink		10	0
Tobacco		5	0
Laundry		5	0
Servant		10	0
Entertainment		10	0
Saving	1	0	0
Fuel and Light		10	0
Miscellaneous including tax	1	0	0
	£17	5	0

The Committee declared: 'A young man beginning life as a worker expects sooner or later to be coupled. In the meantime he may have a girl-friend to care for, who may later become his wife. Or he may have an old mother or father, brother or sister, nephew or niece who, by reason of our custom and tradition, he is also expected to look after. For these reasons we consider that the sum of £2 15s. be added to £17 5s. and the minimum wage be fixed at £20 per month.'

Could Nigeria afford a minimum wage of £20 per month? The Committee said she could, and suggested austerity measures including a cut in the salaries of top posts as one of the ways of saving money to meet this objective. It declared: 'We cannot but express our disappointment that, at a time when there is a popular demand for a reduction in the salaries of top posts with a view to bridging the gap between them and those of the lower posts, members of the Federal Parliament should go out of their way to vote a £200 increase for themselves. When it is remembered that Nigeria is to pay £1,000 as salary for less than 12 weeks work, the practice of certain legislators using the floor of Parliament to criticise workers becomes a reprehensible and dangerous pastime. Parliamentarians making pious appeals for sacrifices and hard work must learn to teach by examples and not by precept.'

The Committee said that Government transport arrangements

for public servants made those in the senior segments of the public service spoilt babies and those in the junior segments beasts of burden. Government gave loans to senior civil servants to purchase vehicles; it paid these officers a certain amount of money called 'basic car allowance' to enable them to repay the loan thus advanced, and in addition paid mileage allowance when the officers used their cars in executing official duties. A junior civil servant might be given a loan to purchase a bicycle, a scooter or a motor cycle. Not only was he denied basic allowance, but in most cases the amount paid to senior civil servants as basic allowances was much higher than the monthly salary of a clerk or a technician in government service.

The Committee made a number of recommendations. Among them were municipalisation of public transport in the big industrial and commercial centres; building of low cost housing for workers; the introduction of a 40-hour week; the abolition of certain privileges like car basic allowance, children's separate domicile allowance, outfit allowance, rent subsidy, overseas leave and local leave for senior officers.

In a document issued in 1961 and entitled *Objectives of the TUC(N) 1961–62 Programme*, the Congress classified its objectives into two main headings – short term and long term.

The short term objectives were stated as consisting of the following:

(i) strengthening and reorganising the central secretariat by providing an adequate and competent staff to conduct the affairs of the TUC(N);

(ii) instituting procedures to facilitate orderly and efficient conduct of the administrative tasks at the organisation's central office; defining the responsibilities and duties of all grades of officers and employees and laying down effective machinery for proper supervision and co-ordination of efforts;

(iii) ensuring adequate protection and maintenance of all TUC(N)'s property both at central and regional levels;

(iv) extending still further the area of co-operation and consultation with Government at Federal and Regional levels, and with Associations of Employers in advancing and protecting the vital interests of labour; and in insisting upon the full recognition of the TUC(N) to give advice and to be consulted on all matters pertaining to the social and economic developments of Nigeria, especially those bearing upon labour;

(v) stepping up the publicity and information services of the TUC(N) with a view to making its work and programme more widely known and understood among the workers and the general public, both at home and abroad;

(vi) improving TUC(N) income as well as that of its affiliated unions and instituting systems of financial control;

(vii) promoting special publicity campaigns throughout the country by way of mass meetings, labour rallies, conferences, discussions so as to counteract and defeat the malicious propaganda of enemies of the free trade union movement, and at the same time to strengthen and fortify the morale of its adherents;

(viii) improving the structure of the trade union movement of Nigeria where possible by effecting amalgamations or federations of overlapping and fragmented trade unions, and to encourage the development of national trade unions along industrial lines.

(ix) encouraging and supporting the activities of such international trade secretariats which maintain liaison with the ICFTU;

(x) conducting intensive training projects among leading trade unionists and staff members purposely designed to produce cadres for the effective execution of the short-term objectives of the TUC(N).

(xi) improving lines of communication between

(*a*) officers of the TUC(N) at all levels;
(*b*) officers and employees;
(*c*) central Office and Regional offices;
(*d*) officers (both central and regional) and affiliated unions;
(*e*) affiliated unions and their respective membership;

(xii) assisting a selected number of affiliated unions to advance their organisational and educational tasks within their defined spheres of jurisdiction, the specific tasks being:

(*a*) to embark upon membership campaigns with a view to increasing union membership;
(*b*) to improve each union's financial position through increase in the number of regular dues-paying members;
(*c*) to establish sound administrative machinery for efficient conduct of each union's business;
(*d*) to undertake educational projects aimed at improving the quality of membership and stimulating greater

participation in union business at national, local and workshop levels;

(*e*) to strengthen each union's collective bargaining position in every possible way, so that the union will be able to discharge its obligations to satisfy its membership's needs for higher real wages and improved conditions of employment;

(*f*) to improve TUC(N) services to affiliated unions by way of supplying data and literature, tendering advice, helping during negotiations and industrial disputes, intervening during squabbles between one union and another and between officers and/or members of the central working committees or at other levels, and generally to represent and give a national voice to the trade union movement on all matters affecting labour;

(*g*) to establish and develop an efficient directing and co-ordinating machinery by way of a Joint Committee of the ICFTU, the TUC(N) and the International Trade Secretariats, which will ensure the realisation of these objectives.

The long term objectives were stated as consisting of:

(i) organising all the workers of Nigeria within the trade union movement in the shortest possible time;

(ii) projecting uncompromisingly the concepts and principles of free, democratic trade unionism within the framework of the liberal democratic structure of our independent state of Nigeria;

(iii) attaining a position of complete independence in labour policy and finance for our trade union movement;

(iv) striving unceasingly to protect and promote the social and economic interests of Nigerian workers, and to resist at all times any encroachment, from whatever source, on the rights, freedom and privileges of the workers;

(v) co-operating with Governments, employers and other sections of our community in the task of developing the economic resources of Nigeria and to ensure for each of the major factors of production a just and equitable share in the proceeds of industry;

(vi) strengthening still further our ties and fraternal relationship with the free international labour movement, more especially with our immediate neighbours on the continent of Africa.

As to realising the short-term objectives, the TUC(N) said it would be unrealistic and unrewarding to dissipate energies on its ninety-eight affiliated unions spread all over the country. Such an exercise would require a large army of trained personnel, enormous financial resources and a highly competent organisational apparatus which the Congress could not afford. Consequently it decided to concentrate its activities in ten major industrial sectors as follows:

(i) *Mining and Extractive* – which included tin, coal and petroleum;
(ii) *Services* – which included manual and non-manual workers employed by the Federal and Regional Governments, Local Government bodies and quasi-governmental institutions like public boards and corporations;
(iii) *Mercantile;*
(iv) *Distributive Trades;*
(v) *Communications* – which included telephone, telegraph, and external communications;
(vi) *Banking* – which included banking and insurance services;
(vii) *Woodworking*;
(viii) *Building Trades;* and
(ix) *Textiles.*

The implementation of this programme was just beginning to take shape when the All-Nigeria People's Conference began in Lagos in August 1961. The outcome of that conference marked yet another turning-point in the chequered history of organised labour in Nigeria. We shall be returning to this matter presently.

The Nigerian Trade Union Congress followed a programme of action identical to the above but with a slightly different approach. On January 23, 1961, the Congress addressed a memorandum to the Prime Minister demanding an improved national minimum wage. The memorandum said that 'there are some workers in our Federation today whose policy is to eat only a single meal a day because their pay is incapable of sustaining anything beyond this. Others, with their families, share the same under-sized rooms with several working families because they cannot maintain one room exclusively.' The memo listed poor wages, inadequate housing, the 5 per cent hardship allowance recommended by the Mbanefo Commission, Nigerianisation and vocational training and unemployment as major problems causing workers anxiety and concern. It demanded the reclassification of jobs into General Labour, Semi-skilled and

Skilled as a means of eliminating the inequities in the wage structure, and demanded the payment of £4 per week minimum wage. The memorandum called for the establishment of a Ministry of Housing, and expressed surprise at the Government's attitude towards the payment of a 5 per cent hardship allowance, and called upon Government to 'co-operate with the proposals of its own commission'. It declared, with reference to Nigerianisation, that 'Nigeria can no longer tolerate interference in her own affairs, and the only insurance to check this is the appointment of indigenous officers to positions of responsibility'. Finally the memorandum called for more job opportunities for thousands of idle hands in the country, the abolition of the daily pay system of wage payment, and the provision of transport, leave and free medical facilities for workers not enjoying these privileges.

At its first Annual Congress held in Jos in September 1961, the NTUC adopted a programme of reorganisation of unions on an industrial basis, prepared by its Secretary for National Organisations, Nehru Amaefule Ikoro. Under the programme, the 371 registered unions in the country were to be regrouped into twenty-five industrial and general unions as follows:

(i) *Union of Railwaymen* –covering all existing unions in the Railway;
(ii) *Ports and River Workers' Union* – covering all trades in Nigerian Ports and Inland Waterways;
(iii) *Mines Workers' Union of Nigeria* – covering all the coal, tin, surface and underground mining workers in the country;
(iv) *Catering, Hotel, Restaurant, Bar Tenders Employees' Union;*
(v) *Maritime, Seafarers', Stevedores', Warehousemen's Union* – covering dock workers, seamen, and other allied workers;
(vi) *Chemical and Research Workers' Union;*
(vii) *Oil, Air and Petroleum Workers' Union;*
(viii) *Textile, Pottery, Pioneer and Garment Industries Workers' Union;*
(ix) *Municipal, Local Authority and General Workers' Union;*
(x) *Brewery, Distillery, Cigar and Soft Drinks Employees' Union;*
(xi) *Furniture, Brick, Clay, Carpenters', Woodworkers', Woodcarvers', Joinery and Masons' Union;*
(xii) *Beauty Culturists', Hairdressers', Cosmotologists' Union of Nigeria;*
(xiii) *Power, Electrical, Radio and Electronic Employees' Union;*

(xiv) *Plantation and Forestry, Agricultural and Veterinary Workers' Union;*
(xv) *Union of Building Trades, General Construction and Sawmill Workers;*
(xvi) *Civil Service and Public Employees' Union;*
(xvii) *Teamsters, Retail, Distributive Trade and Commercial Workers;*
(xviii) *Telecommunication and Postal Employees' Union;*
(xix) *Banking, Insurance and Social Security Workers' Union;*
(xx) *Decorators, Painters, Printing and Bookshop Workers' Union;*
(xxi) *Auto, Metal and Amalgamated Engineering Employees' Union;*
(xxii) *General Transport Workers' Union* – covering truck pushers, airways, motor drivers, taxi drivers but excluding railway porters;
(xxiii) *Medical, Health and Welfare Workers' Union;*
(xxiv) *Journalists', Vendors', Newspaper Guild Union of Nigeria;*
(xxv) *Musicians and Artists, Broadcast, Cine and Cultural Employees of Nigeria.*

The following objectives were to be achieved: 'A press, a trade union secretariat built by our sweat, a labour college before two years, improved wages before six months, a movement robust, militant, democratic, with all the organisational characteristics of modern proletarian Pan-Africanist maturity.' An anti-ICFTU day was to be celebrated. All workers were to possess one type of membership card issued by the NTUC and for which it would collect 1s apiece. Unions would not be required to pay monthly dues to the Congress, but individual union members could pay dues to their unions.

The educational programme as outlined by W. O. Goodluck, Secretary for Foreign Affairs and Education, envisaged increased exchange of visits between NTUC leaders and supporters and 'socialist countries' and 'socialist trade unions' in Eastern Europe, the USSR and the Peoples' Republic of China. It recalled the great number of Nigerians who had been behind the Iron Curtain at the instance of the NTUC or through its channels.

In his report on activities, the General Secretary, S. U. Bassey, said that the NTUC membership had risen from fifty-five unions representing 184,612 workers to seventy-five representing 222,466. How reliable this claim was may be measured from the fact that a little over that figure was the total strength of organised labour in the country, and the Congress was known in any case to be less representative than its rival, the TUC(N). Bassey also reported on the appalling situation of the workers in the mines at Jos and the efforts of the NTUC to help ameliorate their grievances. 'It is now history', the report went on, 'that this is the second time we have as comrades been collectively compelled, in the vital interest of the movement, to apply discipline against Mr. Nzeribe. The first instance was in the All-Nigeria Trade Union Federation. At that time he was asked to resign because the Federation found his tactics too difficult to understand. . . . We have found him guilty of organisational opportunism, excessive duplicity, inactivity and vulgar ambitions.' It was also reported that the NTUC had presented an Opel car and a purse of £100 each to M. A. O. Imoudu and S. O. Oduleye respectively, two of the four railway union leaders jailed after the 'Emerson Must Go' demonstration. In addition it was decided to build a house for Imoudu 'as a permanent reward for his sacrifices for the working class of Nigeria'.

The report said that delegations of trade union leaders had been received from the Ghana Trades Union Congress, the Italian Confederation of Labour, and the South African Congress of Trade Unions, and mutual friendship agreements were signed between the representatives of these organisations and the NUTC. These agreements condemned colonialism without reservation and commended 'the laudable efforts of the brave and patriotic African working class who, in their heroic struggle, have beaten hollow the imperialists and their lackeys to establish the positive All-African Trade Union Federation at Casablanca'. The NTUC delegation had also visited Ghana, Guinea, Mali, Czechoslovakia, East Germany, the USSR, the Peoples' Republic of China and Italy 'to promote mutual understanding between our Congress and some friendly trade union organisations abroad, and to popularise the effectiveness of the NTUC. The delegation signed a pact of labour solidarity and friendship with the communist Confederation of Free German Democratic Trade Unions (FDGB) on world peace, international understanding, peaceful co-existence, and the establishment of a free demilitarised city of West Berlin. As a result of this agreement the FDGB offered the NTUC cars, typewriters, duplicating machines, bicycles, motor cycles, cinema projectors, a printing press and scholarships tenable in East German universities and technical colleges.

Finally, the report referred to the Labour Reconciliation Committee set up by the All-Nigeria People's Conference in August 1961, and declared: 'Whatever may be the recommendations of the committee, one thing must be made quite clear to all the delegates attending this conference and to all the affiliated unions of Congress: that we welcome the move to unite labour in this country and we in the past worked earnestly towards the realisation of unity. But the greatest obstacle has always been and will continue to be the existing marriage between the TUC(N) and the ICFTU. We make bold to say that as long as the TUC(N) remains an affiliate of the ICFTU the possibility of unity between the NTUC and TUC(N) is far remote if not impossible.'

If the workers and people of Nigeria were in any doubt as to what the NTUC was and has continued to be, that doubt was dispelled by the role it played in the December, 1961, strike of Lagos municipal bus drivers. Most NTUC top officers were involved in organising and executing the strike. At the time of the strike there were five unions catering for LMTS workers, and these unions formed the Federation of Lagos Municipal Bus Workers, of which V. M. I. Jack, later chairman of the Lagos District Council of the United Labour Congress, was the General Secretary. A dispute occurred among the leaders of the drivers' union, and this led some of them to invite Samuel U. Bassey to come and organise the bus drivers. Bassey's acceptance of the invitation had a far-reaching consequence for union organisation and industrial relations in the LMTS. Apart from being the General Secretary of the NTUC, he was also a well-known red cell. For his part, Jack was a fire-eater, a fanatical TUC(N) supporter and a believer in the cause of free trade unionism. With two men of such conflicting ideological orientation in the LMTS, it meant that union organisation as well as labour management relations in that establishment had been exposed to ideological warfare between the TUC(N) and the NTUC. Against this background subsequent events must be considered.

Late in 1961, the Federation of Municipal Bus Workers declared a dispute with the LMTS management over improved conditions of employment. A conciliator was appointed. He was still on his assignment when Bassey called out the drivers on strike, apparently in an effort to demonstrate that he was more 'dynamic'. The strike was unique on many considerations. First, it was organised and executed without a dispute, first being declared as is usual if the strikers want the Ministry of Labour to intervene, which in this case they wanted. Consequently the LMTS authorities argued, and continued to maintain, that there was no dispute between them and their employees, and therefore the strike was un-called for. Ministry of Labour officials supported their stand. Secondly, the reason for the strike was not quite clear, and did not enhance the prestige of the organisers. The drivers gave the impression that they were on strike over issues they had not even raised as a grievance. It took some lecturing at the Ministry of Labour for this elementary procedure to be appreciated. Thirdly, the strike was acutely timed (December 24) and might have succeeded had it not been for the method employed. Members of the public badly needed a bus transport service for the heavy shopping of the Christmas season. The great hardships imposed by the strike alienated whatever sympathy the public had for the drivers. Fourthly, the strike was not just a strike but a combination of strike and sabotage. All buses were ordered to be removed from the roads and the workshops to Oshodi Terminal, where packets of six-inch nails had been procured to puncture the tyres as soon as the green light was given by the man who master-minded the operations. The leakage of the plan a few minutes earlier, coupled with the timely action taken by the LMTS chairman, Frederick S. McEwen, saved the situation. Fifthly, the strike was organised just after Bassey's return from Moscow, where he had attended the fifth world congress of the WFTU. Newspaper reports quoted Congress as having discussed, among other things, a programme of trade union action which would bring the world's trade union movement under the canopy of international communism through various devices. Among the devices might be the often-quoted charge of V. I. Lenin in his *Infantile Disease of Communism* where he advocated 'the use of all strategems and artifices, the adoption of illegal methods, occasional silence, occasional concealment of the truth, for the sole purpose of penetrating the trade unions, staying there and still carrying out the communist assignment.'[1]

Appeals were made to the drivers to call off the strike and follow the normal procedure if they had any grievance. Their failure or, to be more accurate, the failure of some of them to heed these appeals cost 107 men their jobs. Some of them had had more than ten years' meritorious service and lost all their entitlements. Later the rumour spread that the men held out because the organisers of the strike said that it would last for at least three months and they had the money from their overseas friends to pay their salaries for that period. The hopes eventually became forlorn, and the men lost on both the swings and the roundabouts.

The effects of the strike were as dramatic as the strike itself. Bus drivers kicked out Bassey – paving the way for the amalgamation of the five unions in the LMTS a few months later. There was a political change as well – in the attitude of the top leadership of the NCNC to NTUC. Hitherto it had been one of almost unqualified support for the Congress, either because of its daily denounciation of imperialism and of ICFTU, and its loud claims that it was the only Nigerian trade union organisation which believed in Pan-Africanism.

This was the general trade union situation until that historic meeting at King's College, Lagos, in August – the consequences of which we shall now consider.

REFERENCE

1. *Brief History of the International Labour Movement* (ICFTU Publication), page 23.

19

BEFORE AND AFTER IBADAN

Before and shortly after the attainment of independence, it was popularly felt that Nigeria had not been playing the role expected of her in African affairs. Because of her size, her strategic geographical location, her manpower and other resources, and more important, her belief in, and practice of liberal democracy, she was in a better position than any other country to offer leadership to Africa. It was partly in order to satisfy this popular desire and partly in order that the Nigerian Government could be better informed about Africa that Sir Abubakar Tafawa Balewa, then Prime Minister, appointed Dr. K. O. Mbadiwe, the vanquished leader of the abortive 'Zik Must Go' episode[1] of 1958, as his Personal Adviser on African Affairs.

In 1961 Dr. Mbadiwe, aided by a small preparatory committee of public-spirited Nigerians, organised the All-Nigeria People's Conference held in the King's College Hall, Lagos, from August 19 to 21. The theme of the conference was 'The Role of Nigeria in African Affairs'. The name of the conference was apt, for its composition was truly All-Nigerian Representatives of organised bodies from all parts of the country attended. They spoke and behaved as Nigerians and not as northerners or westerners, easterners or mid-westerners or Lagosians, nor did they talk in terms of tribe. Hardly since the tripartite division of the country had the people of Nigeria had such a common forum, nor had the extremists, the moderates, and the rightists had such an opportunity to talk and speak their minds without the fear of reprisals. Most of the 500 delegates, who comprised some of the best brains from the universities, the professions, the political parties, journalism, the trade unions, and student, youth and women's organisations, would admit that they had never before seen a better demonstration of the spirit of one Nigeria.

The All-Nigeria People's Conference appointed a number of Committees to facilitate its work. Among them was the Labour and World Economics Committee, whose chairman was Dr. S. A. Aluko. Other members of the Committee were Dr. P. N. C. Okigbo, Chief

O. A. Fagbenro-Beyioku, Lewis U. Agonsi, Ojo Odonjo, E. C. Okei-Achamba, R. U. Onyia, M. A. O. Imoudu, C. P. Ngene, O. Badamosi, Wogu Ananaba, N. F. Pepple, W. O. Goodluck, Zeal Onyia and Alhaji Abdullahi. In its report, which was unanimously adopted by the Conference, the Committee pointed out that labour was one field in which Nigeria could play a leading role. But it emphasised that the Nigerian labour movement could not play that role as long as it was divided. To lead others the movement must first put its own house in order, and that meant that unity must be achieved. The Committee recommended the appointment of an *ad hoc* committee to reconcile the TUC(N) and NTUC. After the adoption of the committee's report Alhaji H. P. Adebola, TUC(N) President, and M. A. O. Imoudu, NTUC President, made statements each welcoming the recommendation and pledging the co-operation of his organisation. The Conference then appointed a seven-man Labour Reconciliation Committee made up of the following: Alhaji Ibrahim Jalo Waziri, Speaker of the House of Representatives, chairman; the Rev. Dr. J. O. Lucas, Chief Kola Balogun, C. C. Mojekwu, Dr. Tunji Otegbeye, E. T. Orodi, and Dr. S. A. Aluko.

The Labour Reconciliation Committee held its first meeting on September 27, 1961, and continued in the second week of October. Both the TUC(N) and the NTUC submitted memoranda outlining their cases. Because of their importance these documents are reproduced as appendices. Members of the Reconciliation Committee began to assess the quality of NTUC leadership from a strange incident, which happened just before negotiations began. The NTUC had submitted their case a few days before the October meeting, in a memorandum signed by Imoudu and S. U. Bassey. A few minutes before the meeting, another memorandum purporting to be the official case of the NTUC was distributed. This one was signed by Imoudu and Ibrahim Nock, newly-elected General Secretary of the NTUC, and the interesting thing about it was that it contained nothing new except Nock's signature. It took the characteristic forthrightness of C. C. Mojekwu to remind NTUC leaders that the meeting was not the appropriate platform for them to advertise their quarrels or for Imoudu to prove his inability to lead. The committee completed its assignment on October 12, when the following agreement was signed by members of the Committee and the representatives of the TUC(N) and the NTUC:

> The Settlement Committee appointed by the All-Nigeria People's Conference to settle the rift in the Nigerian labour movement met representatives of the Trades Union Congress of Nigeria – TUC(N)

– and the Nigerian Trade Union Congress – NTUC – in the Senate Building, Lagos, on Wednesday, September 27, 1961, and on Tuesday and Wednesday, October 9 and 10, 1961, for negotiation and reconciliation.

After detailed and frank exchange of views and negotiations, the representatives of the TUC(N) and the NTUC agreed as follows:

(i) that there should be only one central trade union organisation for all Nigerian trade unions, and that the central labour organisation should be known as and called 'The United Labour Congress';

(ii) that a Caretaker Committee, consisting of twenty members, ten members each from the TUC(N) and the NTUC, be set up to work for the achievement of a unified central labour organisation. The membership of the Committee was agreed to be as follows:

TUC(N)	NTUC
1. Alhaji H. P. Adebola	1. Mr. M. A. O. Imoudu
2. Mr. N. A. Cole	2. Mr. S. U. Bassey
3. Chief Fagbenro-Beyioku	3. Mr. S. O. Khayam
4. Mr. L. L. Borha	4. Mr. P. B. Olanrewaju
5. Mr. Ayodele Adeleke	5. The Rev. V. I. Oshinaga
6. Malam Yakubu Kaile	6. Mr. P. I. Okoye
7. Mr. E. U. Ijeh	7. Malam Ibrahim Nock
8. Mr. O. Zudonu	8. Mr. W. O. Goodluck
9. Mr. Wogu Ananaba	9. Mr. S. O. Oduleye
10. Mr. N. F. Pepple	10. Mr. A. Ikoro

It was further agreed that the Caretaker Committee will elect the *pro tem* officers. The Conciliation Committee agreed to continue to make itself available to the Caretaker Committee for regular consultation;

(iii) that while recognising the right of the individual trade unionist to believe in any brand of political ideology, the TUC(N) and the NTUC, nevertheless, take cognisance of the events which led to disunity within the Nigerian trade union movement in the past and agree, therefore, that in the interest of permanent unity communism, capitalism, fascism and national political partisanship shall not be projected in the Nigerian labour movement;

(iv) that both the TUC(N) and the NTUC are quite prepared to accept the verdict of the Nigerian workers on the issue of international affiliation. Towards this end both the TUC(N) and the NTUC agree that there should be a joint unity conference of the two organisations at a place easily accessible to the Nigerian trade union delegates to take a decision on the question of international affiliation. The conference should be presided over, for the purpose, by an independent chairman, acceptable to both the TUC(N) and the NTUC, and voting at such conference should be by secret ballot;

(v) that as a matter of procedure, no trade unionist should go abroad to speak or act on behalf of the Nigerian central labour organisation unless he is nominated by the Executive Committee of the central labour organisation, or by such other competent body charged with such nomination by the central labour organisation;

(vi) (*a*) that the TUC(N) and the NTUC agree to pool their assets and liabilities together;

(*b*) that the Federal Government should co-operate more fully with the trade unions for the effective and efficient operation of the check-off system. To this end the TUC(N) and the NTUC and the Reconciliation Committee appeal to the Ministry of Labour to withdraw such instructions and regulations restricting the effective and immediate operation of the check-off system;

(*c*) that the employers, Governments and the central labour organisation should accept the principle and the operation of the 'closed shop system';

(*d*) that, as much as is compatible with the independence of trade union organisation in Nigeria, the Federal Government should assist the Nigerian central labour organisation;

(*e*) that the existing paid officials of both the NTUC and the TUC(N) should be retained by the new organisation and that the principle of parity should be kept in mind as new officials are appointed.

(vii) the Reconciliation Committee, the TUC(N) and the NTUC appeal to all trade union leaders and organisations to give every support to the new spirit of unity being fostered by their leaders in the interest of peace and tranquility, and of the welfare of the workers of Nigeria.

The inaugural conference of the ULC was fixed for February 1 to 3,

1962, and physical arrangements were left with the Caretaker Committee, which held a meeting on December 16, 1961, to consider and determine the basis of representation. After five hours' discussion, no agreement was reached. A second meeting was held on January 15, 1962, when it was agreed:

(i) that the founding congress would be held from March 1 to 3 and not February 1 to 3 as originally planned;
(ii) that every registered trade union affiliated to the TUC(N) and the NTUC would be represented at the conference on the following basis: unions with membership below 1,000 three delegates; unions with membership above 1,000 five delegates;
(iii) that membership would be determined on the basis of the latest figures with the Registrar of Trade Unions;
(iv) that any other registered trade unions not affiliated to either the TUC(N) or NTUC could, if they chose, send an observer to the conference, but such observers would not speak or vote.

The Committee met again on February 17 to finalise arrangements for the founding congress. Contrary to popular expectations, however, members were told by Robert Onyia, leader of the NTUC delegation, that the NTUC were no longer prepared to continue the talks unless four conditions outlined in their memorandum to the Prime Minister and copied to the chairman of the Reconciliation Committee were satisfied. These conditions were:

(i) that the Federal Government should enact a law prohibiting international affiliation;
(ii) that non-affiliates of the TUC(N) and the NTUC be permitted to attend and to participate in the deliberations of the founding congress of the United Labour Congress;
(iii) that Irving Brown of the American Federation of Labour and Congress of Industrial Organisations, who the NTUC claimed to have been working with the TUC(N) but who in fact had not visited the country in February 1962, be ordered to quit Nigeria immediately;
(iv) that George Francis McCray, Vice-Principal and Director of Extra-Mural Studies of the ICFTU African Labour College in Kampala be declared a prohibited immigrant in Nigeria.

The chairman appealed to the NTUC to reconsider their decision particularly because of the October 1961 agreement, and Imoudu's pledge that his organisation would co-operate to the fullest for the realisation of labour unity in the country. When the appeal appeared to have had no response, the chairman declared in a stern voice:

'If you press this point and make it impossible for the conference to hold on March 1–3 as scheduled, we shall be obliged to record that responsibility for the failure to achieve unity in the labour movement rests on your shoulders.' Finally the chairman announced with great disappointment: 'There will be no conference on March 1–3; rather the Caretaker Committee will hold another meeting sometime in the middoe of March.'[2]

Three important developments would appear to explain the NTUC's change of attitude. Both the TUC(N) and the NTUC went into the field immediately after concluding the October agreement. At the commencement of the NTUC country-wide tour, Imoudu boasted that he would 'finish' the TUC(N) in two weeks. By the time the tour was over it was clear that instead of the TUC(N) it was the NTUC that had been 'finished'. Many unions had deserted the organisation and declared for the TUC(N). As a result the comparative strength of the two organisations was TUC(N) 179 affiliates and NTUC 69. It was anybody's guess what this might mean in terms of the number of workers these unions represented, since statistics were unreliable on account of widespread book membership.

Secondly, it was reported that the NTUC were severely reprimanded by the fifth World Congress of the World Federation of Trade Unions held in Moscow in December 1961 for being a party to an agreement setting up a labour organisation whose constitution specifically forbade the projection of communism. The communists who gathered in Moscow felt that this was the greatest possible betrayal of international communism.

Thirdly, an attempt by a TUC(N) top official to cause disaffection and break the solidarity of the organisation had failed. Nneamaka Chukwura, an Assistant Secretary of the NTUC, made serious allegations of maladministration, fraud, squandermania, nepotism, favouritism, misappropriation of TUC(N) funds and unauthorised reversion of Executive Council decisions and non-rendition of accounts by the responsible officer of the TUC(N). Chukwura's letter was widely distributed to TUC(N) affiliates and the Press, and the allegations formed the subject of a leading story in *The West African Pilot* of February 14, 1962, under the streamer headline 'TUC(N) in £8,000 Row'. A meeting of the TUC(N) Central Executive was summoned to consider the allegations. The meeting, attended by members from various parts of the country, 'took up each of the allegations and called upon Mr. Chukwura to prove or substantiate all or any of them. Mr. Chukwura was unable to do so. The meeting went through the account books and the statements of account presented by the responsible officers of the Congress, but Mr. Chukwura did not challenge any entry or expenditure item.'[3] In the circumstance the Executive unanimously passed a vote of confidence in the Trustees of the Congress having been satisfied that 'there was no substance whatsoever in the allegations'.

The NTUC's own reasons for backing out of the unity talks are worthy of examination. In their memorandum to the Labour Reconciliation Committee the NTUC said they were opposed to affiliation to either the WFTU, the ICFTU or the IFCTU. Nevertheless, they would respect the verdict of Nigerian workers on the issue of international affiliation. According to the October 1961 agreement, the verdict of Nigerian workers was to be known at Ibadan. Since they often claimed to command the support of the majority of registered trade unions in the country, these should have gone to Ibadan and used their majority to block international affiliation by voting against it. By not co-operating to see the issue settled in this manner, which was in keeping with their original suggestion, the NTUC were, by implication, telling the Federal Government and the world at large, that they did not command the majority support they claimed. But the NTUC request is most reprehensible when considered from the point of view of its likely effect on the trade union movement as a whole, and on the Government of Nigeria. With the possible exception of those countries where trade unions are an arm of the government, it has been the unanimous desire of organised labour throughout the world that Governments should, as far as possible, not interfere with trade union rights. In fact the history of the trade union movement and of the international movement has been one of consistent struggle in defence of trade union rights. For a trade union organisation, therefore, to advocate the curtailment of these rights, apparently in pursuance of the policy to 'destroy the ICFTU and its supporters in Africa', suggests that straight thinking among some union leaders in Nigeria had suffered a serious derailment. Moreover, before March 1962, Nigeria had ratified ILO convention 87, which guarantees freedom of association to the workers of Nigeria. The NTUC request meant that, having accepted the principle of freedom of association the Nigerian Government should turn round like a rascal and pass laws negating these principles.

The NTUC demand could also be considered in relation to its timing. Before the demand was made, the conference had been fixed for March 1–3. Those making it knew that Parliament was in recess, and could not, therefore, pass a law prohibiting international affiliation before March 1. Clearly, therefore, the main purpose of making the demand was to draw a red herring across the trail and prevent the conference from taking place as planned.

Another meeting of the Caretaker Committee was held on March 17. This meeting was attended by members of the Reconciliation Committee and the Steering Committee of the All-Nigeria People's Conference led by Dr. K. O. Mbadiwe. Discussions centred around the resolution of the deadlock on unity. Dr. Mbadiwe addressed the meeting and reminded the leaders of the TUC(N) and the NTUC of the pledge which their presidents gave to the nation in August 1961. Excepting those who probably had reached the point of no return, his speech touched the soul of most of those present and aroused a sense of mission hitherto unknown in some of the labour leaders. It appeared this meeting had begun well; but it was only a lull. After a few minutes, it returned to the situation of February 17 with the NTUC insisting that unless their four demands were met they would not co-operate. It took a recess and some lobbying to get their leaders to retract, and to persuade the leaders of the TUC(N) to consider two compromise suggestions in the interest of unity. These suggestions were that all registered trade unions in the country willing to do so should be permitted to participate in the deliberations of the Ibadan conference, and that representation at the conference should be on the basis of the agreement reached at the meeting of the Caretaker Committee on January 15. The first suggestion arose from the feeling that an important controversial issue like international affiliation should not be left entirely to the affiliates of the TUC(N) and the NTUC, who had a vested interest in the matter. Uncommitted unions should be brought into the picture as a countervailing force, and any decision then taken on the subject would represent a majority opinion of workers' representatives and not just the opinion of vested interests. Both suggestions were accepted by the TUC(N) and the NTUC, and the inaugural conference of the ULC was finally fixed for May 3–5, 1962.

It was held as planned, in the Trenchard Hall of what was then known as the University College, Ibadan. A series of dialogues took place before the opening session on May 3. On the eve of the conference Ene Henshaw, TUC(N) Assistant General Secretary, alleged in a telegram to the Inspector-General of Police that John Tettegah had sent fifty armed hooligans from Ghana to sabotage the conference; he said that the names and address of the hooligans could be given on request. Henshaw's allegation was widely publicised by the press and radio Nigeria, and excited the just indignation of many Nigerians, who had become thoroughly disgusted by Ghana's persistent interference in the affairs of the Nigerian trade union movement. Outside Trenchard Hall itself many things were happening. NTUC activists were busy with their opposite numbers from the

Nigerian Youth Congress, the Students' Union of University College, Ibadan, and a host of other front organisations which would appear to have sprung up purposely for that conference, distributing anti-ICFTU literature and campaigning among delegates to vote against international affiliation.

TUC(N) activists countered by distributing the February 1962 issue of *The Voice of Labour* containing the front-page editorial headed 'The Choice Before You'. That issue also contained a photostat copy of a letter from Prague in which the WFTU declared, among other things, that 'our objective in Africa is to destroy the ICFTU in Africa and destroy its supporters in Africa'. Delegates, particularly those from uncommitted unions, read the paper with avidity. Those who had no copies rushed for some. In the stampede more than 2,000 copies disappeared. It was generally thought that most of them had found their way into the hands of delegates who needed them, and of the thousands of observers waiting to be admitted into the hall, but in fact the mad rush and the mysterious disappearance of the copies had been organised by NTUC activists in an all-out effort to make it impossible for workers' representatives to hear the other side of the story and know the facts about democracy, socialism, totalitarianism and communism with a view to making up their minds as to which system the workers of Nigeria should embrace. A little way outside Trenchard Hall three determined young men were busy tearing into shreds copies of *The Voice of Labour* and swearing against some of their colleagues for not alerting them earlier to the distribution of such a 'dangerous document'.

The conference began at about 10 a.m. and was presided over by Alhaji Ibrahim Jalo Waziri, Speaker of the House of Representatives. With him were Dr. K. O. Mbadiwe, Chairman of the Steering Committee of the All-Nigeria Peoples Conference; Alhaji A. A. Koguna, Parliamentary Secretary to the Federal Ministry of Establishments and Chief of Credentials; A. K. Blankson, Chairman of the Federal Loans Board and Chief Electoral Officer of the conference; Dr. J. O. Lucas, an eminent clergyman and chairman of the Preparatory Committee of the conference; and Okoro Okarevu, African and Foreign Affairs Officer of the NCNC and Secretary of the Steering Committee of the All-Nigeria Peoples Conference. Okarevu succeeded Dr. S. A. Aluko as Secretary of the Labour Reconciliation Committee when Dr. Aluko left on a study visit to the United States in March 1962. Messages of goodwill were received from various individuals and organisations, including one from John Tettegah, which met with a very hostile reception. The opening session ended with an inspiring address from Dr. K. O. Mbadiwe. The business session opened in the afternoon with the checking of credentials. At the end of the exercise, which lasted the whole afternoon, the Chief of Credentials announced that 1,205 delegates were attending the conference and each had been issued with an admission ticket.

On the second day, the conference considered clause by clause the draft constitution of the United Labour Congress. The constitution was unanimously adopted after minor amendments. A motion for the formal inauguration of the ULC and for the dissolution of the TUC(N) and NTUC was moved by Amaefule Ikoro of the NTUC and seconded by Lawrence Borha of the TUC(N) and was unanimously carried. The time was 12 noon, and the conference adjourned for lunch.

The afternoon debate opened on the controversial issue of international affiliation. Originally intended to last for half an hour, the debate took up the whole afternoon session. There were four speakers for and four against, and it was agreed from the outset that voting on the issue should be by secret ballot. One of the speakers, Chief A. O. Fagbenro-Beyioku, not only supported international affiliation, but moved a formal motion that the ULC be affiliated to the International Confederation of Free Trade Unions and the African Trade Union Confederation. When the motion was seconded the chairman ruled that it would be dovetailed into the general issue of international affiliation. Those in favour of the motion would show by voting for international affiliation; equally, those against it would show by their vote. Voting could not take place that evening because it was already late and the hall was booked for another event. It took place the following morning. Two ballot boxes marked YES and NO were displayed. Before taking them to the polling booth the Chief Electoral Officer explained the electoral procedure. Every accredited delegate was to come to the rostrum, collect a ballot paper and proceed to the polling booth. Those in favour of international affiliation and by implication the motion of Chief Beyioku were to cast their votes in the box marked YES; those against were to cast their votes in the box marked NO. The voting took the whole morning session, and the result announced just before lunch break showed 659 in favour and 407 against.

The conference reassembled at 2.30 p.m. to elect officers. Many delegates took their seats before that time. When the hour struck, however, Imoudu and his supporters were nowhere to be seen. The chairman waited till 3.40 p.m., when the Chief Electoral Officer called for nominations for the office of President. Alhaji H. P. Adebola was nominated and this was duly seconded. There being no other nomination Adebola was declared elected unopposed. Two important events took place at this stage. Dr. K. O. Mbadiwe came in and made a passionate plea. He said that, although he realised Adebola's election was unanimous, yet he would like a vote to be taken and a record of its result kept. The vote was about to be taken when a deafening noise was heard from outside the hall. The police officers on duty reported that it was Imoudu and his supporters seeking admission. The chairman ordered that they be admitted. Just then a group of men led by Imoudu singing Ojike's freedom song trooped in. They presented a letter to the chairman. Before leading them in a walk-out, Imoudu declared that he and his supporters were not going to join the new organisation as long as it was affiliated to an internal labour organisation. When they had withdrawn, those present were counted and the number was 659. Adebola was elected by the same number of votes and so were other officers.

That evening Imoudu and his supporters gathered at a corner in Ibadan and founded what was then known as the Independent United Labour Congress. Its principal officers were M. A. O. Imoudu, President; Amaefule Ikoro, Secretary; and Nnewedim Anunobi, Nigerian Representative of the International Federation of Christian Trade Unions, Treasurer. The IULC said it would not be affiliated to any international organisation except the All-African Trade Union Federation. Its first notable activity shortly after its inaugural meeting was to challenge the credentials of the Nigerian Workers' Delegation to the ILO conference in 1962. The striking thing about the IULC objection was that it did not originate from Nigeria. According to the ILO Credentials Committee Report 1962, the Committee 'had before it an objection to the nomination of the Workers' Delegation of Nigeria obtained in a telegram sent from Accra on June 6, 1962'. The telegram was followed by a 'letter purporting to come from Lagos dated June 7, 1962, from the Independent United Labour Congress of Nigeria'. The objection was rejected.

The decision on international affiliation seemed to have annoyed not only Imoudu and his supporters but also the Nigerian press and certain Nigerian journalists. On May 7 all sections of the national press published an IULC statement blaming the conference chairman and Dr. K. O. Mbadiwe for the failure of the Ibadan conference. The statement accused them of responsibility for inserting international affiliation in the agenda contrary to the provisions of the ULC constitution. Other points made in the 800-word statement were that representatives of deregistered unions were admitted and allowed to participate in the deliberations of the conference; that some unions with less than 300 members had as many as five delegates instead of three; that there was large-scale impersonation; and voting on international affiliation was a violation of Article 1 (15) of the constitution which permits the 'maintenance of fraternal relationships with international trade union organisations as shall be determined by congress in accordance with its constitution'. Almost all the sections of the national press joined the IULC in making the conference chairman and Dr. Mbawide scapegoats and in expressing their opposition to international affiliation. Commenting on the outcome of the Ibadan conference, the *West African Pilot* said that 'the Ibadan peace talks have ended in a disastrous failure. The hopes of establishing an independent united labour movement are now dashed. . . . The cause of the strife all these years has been the question of foreign link. Adebola supports foreign affiliation. Imoudu doesn't. . . . We agree with Imoudu that tying our trade union movement to the chariot of alien bodies is not only inconsistent with our foreign policy but also in our domestic affairs. The saying that he who pays the piper dictates the tune is true even in trade union movements. It should have occured to those who voted for foreign affiliation that those alien bodies are not charitable or philanthropic organisations. They must have a purpose for what they are doing.'[4]

Ebenezer Williams in a front page comment in the *Morning Post* observed that 'Alhaji H. P. Adebola rode some of his human horses last week. So did Mr. Michael Imoudu. And I am tempted to suggest that the "riding in majesty" will continue for some time because the Nigerian worker prefers to be ridden to riding, to be exploited mentally and physically by the secretaries he pays. Alhaji Adebola has won no victory; let him be told that. Imoudu is right on this occasion, if he sincerely meant that the Nigerian Trades Union Congress should not be affiliated to any foreign body; but in the face of the annoying fact that he has been hobnobbing with communists and publicly come to the defence of the Ghana TUC and the AATUF, let him be told that his talk about the Independent United Labour Congress is a piece of rubbish fit only for the silly crowd that shout in unison with him. . . . Mr. Imoudu cannot expect, as the minority faction, to secure Government recognition, even though the principle on which he has broken away is understandable. And Adebola cannot expect that Government will deal with him even though he represents the majority view, because the question of affiliation over which he has secured the support of the majority runs counter to Government policy, and will put Government into unnecessary embarrassment in the manner in which it has been handled, just as the question of affiliation cannot be said to be in accordance with the provisions of the ULC itself. It would be unfair and unreasonable for Government to take sides by giving recognition to the Adebola faction when all that faction has succeeded in doing is in gathering a motley crowd, whose votes are as suspicious as those of the Imoudu crowd to submerge the principles dear to Imoudu to those dear to Adebola.' Ebenzezer Williams suggested that Government should 'puncture Adebola's so-called victory' by placing a ban on ICFTU; test Imoudu's sincerity by stopping his globe-trotting, and seal all the borders to itinerant trade unionists and censor the mails of all trade unionists.[5]

He had earlier tried to convince the public that the Ibadan conference would be another fruitless exercise. In a satire captioned 'In Search of Unity' published in the *Morning Post* of May 5, Ebenezer Williams wrote: 'Sansa, thug on Campos Square, Lagos, was due to vote in today's election of the United Labour Congress of Nigeria. He had passed through the gate as a representative of the Ilorin Progressive Union. When I asked him how many people were in his union, his reply was prompt: "1,000". When I further queried as to how his union of 1,000 members came to have such a paltry representation he was for the occasion temporarily dumb. I giggled. Then I presented the elector to Robert Oniya as representative of Ilorin Progressive Union, truly and fully armed with accreditation card to elect the President General of the United Labour Congress of Nigeria. And poor Robert he laughed as I had never seen him laugh before. I now openly joined in the laugh, and Sansa walked away perturbed not about the future of trade unionism in Nigeria but as to whether or not he had done his duty of impersonation well.'

It was this apparent attempt to run away from the facts, not to face realities, and to justify continued irresponsibility in the trade union movement by even the Fourth Estate of the Realm that compelled the writer to declare in an article headed 'Aftermath of Ibadan Conference' that

> Two simple facts have been established from the incidents which marked the close of the unity conference held at Ibadan recently. The first is that it was not international affiliation as such that divided the former Trades Union Congress of Nigeria and the splinter Nigerian Trade Union Congress. The second is that there are still people in Nigeria, in and outside the labour movement, who do not want our trade union organisations to be run on democratic principles. The events of May 5 have vindicated the stand of the former TUC(N) that the cause of division in our labour movement has not been the relationship existing between the TUC(N) and the ICFTU. Rather it has been the communist dogmatism of certain elements in the labour movement – a dogmatism which

makes it impossible for them to recognise and respect the first essence of democracy that the minority may have its say, but the majority must have its way. Of course, every intelligent person knows that all communist-oriented trade unionists do not scruple to take advantage of democratic practices to supplant democracy and impose their pet dictatorship. . . .

It has been argued that the question of international affiliation ought not to have been allowed to be debated at the conference because it contravenes Article 1 (15) of the constitution of the United Labour Congress. Such an argument ignores the fact that the matter was specifically referred to the conference for determination at the instance of the two major parties to it – the TUC(N) and the NTUC. Granting for the sake of argument that the constitution did not provide for international affiliation but for maintenance of 'fraternal relationship, the question then arises as to how the fraternal relationship may be maintained. Clearly fraternal relationship does not consist in a mere exchange of messages of goodwill; association with other trade union organisations by means of affiliation is a positive expression of fraternal relationship. Yet Article 1 (15), by including the words 'as shall be determined by the Congress', clearly authorises the Congress to determine the nature of the fraternal relationship to be established.

Almost all the sections of the Press have been unanimous in blaming the conference chairman and Dr. K. O. Mbadiwe for ever allowing the question of international affiliation to be debated. Could the chairman and Dr. Mbadiwe have been worthy of their charge if they had barred discussion of the major issue referred to the conference for a decision? Yet Imoudu and his lieutenant Amaefule Ikoro were a party to the Preparatory Committee which drew up the agenda which included debate and voting on international affiliation. The truth is that Imoudu and his supporters calculated that they would carry the day at Ibadan. That was why they ever agreed to participate in the voting. When however the result of the poll worked against them they had cause to complain. Obviously if the voting had favoured them there would have been no time to vent spleen and find scapegoats in Jalo Waziri and Dr. K. O. Mbadiwe. . . .

One thing must be said. Nigerian workers went to Ibadan to found a new central labour organisation. But they also went there to do something else. They went there to:

(i) demonstrate their faith in free trade unionism as against a controlled movement;

(ii) show clearly to their country and the world at large those of them who are loyal citizens of Nigeria and those whose loyalty is first to Ghana before the country of their birth.

It is significant that Imoudu and his group who decried international affiliation on May 4 should decide on May 8 to accept international affiliation. And the international organisation which appealed to them was the still-born baby known as the All-African Trade Union Federation, whose connection with the Communist World Federation of Trade Unions is no longer a secret. Clearly, therefore, Imoudu's noise against international affiliation is a smokescreen. The old man is not against international affiliation: he is all out for it. But he wants affiliation to the Communist international which would enable his principals in Prague and Ghana to achieve the 'common political objective' indicated in the sensational letter from Prague last July'.[6]

Unity within the IULC was short-lived. In 1963, Anunobi broke away from his colleagues and founded the Nigerian Workers' Council, which is an affiliate of the International Federation of Christian Trade Unions. A few months after, and following a series of disagreements, matters came to a head in the IULC itself. The Executive held a meeting, removed Imoudu and Ikoro from office and substituted for them W. O. Goodluck and S. U. Bassey. The meeting also resolved to change the name of the organisation to the Nigerian Trade Union Congress.

In February 1964, representatives of twenty-one registered unions formed the Labour Unity Front. Its principal officers were Abayomi Alabi Ishola, President, and Gogo Chu Nzeribe, Secretary. The Front claimed to have worked out 'a programme of action to bring about the immediate unification of all factions of the Nigerian trade union movement into one single, respected, dynamic and progressive central trade union organisation in the country'. Not much came out of its efforts because of mutual distrust. Efforts by the NTUC, NWC and LUF to achieve the same objective early in 1966 failed for precisely the same reason.

REFERENCES

1. Popular name for a campaign organised by a militant group in the NCNC hierarchy demanding Dr. Azikiwe's removal, after the NCNC was returned to power in Eastern Nigeria in 1957 and Azikwe was accused of breaking election pledges.
2. *The Voice of Labour*, February 1962.
3. Ibid.
4. *The West African Pilot*, May 7, 1962.
5. *Nigerian Morning Post*, May 7, 1962.
6. *Daily Telegraph*, May 12, 1963.

20

THE 1964 GENERAL STRIKE

The Federal Government did not pay any attention to the workers' claim for a wage increase made in the Zudonu Committee Report forwarded in 1961 by the Trades Union Congress of Nigeria. A similar claim made by the NTUC was treated in the same way. The rivalry between the two organisations made it impossible for them to think of working together to achieve the common objective of winning wage increases for the workers. Moreover, the decision of the All-Nigeria People's Conference to set up a Committee to reconcile both organisations tended to create the impression that it was unwise for either of them to dissipate energy in the meantime over fruitless wage agitation. It was clear from the manner in which the Government had treated their wage claims that only a united central trade union organisation could force the Federal and Regional Governments to act. From August 1961, therefore, till after the Ibadan unity conference, agitations for a general wage increase were put in the shade. All efforts were devoted to achieving unity, which the Ibadan conference promised. When the conference ended and failed to achieve its purpose the United Labour Congress of Nigeria, which had succeeded both the TUC(N) and the NTUC, took up the mantle of wage agitation where its predecessors had left it.

It forwarded a memorandum to the Federal Government demanding a general revision of wages and salaries and the introduction of a national minimum wage. A copy of the Zudonu Committee Report, which formed the basis of the demand, was enclosed. As no reply had been received after a long time, the Congress sent a reminder, and spoke this time in the only language that appeared to impress the Federal Government in industrial matters. That language was a threat of a general strike if the Government did not concede the demands, or express willingness to negotiate within a certain date. As the deadline drew nearer panic and hysteria seemed to take control of Government circles. On August 20 the Federal Minister of Establishments and Service Matters held a meeting with a ULC delegation. Notes taken at that meeting lead to one of two conclusions. Either the Minister was incompetent to speak for the Government, or the Government itself was extremely tactless in handling labour problems. According to the notes, the Minister told the delegation that it was not an opportune moment to make wage claims. The Government concern was how to find employment for the unemployed. That was one of the main objectives of the Six-Year Development Plan for which ULC co-operation was needed. The Government was not in the mood to negotiate in a manner that would be advantageous to labour. Employers in the private sector were complaining of lack of funds to run their businesses. They claimed that they always followed Government examples in paying wage increases. If wages were now increased, the increases would ruin private employers and the Government. If there was money in the kitty, he would advise the Government to deploy it in providing more jobs and not in paying increased wages.

Sharp exchanges between the Minister and members of the delegation followed, the main points made being:

By the Delegation

(i) that Government could not hope to build a robust economy by maintaining a debtor working class;

(ii) that there was no disagreement over the ULC's contention that there had been a considerable increase in the cost of living since the Mbanefo Commission awards. That being the case the proper thing for the Minister to do was to arrange for discussions to open at the earliest possible moment with the appropriate Ministry with a view to finding out how the matter could be resolved amicably. The Minister's suggestion that the Congress should give up the demand was, to say the least, disappointing;

(iii) that the important question of introducing a national minimum wage was not a matter to be discussed at a Whitley Council meeting. Congress wanted to negotiate with Government on the matter, not as an employer but as a State authority.

By the Minister

(iv) that Government could not negotiate with the Congress but with its affiliates. If this condition was unacceptable, could Congress quote precedents when Government had negotiated with central labour organisations? (Precedents were quoted.)

(v) that negotiation could not be started in the face of a strike threat. If Congress was serious about negotiation it should first withdraw its strike threat to enable negotiation to be conducted in a friendly atmosphere.

At the end of the discussion it was agreed that the Minister would submit the Congress' claims to the various Governments of the Federation for consideration. When their comments were received another meeting would be convened. On the basis of this agreement the strike threat was withdrawn. Apart from the fact that it took an unduly long time to hear from the Government, the information conveyed to a ULC delegation, which met the Minister later, gave the impression that the Federal and Regional Governments were not playing fair with the Congress. Information had been received before this meeting that all the Governments of the Federation were unanimous in refusing to consider the workers' claim for wage revision; wage increases would upset the Six-Year Development Plan, since no provision for them had been made during the formulation of the Plan. This argument soon became a convenient excuse to deny workers their just demands, and was echoed with glee by Government spokesmen in and out of season. The statement alleged to have been made by the Industrial Relations Commissioner during the conciliation talks in the dockworkers' strike of February 1963, is a case in point.[1]

The General Manager of the Nigerian Ports Authority was reported to have announced the Authority's willingness to pay whatever wage increase could be arrived at after negotiation, provided the Federal Government had no objection. The IRC was reported to have told the meeting that the Government was opposed to granting any increase to dockworkers because such an increase would set in motion a series of agitations for wage increases which would adversely affect the Six-Year Development Plan. Stevedoring contractors who had contracts with the NPA were said to have also expressed willingness to pay increased wages in an effort to find a solution to an agonising problem; their offer was given a cold reception because of Government opposition. That evening Radio Nigeria announced that the NPA had given its stevedoring contractors forty-eight hours to supply labour to load and unload ships at Lagos and Apapa Quays or face the danger of losing their contracts. The ultimatum added fuel to the fire.

In the early hours of the following morning some contractors brought lorry-loads of people to break the strike. The strike-breakers clashed with picketers. In the mêlée which followed several strikers were wounded and many were taken into police custody. News of similar incidents were reported in Port Harcourt, Sapele and Warri. Two days after, the press published the sad news that a striking dockworker, apparently wounded in the encounter with the police, had died, and although the police later denied the newspaper story, the tendency among members of the public was to believe it. Several strikers lost their jobs. Others suffered severe injuries and many were prosecuted for conduct likely to cause a breach of the peace. In terms of results, the strike was a failure, but as a test of workers' solidarity it provided an interesting case study.

The brain behind the strike was Sidi Khayam, General Secretary of the National Council of Dockworkers and Seamen, and Deputy President of the Independent United Labour Congress, Khayam reports that the IULC was fully behind them when they were planning the strike; when the strike began they also gave them a moral support and promised to call out other IULC affiliates in sympathy. But that was all. When the zero-hour struck the IULC did not show up, and none of its affiliates came out in sympathy. It was the ULC, a rival organisation, that came to their aid. The ULC General Secretary and his Director of Organisation stood with the Council in its greatest hour of trial. The ULC imposed a levy of £3 on each of its affiliated unions to help the Council defray the legal expenses of the men being prosecuted.

The dockworkers' strike was still fresh in the public mind, when certain important developments took place in the political arena. A frightened Government, apparently haunted by the nemesis brought about by its own misdeeds, tried to find an easy answer to some of its problems. It proposed an all-party Federal Government, which would have meant the end of an official Opposition in Parliament and, by implication, the sealing of the one medium of information by which the public were kept constantly informed of the achievements and failings, the broken pledges, the corruption and graft of some of the key figures in the Government of Nigeria's First Republic. To add insult to injury, it also proposed a Preventive Detention Act. Nigerians from all walks of life, who had been watching with interest how these things had been working in other African states, felt called upon to accept a challenge. Most organised bodies in the country roundly condemned these measures. The United Labour Congress of Nigeria spoke out gallantly on behalf of organised labour. In July, 1963, it addressed the following open letter to all political leaders, all legislators, and all the Governments of the Federation of Nigeria:

> In the name of Nigerian workers and your compatriots, the United Labour Congress of Nigeria greets you!
>
> On July 25, you will assemble for the all-important Conference to decide the question of a Republican Government for Nigeria. In this final act of shedding completely the remnants of

the colonial trappings of our national sovereignty, we join you and support you whole-heartedly because we believe that it is just and proper that a truly sovereign Nigerian national should not, in the direction and management of her own affairs, be tied either in form or in fact to the farcical approval of a foreign monarchy, no matter the close ties of friendship deriving from our past association.

You are reminded that in the long-drawn struggle for national independence, the workers of Nigeria fought side-by-side with you; they were massacred at Iva Valley coal mines; they were bulleted at Burutu, they were bludgeoned and tear-gassed and buffeted because they fought for the dignity of man in Nigeria and for the freedom of the fatherland. Nigerian labour stands today, as it stood then, for the dignity of man, for the liberty of the individual and for the untramelled freedom of the fatherland.

Our fight for freedom was dedicated to the proposition that every worker, every citizen, in independent Nigeria must be a man of dignity with the right to the pursuit of, and guaranteed the means to attain, happiness in individual liberty and freedom; that he will be a man who can raise a family in congenial surroundings, in a comfortable home, assured that his children will possess equal opportunity in education, in business and in politics; that he and his family will enjoy a fair share of the national prosperity, secure and free from hardship, privation and wants; that he must know he is the happy citizen of a great new nation.

After nearly three years of dynamic experiment as masters of our own destiny, the fine hopes and reasonable expectations, born of the splendid prospects that heralded and marked the celebration of independence, are becoming increasingly confused and darkened by the statements and doings of politicians and Governments. The workers are baffled and fearful, disillusioned and frustrated. What accounts for these unhappy circumstances of the worker forms the subject of this open letter.

First: *The Preventive Detention Act*

The Preventive Detention Act is the most reckless invitation to a new crisis in the nation. It introduces our young democratic country most deplorably on the path to every type of totalitarian rule which leads inevitably to the violation of human dignity, and the destruction of man's freedom and the rule of law. The United Labour Congress has no political affiliations, and for this reason it takes the liberty of recalling the memorable event of November 16, 1960, on the occasion of the inauguration of the first Nigerian Governor-General of Nigeria, and of drawing your attention to certain passages of his most inspired and most inspiring inaugural address – *Respect for Human Dignity*. We quote: '. . . This definition of representative democracy, as it has been adapted to Nigeria, is based on the concepts of the rule of law and respect for individual freedom which have been bequeathed to us during our political association with Britain. These notions are the foundations upon which have been built the pillars of our parliamentary government. Without respect for the rule of law permeating our political fabric, Nigeria would degenerate into a dictatorship with its twin relatives of tyranny and despotism. I hold that the arbitrary exercise of power without the restraining influence of the rule of law must be condemned as a fundamental departure from constitutional government. Any justification of such untramelled exercise of political power is, to me, an outrage on human conscience and a gross violation of basic human rights.

'With this concept of the rule of law, we have inherited the idea of individual freedom, which is the sheet-anchor of democratic institutions. The sanctity of the person, the right of a person to fair and public trial, the assumption of the innocence of an accused person until he is proved guilty: these are examples of the basic human rights which feature our Constitution and which I have sworn today to uphold. But there are other ancillaries to these elements of liberal democracy. I have in mind religious freedom – freedom of thought, freedom of conscience, freedom of worship, the independence of a responsible judiciary, which is conscious of its responsibilities in a democratic society, and the existence of an untarnishable public service whose members are appointed or promoted strictly on the merit of their qualifications and good character and not on any other extraneous criteria.'

We emphasize that in our considered view the introduction of the Preventive Detention Act will be a most shameless, a most outrageous denunciation of that fitting declaration by the Governor-General which Nigeria presented to the world on November 16 as a testimony of her stature, nationhood and maturity. We state that it will be a national shame that while yesterday Nigerians – politicians, legislators, Governments and the people alike – as one man rose to condemn the Preventive Detention Act of Ghana and the whirlwind of calamities it set in motion in that country, our political leaders and legislators and Governments should today wish to join the bandwaggon of the condemned. The ULC cannot and will not join in that betrayal of the Promise of Nigeria.

Indeed, it would be a great tragedy if our independence, begun in the teeth of imperialist opposition and suppression, forged with supreme courage and sacrifice, and brought to fruition with such inspiration and high hope, should now on the very eve of gaining complete mastery of our own fate be blighted with the introduction of a Preventive Detention Act that curtails the necessary expressions of human dignity. However genuinely motivated and however well intentioned those behind the new measures may be about the security of the State, we tell them that the contemplated Preventive Detention Act can only defeat the very purpose for which it is intended and that Nigeria will have taken the first fatal step which completely negates the fundamental inspiration of our anti-colonial struggle – Freedom and Liberty. We detest the contemplated Preventive Detention Act with every vein in our being, we reject it unequivocally and we address to you a solemn appeal to drop it as bad business.

Second: *The Call for a National Government*

In recent public statements some of you have lent vigour to the idea of an all-party national government in the country with a life span of 15 years for a start. This idea is being justified by appeals designed to whip up a false sense of national emergency. What today constitutes our national emergency, indeed our national crisis, is not the existence of the Opposition in Government but the reckless neglect of the economic well-being of the workers, the vindictiveness of our national politics, the ridiculously excessive political party patronage heaped on a small élite in our society, the excesses of those public men and women whom the spoils of office have bought and clothed with material splendour and economic affluence totally out of tune with the realities of the economy of the country. Oh, yes, we know how concerned you all are about this unhappy situation, but we demand that you today honestly address yourselves as our leaders to doing some sensible thing about it. To woo or bribe an official Opposition out of existence is not democratic government and certainly not the answer to our national emergency.

A government without an official Opposition is an organised deceit of the people. It is the beginning of the first treacherous strokes of dictatorship. You are all knowledgeable men and remember only too well the saying which immortalises the finest concept and practice of democracy:

Let the minority have its say,
But the majority must have its way.

This is the form of government we can co-operate with and will defend.

Third: *The Economic Distress of the Workers*

Shortly before and since independence, Nigerian workers have been pleading with you to carry out a thorough review of salaries and wages, redraw the wage structure and generally to improve their working conditions. Quite apart from the economic arguments which justify this demand as an urgent national necessity, we pointed out that such an undertaking was a necessary memento not only to our break with colonial Nigeria but also to the contributions which we made to independence, as well as an incentive in the formidable task of nation-building. So far you have left our appeals to go unheeded. This is not astute statesmanship. It is unnecessary provocation and an unenlightened invitation to industrial strife and discord of a magnitude that could prostrate the body of the nation's economic growth disastrously. While there is still some restraining element in our tempers and disposition, we call upon you to heed our cries, our appeals and our demand for economic justice based on an equitable redistribution of the national income. Those who, because they govern, enjoy the good things of life and wish to continue to do so should take a lesson from history, and keep themselves constantly reminded that a thousand preventive detention acts or such other tyrannical laws have succeeded to hold down an aggrieved populance only for a short time – not all of the time. If you, dear compatriots, would let us, we would urge you to live the preachment that 'there is enough for the need of all but not for the greed of the few'. We urge you, dear compatriots, to be statesmen more and more every day and not opportunist politicians; to be re-imbued with the pulsating inspiration which permeated our nationalism in the days of the colonial struggle and redeem your promise to the workers and the masses of our people that their welfare, their well-being and their aspirations would be the highest order of the land in independent Nigeria.

In your luxurious surroundings, in your residential palaces far removed from the squalor of the worker's living conditions, from his privation and generally depressed economic condition, you, dear compatriots, may be sitting on a powder-keg. We do not begrudge you, but we give a timely warning. Please understand us properly. We want you to understand the present, and live it in accordance with the tenets of social and economic justice, so that we can all avoid the catastrophes of tomorrow.

We conclude with this solemn appeal:

> Drop the contemplated Preventive Detention Act;
> Abandon the idea of an all-party government without official opposition;
> Stand for the human dignity of every citizen;
> Defend our national freedom and our personal liberty;
> Heed the workers' demand for salaries and wages review;
> Forward with democracy;

and Nigeria shall be the greatest among the great nations of the world.

Yours sincerely,
L. L. BORHA,
General Secretary,
United Labour Congress Nigeria.

It is to the everlasting credit of the Action Group Opposition that it did not succumb to this bait. Its courageous stand against an all-party Government, coupled with the overwhelming opposition of most organised groups in the country, forced the Federal Government to withdraw the Preventive Detention Bill. Victory in the struggle encouraged agitation over the wage claim. Since the fruitless meeting with the Federal Minister of Establishments and Service Matters, the ULC had been considering how best to pursue the wage claim with the support of other labour leaders whose unions were not affiliates of the Congress. A direct personal approach could not be considered for two reasons. First, the subversion of the ULC and its affiliates by the NTUC and other splinter organisations had severely strained the personal relationship of ULC leaders with their counterparts in other organisations. To approach them on a question such as this would create the undesirable impression in those being approached that without them and their support the ULC was incapable of discharging one of its basic functions. Secondly, there was still lingering suspicion and distrust among former members of the Marxist Group, many of whom were in the opposing camps in the labour movement. The moderates in the ULC did not believe that the extremists in the NTUC were genuinely interested in advancing the economic interests of the workers of Nigeria; they believed them rather to be so fanatically committed to communism that they would exploit the genuine grievance of the workers to advance the communist cause in Nigeria.

As time went by and the failures, the abuses and the unfulfilled hopes of the workers for an independent Nigeria became more and more glaring; as attempts to convince the Federal and Regional Governments that it would be in the interests of themselves and the nation as a whole to consider the workers' plight – against the background of soaring prices and of the considerable salary increases which legislators had voted for themselves – failed, even the moderate erstwhile Marxists began to have second thoughts about the need to work with their former colleagues. It became increasingly clear that, in order to win higher wages, improved working conditions and better housing for Nigerian workers, which were among the key objectives outlined in ULC's First Policy Statement of May 25, 1962, it might be necessary even to sup with the devil.

In May 1963 the first Annual Congress of the ULC adopted a resolution authorising the Central Executive to press for a general revision of wages and salaries. Three months later, the first Annual Delegates Conference of the Eastern District Council adopted another resolution urging the ULC to set up a Political Action Committee 'which will have as its primary objective the propagation of a socialist welfare state and the furtherance of the workers' power and influence in the national politics of Nigeria . . . and to proceed to establish proper liaison between it and other organisations, political or otherwise, that subscribe to the principles of a socialist welfare state in Nigeria.' The following month a representative meeting of Presidents and General Secretaries of ULCN affiliates in Lagos adopted a resolution appealing to 'all trade unions outside the ULC to abandon their strifes and futile dissensions and return to or come within the fold of the United Labour Congress as a proper and recognised platform for the prosecution of the grievances of Nigerian workers'. Finally, the meeting requested the ULC Central Executive to arrange a meeting of all unions in Lagos to take a decision in favour of country-wide industrial action in furtherance of the ULC's demand for wage and salary revision and improved conditions of employment.

A representative meeting of all registered unions in Lagos was convened on September 12, 1963. That meeting endorsed a statement issued earlier that same day by the ULC General Secretary, Lawrence L. Borha, on the Government's statement on the workers' claim for wage revision. The ULC's statement reads:

> The ULC has received a statement by the Federal Ministry of Establishments outlining the position of the Governments of the Federation on Congress' demand for a general upward revision

of wages and salaries of junior civil servants as well as junior employees in private establishments, a review of the whole structure of salaries and wages as well as conditions of service, including the daily-paid question, and the introduction of a national minimum wage.

After careful consideration, the Congress takes the position that the statement, even as a tentative offer, is most unsatisfactory, because it reveals once again the agonising fact that the Governments are unwilling to grapple courageously with the basic and fundamental question raised by Congress' demands.

In this connection, it is necessary to re-emphasise that Congress did not address its demands to the Governments necessarily as employers but as *the authority of State*, which not only has direct responsibility to protect workers in *all sectors* of wage-employment in the country, but also the obligation to bring about a more rational economic structure, the first steps towards which in our view is a complete overhaul of the existing colonial wage structure.

It is clear that when the Governments spoke, as they did in the present statement, merely as civil service employers, they have once again shirked their responsibility to the workers in the private sector of the economy. It was precisely to avoid a further perpetuation of the neglect and discriminatory practice directed in the past against non-civil service employees in these matters that Congress considered it necessary to call for a Commission, call it a special panel, with comprehensive terms of reference to carry out a thorough review so that the anomalies which exist as between the foreign-oriented upper stratum and the domestic-oriented lower stratum of the existing wage structure may be removed once and for all.

On the question of a national minimum wage, the Congress is unable to agree that there is justification for Government's refusal, in fact no single justification was offered.

Although desirable that wage differentials based solely on zonal wage-rates should be eliminated, nevertheless Congress considers that the proposals to set up wage-fixing machinery at certain local levels lacks effectiveness by reason of the severely circumscribed competence which such machinery will exercise. There should be a new wage charter now upon which wage committees may work subsequently. In any case there should be a permanent wage regulating Council at the national level as a prerequisite to local wage-fixing bodies.

In the light of the foregoing, the ULC finds the proposals of the Governments unacceptable.

The meeting took two other important decisions. The first was the setting up of a Joint Action Committee of Nigerian Trade Unions (commonly referred to as JAC) to prosecute the wage demand; and the second was a general strike on September 27, 1963, if the demand was not met within that deadline. No effort was made by the Government to concede the demand. So a day's lightning strike took place on September 27, 1963. To contain the strike Government appointed a six-man commission of enquiry with the following terms of reference:

(i) to investigate the existing wage structure, remuneration and conditions of service in wage-earning employments in the country and to make recommendations concerning a suitable new structure, as well as adequate machinery for a wages review on a continuing basis;

(ii) to examine the need for:

- (*a*) a general upward revision of salaries and wages of junior employees in both Government and private establishments;
- (*b*) the abolition of the daily-wage system; and
- (*c*) the introduction of a national minimum wage;

and to make recommendations.

The members of the commission were Mr. Justice Adeyinka Morgan, Chairman; Mr. S. O. Sodipo, Secretary; Malam Abdu Gusau, O. I. Akinkugbe, C. O. Nwokedi, Chief T. E. A. Salubi, and Dr. T. M. Yesufu. The Morgan Commission began its work in October 1963 and ended in April 1964. It received memoranda from 258 organisations and individuals, and took oral evidence from fifty-five persons. Considering the circumstances leading to its appointment, one would have expected that the Commission's Report would have been published with despatch. For some unexplained reason the Report was not published as expected, in spite of considerable agitation from trade unions. The JAC tried without avail to persuade the Government to publish the Report and kill ugly rumours spreading around the country. A mass meeting held at Surulere on May 30 mandated the Joint Action Committee to organise a general strike on June 1 if before that day the Government did not release the Morgan Report. The meeting also decided to stage a demonstration against the Government's handling of the Report and the continued ban on public meetings and demonstrations in the Federal Territory of Lagos.

The decision to demonstrate was significant. It was perhaps the second well-known occasion in Nigerian labour history when workers, knowing the probable consequence, had decided to defy the law. During the discussion on the suggestion for a demonstration, someone called attention to the ban on public meetings which was still in force. Popular indignation against Sir Abubakar's Government's decision to continue, ever since 1962, to deny the people the right to meet and to demonstrate killed any appeal to reason. On taking the decision, the meeting constituted itself into a mile-long demonstration, which made its way peacefully to the head office of the United Labour Congress at 97 Herbert Macaulay Street, Ebute-Metta. Here two schools of thought emerged. One, led by Alhaji H. P. Adebola, who led the demonstration from Surulere, felt that it should now disperse, having achieved its objectives – which were to express workers' resentment against the delay in releasing the Morgan Report, and their opposition to the continuation of the ban on public meetings and processions in the Federal Territory. The second school, led by Michael Imoudu, held a different view. It was true, Imoudu argued, that the ban on demonstrations had been defied, but the defiance would not be effective if it stopped at Ebute Metta. It must be carried on to Lagos to convince Sir Abubakar and his Government that workers were angry. If anybody felt unable to lead the demonstration, he was prepared to do so. The crowd yelled 'Imo, Imo'. In order not to allow Imoudu to take credit for a job well begun, Adebola agreed not only that the demonstration should continue but that he would continue to lead it.

From 97 Herbert Macaulay Street, the demonstrators went on without incident until they reached Iddo Carter Bridge, where they clashed with the police. In the scuffle which ensued, Adebola received a fractured arm and a battered head. Several other labour leaders received injuries, while some were removed to the hospital unconscious suffering the effects of tear gas and severe beatings by the police. That evening the Iddo incident featured prominently in the Radio Nigeria news bulletin, and many workers in the Federal Territory who heard the news wept. Radio Peking 'lustily reported the mischievous news of the death through Police action of that arch-imperialist stooge and reactionary trade unionist Alhaji H. P. Adebola'.[2]

From his sick bed Adebola spoke the following day to the workers and the nation. He said that the general strike planned by workers would begin the day after and continue until their demands had been met. True to his word the strike began in Lagos as planned, and hit all Government offices and industrial undertakings, except those on the essential service list. Big department stores and small companies engaged in retail and distributive trades all equally were affected. By the next day practically all the industrial life of the nation had come to a standstill. The Government tried on June 3 to contain the strike by releasing the Morgan Report and its White Paper on the Report. This added insult to injury, for the Government refused to pay the wage rates and salary scales recommended – a striking departure from practices which had become more or less a tradition in the history of wage fixing in Nigeria. The following are some of the main areas of disagreement between the Government and the Commission:

MORGAN COMMISSION	FEDERAL GOVERNMENT
(i) *The Principle of Living Wage.* The commission felt that Nigerian workers should be paid wages high enough to enable them to support themselves and their families. This the Commissioners called a Living Wage. To support their recommendation the Commissioners quoted a similar recommendation made by the Bridges Committee of 1941 and Despatch No. 607 of April 15, 1955, addressed to the Secretary of State for the Colonies by the Governor-General of Nigeria in which the latter was credited with having said that the Nigerian Government had accepted the policy of taking family responsibilities into consideration in the fixation of wages.	The Federal Government argued that in recommending a living wage the Commission departed from the fundamental concepts and pattern of expenditure on which the existing wages were based. In doing so the Commission directed its mind to 'the balanced diets based on local foodstuffs drawn by dieticians. By deriving the new wage structure from its own suggested pattern of living, the Commission has increased the existing minimum wage by 58 per cent in some cases, and in others by 100 per cent, whereas the pattern of the cost of living index would have produced an increase of say 15 to 20 per cent. Whatever consideration might have led the Commission to reject the existing pattern of family expenditure upon which the current cost of living was based, the Government could not accept all the components of the revised pattern as realistic.
(ii) *National Minimum Wage.* The country was divided into four Zones and minimum wages recommended as follows:	
Zone 1: Lagos up to within a radius of 16 miles and Port Harcourt: £12	*Zone 1*: Federal Territory of Lagos: £9 2s. per month or 7s. per day

Zone 2: Jos urban area including the minesfield; the urban areas of Kaduna, Kano and Zaria; Aba, Enugu, Onitsha, Umuahia; Ibadan, Benin City and Burutu: £10	*Zone 2*: Whole of Western and whole of Mid-Western Regions: £7 16s. per month or 6s. per day
Zone 3: Eastern Nigeria, Western Nigeria, and Mid-Western Nigeria excluding areas in Zones 1 and 2: £8	*Zone 3*: Whole of Eastern Region: £7 16s. per month or 6s. per day
Zone 4: Northern Nigeria excluding areas in Zone 2: £6 10s.	*Zone 4*: Kaduna and Kano urban areas: £6 12s. 2d. per month or 5s. 1d. per day
	Zone 5: Urban areas of Jos, (including minesfields) Zaria, Sokoto, Gusau, Bauchi, Gombe, Lokoja, Katsina Province, Kano Province (excluding urban areas) Kabba Division: £6 1s. 4d. per month or 4s. 8d. per day
	Zone 6: Zaria, Sokoto, Bauchi Provinces (excluding urban areas in 5) Gashaka-Mambilla Native Authority: £5 6s. 2d. per month or 4s. 1d. per day
	Zone 7: Niger and Kabba Provinces (excluding Kabba Division and Lokoja urban area), Bornu, Ilorin, Adamawa and Sardauna Provinces (excluding Gashaka-Mambilla Native Authority): £4 15s. 4d. per month or 3s. 8d. per day

Note: It was explained that 'it has been found necessary to retain four Zones in the Northern Region in order to reflect the difference in cost of living in certain rural areas, and also to maintain an equitable wage pattern'.

Salaried Staff

Salary	*Increase*
Up to £318 p.a.	£36 p.a.
£319–£432 p.a.	£24 p.a.
£433–£588 p.a.	£12 p.a.

Salary	*Increase*
£78–£90 p.a.	To be brought in line with revised annual minimum for daily paid employees.
£91–£318	£18 p.a.
£319–£432	£12 p.a.
£433–£588	£6 p.a.

(iii) *Application of Recommendations Regarding Wages and Salaries*: Government should take the necessary legislative measures to ensure the enforcement of salaries and wages recommended. For this purpose necessary amendments should be made to the Wages Board Act. Junior employees in the private sector who came within the wage groups affected by the increases recommended should also benefit. The Government should create appropriate machinery to enable junior employees to negotiate with employers who ignore the increases recommended.

Government did not consider it necessary to enforce minimum rates without due consideration of the peculiar circumstances within each industry and the ability of the employer to pay. The tradition in the country had been for private employers to pay rates paid by Government because the employers realised that it was in their own interest to do so. Moreover, it would appear that both employers and trade unions did not want state intervention to take the place of collective bargaining in the private sector of the economy.

(iv) *Effective Date of Payment of New Wage and Salary Increases*: The commission recommended that the new wage and salary scales be paid with effect from October 1, 1963. Any other day later than that date, and considering the circumstances leading to the appointment of the commission, would be a breach of faith with the workers.

Government could not assume the financial burden of paying nine month's arrears without jeopardising the financing of the Six-Year Development Plan, and consequently the future development of Nigeria. The financial burden of heavy arrears would cripple production in the private sector of the economy, and might lead to general inflation as well as worsen the unemployment situation in the whole country. For these reasons the new salary scales and wage rates would be effective from April 1, 1964.

Apart from the areas of disagreement, agreement was recorded in many areas. The main recommendations accepted by the Government were:

(i) Legislation should be introduced to ensure that each employer publishes his conditions of employment and workers' entitlements and makes copies available to workers;

(ii) The Labour Code Act should be revised to guarantee certain basic minimum rights to all categories of workers with special reference to termination notices, leave entitlements, sick leave and medical care;

(iii) Wages and salaries should be paid twice monthly;

(iv) A statutory National Dock Labour Board should be established to deal with all aspects of stevedoring and dock work, including the operation of dock labour registration schemes;

(v) Except in cases of casual or seasonal labour, unestablished staff should be given the same conditions of service as established staff;

(vi) A National Joint Industrial Council for each major industry or group of similar industries or employments should be established. Members should be appointed by the Federal Minister of Labour after consultation with both sides of industry. The Council should assume the status of Wages Boards, and all agreements negotiated should be submitted to the Federal Ministry of Labour for registration under the Act. It thus becomes legally enforceable.

(vii) There should be a National Wages Board to regulate wages and conditions of service for unskilled and semi-skilled labour;

(viii) A National Wages Advisory Council should be established to observe, co-ordinate, and advise on all aspects of wages policy;

(ix) An industrial court should be set up to adjudicate on industrial disputes;

(x) The Trade Disputes (Arbitration and Inquiry) Act should be amended to make provision for compulsory arbitration;

(xi) The Trade Disputes Act should be amended to make strikes and lock-outs illegal until a dispute has been referred to the Minister of Labour, who should within a month take steps to effect settlement by negotiation, and/or arbitration. It should be illegal for either side to strike or lock out until after three months from the publication of an arbitration award.

(xii) Labour legislation should be reviewed so as to bring it up to date and codify it in one Labour and Industrial Relations Act.

(xiii) The minimum number of persons who could form a trade union should be revised upwards. The present minimum of five is too small;

(xiv) The Trade Union Act should be amended to prevent employers from interfering unduly with Trade Unions;

(xv) It should be made illegal for one person to be Secretary, Treasurer, or an executive member of more than one registered trade union at the same time. Any person convicted of a crime involving dishonesty or fraud should be disqualified from acting as official or executive member of a trade union for at least three years from the date of conviction;

(xvi) It should be illegal for an employer to refuse to recognise a duly registered trade union;

(xvii) A National Joint Negotiating Council to deal with the remuneration and conditions of service, gradings, etc., of teachers should be established.

On many considerations, the Morgan Report is a revolutionary document – not just because it undertook to do some of those things that it ought not to have done, but because some of the members of the commission had the courage to attack certain injustices which, all along, had rankled in the minds of all decent people, but which men of influence for varying reasons had either failed to pinpoint or struggled to see them removed. In their Minority Report C. O. Nwokedi and O. I. Akinkugbe recommended a general downgrading of salaries of posts in the upper segment of the public service. In making the recommendation the two commissioners accepted the argument often advanced by trade unions in Nigeria and by some Nigerian economists that the salaries of these posts were colonial in content and structure and not related to the capacity of the national economy, nor to the degree of responsibility shouldered by the beneficiaries. The commissioners declared: 'We advocate a complete break with this humiliating past and would recommend one which would be a challenge to our nationhood and patriotism.'[3] A first step in this direction, they added, was to reduce wasteful spending in public corporations by levelling down the salaries of corporation officials to the rates paid to their counterparts with comparable qualifications, experience and responsibilities in the public service. The commissioners also advocated the abolition of car basic allowance, holding that the continuance of this allowance as a policy had been a disincentive to the rapid evolution of a more efficient system of transport.

Dr. T. M. Yesufu in his own Minority Report said of the Inducement Addition: 'If, as appears to be the case, the basic salaries recommended by Mr. Gorsuch were calculated to reflect Nigerian conditions, there seems to me to be no justification whatsoever to pay an "Inducement Addition" to any indigenous officer. I therefore recommend that this element of Inducement Addition should be separated from all salaries attached to super-scale posts and that only expatriate officers should henceforth be entitled to draw it.' Dr. Yesufu said that, from information supplied to the commission, the amounts being spent by the Federal Government on payment of car basic allowance had been rising steeply. Between 1960–61 and 1962–63 the figure had risen by about 58 per cent. During the same period the amount spent by the Federal and Regional Governments on the same item were as follows:

GOVERNMENT EXPENDITURE
ON BASIC ALLOWANCES 1960–63

Government	*1960–61* £	*1961–62* £	*1962–63* £
Federal	318,000	436,558	503,415
North	331,153	374,390	389,714
East	224,809	257,077	288,964
West	355,824	412,312	498,026

In 1962–63, the proportion of the expenditure on motor car basic allowance to the recurrent estimates of the Governments was Federal 0·8 per cent; Northern Regional 1·8 per cent; Eastern Regional 1·5 per cent; and Western Regional 2·4 per cent. Dr. Yesufu supported the recommendation of his fellow commissioners that car basic allowance be abolished forthwith, and added: 'Whatever may be the state of the public transport system, it appears to me that there is very little justification for a situation whereby the Governments disburse from about one per cent to 2·5 per cent of their revenue as allowances to a few thousand public servants to maintain private vehicles. . . . In their place Government should introduce enhanced mileage allowances to be paid only on occasions when an officer uses his car in the public interest.' Dr. Yesufu also recommended the abolition of children's separate domiciled allowance. The Government should, as a matter of policy, cease providing quarters for Nigerian officers. After making provision for expatriate staff, surplus Government quarters should be sold, preference of purchase being given to Nigerian officers. As an interim measure for raising revenue, rents payable in Government quarters should be increased to 10 per cent of an officer's salary, subject to a maximum and a minimum of £240 and £120 per annum respectively.

The Government made no serious attempt to come to terms with JAC leaders until attempts to break the strike by threats and victimisation of strikers had failed. As the strike entered its fifth day the Prime Minister ordered workers back to work within 48 hours and warned them that failure to comply would be met with summary dismissal. Striking workers merely treated the warning as a joke. JAC leaders retorted in a strike bulletin: '*The strike continues*'. A mass meeting later adopted a resolution giving the Prime Minister a 48-hour ultimatum to resign his position. In Port Harcourt, Aba, Enugu and several other towns in Eastern Nigeria, politicians as well as businessmen demonstrated their sympathy with workers by carrying palm fronds – an action which soon became a recognised sign of sympathy with the strikers. Those who failed to carry them were marked as traitors to the common cause and molested or ostracised. It was in the midst of this deteriorating situation that the Government made a positive move to end the strike. On June 7 and 8, an exploratory talk was held between JAC leaders and representatives of the Federal Government. While the talks were going on it was reported that the Government had issued queries to some 10,000 civil servants in Lagos. This almost broke down the talks, but wise counsel eventually prevailed. On Saturday, June 13, it was announced that the giant strike had been called off on the following terms:

(i) that the strikers would not be victimised in any way;
(ii) that the dismissal and warning notices already served on strikers would be withdrawn;
(iii) that the strikers would not be penalised for the period of their absence from duty on account of the strike, which period would be treated as leave with full pay and without prejudice to leave already earned;
(iv) that a negotiating body on which the Governments of the Federal Republic of Nigeria, the private employers and the Joint Action Committee of Nigerian trade unions would be represented, would be set up immediately and commence negotiations on Monday, June 15, 1964, at 5 p.m.;
(v) that the negotiations would be conducted on the basis of the Morgan Commission Report; and

(vi) that, in consideration of the conditions stated above, the strike was thereby called off.

Workers went wild with joy when the terms were read at a mass meeting that afternoon. They rejoiced not only because the strike was a huge success, but because they had won an unprecedented concession which, if care were not taken, might haunt future labour–management relations in Nigeria like a spectre. Never in the history of strikes in Nigeria, particularly of strikes lasting more than one or two days, had the employer undertaken to pay workers during strike period. The concession might be defended by all the parties to it on the ground that the 1964 General Strike was not in the real sense the normal strike involving a physical withdrawal of labour. It was a sit-down strike; technically, they had not absented themselves from work and could therefore claim their pay. It might also be argued that the economic disruption of the country that resulted from the strike was such as to justify any price being paid to bring the nation back to work and to stave off the threatened disaster.

Against what admittedly was a good concession for the workers stood the national interest. Here arises the important question of the cost to the nation of the General Strike. Estimates vary. The Government-sponsored *Nigerian Morning Post* estimated the cost at £240,000 per day when the strike was only five days old.[4] *The Sunday Times* Industrial Correspondent said the country lost £14 million during the 13 days.[5] *The West African Pilot* quoted experts as estimating the cost at between £10 and £20 million.[6] Would so much desperately needed money have been lost if those who governed Nigeria's First Republic had given the workers' claims the attention and consideration which would have assured them that the agitations for independence had really been meaningful and rewarding exercises? There might have been no need for the Morgan Commission if the recommendation of the Mbanefo Commission – that a machinery be set up for periodical review of wages and salaries – had been accepted and implemented. The Commission found that commissions of enquiry often resulted in the payment of large-scale arrears, which adversely affected the economy.

The negotiating body appointed to negotiate on the basis of the Morgan Report began its work on June 15. The Governments of the Federation were represented by Dr. K. O. Mbadiwe, J. C. Obande, Alhaji Waziri Ibrahim, Chief J. M. Johnson (Federal); Z. Mustafa Ismail (North); H. U. Akpabio (East) and J. U. Umolu (Mid-West): the employers by D. Fleming, J. Ade Tuyo, C. E. Abebe, A. D. G. Paxton and D. A. Borrie: and JAC by H. P. Adebola, W. O. Goodluck, N. Chukwura, M. A. O. Imoudu, E. C. Okei-Achamba, H. W. Ugwuala, J. O. James, E. N. Okongwu, L. L. Borha and S. U. Bassey. After two weeks of protracted negotiations an agreement was signed on June 29, 1964. Among its many provisions were the following:

(i) (*a*) The Government should provide an adequate machinery through the Wages Board Act to deal with the application of the minimum wage rate for each area to the private employers, and the Wages Board Act should be suitably amended for this purpose.
(*b*) Other junior employees in the private sector within the range of salary and wage groups affected by the recommended increases should also benefit from them.
(*c*) The Government should create appropriate machinery to enable junior employees to negotiate with employers who ignored the recommended increases.

(ii) Grading teams should be set up as a matter of urgency to examine the regrading of certain posts. The question of grading should be kept under constant review. The National Council of Establishments should ensure that persons performing identical duties in different regions were equally remunerated.

(iii) (*a*) Instead of the old division of labour into General Labour, Special Labour, and Skilled artisans, the following division was agreed: Unskilled and Semi-skilled; Artisans.
(*b*) The unskilled and semi-skilled should be accommodated within a 13-point scale.
(*c*) Unskilled labour would run from the minimum of the wage scale and terminate on the 8th point of the scale; and semi-skilled labour would run from the 5th point of the wage scale and terminate on the 13th point of the scale;
(*d*) The existing Special Labour Grades I, II and III should be classified as semi-skilled labour. The details of the application of this principle to established semi-skilled labour would be worked out.
(*e*) The unestablished artisans would run the same scale as their counterparts who were established.

(iv) The country should be divided into Six Areas and the agreed minimum WAGE RATES applicable in the different Areas of Classification were as follows:

Area	Territory covered	Agreed minimum rate per month of 26 days and per day
I.	Federal Territory of Lagos (including a radius of 16 miles from Timubu Square, and referring to employees of the Federal Government and the private sector.	£10 per month or 7s. 8d. per diem.
II.	Whole of Western, whole of Mid-Western, and whole of Eastern Regions.	£8 2s. 6d. per month or 6s. 3d. per diem.
III.	Kaduna and Kano Urban areas.	£6 18s. 6d. per month or 5s. 4d. per diem.
IV.	Urban areas of Jos (including Mine-fields), Zaria, Sokoto, Gusau, Bauchi, Gombe, Lokoja, Katsina Province, Benue Province, Kano Province (excluding urban areas), Kabba Division.	£6 7s. 10d. per month or 4s. 11d. per diem.
V.	Zaria, Plateau, Sokoto, Bauchi Provinces (excluding urban areas in IV) Gashaka/Mambilla Native Authority.	£5 10s. 6d. per month or 4s. 3d. per diem.
VI.	Niger and Kabba Provinces (excluding Kabba Division and Lokoja urban area), Bornu, Ilorin, Adamawa and Sardauna Provinces (excluding Gashaka /Mambilla Native Authority).	£5 4s. 0d. per month or 4s. per diem.

(v) The DAILY WAGE SYSTEM should be gradually abolished and all skilled workers should be transferred to the PERMANENT ESTABLISHMENT as follows:
With effect from 1.4.65: All those with 15 years and over continuous service;
With effect from 1.4.66: All those with under 15 years continuous service;
With effect from 1.4.67: All those with less than 10 years but over 5 years continuous service.
Subsequently, all skilled workers with 5 years and over to be absorbed.

(vi) No Junior employee in the private sector should earn less than what is agreed for Area 1 of wage-earners.

(vii) The agreed salary increases for junior employees were as follows:

Salary range	*Salary increases*
Up to £318 per annum	£24 per annum
Above £318 per annum to £432 p.a.	£16 per annum
Above £432 per annum to £588 p.a.	£8 per annum

(viii) The minimum wages and increases agreed should also apply to persons of equivalent status in the Public Corporations, to teachers and nurses, and other junior employees of Local Authorities.

(ix) Any minimum wage and increase agreed should also apply to junior employees in the private sector and legislation should be introduced to provide the machinery for negotiation.

Although it was basically an *ad hoc* body most workers and their friends hoped that the JAC would pave the way and eventually become Nigeria's central labour organisation in a unified labour movement. This cherished hope was frustrated by the activities of certain members of the JAC itself. Alhaji H. P. Adebola, ULC President and former Joint Chairman of the JAC, enumerated these activities in his presidential address to the second biennial congress of the ULC held at Port Harcourt in 1965. Alhaji Adebola said:

> Immediately after the formation of the JAC, the NTUC felt it was an opportune time for them to work havoc against the ULC. First and foremost they wrote a letter without our knowledge urging the Federal Government to withdraw the official recognition accorded to the ULC even though we were working together in the JAC. In the second place they took advantage of our coming together to go round some of our affiliates with a view to disorganising them, an act which otherwise they could not have been able to do if we had not come together at all. . . . When the JAC was formed we of the United Labour Congress thought it was only for the purpose of using it to obtain benefits for the workers of Nigeria, but members of the NTUC took the opportunity to advocate and further the interests of the Socialist Workers and Farmers Party.

Lawrence Borha showed how these interests were furthered. In his report on activities to the same Congress he said, under the subheading 'The Formation and Disbandment of JAC':

> The climax came in December during the Federal Elections when these people started to 'chase the hounds and run with the hare'. In the open they proclaimed their support for a particular alliance and underneath they engaged in frenzied house-to-house campaign against that very alliance. As a way of testing their honesty of purpose they were called upon to withdraw their candidates who were contesting against the official candidates of that same alliance. They not only refused to withdraw but also went to solicit financial

help from another party which is a deadly rival to the alliance they claimed to support. This act of political treachery and perfidy revolted our sense of patriotism and code of behaviour. All this culminated in the disbandment of the JAC in Lagos as well as in certain other Regions.

Although, immediately the ULC and the NWC pulled out of it, the JAC died in Lagos, and the Western, Mid-Western and Northern Regions, it remained alive in the East for several months. Eastern workers found in the JAC a more uniting force than anything they had previously known. Its demise in the East followed NTUC attempts, in the name of JAC, to disorganise certain ULC affiliates and create ill-will among the workers. Its agents showed no scruples in assassinating the characters of workers' leaders in the Region of proven worth and selflessness. Both the committed and uncommitted unions felt called upon to take a stand. 'Thus far, but no further', they cried. In unison they withdrew from the Eastern JAC, which from then became a façade existing more or less on the pages of newspapers and over the radio network.

REFERENCES

1. Synopsis of Dockworkers' Strike: A Report to ULC Central Executive Council, February 1962.
2. Report on Activities presented to 2nd Biennial Congress of the ULC, 1965, page 14.
3. Morgan Commission Report, 1964, page 49.
4. *Nigerian Morning Post*, June 6, 1964.
5. *Sunday Times*, June 14, 1964.
6. *West African Pilot*, June 15, 1964.

21

LABOUR IN NIGERIA 1966

Four important things happened in Nigeria in 1966. On Saturday, January 15, a military coup ousted the nebulous Government of Sir Abubakar Tafawa Balewa. By a twist of fortune, power eluded the organisers of the coup, and fell into the hands of Major-General J. T. U. Aguiyi-Ironsi, General Officer Commanding, Nigeria's Armed Forces, who was neither involved in the planning nor in the execution of the coup. Six and a half months later General Ironsi's Government was overthrown by another coup which brought Lt.-Col. Yakubu Gowon, Ironsi's most trusted aide, to power. During the second coup General Ironsi, Lt.-Col. Francis A. Fajuyi, Military Governor of Western Nigeria, and about 300 officers and other ranks of Eastern Nigerian origin were killed by their colleagues of Northern origin. Before the second coup an incident took place in Northern Nigeria that began the dangerous erosion of Nigerian unity. On May 29 about 3,000 defenceless civilians of Eastern Nigerian origin were killed in widespread riots. The pattern of killing and the timing of the riots suggest that they were carefully planned. Between September 29 and October 1 Easterners were killed, maimed, and brutally assaulted in several places in Nigeria, and thousands were made refugees in their own country.

This book is not concerned with the circumstances leading to the events here outlined; nor are we concerned with their planning and execution. What interests us is the role which the workers and their organisations played, and the effect of that role on the trade union movement in general and in Eastern Nigeria in particular.

All the national trade union centres joined hands with other organisations in welcoming the first military coup, which was popularly hailed as a blessing to the country. No such reception was accorded the second coup whose propriety has often been questioned. Other organised groups showed an identical attitude to the second coup as was shown by the trade union movement. The situation was different in Northern Nigeria, where men, women and children took a day off to celebrate not only the success of the coup but also the reward that 'God, in his power, has entrusted the responsibility of this great country of ours, Nigeria, into the hands of another Northerner'.[1] Leaders of the Northern Federation of Labour and its affiliated organisations moved a step further. They exploited the success of the coup to cause fear and despondency among Easterners working or doing business in that region. They campaigned in offices, workshops, department stores, markets, schools, hospitals, post offices and federal research stations demanding the removal or withdrawal of Easterners from Northern Nigeria. A 'Secret Society' soon emerged threatening expatriate employers with reprisals if they did not dismiss employees of Eastern Nigerian origin. 'Away with Ibos,' 'Down with Easterners,' 'North for Northerners' – these were some of the slogans posted at important places in some Northern Nigerian cities.

Walter Partington writing in the *Daily Express* of October 6, 1966, reported that some British housewives in Kano had taken refuge in the city's Central Hotel (some under assumed names) after threats that they faced death unless they sacked their Ibo employees. A woman from Southport, Lancashire, who preferred to be called Mrs. X, was quoted as saying: 'My husband and I are terrified. We got a letter signed "Secret Society". It threatened to cut our throats and hang our bodies outside the city gates if we did not sack our twenty Ibo workers.'

Some Easterners working in Federal establishments tried to secure transfers outside Northern Nigeria. Their applications were still under consideration when the worst of the massacres took place all over Northern Nigeria and certain parts of Western Nigeria and the Federal Territory of Lagos. In Lagos and parts of Western Nigeria and the Federal Territory of Lagos troops of Northern Nigeria origin alone did the killing. In the Northern Region, people from nearly all walks of life participated. Motley crowds armed with matchets, spears, and poisoned arrows attacked Easterners in their homes, in streets and markets, killing, maiming and wounding thousands. Soldiers moved from office to office, workshop to workshop, and other places of business with lists of workers of Eastern Nigeria origin prepared by their Northern colleagues. Where there were no lists Northern workers identified the Easterners among them. These were called, marched out, lined up and shot. At railway stations, motor parks, airports and every possible escape route, Northern soldiers, sometimes aided by police, hounded Easterners and shot them. Pregnant women were also killed, their stomachs cut open and the unborn children slaughtered 'so that they might not become another Azikiwe or Ojukwu'.

When the situation was eventually brought under control a conservative estimate put the figure of the dead at about 20,000. The actual number may never be known. The killings had a three-pronged effect. In Northern Nigeria the sudden disappearance of Easterners, who constituted a majority of the skilled labour force, had two immediate effects. Essential services were dislocated. The wage bill for skilled personnel rose. Retail trade almost came to a standstill because the men and women with the initiative, drive and know-how were also not there. As a result prices rose. The story has been told of the tremendous loss which the Nigerian Railway Corporation sustained when a Railway official tried to prove that what one man could do another could also do. The experiment was made after the September 29 pogrom. One of those who always felt that Easterners had not given him an opportunity to prove his mettle eventually found an opportunity when most locomotive engine drivers had either been killed or had fled their jobs. He took one of the most expensive diesel-engined trains on a journey, but he had not gone far when the diesel engine was shattered. Friends and well-wishers of Nigeria were shocked and disappointed when they read advertisements for posts in the Northern public service in which Northern Nigeria was prepared to pay expatriates as much as three times what it could have paid had it employed Nigerian citizens from the East, West or the Federal Territory of Lagos. As if to cover up the reason for this waste, some advertisements made the false claim that the skills required were not available in Nigeria.

It was probably in trade union circles that the impact of the killings was felt most. In Northern Nigeria, Easterners constituted about 70–75 per cent of the district and branch officials and members of district and branch executive committees of national unions. Their sudden absence left a vacuum in the leadership cadre of the movement in Northern Nigeria, and adversely affected the incomes of most national unions as well as their general administrative arrangements.

In the East, the killings brought three things in their train. First, there was the justified indignation at the manner the Northerners had treated their fellow-countrymen and the incredible acquiescence of the law enforcement agencies in this wanton destruction of lives and property. The pathetic appearance of the maimed, the orphaned, the widows, and the traumatised excited feelings almost beyond control. It was this situation that forced the Eastern Military Governor to order all non-Easterners to leave Eastern Nigeria in their own interest. Secondly, some of those who returned swore never again to live outside Eastern Nigeria or in any place where evilly disposed persons would exploit their ethnic origin to compose, sing and teach hymns of hate against them just because they were of that ethnic group or origin. Thirdly, the killings created panic among Easterners working in the Federal Territory and Western Nigeria. Most of these people felt their lives to be insecure, and deserted their jobs. They soon joined the band of what the *Nigerian Outlook* called the 'Returnees'. Thus Eastern Nigeria, almost overnight, became saddled with one of the greatest refugee problems in modern times.

During the unprovoked massacres of Easterners none of the four national centres did anything to demonstrate that it was a free agent, a fearless spokesman and a defender of the workers and fundamental human rights. None had a programme or took any action to initiate a programme to aid the needy and the helpless. The United Labour Congress of Nigeria, which tried to do something, did not rise from its stupor until there had been criticisms from almost every quarter. Even then, the thousands of members it often claims did not raise an appreciable amount such as a respectable organisation could present with honour. It could only muster the courage to think of a relief programme when the much maligned ICFTU, the AFL-CIO and the PTTI had made substantial donations.

It must be remembered that a great percentage of the dead, the destitute, the refugees in their own country, the maimed, the traumatised, were workers and members of workers' families. Many of these workers were either district or branch officials of national unions affiliated to these national centres. Their contributions, though small, had been helping in some ways to maintain these organisations. The leaders of the national centres derived their authority to function partly from the votes of these workers or their representatives. No leader of a national trade union centre in Lagos running for office had failed to solicit the support of Eastern workers or workers of Eastern Nigerian origin. They did this because of the importance they had always attached to their votes and because of their sincerity in fighting a cause. The importance of Eastern workers to the Nigerian trade union movement is clearly shown by the significant roles they played at the conferences, rallies and other trade union activities organised by the national centres after 1959 and in particular by their wonderful performance during the General Strike of 1964. In the light of these salient facts, and considering the role they played during the 1964 Federal Elections, when the question of fair elections was the main issue at stake, the apparent levity with which Nigerian trade union leaders treated the pogrom of 1966 and the enormous problems it created must strike one as alarming. A critical observer may ask whether their attitude was a mere error of judgment; gross incompetence in discharging their responsibilities; prompted by a desire to minister to the persecution mania of the gunmen and the motley crowds from Northern Nigeria; an indirect way of telling the victims 'you are Easterners, so we can't help you'; or 'since it did not happen to our people (meaning people of our tribe or members of our own organisation) we don't care.' History may yet answer these questions. Eastern Nigeria workers may forgive, but they may never forget.

It was this disappointment, this utter disillusionment with the leadership in Lagos, that inspired a group of Eastern trade unionists to found on October 8, 1966, the Eastern Nigeria Trade Union Rehabilitation Committee to 'devise means best suited to rehabilitate our helpless refugees arriving from the troubled areas of the Republic'.[2] Members of the Committee were S. C. Okafor, C. A. Udensi, F. O. Nwangwu, Miss Uzodinma, N. Anunobi, A. N. Onobia, N. E. Osundu, B. E. Egbunobi, E. O. Bassey and R. Akoma. Later a conference of trade unions in Eastern Nigeria decided that all unions in the region should sever connections with national centres in Lagos. The conference inaugurated the Eastern Nigeria Council of Trade Unions, and elected B. M. Udokporo, General Secretary of the Eastern Nigeria Development Corporation and Allied Workers Union, as its Chairman and Ralph E. Nwosh, General Secretary of Independence Brewery Workers Union, as General Secretary. The birth of the ENCTU has adversely affected the fortunes of the ULC, the NTUC, the NWC and the LUF in Eastern Nigeria.

REFERENCES

1. *New Nigerian*, September 30. 1966.
2. *The Statesman*, Aba, October 11, 1966.

22

FACING THE FUTURE

> It is true that as representatives of the workers it is your duty to strive to improve the working conditions and living standards of your members. That also is the aim of your Government. But your duty does not end there. Those of you who have been entrusted with the leadership of the trade union movement have another equally important obligation. You should educate your members to appreciate their economic, social and civic responsibilities towards the state and the community. . . . You and your employers have contributed, in no small measure, to the remarkable progress which this country has made in recent years, but this progress is yet a beginning.—*Message of Goodwill to the First Annual Conference of the Trades Union Congress of Nigeria, April 1960, from Sir Abubakar Tafawa Balewa.*

In these words the late Prime Minister of Nigeria outlined some of the responsibilities of the Nigerian labour movement. Other responsibilities of the movement were enumerated in Part One of ULCN policy paper entitled *A Programme for the Future* published in May 1962. The paper says that . . .

> . . . the fundamental and enduring concern of the honest trade union is the welfare of the worker and his family. The genuine trade union is above political or compromise betrayal of the worker's interest; it is independent of the government and employers, and free of extraneous control. The genuine trade union works (as the United Labour Congress of Nigeria promises to do) for social justice and national progress. It works for these great ideals on their most meaningful level – the greatest good of the greatest number. The concern of the genuine trade union is that the worker is adequately paid for his labour, that his family has decent food and housing, that his lifetime of toil yield dignity for himself and a happier prospect for his children.

The paper lists the social objectives of the trade union movement as

– Fair wages for every worker;
– Good working conditions for every worker;

- Equal pay and good conditions for work of equal value;
- The right of every worker to choose his own job, his own union, his own political party;
- Full employment;
- Universal free education;
- Universal free health care;
- Better housing for all;
- New and modern industry for Nigeria;
- Modernisation of agriculture;
- Trade union freedom.

To be able to discharge these responsibilities the trade union movement must reconstruct itself with a view to commanding the respect, the influence and resources, both human and material, without which these lofty aspirations would be mere day-dreaming. More than that, it must move from a talking to an action stage. The movement's difficulties are largely due to the multiplicity of unions in the country, the lust for office, outright indiscipline, the dishonesty of some union leaders, and lack of union democracy in the conduct of union affairs. In the following pages an attempt will be made to examine these problems and to suggest improvements in order that the challenging tasks of the future can be met.

There are other factors apart from those examined in Chapter 13, responsible for the multiplicity of trade unions in Nigeria. Some critics have tried to blame it on that section of the Trade Union Act which authorises five persons to register a union. Careful examination of the problem, however, shows that much ado seems to have been made about nothing. The British Trade Union Act, from which the Nigerian Trade Union Act was adapted, has a similar provision: in Britain seven people can register a union. Until a few years ago the Trade Union Acts of Uganda, Kenya, Tanzania, Sierra Leone, Gambia, and the former Central African Federation had similar provisions. Yet the mere existence of these provisions did not necessarily make the workers of these countries to set up inconsequential house unions such as predominate on the Nigerian trade union scene.

The truth about union multiplicity in Nigeria is that the movement had a poor foundation. Although the reason for founding it was basically economic, its organisation and functions were bedevilled by the political situation of the day. Organisation of unions on the proper lines and basic trade union functions were relegated to the background, and political agitation took the helm. This explains why the top leadership of many Nigerian trade unions seem to be politicians more than they are trade unionists. The situation might have been reversed given two conditions. First, there was no James Patrick willing to show all the ropes to the budding movement in Nigeria even at the risk of losing a career; Nigeria was not as fortunate as Kenya in this respect. It is true that we had Labour Officers (Trade Unions). Some of them were devoted, sincere and hard-working trade unionists seconded to the colonial service from the British trade union movement. Given a free hand they might have done for Nigeria what James Patrick did for Kenya. They failed, apparently because of difficulties placed in their way – difficulties arising out of colonial policy.

Secondly, there was no programme from the national centre outlining the type of unions considered suitable for Nigeria and how to set about creating them. The absence of such a programme played dangerously into the hands of unscrupulous employers. The early unions were founded when there were several grievances requiring solution; workers wanted an opportunity to discuss these grievances with their employers. Since discussion could not take place without unions being formed and registered and since the law did not provide for mandatory recognition of a registered union, some employers, particularly those vehemently opposed to trade unionism, felt that this was an opportunity to work within the law and yet weaken the movement. They suggested – and unsuspecting workers readily accepted – that membership of the unions must be confined to employees of the particular firm. Slowly, steadily, the same pressure as was applied by the early employers was copied by others. Some workers themselves unwittingly lent support to this conspiracy. Not infrequently it has been reported that workers refuse to team up with their colleagues employed by other companies, arguing that it is because their interests are not identical.

Another factor responsible for multiplicity of unions would appear to be the membership provision of the specimen constitution given to trade unions applying for registration. This specimen, which was first produced in the early 1940's, was adopted word for word by most of the unions. But for a few possible exceptions none has tried to amend its provisions or improve upon them. The membership provision referred to above says, among other things, that 'membership of the union is open to workers employed in this industry'. Since union jurisdiction is not clearly defined in the specimen constitution, and since the union applying for registration may be Mustafa Trading Company Workers' Union, or Northern Dawn Workers Union, or Ikechukwu Engineering Workers' Union, it follows that the word 'industry' meant 'establishment' or 'company' – not a group of companies or establishments engaged in a particular industrial activity.

Within recent times, say the last decade, the multiplicity of trade unions has increased as a result of the activities of a group of men whom Dr. T. M. Yesufu has chosen to describe as 'trade union promoters'. This is a group of men who go about organising new house unions and becoming paid secretaries of each of them, or plotting the removal of existing incumbents in order to take over. Some work for themselves while others are employed by older hands in the movement. The irony of their operation is that almost every one of them talks glibly about the multiplicity of trade unions in the country and the need for big unions to strengthen the bargaining power of workers. Yet, in spite of their apparent concern about the problem, their activities complicate the matter. They not only register house unions but in some cases they spread the lie that workers engaged in identical trades or industries should not co-operate with their colleagues employed by different companies to form one strong union because the workers have no common interest. Why do they behave in this manner? There are probably two reasons: cupidity and the desire to satisfy the conditions laid down by the Government for dealing with central labour organisations in a country menaced by splits in the national trade union centre. As a rule trade union promoters are not paid much, but their aggregate income is usually higher than it would be if they were each paid by a single union. The desire to make more money would appear to explain why some people prefer the wrong thing to the ideal. The second reason is connected with the first. Since it became clear that the Government of Nigeria would deal with any national centre commanding the support of the majority of registered trade unions, the forces behind the perennial splits in the labour movement have strengthened their activities. One of their strategies has been to recruit activists as organisers to register unions. By becoming paid secretaries of these organisations these organisers ensure that the unions affiliate to the national centre of their choice. In the case of existing unions their tactics has often been to plot the removal of the paid secretary by bribing and corrupting the union executives and getting them to appoint their newly-found friends. On achieving this objective they get the union to change its national centre affiliation by the same method of bribery and corruption. In doing this they sometimes violate some of the rules of the game. It has been reported that during the test of strength between the TUC(N) and the NTUC in 1960 and 1961, NTUC activists not only offered inducements in cash and in scholarships tenable in communist countries to get unions to disaffiliate from the TUC(N) and join the NTUC, but also offered heavy subventions to unions not operating check-off in order that they might not harrass their members about dues payment.

Table 8 shows the number of unions in the country from 1940 to 1966 and the strength of organised labour during the period. Table 9 shows the pattern of development, and shows also that more than half of the total number of registered trade unions in the country have membership strengths of under 1,000 – the strength of branch unions in industrialised countries.

Table 8

REGISTERED TRADE UNIONS 1940 – MARCH 31, 1966

Year	*No. of Regd. Trade Unions*	*Membership*
1940	14	4,629
1941	27	17,521
1942	80	26,275
1943	85	27,154
1944	91	30,000
1945	97	Unknown
1946	100	52,747
1947	109	76,362
1948	127	90,864
1949–50*	140	109,998
1950–1	144	144,358
1951–2	124	152,230
1952–3	131	143,282
1953–4	152	153,089
1954–5	177	165,130
1955–6	232	175,987
1956–7	270	198,265
1957–8	298	235,742
1958–9	318	248,613
1959–60	347	259,072
1960–1	360	274,126
1963	399	375,354
1964	487	416,082
1965	600	486,430
1966	625	490,905

* Financial year April 1, 1949, to March 31, 1950.

Table 9

PATTERN OF UNION STRENGTH, MARCH 31, 1966

Strength	*No. of Unions*
1–50	102
51–250	245
251–1,000	157
1,001–5,000	53
5,001–10,000	9
10,001–20,000	7
20,001–50,000	1
Over 50,000	1

The first approach in reconstructing the trade union movement is to determine what types of union may be considered suitable for Nigeria. Unions are generally classified under three main headings – craft, industrial and general workers'. The craft union, being an organisation of workers of a particular skill or trade, cannot be considered suitable for Nigeria for two main reasons. There are very few skilled men in any trade in the country, and these few men cannot maintain a union. An ideal union for Nigeria must be self-supporting; it must have the resources – human and material – to render effective service to its members and contribute its quota in community and national affairs. For it to acquire these prerequisites it must have an adequate dues-paying membership potential. No particular skilled trade, except the teaching profession, has that potential. Industrial and general workers' unions appear to be the only types of union suitable for Nigeria. Being organisations which draw their membership from workers employed in the same or similar industries, irrespective of their skill, they offer prospects of adequate dues-paying membership potential and, thus spread the financial burden of running the union over many more heads. If this advantage were coupled with a high dues rate as is the case in other parts of the world, the viability of the union would be assured, which would enable the unions to engage in such beneficial schemes as workers' education and consumer and housing co-operatives, which aid the economic and social development programmes of the nation.

The job of reconstruction may be approached in three ways. Since there is agreement on industrial unionism the first thing is to determine into how many industrial classifications may the industries in Nigeria be classified. In this connection Table 10, the ULC's reconstruction proposals of 1962, and the recommendations of the

Table 10 UNITED LABOUR CONGRESS' RECONSTRUCTION PROPOSALS 1962

No.	*Existing Union*	*Proposed Union*	*Jurisdiction*
	GROUP A–AGRICULTURE, FISHERY & FORESTRY		
1	(i) Dunlop African Workers' Union (ii) Pamol African Workers' Union (iii) Oban (Nigeria) Rubber Estates Employees' Union (iv) S. Thomopolous Workers' Union (v) Forestry & Agricultural Workers' Union (vi) Federal Fisheries Workers' Union (vii) Eastern Fisheries Workers' Union (viii) Union of African Agricultural Technical Workers (ix) Forestry Technical Workers' Union (x) ENDC Workers' Union (xi) WNDC Workers' Union	NIGERIAN UNION OF AGRICULTURAL & ALLIED WORKERS	All classes of workers (manual and non-manual engaged in agriculture (whether farming or livestock rearing), fishing and forestry whether employed by public corporations or private enterprises.
	GROUP B–CATERING		
2	(i) Federal Palace Hotel African Workers' Union (ii) Domestic Workers' Union (iii) Federation of Hotel Workers of Nigeria	CATERING & ALLIED WORKERS UNION	All classes of workers engaged in catering trade including domestic servants.
	GROUP C–COMMERCE, RETAIL & DISTRIBUTION		
3	(i) Barclays Bank DCO African Staff Union (ii) United Bank for Africa Staff Union (iii) Bank of West Africa Staff Union (iv) ACB Staff Union (v) Royal Exchange Assurance African Workers' Union	UNION OF BANK & INSURANCE EMPLOYEES	All classes of workers engaged in banking and insurance industry.

No.	*Existing Union*	*Proposed Union*	*Jurisdiction*
	(GROUP C – *Continued*)		
4	(i) Ollivant African Workers' Union (ii) Holts African Workers' Union (iii) P.Z. African Workers' Union (iv) A.G. Leventise Workers' Union (v) K. Challarams & Sons Ltd. Workers' Union	SHOP, DISTRIBUTIVE & ALLIED WORKERS' UNION	All classes of workers engaged in retail and distributive trades including skilled and unskilled workers engaged in repairing of vehicles employed by companies which combine vehicle distribution and repairs with retail trade in shops.
	GROUP 'D' CONSTRUCTION & WOODWORK		
5	(i) Building & General Employees' Union (ii) Micheletti African Workers' Union (iii) Contract and General Workers' Union (iv) Aiyedade Carpenters' Union (v) Aiyedade Bricklayers' Union (vi) Association of Construction and Civil Engineering Workers of Nigeria (vii) Association of Garage Employees (viii) Costain and Allied Companies Technical and Clerical Workers' Union (ix) Nemco Workers' Union of Nigeria	CONSTRUCTION & GENERAL WORKERS' UNION	All classes of workers engaged in construction work, whether building, road or bridges, employed by various contracting firms foreign and indigenous.

ULC'S RECONSTRUCTION PROPOSALS 1962 (*contd.*)

No.	*Existing Union*	*Proposed Union*	*Jurisdiction*
	(GROUP 'D' – *Continued*)		
6	(i) AT & P Workers' Union (ii) British West African Timber Company African Workers' Union (iii) Nigerian Union of Carpenters and Cabinet Makers	WOOD AND FURNITURE WORKERS' UNION	All classes of workers (save those on managerial or executive position) engaged in wood work either in felling or logging, sawing or furniture manufacture.
	GROUP 'E' DOCKS & SHIPPING		
7	(i) Nigerian Dockers Transport and General Workers' Union (ii) Bakare Dock Workers' Union (iii) Nigerian Stevedores and Dock Workers' Union (iv) Port Harcourt Dock Labour Union	UNION OF NIGERIAN DOCKWORKERS & STEVEDORES	Workers engaged in dock work and stevedoring business at all ports, and dockers in Nigeria, whether employed by public authority or private enterprises.
8	(i) Elder Dempster Lines African Workers' Union (ii) Holland Line African Workers' Union (iii) Nigerian National Line African Workers' Union (iv) Government Coastal Agency Workers' Union (v) French West Africa Lines Workers' Union (vi) Customs and Excise Maritime Staff Union	NIGERIAN UNION OF SHIPPING TRADES WORKERS	Workers engaged in shipping trades whether employed by public authorities or private business enterprises, but does not include seamen.

No.	Existing Union	Proposed Union	Jurisdiction
	GROUP 'F' ENGINEERING & METAL		
9	(i) Electrical Workers' Union (ii) NESCO African Workers' Union (iii) NBC Engineering Workers' Union (iv) ECN Clerical Workers' Union	ELECTRICAL TRADES & ALLIED WORKERS' UNION	Skilled and unskilled workers including white collar workers engaged in electrical trades.
10	(i) BEWAC African Workers' Union (ii) M. & K. African Workers' Union (iii) Joe Allen & Co. African Workers' Union (iv) SCOA Workers' Union	UNION OF AUTOMOBILE ENGINEERING WORKERS	Skilled, semi-skilled and unskilled workers including white collar workers engaged in motor marketing or repairing jobs.
11	(i) Amalgamated African Staff Clerical and Technical Workers of Metal Containers (ii) Dorman Long and Amalgamated Engineering Workers' Union (iii) African Metal Workers' Union	STEEL, METAL & ALLIED WORKERS' UNION	All classes of workers, including white collar workers skilled, semi-skilled, and unskilled, engaged in metal and steel industry.
	GROUP 'G' MINING		
12	(i) Northern Mine Workers' Union (ii) Middle Belt Mine Workers' Union	MINE WORKERS' UNION OF NIGERIA	All classes of workers engaged in mining industry whether coal, tin, zinc, lead, gold or silver, but not including mineral oil.

ULC'S RECONSTRUCTION PROPOSALS 1962 (*contd.*)

No.	*Existing Union*	*Proposed Union*	*Jurisdiction*
	GROUP 'H' MUSIC & ARTS		
13	(i) Nigerian Union of Musicians	NIGERIAN UNION OF MUSICIANS & ARTISTS	All classes of musicians and artists whether employed or self-employed.
	GROUP 'I' PUBLIC SERVICES		
14	(i) Northern Civil Service Union (ii) Eastern Treasury Staff Association (iii) Eastern Nigerian Messengers' Union (iv) Messengers' Northern Region Union (v) Civil Service Union Eastern District (vi) Civil Service Union Western District (vii) Eastern Government Stores Workers' Union	PUBLIC SERVICES CLERICAL & ALLIED WORKERS' UNION	White collar workers (including messengers and cleaners) employed by the various Governments as well as local authorities.
15	(i) Public Utility Technical and General Workers' Union (ii) Eastern Nigeria Land Surveyors Union (iii) Union of Survey Draughtsmen (iv) Northern PWD Workers' Union (v) Civil Service Drivers' Union (vi) Geological Survey Workers (vii) Federal Produce Inspection Technical Staff Union (viii) Produce Inspection Junior Staff Union Eastern Nigeria	PUBLIC SERVICES TECHNICAL & GENERAL WORKERS' UNION	Skilled and unskilled workers employed by the Federal and Regional Governments.

No.	Existing Union	Proposed Union	Jurisdiction
	(GROUP 'I' – *Continued*)		
16	(i) Nigeria Union of Local Authority Staff (ii) Northern NA Staff Association (iii) Tiv NA Workers' Union (iv) Ilorin NA Workers' Union (v) Bornu NA Workers Union (vi) Daura NA Workers' Union (vii) Enugu Municipal Workers' Union (viii) Calabar Divisional District Council Staff Union (ix) Onitsha Urban District Council Workers' Union	NIGERIAN UNION OF LOCAL GOVERNMENT WORKERS	All classes of workers employed by the various local government bodies and local authorities (including skilled and unskilled workers) but not including Medical and Health Workers.
17	(i) Nigerian Nurses' Association (ii) X-Ray Technical Workers' Union (iii) Medical Laboratory African Association (iv) Nigerian Leprosy Service Workers' Union (v) Sanitary Workers' Union (vi) Voluntary Agency Hospital and General Workers' Union (vii) Medical Technical Workers' Union (viii) UCH Technical and General Workers' Union (ix) Northern Nigeria Rural Medical Workers' Union (x) Veterinary Laboratory Technical Staff Union (xi) Union of Animal Health Workers of Nigeria and Cameroons (xii) Nigerian Union of Dental Technologists	NIGERIAN UNION OF MEDICAL & HEALTH WORKERS	All grades of workers engaged in medical and health work whether employed by Government, Public Corporations, Voluntary Agencies, Local Government Bodies or Private Nursing Homes, but not including Doctors, Dentists, Opticians or any other Professional Occupation in the Upper Segment.

ULC'S RECONSTRUCTION PROPOSALS 1962 (*contd.*)

No.	*Existing Union*	*Proposed Union*	*Jurisdiction*
	(GROUP 'I' – *Continued*)		
18	(i) Federal Education Department Workers' Union (ii) Nigerian College of Arts, Science and Technology Technician and General Workers' Union (iii) Rural Training Centre Workers' Union	NIGERIAN UNION OF EDUCATION & GENERAL WORKERS	All classes of workers employed by educational institutions in Nigeria but not including teachers.
	GROUP 'J' TRANSPORT & COMMUNICATION		
19	(i) Nigerian Transport Staff Union (ii) Railway & Ports Transport Staff Union (iii) Train Guards Union (iv) Nigerian Ports Authority Clerical Workers' Union	TRANSPORT (CLERICAL) WORKERS' UNION	White collar workers employed by Nigerian Railway Corporation, Nigerian Ports Authority, Inland Waterways Department or such other employers in the transport industry including air and road.
20	(i) NPA Workers' Union (ii) NPA Labourers' Union (iii) Marine Engineering Assistant and Allied Workers (iv) Railway Technical Staff Association (v) Railway Permanent Way Works Union (vi) Association of Loco. Drivers, Firemen and Allied Workers (vii) Inland Waterways Eng. Workers	TRANSPORT (TECHNICAL) WORKERS' UNION	Skilled and unskilled workers employed by the Nigerian Port Authority, Nigerian Railway Corporation, Inland Waterways Dept. or such other employers in the transport Industry, but not including dock workers.

No.	Existing Union	Proposed Union	Jurisdiction
	(GROUP 'J' – *Continued*)		
21	(i) Marine Floating Staff Union (ii) Deck Staff Union (iii) Delta Pilots' Union (iv) Hydrological Survey Workers' Union (v) NPA Firemen, Greasers, Technical & General Workers' Union (vi) ED Lines Floating Staff Union (vii) Seafarers' Service Union of Nigeria	UNION OF SEAFARING & ALLIED WORKERS	Skilled or unskilled workers engaged in light vessels or launches employed by NPA Inland Waterways Department or private employers in seafaring service.
22	(i) Amalgamated Union of Lagos Bus Workers (ii) Armels Workers' Union (iii) Khalil & Dibbo Bros. Workers' Union (iv) Trans-Arab Workers' Union (v) Nigerian Motor Drivers' Union (vi) Federal Taxi Drivers' Union (vii) Motor Stevedores' and Catering Staff Union (viii) Lagos-Abadan Kia-Kia Bus Drivers' Union (ix) Elias Khawam & Bros. Workers' Union (x) Nigerian Motor Ticket Collectors Workers' Union (xi) Western Region Taxi Drivers' Union (xii) Motor Drivers' Union, Warri (xiii) Sapele Motor Drivers' Union (xiv) Northern Nigeria Motor Drivers' Union	ROAD TRANSPORT AND GENERAL WORKERS' UNION	All classes of workers engaged in road transport industry, whether employed by public Corporations, private enterprises or individuals.
23	(i) P & T Telephonists' Union of Nigeria (ii) Union of Telegraphists, Teleprinters and Phonogram Operators (iii) Aeronautical Workers' Union of Nigeria	COMMUNICATION WORKERS' UNION	Workers in communication industry, whether telephonists or wireless operators.

ULC'S RECONSTRUCTION PROPOSALS 1962 (*contd.*)

No.	*Existing Union*	*Proposed Union*	*Jurisdiction*
	GROUP 'K' OIL, CHEMICAL & GAS		
24	(i) Shell D'Arcy Workers' Union (ii) BP Workers' Union (iii) Consolidated Petroleum Workers of Nigeria (iv) Texaco African Workers' Union (v) Esso Workers' Union (vi) Union of Shell Operatives (vii) Nigerian Cement Industry Workers' Union (viii) Alagbon Workers' Union	OIL, CHEMICAL & ALLIED WORKERS' UNION	All classes of workers engaged in oil chemical and gas industries whether exploratory or marketing, natural or compressed gas.
	GROUP 'L' PRINTING & PAPER		
25	(i) Union of Printers and Allied Workers of Nigeria (ii) Nigerian Printing and Publishing Company Workers' Union (iii) Niger Challenge Staff Association	UNION OF PRINTERS & ALLIED WORKERS	All classes of workers engaged in printing and paper industry but not including editorial staff news and periodicals.
	GROUP 'M' TEXTILE & COTTON		
26	(i) Union of Textile Workers of Nigeria (ii) Northern Textile Workers' Union (iii) Northern African Workers' Union of Messrs. BCGA	UNION OF TEXTILE AND ALLIED WORKERS	All classes of workers engaged in Textile or cotton production.

Morgan Commission of 1964 on the setting-up of joint industrial councils are a fairly good working basis. In making the recommendations, the Morgan commission outlined certain guiding principles which may be adopted with certain modifications in determining the number of unions adequate for Nigeria and demarcating the jurisdiction of each union. In the case of private industry, they said that 'it is important to ensure that the type of industries within the purview of a Joint Industrial Council are sufficiently similar in terms of occupations, activities and general economic conditions. On these grounds, it is important to keep the number of Councils and demarcation of jursidiction between them constantly under review, merging existing ones and establishing others whenever necessary.' The commissioners then recommended the setting up of the following joint industrial councils:

1. *National Joint Whitley Council 'A'* to deal with salaries and conditions of service of administrative, senior professional and technical personnel who fall within a scale of salary the initial point of which is not less than £621 per annum.
2. *National Joint Whitley Council 'B'* to deal with the salaries and conditions of service of the executive, clerical, and junior technical, as well as other grades of occupations, the initial salary of which is below £621 per annum, and excluding persons in the unskilled and semi-skilled labour grades.
3. *National Joint Negotiating Council for Local Authority Staff* to deal with the salaries and conditions of service of all categories of local government and native authority staffs, excluding the unskilled and semi-skilled labour grades.
4. National Joint Negotiating Council for Teachers.
5. Shipping and Shipping Agencies.
6. Stevedore and Docks.
7. Road Transport.
8. Air Transport and Travel Agencies.
9. Mining, Oil Exploration, Production and Refining.
10. Food and Drinks, including Brewing, Mineral Water Production, Food Processing and Animal Foodstuffs.
11. Textile and Clothing Manufacture.
12. Paints, Chemicals, Vegetable Oil Processing.
13. Rubber Manufacturing and Retreading.
14. Cement Manufacture and Concrete Products.
15. Engineering and Metal Products.
16. Agriculture, Timber and Plantations.
17. Commerce, Banking, Insurance and allied trades.

18. Hotels, Catering and Entertainment, excluding Radio and Television.
19. Technical Sales and Services.
20. Petroleum, Gas and Oil Marketing and Distribution.
21. Motor trade.
22. Printing, Information and allied trades, excluding Radio and Television.
23. Building and Civil Engineering.
24. Radio and Television.
25. Marketing Boards and Finance Corporations.
26. Development Corporations.
27. Electricity including Niger Dams Authority.
28. Railway.
29. Ports.
30. Coal.

The second stage in reconstructing the movement may be to find ways and means of reaching agreement on the number of unions considered suitable for the country. The co-operation of all interests (Government, employers and trade unions) is necessary in this exercise to avoid the possibility of one or two of them raising an objection and justifying its action with the charge that Convention 87 of the International Labour Organisation is being violated. Those likely to raise this protest may do well to take a dispassionate look at the matter and ask themselves whether the trade union situation in Nigeria does credit or discredit to the country. If discredit, should Nigerians not try to right one of the wrongs in their society? Those who think that freedom to organise is a licence to trade on that freedom must realise that the administering authorities of a country have power under ILO constitution to take action on any labour matter in the national interest.

The Morgan Commission has recommended the setting-up of thirty joint industrial councils for thirty industrial groups. It can be agreed that one union and one union only be allowed to exist in each industrial classification; that workers engaged in other types of work not falling within any of these industrial classifications can be organised in a general workers' union; and that unions should cater for the interests of all grades of workers not holding managerial or supervisory positions in industry, whether or not such workers are union members. This is an attempt to introduce into industry the concept of majority rule as applied in Government. The question of allowing one union only to exist in an industry is a sad omission in the Nigerian Trade Unions Act. The Uganda Trade Union Ordinance of 1952 specifically provides that the Registrar of Trade Unions shall refuse to register a new union if any other union or employees' association registered under the Ordinance is sufficiently representative or is likely to become sufficiently representative of the interests in respect of which an application is made. The same provision features in the new Trade Unions Act passed by the Uganda Parliament in 1965. Had there been such a provision in the Nigerian Trade Unions Act, there might be fewer unions than there are today.

The third stage is to ensure that the Trade Unions Act is amended or repealed and a new Act incorporating the desired changes introduced. The movement, in co-operation with the Ministry of Labour, should work out a detailed programme for giving practical effect to the fusion of many of the existing unions into the new industrial structure. In doing this, care must be taken not to allow any loopholes for unscrupulous characters to exploit for their own ends. The Government should ensure that existing unions contracting amalgamations must, at amalgamation conferences, and before the election of officers, complete all formalities for surrendering their assets and liabilities to the new organisation. It is not safe, as is proved by experience, to leave these details to the initiative and goodwill of office-bearers of existing unions, some of whom may be defeated in the elections that follow. These people will exploit their defeat in order to obstruct the smooth working of the amalgamation. To avoid this embarrassment the new Trade Unions Act should contain a similar provision like Section 5 (1) (*d*) of the Uganda Trade Unions Act, 1965. Provision should also be made for the Registrar of Trade Unions, whenever he is in doubt as to the representativeness of a union, to conduct an election in any industry, establishment or company to determine the views of workers. This is necessary for two reasons. Splits have quite often occurred in Nigerian unions because of the workers' opposition to bad leadership. Workers try as best they can to change a bad leader, and every attempt is frustrated by undemocratic methods of conducting union meetings, and by the bribery and corruption of the membership or of trusted leaders. Secondly, there may be occasional jurisdictional disputes between an industrial and a general workers' union. When such a dispute arises it is necessary to obtain the views of the workers concerned as to which union they wish to join, and which union should therefore be certified for collective bargaining purposes. Such an election must be by secret ballot, and decision should be by a simple majority of 51 per cent of the total number of people voting.

If the problems of multiplicity of individual unions have been solved, the problem of more than one national centre remains. The National Labour Advisory Council appointed a sub-committee in 1965 to review the Trade Unions Act and make recommendations. One recommendation of that Committee was that the national trade union centres should come within the ambit of the Trade Unions Act. This means that they must be registered and, when registered, must comply with the provisions of the Act. The condition for registration of a national trade union centre is that it should command the support of 40 per cent of all registered trade unions in the country. The committee said its aim was to achieve one national centre. If this was in fact the aim, then some of the most important conditions for achieving that objective have been either forgotten or ignored. In the first place 40 per cent is not by any consideration majority support. In the second place a simple majority is difficult if not impossible to attain under present conditions in Nigeria unless membership of the national trade union centre is made mandatory for all registered trade unions. This is dangerous and not worthy of consideration because in certain respects it violates Convention 87 of the ILO. A way out seems to be a change in Government policy. If the Government recognises a national trade union centre, it must, as is the practice all over the world, deal with that national centre and that national centre alone in all labour matters. On no account must it deal with so-called 'neutral' or 'independent' unions. The failure of the First Republic to stick to this policy was one of the things that bedevilled all efforts to achieve unity in the national centre. Individuals looking for patronage went about shouting slogans of 'independence' and 'neutrality' and frustrated every effort of their organisations to team up with other unions to form a strong national centre in the country. Politicians who did not know the undercurrents were carried away by these slogans, and frequently appointed nominees from these unions to policy-making and advisory bodies set up by the Government. In some instances they were selected to represent Nigerian workers on Nigerian delegations to ILO conferences. In other parts of the world governments accept the principle of labour representation on public boards in the belief that organised labour has a contribution to make in national and community affairs; that contribution is made through their chosen representatives. It follows therefore that, if the workers or their representatives are denied the right to choose these representatives, the objective is defeated.

Unity in the national centre is only one of several of the Nigerian labour movement's problems. A foreign observer said early in 1966 that Nigerian workers had trade unions but no trade union movement. What he meant, briefly, was that Nigerian workers and their individual unions had not cultivated that loyalty, discipline and mass support, moral and financial, for their national centres which characterise the trade union movements of Western democracies where there are free trade unions – in which the majority of Nigerian workers believe.

By far the greatest problem facing the trade union movement in Nigeria is how to procure adequate income with which to function. Table 11 shows the income and expenditure of the United Labour Congress of Nigeria, the largest of Nigeria's four national centres, from April 1, 1963 to May 3, 1965. The information from the ULC gives a representative picture of the financial position of the trade union movement. Table 11 seems to confirm one of the allegations often made in the country that the Nigerian labour movement is almost wholly financed from outside, which, to say the least, is a sad reflection on Nigerian nationhood. Apart from the fact that it weakens Nigeria's position internationally, it also constantly puts Nigerians in the embarrassing position of defending the indefensible and inviting derision whenever they try to prove that in this matter he who pays the piper does not necessarily call the tune.

Table 11

UNITED LABOUR CONGRESS OF NIGERIA: INCOME AND EXPENDITURE APRIL 1, 1963, TO MARCH 31, 1965

Year	*Affiliation Fees*			*Dues*			*ICFTU Grants*			*Total Income*			*Total Expenditure*		
	£	s.	d.	£	s.	d.	£	s.	d.	£	s.	d.	£	s.	d.
1963	22	1	0	744	2	0	8,788	3	5	9,554	6	5	10,861	9	2
1964	15	15	0	179	4	11	3,564	5	2	3,659	5	1	3,290	12	4
1965	12	12	0	48	15	8	1,748	0	2	1,799	7	10	1,880	19	7

Why do Nigerian workers and their unions not support their national centres financially? There are probably five main reasons. First, the national centres have hardly functioned in a manner that would inspire their affiliates willingly to pay their dues. Officers are not often available to render services when needed; the secretariats are often closed at times when it is convenient for workers to call seeking advice and guidance on pressing problems which they expect the national centres to help them solve. Secondly, the general administration and in particular the financial administration of the organisation is so inefficient that the unions think it sheer waste to continue paying money which would not be properly handled. This, strictly, is not a convincing argument for unions to refuse payment of dues, but emphasises the need to keep a watchful eye on the management of union money and for unions to insist that qualified and trustworthy people be voted into office or appointed to financial positions. Thirdly, there has been hardly any firmness in handling the financial affairs of the national centres. From the days of the first Trades Union Congress of Nigeria to the present four national centres, no leader has had the courage to apply that provision of the constitution of the national centres which stipulates that affiliated unions in default of dues payment for a given period should be penalised. One leader after another has succumbed to the blackmail that if this clause of the constitution is invoked it would scare away member unions. The problem has been aggravated by the perennial divisions in the labour movement, and has strengthened the blackmailers and lessened their scruples still further. Fourthly, the financial assistance given by ICFTU and other international bodies would appear to have been a disincentive for dues payment. Until these aids began pouring in to Nigeria, unions were at least trying their best to keep their organisations going, though in a modest way, by paying their dues and other subscriptions. One of the main causes of dissension in the TUC(N) in early 1962 was a statement made by a leading trade unionist at a meeting of the Congress' Central Executive when the meeting was discussing TUC(N) finances. To him ICFTU affiliation would have a meaning the day grants from the ICFTU International Solidarity Fund would be shared out to affiliated unions and their leaders. Fifthly, there have been instances or allegations of fraud and misappropriation of funds in the national centres; Nigerian workers and their organisations are easily carried away by allegations of this nature. Often the allegations may relate to monies which the workers did not contribute, yet they engage in endless recriminations over other people's money. A leading trade unionist in recent years threatened to campaign against further payment of dues to a national centre because, according to him, the responsible officers had failed to render a satisfactory statement of account of the monies received from an international organisation.

The attitude of some Nigerian trade union leaders to financial assistance from abroad raises a number of questions about the aids themselves. Why the aids? Is the obtaining of money the main consideration determining the international relations of Nigerian trade unions? In view of the hostile propaganda made out of the financial assistance received from international organisations, should these organisations not be called upon to stop their aids or subject it to critical review? Financial aid is now coming to Nigerian trade unions from many sources. The free trade unions of the world are making contributions through the ICFTU, the affiliates of the International Federation of Christian Trade Unions (now the World Confederation of Labour) contributing their own quota through the IFCTU, while the communists are making theirs through the WFTU, its affiliates and other communist front organisations. The main reason for this aid was to help the recipient organisations to organise for strength. It was never intended that any of the donor organisations should take over the responsibilities of the workers of Nigeria to finance their own organisations. If the purpose of the aid has been misunderstood, if the workers of Nigeria have taken the benevolent gesture of international organisations as a licence not to support their organisations, then the fault is not necessarily that of the donor organisations or a case against international aid, which was offered in a sincere spirit of international solidarity. It is a sad reflection both on those who lead and those who follow in the unions.

It has often been said that getting money is the main consideration determining the international relations of Nigerian trade union organisations. Gogo Nzeribe asserted this in an interview with a Lagos magazine.[1] How true is this assertion? Until 1959 the Nigerian labour movement did not accept money from any international trade union organisation, although individual trade union leaders had been lining their pockets. In 1951 an ICFTU visiting mission reported that it was very much impressed that the labour movement in Nigeria declined financial aid, saying that it wanted to finance its own operations from its own resources. 'Credit', it said, 'must be given to the unions for not wishing any direct financial aid, because, they claim, although the struggle will be hard, it is the more honourable way and most likely to have the desired lasting stability'.[2] As had been stated earlier, the decision to accept financial assistance was taken to make it impossible for certain individuals in the labour movement to continue endlessly to trade with the name of Nigerian workers. It is not easy to say with certainty what other organisations have done or are planning to do. But the ICFTU seems to be keeping to its policy that financial aid to its affiliate is temporary. As will be seen from Table 11, ICFTU aid has been diminishing since 1963. Lawrence Borha, ULC General Secretary, seemed to have seen the handwriting on the wall when he warned:

> The time has come for Nigerian workers to decide whether they want a trade union at all and, if they do, to be told in plain pointed language that it is their responsibility to finance the run-

ning of their organisations; that they cannot shirk their responsibility and yet expect to have a stable, virile and effectively serviceable trade union organisation. We must seriously remind ourselves that we cannot eat our cake and have it. The present subscription rate of one penny per member per month is probably the lowest subscription rate in the world payable to a national centre. It is regrettable that a wage-earner, however low his pay packet, should be so unwilling or claim inability to pay one penny every month or one shilling per annum for the services he derives for his membership in his union or of the Congress. The conference should be aware that the Central Executive has taken the attitude that while it will continue to uphold ULC affiliation to the ICFTU, it proposes henceforth to unburden the ICFTU (and those workers of the free labour world who subscribe the finances of the great International) of continued financial support to the ULC. Thus we must make up our minds to face the inevitable, namely that our members must provide the funds for the administration and maintenance not only of their individual unions but also of their national trade union centre.[3]

It seems that diminishing financial aid is a step towards total withdrawal. This raises the all-important question of financing Nigerian centres when international aid is withdrawn. For good or ill, the national centres have existed since 1959 on the sufferance of international aid. Without this aid there might have been no national centres in Nigeria. If the aid must be cut off, an alternative means must be found of financing the national centres; otherwise Nigerian workers might as well say good-bye to national centres. The traditional way of financing national trade union centres is regular payment of dues by its affiliates. So far this has not worked in Nigeria mainly because affiliated unions either do not see the need to pay, or pressure has not been put on them to do so. In some cases failure to pay has been due to the laziness or neglect of duty of certain officers or officials, who get away with their shortcomings because the membership seldom expresses displeasure or tries to see that an unwilling official is disciplined. In such a situation as this, dues collection may be tackled in two ways. One way is for the affiliated unions to complete a bankers' order (in triplicate: one copy to their bankers, another to the national centre and the third for their own records), which should be varied annually to reflect union membership and turnover. Another way is the deduction of union dues at source: it should be worked out what percentage of a worker's union dues should be paid to the national centre, and on this basis the affiliated union and the national centre can agree to ask an employer operating check-off to deduct the amount due to the national centre and remit it direct to the organisation or its bankers. This is the arrangement in Ghana. The constitution of the new Ghana TUC provides that 35 per cent of the union dues paid by a worker shall be paid to the TUC, to which the employers remit it after deducting it from the proceeds of the check-off. A similar arrangement in Nigeria would go far towards solving the financial problems of national centres.

How does democracy work in Nigerian trade unions? Union democracy means that all members have an equal right to participate in deliberations on union affairs; that decisions must be made by the responsible officers or properly constituted meetings of the appropriate organs of the union structure; that at union meetings decisions are taken by majority vote; that when once a decision has been made every member of the union has to comply, whether or not he was in favour of the original proposition leading to the decision; that, although the majority will have its way, the right of the minority to express its views is not only recognised but seen to be preserved; that all members have an equal right to vote and to be voted for, to hold office, to express their views on the activities of the union and its officers and finally to be consulted on the conduct of union business. It also means that, while union members have the right to criticise the work of those they employ to serve them, full-time salaried officials must be given freedom of action to discharge their responsibilities to the best of their abilities and in the interests of the union.

To observe some Nigerian unions at work is to appreciate the difficulties of the trade union movement. It is not uncommon to see that only a certain group of persons catches the chairman's eye at union meetings, namely those most likely to rubber-stamp the performance of the officers; individuals likely to question why certain things were done or not done may never be noticed. If by chance the critics win recognition and vent their spleen, they go down in the black list as persons subverting the union and its leadership. There are, of course, those critics who never see anything good in the union or in the performances of union leadership – usually, who are angling for office. To them nothing is right unless they have done it themselves. They exploit every mistake, and show no scruples in creating the impression that, if they are given an opportunity, there will be some improvement. Often they get this opportunity, but it is at this stage that workers find that all that glitters is not gold. At some union meetings, matters are so arranged that certain persons may never be heard at all. They may be recognised by the chairman, and given an opportunity to speak, but their contributions to a debate are drowned by noise specially organised for the purpose, or by shouts of 'Sit down'. Behind this ugly performance may be the principal officers of the union.

One of the commonest complaints heard from Nigerian trade union members is that they or the competent organs of the unions are seldom consulted before certain major decisions are taken. It has often been alleged, for example, that the question of affiliation, national and international, is invariably decided by the General Secretary and the President and sometimes by the former alone; whether a given union should affiliate to NTUC or ULC, NWC or LUF therefore depends largely on the inclination of those officers. This appears to explain why splits often occur when there is disagreement between individual union leaders, and why unity moves in Nigeria often begin and end with union secretaries and not with organisations.

A matter which seems to be causing much concern among union members is the method which, they claim, some union leaders adopt to keep themselves in office when it has become clear that they are no longer wanted by the workers. The story has been told of how a union secretary who knew he might be out by the next union conference defeated the plan. He sent notices of the conference to branches. A few days before the conference he sent another notice announcing a change of venue, but made sure that only those branches he wanted to attend the conference got the second notice. The result was that union delegates gathered at two different places for one conference. The conference held at the second venue did his bidding: it reaffirmed his appointment and elected a new President. Today he is no longer with the union, and the union has been deregistered for a violation of the Trade Unions Act which took place during his tenure; he tells of the deregistration of the union with glee. In another case the fear that they might be thrown out made a union secretary and his entire executive refuse to convene an annual conference for three years. In the end they could not avoid calling one, but when they did not a soul turned up. All the branches of the union had passed votes of no confidence in the secretary and the executive. The efforts of the Registrar of Trade Unions to persuade the members to attend the conference and show their disapproval by voting them out failed.

Some union officers retain their offices by bribery and corruption of union members. Those bribed and those bribing them often betray the fact during election periods. One man makes a nomination, another seconds, and a third shouts 'Unopposed'. As soon as some one shouts 'Unopposed' the whole conference hall becomes rowdy. No opportunity is given to a prospective contestant to come forward. You would think it is a spontaneous reaction from people who appreciate services done, but in fact it is all staged, and at a very high price.

There have been complaints that union members who dare to criticise their leaders are often victimised by these leaders. In some unions fear of victimisation seems to envelop an otherwise vociferous group. For example, in 1962, a branch official criticised the General Secretary of his union and accused him of anti-union activities, introducing politics into Nigerian trade unionism, misuse of union funds, and being the good boy of the Western block and the Federal Government. The accusations were made at a union meeting. The Secretary took legal proceedings against his accuser, claiming £10,000 damages for slander. In his statement of claim the plaintiff said that the defendant meant and was understood to mean that he was 'grossly inefficient, dishonest and unfit for his office as General Secretary' and that he was 'guilty of abuse of office and therefore not worthy of the high office of trust to which he [had] been appointed'.[4]

What began as a trifle and was probably regarded by many union members as an attempt by office-seekers to remove a popular trade union leader became an important law case, and has often been quoted – in certain Nigerian trade union circles – as the reward of courage. Three issues arose out of this case. The first was whether or not a union member or official could be sued and the action entertained by any court of law for a tortious act committed by the member or the official in the course of his union activity. Mr. Justice Reed found that the relevant portion of the Trade Unions Act did not give any immunity to individual members of a union. He cited *Bussy* vs. *the Amalgamated Society of Railway Servants and Bell*, when an English court ruled that 'an action will lie against a member or official of a trade union for a tort committed by him when acting on behalf of himself and all other members of the unions 1906 Acts, 4, only preventing him from being so sued as to render the trade union as such and its funds liable for the tortious act'.

The second issue was whether an action could lie against a union member or official for words uttered at a union meeting attended only by union members, and whether the occasion was privileged as pleaded by the defendant. The court found that what the defendant said related entirely to the plaintiff's fitness to hold office and that 'the fitness of the General Secretary to hold office is a matter of interest to all members of the union. One member of the union has an interest to make a communication on this subject and other members have an interest in receiving that communication. I find, therefore, that the occasion was privileged.'

The third issue was to what extent union members were free to exercise their right to examination and criticism of the performances of their leaders if to exercise that right was to render oneself liable to legal proceedings. It is impossible that the plaintiff's motive for going to court was to get £10,000 from a poor worker, though there is doubt as to whether he could have rejected if it had been awarded by the court. Most likely he went to court primarily to salvage his name and reputation, which he felt had been tarnished by the defendant's utterances. Probably this is one of those few cases when what is legally sound may not be morally justified. The outcome of the case was most disappointing for the plaintiff who lost on both the swings and the roundabouts. The judge emphasised the Court's finding as follows: 'I repeat my finding. It is that the plaintiff was inefficient and unfit for his office as the General Secretary of the Union; that he was not a desirable person for the office and guilty of abuse of office and was therefore not worthy of the high office of trust to which he had been appointed.' The claim was therefore dismissed. Since 1963, the judgment in this case has been powerful ammunition in the hands of the plaintiff's rivals, and has been used to discredit him and members and leaders of any trade union organisation with which he is connected.

A good deal of controversy has arisen in many unions from conflicting interpretations of that clause of the union constitution which authorises the president to 'superintend the work of the union'. This is part of the specimen constitution distributed to workers in the early days of unionism and adopted wholesale by them; very few, if any, of the unions have bothered to improve upon it. Should the President order the General Secretary in the exercise of his functions or should both officers consult and take decisions jointly? Is the General Secretary answerable to the President or to the union Executive? Where workers have confidence in their President, the tendency seems to be for the General Secretary's position to be reduced to that of a glorified clerk, who does only what he is told. The situation is worsened when the President is of the bossy or big chief type, who regards the union as his personal property, in which case the Secretary must always do his bidding or things will be made uncomfortable for him. According to B. M. Udokporo, the problems of the Nigerian labour movement are compounded by:

(i) lack of funds to maintain paid trade union officials;
(ii) vulnerability of paid officials to the votes of no confidence which can be trumped up at any meeting of the union through personal dislikes;
(iii) suspicions based on friendship with management staff;
(iv) willingness of the paid official to allow himself to be used as a political tool.[5]

On the other hand where there is confidence in the Secretary, this confidence may be abused. It is not uncommon to hear of union secretaries being accused of demanding and collecting bribes from their members as a condition for taking up their grievances. Some union officials have also been accused of 'selling out' to managements and politicians and thereby compromising the claims of workers. Apparently it was some glaring abuses of this kind that compelled a group of young trade union leaders, who had attended courses at the ICFTU African Labour College in Kampala, Uganda, to adopt a code of ethics to regulate the conduct of trade union leaders in Nigeria. Article 12 of the African Labour College Alumni Association, Nigeria Branch, reads:

Code of Ethics

The Association exists to render service to the workers and the country, and to promote better understanding among the people of Nigeria. To be able to do so, members must be men of integrity. Every member of the Association shall, therefore, pledge, to conform to the following code of ethical practices:

(i) he shall live among the workers, take part in their activities, and at all times identify himself with their aspirations;
(ii) he shall at all times preach and practise and help to promote the practice or brotherhood wherever he may be, and condemn tribalism and other vices which militate against the attainment of national unity;
(iii) if he is a union official or representative he shall discharge the responsibilities of his office to the best of his ability, and on time;
(iv) as a union leader or representative he shall not demand or receive, either in cash or in kind, compensation or reward (other than the salary and/or allowances attached to his position) for rendering service to his union members – service which he is required to render by virtue of his office;
(v) he shall not demand or receive, and his spouse and children

shall not demand or receive, any reward in cash or in kind, from any employer whose workers' interests he represents;

(vi) in times of trade disputes or threatened trade dispute he shall not accept any gift or reward from any employer, politician, political party, religious denomination, government or government agency;

(vii) he shall not misappropriate union funds or be party to any plan which is tantamount to cheating his union or any other trade union organisation and its members;

(viii) whenever he is voted out of office in his union or in any other trade union organisation in which he holds an office by a properly constituted competent organ of that organisation, he shall within 30 days of the decision, hand over to his successor all the property of the organisation in his possession; shall offer his successor full co-operation and shall refrain from organising a splinter group or subverting the organisation and its leadership;

(ix) he shall, in the interest of the workers and the trade union movement in general, avoid excessive drinking and other immoral involvements;

(x) he shall defend and at all times champion the cause of free and democratic trade unionism in Nigeria and throughout the world.

From time to time the trade union movement has been reminded of the important role it has to play in the social and economic development of Nigeria. To be able to play that role, it must engage in extensive workers' educational activity. Much has been done in this direction, but when this is compared with the need, it can be said that only a beginning has been made. It is not uncommon to see top union officials who do not know what collective agreements are and what some of their main contents should be. There are many union functionaries who have not seen the Trade Union Act, let alone knowing its provisions. Amalgamations have been contracted in Nigeria and then broken out of hand by one of the parties without any reprisals because all the statutory requirements were not complied with during the amalgamation process. Sometimes the breach is organised by paid officials who fail to secure certain positions in the amalgamated body. There are still many union functionaries who think that union money can be spent in any manner they please or that correspondence addressed to them in virtue of their position is their personal property.

In the early stages, labour education was carried out by government officials. Between 1949 and 1951, the Government took a bold step by awarding scholarships in trade unionism tenable in the United Kingdom, and among the beneficiaries of this were B. E. Andem of the UNAMAG, W. K. Garber of the Nigerian Marine African Workers' Union, A. Joseph of the Amalgamated Union of Clerical and Allied Workers, R. N. Okoli of the African Loco Drivers' Union, V. D. Uwemedimo of the Nigerian Civil Service Union, E. O. Songonuga of the Association of Railway Civil Servants, A. F. A. Awolana of the Nigeria Union of Teachers, J. W. Wamuo of the Township Workers' Union, Eastern and Western Provinces, Abubakar Usman of the Gaskiya African Staff Union and N. M. Agada of the Federal Union of Native Authority Staff. The overseas scholarship scheme was abandoned after 1951 because the trade union movement itself did not benefit from it; rather the beneficiaries took the awards as springboards for higher ambitions. On their return from the United Kingdom they accepted better-paid positions either with the Government or with employers in the private sector. Some of those who wanted to remain found it extremely difficult to do so because of the teething problems of the movement. The Extra-Mural Department of the University of Ibadan has been trying since 1952 to fill the gap by organising short courses in industrial relations.

Since 1958 labour education has been carried out mostly by the ICFTU African Labour College in Kampala, Uganda, and the Nigerian affiliates of the ICFTU which, in succession, have been the National Council of Trade Unions of Nigeria, the Trades Union Congress of Nigeria and the United Labour Congress. From 1958 to June 1966, sixty trade union leaders have attended training courses at the Labour College. Most of these men are now holding important positions in various trade unions in the country.

Apart from those attending the regular courses organised by the College, many more Nigerian trade unionists have attended short-term residential courses organised by the national centre in collaboration with the Extra-Mural Department of the Labour College. After 1964 the International League for Social and Co-operative Development had been reinforcing efforts in this direction. Aided by two Nigerian assistants, Mrs. Barbara G. Bowen had been conducting workers' educational classes in the four Regions of Nigeria and the Federal Territory of Lagos. Workers' education reached a milestone in April 1966 with the opening of the Trade Union Institute for Social and Economic Development, jointly sponsored by the African–American Labour Centre and the United

Labour Congress of Nigeria. Its first intake of students was drawn from unions affiliated to the ULC.

Other national centres have also made some efforts in the field of labour education. Some Nigerian trade unionists and other persons not connected with the labour movement have found their way on scholarship to the Soviet Union, East Germany, Czechoslovakia, Bulgaria and the People's Republic of China through the aegis of the Nigerian Trade Union Congress. Although estimates vary, it is generally believed that the number is now over 300. The scholarship winners study various subjects including pure trade union subjects and the fundamentals of Marxism–Leninism. In 1963 the Nigerian Workers' Council organised a seminar in Lagos attended by twenty-five trade unionists; in 1964 it organised another seminar at Aba, and in January 1965 announced that it was building a labour college for Nigerian workers. A parcel of land was acquired along the Ikeja airport road, and a huge signboard was erected.

From this it is clear that the Nigerian trade union movement attaches great importance to workers' education, and in view of what has been done so far, it can be said that the crying need is being met. There is, however, a missing link in the whole exercise. Hitherto the educational programme has been geared towards leadership training. Membership training is just beginning, but for it to have the proper impact it must be tailored to fit the needs of individual unions. Needs are not uniform, neither are problems.

The future of the labour movement cannot be considered in isolation from industrial relations in the country. For it is in this field, more than in any other, that labour's contribution to national economic growth can be measured. In a developing economy such as ours, requiring maximum utilisation of scarce capital resources, development efforts can be adversely affected if the relationship between management and labour is strained. Nearly all authorities in industrial relations agree that differences between management and labour can best be resolved at round-table discussions and that agreements so reached by both sides and signed by them are probably the best kind of settlement that can be reached in any industrial dispute. The machinery for such an exercise is what the authorities call the joint industrial council. As we have seen, the Morgan Commission Report recommended the setting up of joint industrial councils for thirty industrial groups and gave indication of the objectives the councils should endeavour to achieve. The call for the setting up of JIC's is supported only to conform with tradition, JIC's being one of the traditions adopted from British industrial practice. Strictly speaking management and labour do not require a specially constituted and defined machinery to be able to meet and discuss their differences. What they require is the recognition of each other's rights and aspirations. In particular management must recognise that workers, through their organisations, have the right to share in decision-making affecting conditions of employment in the work place. The refusal by certain employers to recognise this right has been the cause of many labour disputes resulting in strikes. Most industrialised countries of the world faced a similar problem at certain points of their history, and tried to solve it by making recognition of trade unions obligatory. Nigeria can do the same. She can go further by removing some of the most obvious causes of industrial disputes in the country. To do this, a permanent machinery must be created for the periodical review of wages and salaries; employers' and workers' organisations must bargain in good faith; employers and employers' organisations must at all times bargain with unions through representatives of their own choosing; and union membership must approve collective agreements before they are signed.

How do JIC's function and how many workers are covered by collective agreements? The Morgan Commission Report contains the astonishing revelation that only 66,000 workers out of a working population of over one million are covered by collective agreements, the distribution being as follows:

Mining Industry	40,000
United Africa Company	8,340
Plantation industry	6,000
Shell-BP	2,300
Nigerian Tobacco Company	1,954
Union Trading Company	1,600

Practices may vary in minor details, but as a rule the JIC's function as follows. Their membership is regulated as follows. The chairman is usually drawn from the employers' side, the vice-chairman from the workers' side. There are joint secretaries, one from the employers' and another from the employees' side. The council considers claims brought up by the workers, or any matter which the employer may refer to it. At meetings the employer provides stenographers to take notes, from which draft minutes are prepared and circulated to joint secretaries for vetting. Then the final minutes are prepared and circulated to members of the council. When at a subsequent meeting the minutes are adopted, they become agreements between the employer and the workers. Only in a few cases have proper collective agreements containing wages rates, hours of work and general conditions of employment been drawn up and signed.

This system has many pitfalls. First, where formal agreements are concluded, both sides engage in time-wasting duplication of activity which could have been avoided had union proposals been made in the form of draft collective agreements, and negotiations based on that draft rather than on the usual lengthy memoranda arguing a case, which any way is usually argued again at negotiation meetings. Secondly, the minutes are often usually loosely worded and thus open to various interpretations. Employers, it must be said, are aware of the privilege that accrues to them in being responsible for producing the minutes; they are also aware of the educational limitations of many trade union leaders. The following extract from the minutes of a JIC meeting is a case in point:

> The Executive Director accepted the union's proposal in respect of subordinate staff to be subject to eight hours work per day from Monday to Friday, but with five hours on Saturday. He also agreed that overtime should be paid for those employees called upon to work in excess of those hours and the union left to his discretion the question of suitable rates.[6]

Thirdly, JIC minutes cannot be easily distributed to workers to enable them to know their rights and obligations, to do this would be expensive and cumbersome. Yet it is generally recognised in modern industrial relations practice that the worker must know his rights and obligations at the place of work. These rights and obligations are contained in the comprehensive collective agreement which not only outlines wage rates, overtime rates, leave conditions, medical facilities and other conditions of employment, but also provides a procedure for the orderly and speedy disposal of grievances without disruption of work or the general economic process through strikes. In most industrialised countries these collective agreements are jointly printed by employers and workers' organisations and distributed to every worker covered by the agreement.

Few of the collective agreements in the country contain a grievance procedure clause. There have been complaints against existing grievance machinery: either the steps that have to be taken are too many or the time spent at each step is so long that it takes an absurdly long time to dispose of a simple grievance. Trade unions have often reported that grievances can take as long as six, nine or twelve months to settle. Surely a worker who has been discharged from his work or is suspended for one reason or another wants to know within a reasonable time whether or not he stands a chance of coming back to his work. That time should not be longer than one month. This brings us to the statutory provisions for disposal of disputes and how they operate. The Trade Disputes Act requires the Federal Ministry of Labour to enquire into the causes and circumstances of disputes before appointing a conciliator. If conciliation fails, either party may request that the dispute be referred to an arbitrator or to an arbitration tribunal. At every stage of this procedure, the civil service machinery works at a characteristically slow pace. When the dispute reaches arbitration stage, matters slow down even further. Some arbitrators take three to four months to make an award, and it then sometimes takes almost as long again for the award to be published. A situation such as this opens the door to suspicion, frustration and loss of confidence in arbitration as an effective instrument for resolving disputes. It is this suspicion and this frustration that is responsible for the very unfortunate impression that prevails in some trade union circles that arbitrators are 'bought', and some of their awards are not based on the merits of the cases presented before them but dictated by considerations arising from behind-the-scenes manouvres by unscrupulous employers.

Without necessarily defending Nigerian arbitrators, certain facts must be borne in mind when considering the probability or otherwise of arbitrators being influenced by bribery and corruption. In the first place the unions must realise that in practical life it is not possible for them always to get everything they ask for. Secondly, an arbitrator wants facts or justification for a claim. This proof or justification is not always forthcoming from unions, because of the way they either prepare or present their cases. There are probably two reasons for this. Many unions lack the trained personnel to handle complicated cases coming before an arbitrator; the precarious financial position of most unions makes it impossible for them to secure the services of men competent to do a good job for them. The employer is not in this position, which must partly explain why he appears to be more often favoured by arbitration awards. Another reason why unions lose many cases is that obviously weak cases are often referred to arbitration against expert advice, either because of pressure brought by the union membership or the insistence of the union leadership. Quite often General Secretaries who insist that matters be referred to an arbitrator do so to keep up the morale of union members and get them to continue to support the union financially, knowing fully well that workers tend to give their fullest support to their unions at the time of struggles with their employer.

A new industrial relations system must seek to remove the weakness of the present system. Unfortunately the recommendations, with particular reference to industrial relations, of the Sub-Committee appointed by the National Labour Advisory Council in 1965, to review the labour laws of the country with a view to codifying them into one Industrial Relations Act, is not helpful enough. The Committee made two important recommendations. The first was that an industrial court be established which would be the highest body to adjudicate in industrial disputes. The chairman and vice-chairman of the court were to be legal men appointed on the advice of the Chief Justice of the Federation; one member must be an expert in commerce and industry and another be an economist. No provision was made for labour representation, or for an expert in industrial relations. The committee's second recommendation was that key industries like the railways, docks and municipal transport be included in the essential services list, which meant the imposition of compulsory arbitration in these industries and the denial of the right to strike. Whatever the merits of an industrial court, it suffers from one weakness which is that it takes a very long time to settle a case. The experience of Kenya is relevant here. To establish an industrial court is therefore to perpetuate what Nigeria should try to avoid. It is sad that, at a time when every step should be taken to secure progress through sound industrial relations, machinery for that purpose should be conceived and provisions made for the representation of other interests to the utter neglect of organised labour.

The recommendation that key industries be included in the essential services list is undoubtedly prompted by a desire to achieve industrial peace. Absolute industrial peace is illusory. As David L. Cole, one of America's leading industrial arbitrators has said, 'industrial peace in the absolute sense is a practical impossibility. It is unrealistic to expect it. But this does not mean that the people engaged in labour relations should therefore regard efforts to move towards a better basis of understanding as a futile exercise.'[7] The road to industrial peace is not compulsory arbitration or punitive measures. Dr. T. M. Yesufu has rightly pointed out that 'complete government control, on the other hand, would be a mark of totalitarian state. Yet, even where there is an approach to the existence of such a state in the modern world, there have been practical difficulties which make it impossible for the government actually to regulate and administer the detailed conditions of employment.'[8]

An objective approach to sound industrial relations in Nigeria is to take organised labour more and more into confidence. In this connection it would not be out of place for Nigeria to look beyond British tradition for a guide. Special interest should be paid by all sides to industrial relations practice in the Scandinavian countries and in North America. The ICFTU African Labour College in Kampala, the Trade Union Institute for Economic and Social Development and Nigerian institutions of higher learning engaged in the study of labour relations have important roles to play in this respect. Only by serious study of other systems can Nigeria fashion a system which is not a slavish adoption of any particular system but geared to suit the social, economic and political realities of Nigeria.

In view of the adverse effects it has had on the development of effective and dynamic trade union movement in the country, the time seems to have arrived for the labour movement to make a final ruling on the connections between trade unions and politics. The clause in the settlement of 1959, that the movement as such shall not be part of any political party but that individual union leaders and members were free to believe in any brand of political ideology, is not strong enough. Almost every trade union movement in the world has had to make a decision aimed at safeguarding itself. The Ghana Trades Union Congress did so when, after being Nkrumah's tool for many years, it emerged again as a free agent of the workers of Ghana on June 5, 1966. On that day an extraordinary congress adopted a new constitution which provided that, 'while recognising and preserving the right of members for exercising their civil rights in the affairs of the nation, the Secretary General and top officials of Congress shall not hold office in any political organisation'. 'Top officials' were defined as the Chairman of the Executive Board, Heads of Departments, Presidents and General Secretaries of affiliated unions and Regional Organisers.

The Nigerian labour movement can make a similar ruling, and add that no full-time salaried official of a trade union, whether individual union or a national centre, should be a parliamentarian. If any such person wants to enter Parliament he should either quit the union job on election by resigning his post or be granted leave without pay during the life of the Parliament. Champions of individual freedom may argue that this is a denial of a fundamental human right, but it is not. In any case there is no such thing as an absolute right: every right is relative. Whether trade union leaders should engage actively in politics or become parliamentarians must be considered against the needs of the unions and of the movement as a whole. What the workers of Nigeria need at present is not an endless prayer to administering authorities to grant wage increases and improved conditions of service, which employers in the private sector can emulate. They need instead to 'organise for strength, educate for knowledge', and use the combined asset to strengthen their bargaining position. To achieve that objective, union officials, be they secretaries or organisers, must devote their attention to their jobs. This is what they are paid for. They cannot render this essential service if they develop split loyalties, such as inevitably follow election to Parliament.

A union leader elected to Parliament has a duty to his electorate as well as to his employers, the union. On the one side of the account he has a duty to consult his electorate on issues before going to Parliament, and report back when Parliament is over – exercises that may take several days. On the other side of the account he has a duty to render service to the union from which he derives his living. With the best will in the world he cannot carry out both functions efficiently. One is bound to be sacrificed to the other. Experience so far has shown that the union is always on the losing side.

REFERENCES

1. *The Spear*, February 1966.
2. Report to ICFTU Executive Board (Document 4EB/12).
3. General Secretary's Report to ULC Congress, 1963.
4. Judgement in Suit No. JD/12/63, Alhaji Haroun Popoola Adebola Vs. Clement Kunle Babayemi in Jos High Court before Mr. Justice N. V. Reed, Acting Senior Psune Judge.
5. 'Problems of Trade Unions in Nigeria' (lecture delivered by B. M. Udokporo at the University of Nigeria, Nsukka).
6. Minutes of a meeting between the BWA African Workers' Union and BWA Management on December 28, 1964, page 4.
7. 'The Quest for Industrial Peace', the first of three Meyer Kestenbaum Lectures given at Harvard University, October 15, 1962.
8. 'The Role of Government in the Field of Industrial Relations with Special Reference to Nigeria' (paper read at ILO Seminar on Industrial Relations, October 15–26, 1963).

APPENDIX I

TUC(N) MEMORANDUM TO LABOUR RECONCILIATION COMMITTEE OF THE ALL-NIGERIA PEOPLE'S CONFERENCE

NIGERIAN CENTRAL LABOUR MOVEMENT: THE PROBLEMS OF UNITY

1. This document is an attempt to summarise as briefly as possible the salient points regarding the intermittent splits in the central trade union organisation of Nigeria with special reference to the current division. The document is therefore presented in the hope that it may serve as useful background information in making an informed appraisal of such splits, and thereby help towards practical steps that may ensure the speedy return of permanent labour unity in Nigeria.

2. At the opening session on September 27, 1961, of this Conciliation Meeting, we made a statement containing certain preliminary objections. For purposes of record and in the interest of all concerned, we beg leave to reproduce hereunder parts of that statement:

> Before proceeding further we like to express, as representatives of the Trades Union Congress of Nigeria, genuine pleasure in coming before this Labour Conciliation Committee, and to say that the Trades Union Congress of Nigeria will co-operate in the Committee's task, in the hope that we may thereby achieve permanent unity in the Central Labour Organisation of this country.
>
> It is precisely because of the above-expressed hope that we naturally feel concerned about anything that might conceivably be prejudicial to the success of the work of this Committee. In this regard we wish to draw attention to a statement which a leading member of the Nigerian Trade Union Congress made on behalf of that Congress in the course of a goodwill address delivered to the first Convention of the Nigerian Youth Congress held recently in Lagos. This Nigeria Trade Union Congress leader claimed that his Congress and the Nigeria Youth Congress work hand in hand, having identical aims and policies, and that the differences in name between the two organisations was in fact one without a distinction. This claim, strange enough, was not denied by the Nigerian Youth Congress. In consideration of this and the fact that the President of the NYC is a member of this Committee, one naturally wonders whether the Nigerian Trade Union Congress is not in effect participating in the judgment over its own case. This fact would seem to lend credence to the rumours which have been circulating that this same President to whom reference has been made has drawn up

prematurely certain conclusions and recommendations with a view to subtly pressing their acceptance on the Committee. Whether these rumours are true or false must at this stage be left to be proved by subsequent events. However, we assure this Committee that these observations are made only because we are anxious that all here participating in this important task may feel satisfied that the Committee's work is being carried out under circumstances not prejudicial to the attainment of our common objective.

All over the world where democratic institutions are accepted as a way of life, the trade union movement has always been regarded as a free and independent organisation, and while we are not prepared in the movement to sacrifice our independence we re-iterate our appreciation for those friends who have shown interest in seeing that there is lasting unity in the Central Labour Movement of Nigeria.

3. We now proceed to present our case. As already mentioned, the Nigeria Labour Movement has had splits in the past for various reasons; but the current split may be ascribed to two main causes: namely, ideological differences and the interference by Ghana Trades Union Congress in the domestic affairs of the Trades Union Congress of Nigeria.

BACKGROUND TO THE IDEOLOGICAL DISAGREEMENT

4. Before the 1945 General Strike, the Nigerian Labour Movement enjoyed a comparatively united existence. But from then, that is after the General Strike up till about the end of 1952, the splits which occurred had been in certain respects due to individual ambition, partly to the preponderance of ill-informed and poorly equipped trade unionists in the leadership cadre, and the differences arising from their individual partisan participation in the various arms of the political liberation movement. It is to be noted that in the period following the 1945 General Strike, a good deal of communist/Marxist reading materials with different propaganda slants had already created considerable pro-communist orientation, principally in the leadership cadre of organised labour. This was strengthened by the covert activities of the then existing communist-Marxist groups in which, up to the time of their dismemberment, some leading trade union and potential trade union leaders were active. Even at that early stage, leading communists were already working hard to forge a bridgehead for infiltrating the Nigerian Labour Movement. What was the objective?

5. It is an open secret that organised labour is usually the first target for ideological capture in a communist strategy to take over political power. This was clearly, and still is, the intention in Nigeria. Today, as then, our labour movement is still being subjected with break-neck urgency to this ideological pressure not only by certain active trade union leaders, but also through the covert activities of other persons outside the labour movement who nevertheless still conceive of organised labour as a potential means to political power. Because of its rosy promises, especially on the

question of our struggle against colonialism and the speedy attainment of political freedom this new philosophy (Marxism) readily attracted a keen and enthusiastic body of students, among whom, as has already been pointed out, were trade unionists and budding trade unionists in the leadership cadre. However, events subsequently proved that this line of the communists was not a disinterested approach to our national problem, and that some of the 'students' including certain trade unionists did not just accept the new philosophy as a weapon to fight and defeat colonialism but as a platform to pursue certain other ends involving, among other things, the murder of fellow-Nigerians in bloody and violent revolution. Certain compatriots who are today rendering creditable service to the country as prized experts in their respective fields were tagged 'bourgeois intellectuals, capitalists, confirmed aristocrats', and listed as first casualties in that satanic plot. It was at this juncture that the more patriotic members of the student body felt called upon to take a stand, and this led to the dissensions which thwarted the execution of those sanguine intentions and to the dismemberment of that convert organisation around 1953.

6. However, the whole incident had established permanently a struggle between those who had become committed wholly and entirely to communism as a way of life and those patriotic ex-members of the communist 'cells' as well as those 'uninitiated' trade unionists who had unequivocally rejected communism as a way of life – a rejection based on a good knowledge of the ideological concepts of the new philosophy *vis-a-vis* what they genuinely believe to be conducive to our national well-being. Thus, although that chapter would appear to have been passed over, the ghost of its division has seemed to reside permanently in the labour movement. The above briefly sketches the background history of the ideological conflict which has since then formed a major factor in subsequent splits in the labour movement of this country including the present split.

7. The second and new factor, which has played a disruptive role in the present split is, simply stated, Ghana TUC's unneighbourly interference in the internal affairs of the Trades Union Congress of Nigeria, an interference which gave leverage to the disgruntled group in the labour movement to force the present split in the TUC(N). We do not wish to dwell at length here on the well-known unhealthy anxiety of Ghana about Nigeria as an overwhelming giant performer in African and the international political scene. The Trades Union Congress of Nigeria has not been the only target of this unwelcome interference by Ghana in the internal affairs of Nigeria. We recall that in January 1960 the Nigerian Delegation (comprising representatives of our major political parties and the TUC(N)) to the All-Africa Peoples' Conference in Tunis returned to this country and condemned with one voice Ghana's attempt to sabotage the Nigerian Delegation at that Conference. We would have liked to feel able to dismiss these acts as the misdirected energy of an innocent child, but the facts relating thereto convince us to the contrary. No Nigerian, unless he were unpatriotic, could fail to take umbrage at such unprovoked and un-

neighbourly interferences. We have nothing against any individual Ghanaian, but we make no apology whatsoever for our resentment against the Powers in Ghana who, vicariously or otherwise, are responsible for the acts we condemn. We shall come back to the details of this to show that our accusation is well founded. But for the moment we return to the beginning of the history of the present split.

8. On March 7 and 8, 1959, a Labour merger-cum-unity Conference was held at Enugu, and it gave birth to the Trades Union Congress of Nigeria. That Conference followed the efforts, among others, of a Joint Committee set up to examine ways and means of achieving permanent unity, and thereby to cure the Central Labour Movement of Nigeria of its recurrent splits.

The Joint Committee, which comprised six representatives each of the then rival two central labour organisations in the country – namely, The National Council of Trade Unions (Nigeria) (NCTUN) and the All Nigeria Trade Union Federation (ANTUF) – signed on January 21, 1959, a unanimous Memorandum of Agreement and also agreed subsequently on a draft constitution which among other things formed the basis of the merger-unity conference referred to above. The following are the exact terms of the Memorandum of agreement:

(i) that the two organisations agree to merge and have a new name and a new constitution;
(ii) that the affiliated unions of both organisations should become *bona fide* members of the new body;
(iii) that a joint merger conference of the two organisations should be held at Enugu on March 7 and 8, 1959;
(iv) that, while recognising the right of the individual to believe in any brand of political ideology, we nevertheless take cognizance of the events which led to disunity in the past; and agree therefore that in the interest of permanent unity, communism, fascism, and national political partisanship shall not be projected in the Nigerian Labour Movement;
(v) that the two organisations agree to set up a Joint Committee, six from each side, to meet the National Labour Peace Committee at Ibadan on January 31, 1959;
(vi) that the two bodies shall submit proposals for a merger conference to the NLPC;
(vii) we agree that the assets and liabilities of the two organisations including existing international affiliation of either ANTUF or NCTUN be taken over by the new organisation.

9. It is pertinent to state that the memorandum of agreement was signed for and on behalf of the ANTUF by Mr. M. A. O. Imoudu and Mr. S. U. Bassey as President and Secretary respectively, while Mr. N. A. Cole and Mr. L. L. Borha signed for and on behalf of the NCTUN as President and Secretary respectively. It is to be stated further that at the time of the

signing of this agreement it was the common knowledge of both parties that the only officially and openly declared international affiliation at that time was the affiliation of the NCTUN to the International Confederation of Free Trade Unions – ICFTU for short. Therefore, both parties by endorsing this memorandum of agreement clearly accepted affiliation of the new organisation to the ICFTU. In fact it is of interest to mention that prior to this stage the ANTUF (under the leadership of Mr. Imoudu and Mr. Bassey) had made application to the ICFTU for affiliation. There are also the additional facts that:

(*a*) the Constitution of the new organisation as approved at the merger-unity conference makes further provision on the question of international association and in this connection Rule II, Clauses (*j*) and (*k*), state as follows:

Rule II (*j*) '*to co-operate with free and democratic international trade union federations* whose aims and objects are acceptable to the Congress'; and

Rule II (*k*) 'to safeguard against the projection of communism or fascism into the Nigerian Labour Movement, but without prejudice however to the right of individuals to believe in any brand of political ideology'; and

(*b*) the Unity conference adopted a unanimous resolution accepting without amendment the merger instrument, that is the memorandum of agreement including its clause vii (see above).

10. Our friends, in an attempt to justify their break-away, have stated that the Enugu Conference decided against affiliation. This is not correct. The facts are that after the Conference had ratified the merger instrument signed by the NCTUN and the ANTUF, Mr. Patrick Okoye, now a leading member of the NTUC, tabled a motion suggesting that the TUC(N) should not affiliate to any international organisation *in the interim*. The motion was ruled out of order by the Conference Chairman on the contention that it sought to reverse the decision of the conference. Having now disposed of the facts as they took place, we submit most emphatically that it was the communist dogmatism of our friends that goaded them into breaking the pledge they made to the Congress Constitution and the merger instrument already discussed that caused the present split.

11. At the risk of over-drawing the obvious, we have to invite attention to the significance of the fourth operative clause in the merger instrument which preceded the Enugu unity conference. That clause was a clear testimony, arising as it did from the concrete experience of both parties, that communism or similar '-isms' had become the one major factor bedevilling unity in our Labour Movement; hence both parties had willingly subscribed to the conclusion that 'in the interest of permanent unity, communism, fascism . . . shall not be projected in the Nigerian Labour Movement'. In our view this conclusion remains as valid today as when it was first endorsed in 1959. But if it is argued that it has not

seemed to work, then the fault must be found not in the conclusion itself but in our friends of the opposite group who just would not or could not abide by an honourable contracted agreement. That this is true will be confirmed by the paragraphs that follow.

12. The Enugu unity conference met in peace and held a peaceful election – at least, so we thought at the time. But by the inevitable will of the workers, only Mr. M. A. O. Imoudu from the former ANTUF leadership was elected into office in the new organisation (as President). However, the elections over, we as leaders of the new organisation put the past behind us, ready to work in co-operation with all those who were prepared to put the interest of the workers above partisan or selfish considerations. We ignored all the facts which we knew about the other colleagues, their aims and objectives in the past. Such was our determination to work together that for a long time we never looked back. But our friends felt differently. Their loss of office and, *ipso facto*, control of the Congress for their own purpose, signalled the birth of unabated intrigues and bitterness from them towards all the principal officers of the Congress, minus Mr. Imoudu.

13. Evidence is there to show that as early as April 1959, barely a month after the formation of the new Congress, a prominent leader of the dissolved ANTUF and now a member of the breakaway NTUC came out with a press statement condemning the Congress for allegedly having failed in its duties. But that first press attack was not to be an isolated case, for soon afterwards more similar attacks appeared in the press from the former leaders of the dissolved ANTUF. The Central Executive of the TUC(N) then felt constrained to invite some of these men for personal discussion, pointing out to them the damage to our new-found unity and solidarity which their press attacks were bound to cause, especially as their statements were completely untrue and unfair. While some of them appeared to regret their error, the others left no doubt that they were not unaware of the harmful effects of their action and that that, in fact, was precisely what they desired to achieve in the hope of creating conditions favourable for their plan to overthrow Congress' leadership. The ANTUF leaders had regrouped and were regularly holding secret meetings at which plans to gain control of the Congress were the main business. These meetings were held usually on Sundays between the hours of 10 a.m. and 1 p.m. at different addresses in Yaba, Surulere and Ebute-Metta.

It soon became obvious that the Enugu merger conference had only achieved an *uneasy unity* and that these disgruntled elements, having regrouped, were again out to shamelessly assault labour unity and the new Congress because and only because they could not gain control of its leadership.

14. At every possible stage they were engaged in sabotage activities against the Congress by subtle campaigns of deliberate misrepresentation of Congress leaders among their members in order to undermine confidence in the Congress, and dissuade them from supporting Congress policies

and Executive decisions. We may mention a few instances of such sabotage. As we discovered later, not infrequently Congress circulars to affiliated unions sent to members of this group as Secretary or President of their respective unions were in many cases not brought to the notice of the Executives of those unions, and the result was the lack of effective participation in Congress activities. For example:

(*a*) the conspicuous absence of many of these men and their members at the first May Day celebration following the unity conference;
(*b*) failure of most of these men and their members to take active part in the Congress protest demonstration in Lagos against the French atomic tests;
(*c*) by falsely representing to the workers that Congress leaders had betrayed their struggle in respect of the WAAC 'loyalty bonus' when in actual fact they knew Congress had discharged its obligations in the matter;
(*d*) complete misrepresentation to workers in the Congress salary struggle by accusing the leaders of maliciously abandoning workers' interest when, as a matter of fact, they were well aware that the contrary was the case. They were vocal in support of the Congress decision at the NEC to boycott the Mbanefo Commission, yet they turned round to accuse the Central Executive of carrying out the boycott. The result of their action was a divided voice which played havoc with labour's interests in so vital an issue.

15. In August 1959, when the National Executive Council (NEC) of the Congress met, cyclostyled literature containing unfounded and damaging statements against Congress leaders (again excepting Mr. Imoudu) were distributed to delegates by the same group. In September and October the same group came out with yet another unfounded story, and tried hard to sell it to the workers that certain Congress leaders were on the payroll of the Nigerian Government, in token of which they (the Congress leaders) had agreed with the Government to hold down workers' demands; they carried the campaign into these leaders own unions. These false and unsubstantiated allegations were circulated by them in their attempt to discredit, for their own purpose, all but Mr. Imoudu in the constitutionally elected leadership of the Congress.

16. In November, the TUC(N) sent an official delegation to the conference of the Preparatory Committee of the All-African Trade Union Federation in Accra, but the dissident group under direction of the Ghana TUC sent a rival delegation to the same conference to discredit the official TUC delegation. We shall return shortly to the details of this humiliating incident. Between the later part of 1959, and early 1960, a pamphlet entitled *The Case for the Overhaul of the* TUC was produced and distributed throughout the country and to the Ghana TUC by the same group. The fact became known later that the Ghana TUC provided the money for the activities of the group.

17. In December the Nigerian Union of Railwaymen Federated had a grave encounter with the Railway Management during the Emerson-Must-Go episode. The TUC(N) mobilised as much support as possible behind the Railwaymen in that struggle, stood by them throughout, and every reasonable person felt that the Congress leaders had acted their part well. While the TUC(N) leadership was receiving the commendation and expressions of appreciation from the NUR(F) the confusion-peddling-group came out in its characteristic way to level attacks in and outside the press against the Congress for alleged failure to help or protect the victims of the Railway crisis. The intention of course was to embarrass the Congress and cause disaffection against its leadership. The appeals made by Congress to all affiliated unions for co-operation and financial support for the NUR(F) were as usual spurned by the members of that same group and, as if to show they had not done their worst, they announced that they had set up an NUR Defence Committee outside Congress' official arrangement. As a result of the outcry of railwaymen against the activities of that group, which activities they considered prejudicial to their best interest, the NUR(F) was obliged in a public statement to dissociate itself from the group's anti-unity and anti-solidarity activities. We could go on citing more instances of that group's acts of sabotage, intrigue and subversion against Congress. However, enough has been said to dispel any doubts that, right from the unity conference at Enugu, the ANTUF group (ostensibly dissolved) came out sworn to take the warpath against the new Congress because they could not take control of it, and to disrupt once again labour unity in this country.

18. It is significant to note that throughout this period we studiously avoided being embroiled in the quarrel which the other group was feverishly promoting. This was not because we lacked confidence in ourselves or conviction in our cause, but because and only because the preservation of unity was more important to us than to engage in the sterile game of downright falsehood and mischievous misrepresentations in which the other group engaged itself with gratification. Later however, they changed tactics and resorted, first, to demanding an emergency Congress (conference) and claimed that they had secured the one-third support required by the Constitution. This claim of course was untrue; for at that time the Congress had well over 112 affiliated unions of which only four officially made application to that effect by February 1960. Consequently the demand lapsed for lack of backing, and so the Working Committee proceeded with its arrangements for the delegates' Annual Congress which was due in April.

19. No sooner were affiliated unions advised of the Annual Congress than the group financed by the Ghana TUC set out on a country-wide campaign tour in the hope of enlisting the support of affiliated unions. The tour ended: the group held a secret meeting at which were present an official of Ghana TUC, a Hungarian official of the WFTU and three East German trade unionists. This meeting was to review their strategy and assess their

chances of success at the impending Annual Congress. But the result of the tour left them in no doubt that on the merits of their own case they could not carry the majority of the Congress delegates by a democratic process, and were therefore bound to lose their condemnation and frivolous charges against Congress leaders. The choice before them therefore was either to go to the Congress and be defeated again, or refuse to go, set up a splinter-organisation, and there and then cause a split. It was not surprising that they chose the latter course and so defeated the Enugu unity which we had achieved barely twelve months before.

20. So far we have spoken of that group as a team, without dwelling on the damnable role played by its individual members in their assigned task of causing the present split. Mr. Gogo Chu Nzeribe, one of the chief architects of the present division, has since become as it were 'a clay-footed idol fallen among its worshippers', for, as has since become known, he was removed by his own NTUC Executive 'in the interest of Nigerian workers'. So we pass him by.

21. Mr. M. A. O. Imoudu, though President of the TUC(N) at the time, worked himself into the unenviable position of running with the hare and chasing with the hounds, for all along he godfathered the subversive group. This fact would seem to account for his rather tiresome attitude in the Central Working Committee where he would preside over a decision at one meeting only to disown the decision the next day or seek to reverse it at a subsequent meeting even without excuse. On March 29, 1960, he was suspended on the grounds of indiscipline and gross breach of the Constitution. In reply he announced *ultra vires* that he had dismissed the entire Central Working Committee members and so once more displayed his complete disregard for the Constitution and group discipline. He proceeded to convene an unconstitutional so-called Annual Congress in Lagos in defiance of the constitutional and official TUC(N) Annual Congress in Kano.

22. As should be expected, Mr. Imoudu's suspension was not without valid reasons and adequate constitutional grounds. It is of interest to mention that the suspension of Mr. Imoudu was on the unanimous decision of all the other 25 members of the Central Working Committee, and the unanimous support of the 30 members of the three Regional Working Committees of the Congress. Gentlemen, we ask, is it conceivable that all these men (55 in number) would or could have conspired unanimously to suspend unjustly a man of Mr. Imoudu's position? Certainly not. At the 1960 April Kano Annual Congress the 351 delegates were also unanimous in their decision approving the suspension and in fact went further to resolve unanimously that Mr. Imoudu be expelled from the Congress and that he should retire from the labour movement in the interest of permanent labour unity in this country. A Congress letter dated March 5, 1960, in which were listed a few of the breaches of the Constitu-

tion, of acts of indiscipline and disloyalty, as well as that dated March 29, 1960, on this suspension, are available.

23. Our friends of the opposition group have tried hard to lay the misleading impression that Mr. Imoudu was disciplined for making a trip to Russia and communist China. We of the TUC(N) do not hold against anybody's personal political opinion, but we insist that it should not be demonstrated at the expense of the workers' collective will as enshrined in the Congress Constitution. Mr. Imoudu went to these countries without even the courtesy of informing the Executive Committee, for reasons, according to him, of security; yet in these places Mr. Imoudu represented the TUC(N) as the head of the Congress. For this he was censured. But when, on his return, under his new inspiration he took the Congress platform to hold forth for his communist ideology and project the same, contrary to our Constitution Rule 11 (*k*); to attack and denounce and falsely accuse his central executive colleagues in matters relating to Executive decisions, again contrary to Rule 5 (*c*) of Congress Constitution; when he came out in defence of the Ghana TUC that humiliated our own TUC on an international platform; when, in fact, he had done his utmost to damage almost irretrievably the unity and solidarity of Nigerian workers by teaming up with the disgruntled group, and when he repeatedly spited the Central Working Committee on every opportunity offered him to justify his actions, the Central Working Committee felt obliged to call Mr. Imoudu to order. His suspension by the Central Working Committee is supported by Congress Constitution Rules 7 (*v*) and 8 (*e*).

24. Our friends of the opposition have argued often that it was the action of the Working Committee in suspending Mr. Imoudu without authority that made them break away. We have already proved conclusively that their argument is an excuse, not the cause of their break away. But granted for the sake of argument that the Central Executive acted *ultra vires*, was their breakaway a constructive and sensible course of action to take? The answer is bound to be a 'No', because the Annual Congress as the supreme and final authority of our organisation was there [for them] to submit their case to [it] for an impartial verdict. No doubt, this could have saved us the present split. But why did they reject this course of action, which the rules of our Constitution and the simple rules of democratic procedure proclaim? The answer is too obvious for words.

25. We recognise that Imoudu has been long in the Nigerian labour movement and, without any intention to deny what contributions he may have made in this long connection, we feel obliged to state frankly that in nearly all splits that had occurred in the labour movement of this country, Mr. Imoudu has been the central figure. We may mention a few cases:

The split in the first TUC of Nigeria in 1948 found Mr. Imoudu at the head of the break-away group which named itself 'the Committee of Trade Unionists' and in 1949 became the 'Nigerian National Federation of Labour' with Mr. Imoudu as President. In April 1950 the warring

NNFL and the first TUC dissolved and inaugurated the Nigerian Labour Congress in August 1950 with Mr. Imoudu as President. But the Congress soon became moribund because of its President's activities. In 1953 the All-Nigeria Trade Union Federation was formed with Mr. Imoudu as President. In 1956 the ANTUF split, because of disagreement in its Executive following Imoudu's unreasonable backing of mismanagement of the affairs of the Federation by the then General Secretary. We have already dealt with the merger of the ANTUF and the NCTUN, the two organisations which brought into being the Trades Union Congress of Nigeria.

26. It will be interesting to note that about three or four years ago his own union, the Nigerian Railway Workers' Union, decided to retire him and launched an appeal for a retirement fund. The response to this appeal fizzled out when Mr. Imoudu himself accused those supporting the appeal of being his enemies who wanted to get rid of him, and threatened that, even where he collected the retirement benefit, he would refuse to go for he was, as he claimed, the life-President of the Union. Gentlemen, does this suggest that Mr. Imoudu is a difficult man?

27. We acknowledge that Mr. Imoudu in the labour movement was the man of the moment in the 'forties and to a certain extent in the early 'fifties. But surely 1961 is not 1941 or 1951. It is not in us to be unkind to old age or dispute a retirement that would seem overdue. We suggest that, if this situation remains undetermined now, Mr. Imoudu may increasingly become, in spite or because of himself, a capillary attraction for dissensions and open disagreements in the labour movement; for there will always be mischief-makers to cash in on this attribute of Mr. Imoudu in order to enact the unhappy situation that is now facing us.

GHANA TUC: ITS ROLE

28. We have stated earlier that Ghana TUC's meddlesomeness in our internal affairs is the second major factor in the present split. We accuse Ghana TUC of being a means for the break-away group's sabotage of Nigerian labour unity which the birth in 1959 of the TUC(N) was meant to foster. The TUC of Ghana, servilely backed by their Nigerian baby, the NTUC, allege that the TUC(N) is opposed to the Pan-African Labour Movement and has on the basis of this allegation sought to justify their divisionist campaign against the TUC(N). Now let us examine the facts.

29. It is on record that the TUC(N) was the first trade union organisation in Africa to take steps to give practical expression to Pan-African labour following the 1958 All-African People's Conference held in Accra. Actuated by the noble sentiments of Pan-Africanism in the sphere of labour, the TUC(N) wrote in August 1959 to the Ghana TUC to consider the possibility of a joint action in protest against the then imminent French Atomic test in the Sahara, and also examine ways and means for closer association. This led to the joint meetings that same month between the two TUCs at the opening of which Mr. John Tettegah, Ghana TUC Secretary and leader of his delegation, declared:

> We congratulate the Trades Union Congress of Nigeria for the initiative in proposing this joint Conference. It is the long-felt desire of the workers we represent that, throughout West Africa and ultimately in the whole of Africa, labour organisations must forge greater unity in meeting the challenges that face them in the emerging independent nations.

During the joint discussions that followed, unanimous support was expressed for the protest against the French atomic tests and we also reached

> complete agreement on the formation of a West African Federation of Trade Unions to cover the English-, French- and Portuguese-speaking areas of West Africa, and consider the present joint meeting the nucleus of the future Federation and mandate the Secretary-General of the Ghana TUC to undertake preparatory talks with the other national centres for a future meeting.

After the joint statement, the meeting also considered the then pending 2nd African Regional Conference of the ICFTU scheduled for November 4–14, 1959, and for which Nigeria was being considered a likely venue. It was noted that the first African Regional Conference of the ICFTU was held in Ghana in 1957 with the Ghana TUC as host. The understanding reached then was that the Ghana TUC would send delegates, at least observer delegates, and the TUC(N) would act as host to the Conference.

30. The Ghanaians seemed happy and went away. But on their return home, we expected, in fact waited in vain for them to write back and keep us informed of further developments, at least in the terms of our joint discussions in Lagos. To our surprise, the next communication from them was a delegation from Accra on November 1, 1959, on behalf of the Ghana TUC to ask us – indeed to order us – to abandon the ICFTU Conference then due to open on November 4, 1959, but to attend instead at Accra a Conference of the Preparatory Committee of the All-Africa Trades Union Federation. Apparently, after the Ghanaians returned from the first visit to us in August, some 'Great Comrade' in Accra must have given contrary orders, and so we here in Nigeria were expected to be on the double quick march!

31. We complained to the Ghana TUC emissary, Mr. John Eburay, that we regretted that the notice from Ghana had been so short on the issue, and that in any case we had given an undertaking, of which they were well aware, that we would play host to so many labour leaders from all over Africa that we could not very well now tell these trade union colleagues: 'Go home, gentlemen, we are finished with you.' A person like Tom Mboya, for instance, would have met such an unfriendly act, and so would others of his calibre. We pointed out too that the demand from Ghana was contrary to our agreement at the Lagos conference. In any case we felt that if we were to take a decision not to carry on with the Lagos

Conference, that was our sole responsibility and not to be ordered by anybody, including the Ghana TUC. However, notwithstanding all this, we told the Ghana TUC emissary that we would send representatives to the Accra Conference but that we would still proceed with the Lagos Conference.

32. On the following Sunday morning, two officers of the TUC(N) paid a courtesy visit to Mr. Eburay in his Ambassador Hotel at about 10.30 a.m. and found him in conference with Messrs. Gogo Chu Nzeribe, S. O. Khayam, A. Ikoro, P. I. Okoye, R. O. Aghedo, R. U. Onyia, M. O. Ewuzie, G. I. Igbokwe, W. O. Goodluck and E. Ifedirah – all of the opposition group, new leaders of the NTUC. Naturally, this meeting suddenly broke up on the entry of the two officers of the TUC(N), and Eburay tried to explain that he had held the meeting under the mistaken impression that Mr. Nzeribe and his friends were officers and members of the TUC(N) Central Executive, and apologised for his 'mistake'. However, the significance of this meeting found explanation in what happened later at the Accra meeting of the Preparatory Conference of the AATUF, to which we sent an official TUC(N) delegation in keeping with our promise to the Ghana TUC emmisary. After the arrival in Accra of the TUC(N) official delegation of two, the Ghana TUC rushed off a message to the Airways to issue three return air tickets to Mr. S. O. Oduleye, Mr. W. O. Goodluck and Mr. E. Ifedirah to attend the same Accra Conference without a word about it to the TUC(N). After the first two days of the Accra Conference, the unofficial delegates from Nigeria arrived and, with the backing of the Ghana TUC as host organisation, contested seat in the conference against the official delegates of the TUC of Nigeria. In consequence of this, the official TUC(N) delegation protested vigorously and made the following statement to the conference:

Statement submitted on the credentials of Conference Delegates by the TUC Nigeria delegation to the Preparatory Committee of the All-African Trades Union Conference holding at Accra, which opened on November 5, 1959.

Mr. Chairman and Brother Delegates,

(i) The official Nigerian delegation wishes to inform you that in view of the fact that this Conference decided to accept only delegates sponsored by their National Trade Union Centres for participation in the business of the Preparatory Committee of the All African Trade Unions Federation;

(ii) and bearing in mind that the Trades Union Congress of Nigeria has been accorded official delegate status through its official delegates who are the undersigned;

(iii) we consider the attitude of this Conference to adopt the mistakes of the Sub-Committee under the directives of the Ghana TUC in inviting unofficial delegates and forcing them on the TUC(N) delegation to participate at this Committee stage of the Conference directly or indirectly as delegates of Nigeria, an attempt to subvert the solidarity of the TUC of Nigeria and to keep it out from the proposed all African Trade Union Federation.

(iv) We therefore declare that we do not consider the composition of the Conference at this stage proper and fitting for the official and accredited delegates of the Trades Union Congress of Nigeria to continue its participation. And we have to announce our withdrawal from the Conference, and therefore we are walking out.

(v) We regret this unfortunate situation, but assure you that the Trade Union Congress of Nigeria will be prepared at any future date, if its official status and position is not improperly assailed, as on this occasion, as representatives of the workers of Nigeria to participate actively in the realisation of the All African Trade Union Federation.

We are,
Yours fraternally,
(1) NWAFOR A. OTI
(2) E. U. IJEH

33. Already, the Ghana TUC were angry because it was clear they could not push us around, and so, following the withdrawal of our official delegates, the Ghana TUC rallied all the official newspapers and radio in Ghana to denounce our delegates as imperialist stooges and blasted the Lagos Conference as an imperialist-organised conference. Yet when in 1957 the Ghana TUC was host to a similar conference, it was not imperialist-inspired! At home here in Nigeria the Ghana TUC agents, Gogo Chu Nzeribe and his group, were also singing the same song. And so Nigeria's labour delegation, indeed Nigeria, was disgraced and humiliated in the conference hall in Accra. We ask you gentlemen as Nigerians to consider this incident very deeply. Ghana TUC wanted puppets, and the opposition group was ready for it without a thought for Nigeria's honour. Of course they wanted to be financed to attain their ambition of controlling the TUC(N) or, in the alternative, break away and run their own show. The basis for the mutual attraction between the GTUC and the Nigerian saboteur group had been laid but alas at the expense of our country's honour and prestige.

34. Shortly after that Accra episode, the Chairman and the General Secretary of the Ghana TUC paid a visit to Lagos for three days and held three secret meetings with the dissident group. This meeting laid the plans for the first [subvention of] £1,800 which the Ghana TUC gave to the dissident group to carry on their campaign of division and their country-wide tour mentioned earlier. As already pointed out the result of that country-wide tour did not encourage the rebel group, and so now, encouraged by Ghana's financial and moral patronage, they turned their back on their original plan to 'capture the TUC(N) by fighting from within'.

35. After the unofficial so-called annual Congress in Lagos under Imoudu and his men, the Ghana TUC paid another visit here in May and told the press that they were in Nigeria to exchange views with the NTUC and that

the Ghana TUC did not recognise the existence of any other central labour organisation in Nigeria. On that occasion plans were laid for the execution of the scholarship game of the NTUC to communist countries. The position today is that the NTUC pass the Nigerian students to Ghana with a travel certificate under some excuses, then Ghana TUC arranges Ghana passports for the Nigerian students or, in the alternative, pass them through the Russian Embassy in Accra to the various 'universities' in the countries concerned without Nigerian passports. As is well known, the Ghana TUC is an arm, indeed, a department of the Ghana Government. It is hardly deniable therefore that its activities are those given approval by the Government of Ghana. It is therefore clear that, in the NTUC/Ghana TUC relationship, the Ghana Government has responsibility, at least vicarious responsibility, for the NTUC/GTUC activities in this scholarship racket which clearly is undermining the international honour and prestige of the Government of our own country. Today there are well over 200 Nigerians in Moscow, 65 to go to China, out of a total of 5,000 scholarships which the NTUC, with the collaboration of Ghana, will pass on to Moscow, China, East Germany, Prague, etc., through this illegal exit. Each of these students pays £50 into the coffers of the NTUC. Not long ago a bitter quarrel erupted in the NTUC camp over the £50 'scholarship fee' of one Nigerian girl now in East Germany because it happened that her sponsor – an officer of the NTUC – passed her off without the usual fee. We make these statements with all seriousness. We have no wish to embarrass any of these 'scholarship winners' by mentioning names. But a good number of these names are available if the Committee is interested. We submit, Gentlemen, that this act of the NTUC is unworthy of any patriotic Nigerian or Nigerian organisation.

36. But we all know how our friends of the NTUC have strenuously denied (at least in the past) knowledge of these scholarships, of their ties to the World Federation of Trade Unions – that communist international organisation reputed for its calm and calculated way of disrupting democratic organisations. Today they cannot effectively deny these things. They cannot say today that their increasing trips to China, Moscow and East Germany and the so-called 'Pacts of Friendships' which they contract in these countries are just accident; that the recruiting of 5,000 Nigerians for communist indoctrination is an accident, that their rapid hostility and unfounded accusations against the ICFTU are just accidents. No. They are an integral part of the anti-Nigerian plan which horrified Mr. Aderogba Ajao, a Nigerian, Mr. Chukwuemeka Okonkwo, a Nigerian, and Mr. Okotcha, another Nigerian, and inspired their revealing stories told to the world recently. The foregoing reveals clearly the reasons behind the war-cry of the NTUC, the communist World Federation of Trade Unions, Ghana-Guinea and their friends against the ICFTU.

WHY WE CHOOSE ASSOCIATION WITH ICFTU

37. Having established beyond doubt that TUC(N) Constitution provides for affiliation and that the merger-instrument at the Enugu Unity Con-

ference endorsed affiliation to ICFTU, we will now examine some other relative facts. We wish to make it quite clear that we are not concerned with the defence of the ICFTU as such but of certain principles which we believe in and which that organisation also believes in. But first of all it is pertinent to our deliberations that the Committee's notice be drawn to the fact that there exists irrefutable evidence to support the claim that the ICFTU has rendered invaluable service towards the growth and improvement of African trade unions during the past ten years of its existence. Such a claim will find ready support by the testimony of about thirty national trade union centres covered by ICFTU affiliation throughout the African continent. So far as the Trades Union Congress of Nigeria is concerned, we offer no apology for our affiliation to the ICFTU. Indeed, we feel convinced of the righteousness of our act in this connection and are prepared to defend it.

38. In the first place the TUC(N) believes in, and in consequence is committed to, the ideological concept of *Liberal Democracy*. On the basis of this belief the TUC(N) recognises its duty to the workers and people of Nigeria to exert its energy and influence at all times towards the promotion of free democratic institutions in our community. Notwithstanding the criticism and slurs which protagonists of totalitarian systems of society may direct against all forms of liberal democratic social institutions, such as the ICFTU and the TUC(N), we believe that in the strivings towards a social order which will adequately provide all citizens with the necessary economic and cultural goods for overall contentment and happiness, mankind must ever remain mindful that *human dignity* must at all times be sacredly upheld and that it is the duty of all citizens to resist any attempt to trample underfoot this essential and indispensable human attribute. In the considered view of the TUC(N), a social order which ignores and relegates to positions of unimportance the voice of the people expressed by the democratic process of majority decision; that frowns upon and rejects freedom of association among all citizens; that glorifies and advocates the rule and absolute wisdom of one man who by some dubious device sets himself at the apex in the hierarchy of a small ruling clique; that imposes by force, if necessary, the will of one man or a small power group upon the majority; that ignores human rights to such essentials as freedom of speech, freedom of assembly and freedom of the individual from the arbitrary decisions and acts of the ruler; that casts aside the rule of law in adjudicating upon differences and disputes between citizens; such a social order will fail in the long run to establish an enduring social order, capable of bringing happiness and contentment to the majority of citizens.

39. We submit that these are the ideological concepts which constitute the foundation of our beliefs, and which provide the motivating force behind our actions in the discharge of our trade union tasks. In this respect, we of the Trades Union Congress of Nigeria are not alone. Consequently, we of our free will have established fraternal ties through affiliation with

the world community of labour, knowing that our principles and ideals are shared by those concerned.

40. We find that both in the written constitution of the ICFTU and in the practical observance of that document there are principles and concepts which coincide with out beliefs and aspirations as trade unionists. In our capacity as members of that international trade union organisation we participate on a basis of unqualified equality with other national centres irrespective of membership, size, geographical region or race. Decisions are arrived at by democratic processes, and at all times we have exercised our right to express freely our points of view and to register our agreement or disagreement in the light of our national interest. Indeed, during our association with the ICFTU numerous decisions have been taken and pronouncements made to world councils in defence of Africans on such burning questions as the apartheid policy of suppression and repression in South Africa, the Algerian liberation struggle, Portuguese atrocities in Angola, the liberation movement against British colonialism in East and Central Africa, Bizerta and the Congo situations, the fight for trade union rights and for economic and social advancement.

41. Because our detractors, under the guise of promoting Pan-African Labour sentiments, have quite deliberately sought to misrepresent the ICFTU as an imperialist organisation, we feel obliged at this juncture to call into evidence the testimony of some well-known anti-imperialist fighters to debunk such a misrepresentation. Nouri Bondali of the Tunisian liberation movement in 1953 said:

> It may be seen that the ICFTU's action in connection with non-self-governing territories has in the last two years been realistic, positive and constructive. We are very glad to see that the ICFTU's attention has been devoted to the problems of Central, West and East Africa, racial problems in South Africa and to the questions of trade union rights in Morocco and the trade union situation in the Middle East. We hope that this action will be continually strengthened and that it will be extended to all those countries where the free trade union movement is still weak and to all countries under a colonial regime where there is, consequently, a permanent danger to trade union freedom.

Also in 1953, Mr. S. Larbi-Odam of Ghana (then Gold Coast) declared:

> Now, on the question of self-government for dependent countries we note with satisfaction the statement of the Executive Board, and also the action which has been taken to convey the terms of this statement to all concerned.

Mr. Mahjoub Ben Seddik of Morocco in 1955 said:

> I should also like to take this opportunity to thank once again, in public this time, Brothers Becu and Oldenbroek for their activities on

behalf of the Moroccan workers, whom they have appreciated at their true worth.

From Rahmoun Dekkar of Algeria came at the Tunis Congress in 1957 yet another testimony:

> In its dramatic struggle for existence and the liberation of Algeria, the Algerian trade union movement has fortunately been encouraged by the sympathy and solidarity which all the workers and the ICFTU in particular have never ceased to show them. The sense of solidarity felt by the ICFTU has revealed itself many times and in many ways, by public declarations which we find highly encouraging, and by taking up the cudgels with various French governments for an end to the violation of trade union freedoms and for the release of trade union leaders held in concentration camps. Resolutions have been approved by the Executive Board, appeals have been sent to the United Nations and a complaint lodged with the ILO.

Mr. Omar Nur Abdi, President of the Somali Workers Confederation speaking in Mogadishu on July 8, 1961, declared:

> We, the Somali Workers' Confederation of Free Trade Unions, with full autonomy of choice and decision, without ever becoming the object of attempts at bribery or intimidation, joined the ICFTU because we found that it provided not only whole-hearted and loyal collaboration in the setting up of our trade union movement, but also because we found and noted that it respected our principles, our freedom of decision and action and the confirmation of the common ideals for which we fight against every form of colonialism and racialism.

Even John Tettegah of the Ghana TUC, speaking at the ICFTU World Congress in Vienna in 1955, said:

> We value this friendship with *the workers of the free world*. . . . For the one European ruling somewhere in Africa or Asia, there will be hundreds like you gathered here, speaking in many towns and cities of Europe and America, supporting the colonial workers in their struggles for improved living standards and national independence . . . what history has been yearning for, the ICFTU has done.

To say more would be superfluous. In the face of these testimonies one must rightly dismiss as completely unfounded the accusation that ICFTU is an imperialist organisation. Thus, if today (and alas so it is) John Tettegah makes common front with the unholy crusade against the ICFTU, the explanation is simple: the ICFTU frowns upon (and so do we of the TUC(N)) state-incorporated trade unions, the new pattern of unionism in Ghana with John Tettegah as General Secretary cum Ambassador Plenipotentiary cum Minister of State in the Republic of Ghana! Gentlemen, what a strange combination! And there can be no greater reason for him and his satellites in Africa to find the waxing strength of the ICFTU represented by

57 million workers in 137 national trade union centres active in 93 countries in every continent of the world, an intolerable inconvenience.

NO LABOUR ISOLATIONISM

42. The TUCN believes that there is an identity of interest among workers of the world, irrespective of geographical location, ethnic group or racial origin. It further believes that human progress is impossible under conditions of isolation and barriers to communication and interrelationship. For this reason the TUC(N), like all other workers' organisations of the world, adheres to the Charter of the United Nations and supports its Specialised Agencies such as ILO, UNESCO, etc. Since progress is a matter of reciprocity, it is patent to all that no national state, whatever its political system or tendency, is content to cut itself adrift from international activities. By the same token, it is preposterous to suggest that Nigerian workers should isolate themselves from the 57 million workers who share with them identity of interests in the international brotherhood of the free trade unions of the world.

43. On the basis of the facts established above, it would be clearly misleading to suggest that the hope for financial assistance inspired our stand in favour of association with international bodies. The affiliation of the big and financially stable national trade union centres in some countries of Asia and Africa to international trade union bodies further confirms that, rather than financial considerations, the identity of similarity of basic beliefs and concepts forms the basis of mutual attractions.

NO GOVERNMENT FINANCING

44. In the rather anxious exercise to find a solution to our problems of unity, it has been suggested in certain quarters that by Government or other non-trade union sources giving substantial financial aid to the central labour organisation of this country, it will be successfully persuaded against international association. This is a fallacy. And we draw attention to the preceding paragraphs for evidence. In any case the TUC(N) vigorously rejects the idea of the labour movement of this country being financed by Government or other non-trade union sources. It may be argued that any Government financial aid would be without strings attached. We know that every Government is interested in curbing the powers of trade unions and since Government as a state instrument has legislative powers, the risk to the freedom and independence of the labour movement is obvious, 'guaranteed strings' or 'no strings attached' notwithstanding. We concede however that Government may legitimately donate to the Movement a 'Labour House' to own as its property and in token of Labour's contribution to the struggle for the country's national independence. A more legitimate task within the Government sphere in seeking to contribute substantially to the financial stability of Nigerian trade unions is to ensure the full and unfettered implementation of the check-off system in every organised industry in the country. The elaborate and cumbersome process

which at present characterises the operation of the check-off is hampering the fulfilment of that objective.

45. One final question within the general context of international association now remains to be cleared and that is, whether TUC(N) affiliation is necessarily or essentially in conflict with the non-alignment policy of the Federal Government of Nigeria. In answer, we quote, first of all, the pertinent part of a parliamentary statement of the Federal Government on August 16, 1960, in reply to an Hon. Members' question:

> The Government is not, at present, considering the advisability of prohibiting Nigerian trade unions and their leaders from having foreign assistance and/or affiliation. It is the declared policy of the Government to foster and encourage the development of sound, independent and responsible trade unions on democratic lines. The Government wishes to preserve the rights of the trade union movement to develop freely, and any restrictions placed on these rights as suggested by the Hon. Member will infringe the freedom of association which the Government seeks to preserve.

Secondly, we draw attention to the position as it is today in a number of other militantly nationalist African and Asian countries within the same category of non-aligned States as Nigeria:

> In Tunisia, Algeria, Morocco, Libya, the Congos, Ivory Coast, Tanganyika, the central labour organisations of all these countries are affiliated to the ICFTU. India, the modern virtuoso of the policy of non-alignment or neutrality, has three central trade union organisations two of which are affiliated to the ICFTU. In Malaya, Ceylon and the Philippines, their national trade union centres are also affiliated to the ICFTU. In all these countries no hue and cry has been raised in responsible quarters that such affiliation has infringed the non-alignment policy of the countries concerned. Finally, neither Nigerian political parties' membership of the Commonwealth parliamentary association nor Nigeria's membership of the Commonwealth has in any serious-minded consideration been judged as a negation of the independence of Nigeria in the management of her external affairs. In the light of these and the fact that the TUC(N), notwithstanding everything else, enjoys complete freedom of choice and of action, we submit that TUC(N) affiliation is *not* in conflict with the declared foreign policy of our country.

46. To conclude our views on this question, we want to state most categorically that the hue and cry being raised by a vocal minority in the Nigerian labour movement against the principle and the act of international association or affiliation is an attempt not only to gratify the ideological promptings of totalitarian trade unions and their adherents but also to disguise their true designs for power and leadership. We have challenged this vocal minority before: we challenge them again to point

to a single act which we of the TUC(N) have committed against Nigeria or Nigerian workers in consequence of our international affiliation.

ALL-AFRICA TRADE UNION FEDERATION: OUR STAND

47. The TUC(N) has been accused of not supporting the Pan-African Labour Movement. This accusation is arrant nonsense because the TUC(N)'s belief in and support for the Pan-African Labour Movement have been demonstrated beyond reproach by the facts that

(*a*) at its insistance in August 1959 a joint meeting between TUC(N) and the Ghana TUC was held in Lagos to further the objectives of Pan-African Labour Movement, and
(*b*) TUC(N) has attended all meetings of the AATUF to which it was invited including the Casablanca Conference, and has reaffirmed over and over again, its readiness to continue to support the Pan-African Labour Movement (see *Independence Manifesto* and *United for Nigeria* TUC(N) publications).

What the TUC(N) has fought against and will continue to fight against within the framework of an AATUF is the attempt of certain national trade union centres like Ghana to trade illicitly on the noble sentiments of the Pan-African Labour Movement or to claim exclusive right to be the sole pattern-setter for Pan-African labour concepts and practice. We will always oppose any form of dictation, domination or neo-colonialism which hides itself behind the great idea of Pan-Africanism. Those who take a contrary stand falsify, in our view, the sentiments of true Pan-Africanism. Finally, we declare, in the words of one of our African trade union colleagues:

> We believe in the unity of all African workers and will make common front with them against any kind of colonialism or imperialism, old or new, of whatever colour it be and from whichever direction it might come. But if we believe in the need for unity in African trade unionism – free and independent of all influence – we also believe in the need for unity and collaboration of all the workers on the international plane, in a free and democratic trade unionism.

SUMMARY

48. In the foregoing paragraphs it has been conclusively established:

(*a*) that the TUC(N) is the *bona fide* central labour organisation of Nigeria, with a duly constituted executive and approved constitution;
(*b*) that the NTUC is a splinter-group which, before the time of its breakaway, unrelentingly attempted to subvert the authority of the TUC(N) in defiance of the Congress;
(*c*) that the communist dogmatism of the group which goes by the name of NTUC has become the major factor bedevilling unity in the Nigerian labour movement and in fact the cause of the more recent splits as well as the present one;

(*d*) that the conduct of the NTUC leadership, dictated by its ideological commitments and leanings, has shown unmistakable evidence that it cannot accept democratic decisions of the majority, that it deliberately engages in a campaign of calumny and slander against any other leadership that does not subscribe to communist ideology, thereby destroying the basis of comradeship so essential to permanent unity;

(*e*) that Ghana TUC's meddlesomeness in the internal affairs of the Nigerian labour movement, coupled with its projection of pseudo-Pan-Africanism, played the role of rallying and aggravating the forces and factors of division in the present split;

(*f*) that, contrary to the inspired accusations by the Ghana TUC and their Nigerian satellite, we of the TUC(N) are dedicated and unrelenting advocates of the labour ideals of true Pan-Africanism.

(*g*) that while the TUC(N) is a truly patriotic *bona fide* trade union organisation, the NTUC is virtually a front organisation and, being so, has with the active collaboration of Ghana engaged in certain activities detrimental to the territorial integrity, the international prestige and honour of our country and the legitimate authority of the Nigerian State;

(*h*) that there is no valid basis for the claim that TUC(N) affiliation to ICFTU led to the present split and that indeed, the claim is simply a red herring drawn across the trail by the NTUC saboteurs of labour unity in order to draw attention away from themselves and escape condemnation for their actions;

(*i*) that the ICFTU is not an imperialist organisation but a workers' organisation pure and simply dedicated to the well-being of all workers, committed to the defence of democratic principles against all who violate them without following any bloc;

(*j*) that the hope for financial assistance is not the great inspiration of international affiliation but rather the mutual attraction arising from common beliefs and identity of interests;

(*k*) that the gospel of labour isolationism is alien to the universal concept of the international brotherhood of the free labour of the world;

(*m*) that the TUC(N) like every democratic institution in Nigeria accepts as basic a belief in liberal democracy and parliamentary government and therefore in a free and democratic society; finally

(*n*) that Mr. Imoudu not infrequently has been a capillary attraction to dissensions and splits in the central labour organisation of this country.

POINTS FOR CONSIDERATION

49. In the light of the foregoing we venture to put forward for consideration of the Committee the following proposals, hopeful that they may offer grounds of achieving permanent unity:

(*a*) that agreement be reached on the ideological pattern for the trade union movement of this country;

(*b*) that a unity conference be convened, to be attended by the affiliated unions of the two sides; that a Preparatory Committee comprising four from each side be set up to undertake the physical arrangements and the preparation of necessary documents for the unity conference;

(*c*) that, in the event of unity and the coming together of the two organisations, officers of the Congress already on full-time appointment shall be guaranteed position and conditions no less favourable than what they enjoyed prior to the merger;

(*d*) that the unity conference be invited to decide the question of international affiliation;

(*e*) that Mr. M. A. O. Imoudu be retired from the labour movement now with a substantial financial retirement benefit, and that a Committee comprising an equal number from both sides be set up to execute the agreed terms of such retirement;

(*f*) that in order to help Nigerian trade unions combat financial instability, Government takes immediate steps to ensure full and unfettered operation of the check-off system in all organised industry in the country.

CONCLUSION

50. Gentlemen, we have perhaps wearied you by the length and detail of this our statement. If that is so, we ask you to bear with us. Our plea is that we consider that in this important task you have the right to know the full facts in order that you may get a thorough and an intelligent insight into what appears to be a chronic malady in our central labour organisation. We have therefore given you the facts without embroidery but as we know and believe them to be true. We trust that the evidence before you will help you discover the root-cause of these recurrent splits and then guide you in finding such a solution as will end once and for all this distressing ill-wind in the trade union movement in Nigeria. It is the confident hope of the TUC(N) that God will grant you, Gentlemen, the wisdom to recognise the truth and the courage to defend such truth – for the ultimate good of our country and its people.

L. L. BORHA
General Secretary,
Trades Union Congress of Nigeria

APPENDIX II

NTUC MEMORANDUM TO THE ALL-NIGERIA LABOUR RECONCILIATION COMMITTEE

HISTORICAL FACTORS OF DISUNITY IN THE NIGERIAN LABOUR MOVEMENT

We do not wish to re-establish the necessity to have unity in our labour movement for we realise that disunity, with all its effects and dangers, has never served the interest of Nigerian workers. We also believe that the only way to defeat this division is to trade the historical roots of it, enabling us to avoid all factors which in future might promote division again.

Today Nigerian Trade Unionism is in the doldrums, impotent, and tends at its best to follow a negative drift instead of asserting itself as a force. This is why, among the workers who today suffer from poor working conditions because of such disunity, the idea of reviving unity within their rank is always very popular.

In going into the past we do not seek to formulate allegations; we would cite such facts as would enable anyone to admit that there is concrete substance in the case we cite. We like to stress that we are definitely optimistic that labour unity can be restored, because NTUC firmly believes that no amount of tactics can confuse the workers into regarding as useful to their interest any policy which propagates splits in their ranks.

We of the NTUC therefore take advantage of this opportunity to cement our common bonds and to come together. So far several efforts made in the past have been negative, because it is the custom, particularly among vested intruders in our labour affairs, acting as diplomatic consultants, to continue to confuse some leaders as to what direction they should lean to whenever an attempt is made to introduce stability in our labour movement. And none could validly suggest that such outside influences would be favourable to the unity of workers, when in fact they are not workers, but imposters. Thus a persistent attempt to create confusion has constantly resulted, whenever there is any unity move, from those who consider labour unity detrimental to their own interest. And resulting from this miscarriage, such moves have flopped again and again.

The truth is that we have inherited differences in our labour movement today from the myth of ideology, whereas our ideology as workers has just one simple content. But the most dangerous anti-labour forces, outside the labour movement itself, have introduced the havoc of a hysterical cry by one section against the other. Resulting from this, our movement has, since a very long period, been plastered with red-baiting, even though there is no shred of evidence that there are communists in our labour movement. But then there are several labour leaders who were formerly called communists who, on turning to accept the award of Government and employers of posts of responsibility, eventually ceased to be labelled 'reds'. This tears to pieces the pretences that they were even really regarded as communists, when they were called these names.

There is no need therefore to present defence or denials about communism. Mr. L. L. Borha for instance was arrested about ten years ago with *Socialist Review* bulletins and was regarded as a communist. But we understand the essence of this charge at that time. Mr. H. A. P. Nwana, a personnel officer in the Ports Authority today, then a labour leader who formerly kept coming into the forefront of 'pro-communists currents', as they call it, was once regarded as a 'Red'.

When a labour leader persistently advocates a boost in workers' wages, and refuses either to be gagged or put in a straight jacket by the Federal Government, the almighty employers, the Ministry of Labour or the forces of ICFTU or MRA [Moral Re-Armament], then in Nigeria he must be a 'Red'. The day he accepts any board post, personnel job, labour officer position or becomes a career representative of the ICFTU, or its Trade Department, he is born again into a leader worthy of the confidence and respectability of all vested interests in Nigeria. From that day his persecution ceases and he finds salvation and comfort with the very opponents of the workers he serves.

This vicious outlook must cease in our labour movement, and labour leaders must begin to refuse to regard such influences as having the right to work out for them their basic attitude towards other leaders. Several leaders have refused to take a post in the Government or employers' side of the fence in Europe; and others have also refused positions of attraction and were not classified as Reds. But in Nigeria you must refrain from speaking the truth, abstain from attacking exploitation of the workers, oppose strike action or the achievement of advanced conditions for workers, in order to enjoy immunity from red labels.

The other day Belgian trade unions, led by their Socialist Party Movement, promoted a long-drawn strike. Though reports colourfully characterised their picketing campaign as strong and vigorous, yet they were not regarded as communist-inspired. The British TUC rather remitted the strikers some financial support. But the British TUC and ICFTU would suggest communism if it all happened in Nigeria. Yet the Posts and Telecommunications strike of 1959 and the Plateau strike of the miners for the Mbanefo Award and proper negotiating machinery in December 1960 were regarded as 'Red'-inspired. Several British labour leaders, who are members of the British Communist Party, participate in the activity of the British TUC. Yet the British TUC inspires hatred and division in our movement against imaginary 'Reds' who don't exist. Such are samples of the core of division in the Nigerian trade union scene. The idea of making money as distinct from the idea of serving the workers, the idea of pleasing Government and fulfilling the employers' definition of what makes a model labour leader, the idea of attending parties called by American consulate and ICFTU officials and parading as big shots in Nigerian high society becomes the overriding, dominant outlook in the new type of unionism established under the auspicies of the *status quo*.

We of the NTUC have always considered it outright fraud or practically treason against the workers to derive the validity of our actions and standards from employers and Government and not from the workers' attitude. This is perhaps why we have always been regarded as heretics in our local labour front. But in order to restore and consolidate the prestige of labour, we need to formulate our own attitude to things, guided mainly by the role which we can play with such policies for serving the workers' interest – no more and no less.

We must reject this policy which has been influential in sowing confusion among the rank of the labour leaders, i.e. declaring people this or that and abandoning the work to be done for workers of the country, scattered all over the place, most of whom are hardly organised. Some labour leaders who constitute government and police informers and who gain some advantage by attributing to others the role of conspirators against Government must be warned to cease or resign.

We have little faith too in labour leaders who are completely opposed to real decent standards for Nigerian workers and who oppose demonstrations and strike action even when there is ample evidence that the workers cannot succeed unless such industrial action is taken. These leaders abuse their position by using it to hold back the advance of workers, and hence become open to the suspicion that they are being pitched against the workers. All these systematically produce division between them and the more honest and militant elements.

While we reject the introduction of any ideology into our movement, as decided at the Enugu Unity Conference, we do not consider that it is right to neglect the problems of the workers and make honest trade unionists the main target of attack. Our Congress has been accused of belonging or affiliating to the World Federation of Trade Unions (WFTU) whereas there is no evidence that we have done any such thing. Whereas if we want to affiliate to WFTU we are free to, since there is no law in Nigeria which forbids it. The tactic behind this distortion is to enable those who affiliate to the International Confederation of Free Trade Unions to be justified. They are never tired of criticising whatever we do. We are free to affiliate to ICFTU or WFTU but we have not and shall not, because we realise that by doing so we shall be faced with the problem of promoting the basis of foreign affiliations by several central trade unions. And since WFTU and ICFTU are antagonistic, their decision will be reproduced in the same degree in our local labour movement. But of course these arguments and considerations do not worry our friends of the TUC(N).

The relation between us and other trade union movements is merely one of mutual co-operation. This same policy applies to other African trade unions whom we treat with fraternal equality. It is therefore revolting to hear the allegations that we are obedient to Ghana TUC or that our activities are financed by it.

While we would not of course repudiate any support from Ghana TUC or other African trade unions, we have not in actual fact received anything from the Ghana TUC. But the sum of £1,800 was received by us from the All African Trade Union Federation, for which we feel immensely grateful. This however does not satisfy the allegation that Ghana TUC has exclusively financed our activity. While we would stress that we have little faith in support from outside in organising our movement, we would also prefer help from African trade unions than from any international trade union organisation which tends to attach a policy of domination to the aid they give in the circumstances. This is why our policy on international affiliation is that of neutrality.

As the world is divided into two camps, so are its labour forces, i.e. WFTU and ICFTU. It is clear that ICFTU is the labour arm of Western capitalism. Why then should we affiliate to it? Was the Enugu Conference absurd to recommend the suspension of affiliation to ICFTU? Is the Federal Government senseless to adopt neutrality as its foreign policy? And does neutrality imply affiliation to either WFTU or ICFTU? Don't we consider it the safest and only sane road towards cementing understanding and unity in our labour movement? It requires no great erudition to arrive at the facts about what is correct, and all those who disregarded the decision of the Enugu policy of neutrality and affiliated the movement with the ICFTU wanted to put an end to unity in our labour movement. It even unquestionably exposes their insincerity, in that they refused, contrary to the constitution and the demand of the majority of affiliated unions, an emergency conference to consider this matter and proceeded undemocratically and secretly to procure this affiliation.

The Federal Government too, while talking of neutrality, openly supports the TUC(N) which violates its doctrine of neutrality by affiliating to ICFTU. In fact the Federal Government has clearly shown indications that it supports ICFTU, both in its attitude during the last ILO African Regional Conference; to its publications and display of hospitality towards ICFTU officials, while showing hostility to WFTU, those pamphlets and books are still banned in Nigeria. There can be no health in our labour Movement if the decision on neutrality in foreign affiliation is not restored. However, it is not correct to say that we oppose financial help from anybody, except it is tied to foreign affiliation and tends to promote laziness and corruption of local trade union leaders. This point defeats the affiliation of TUC to ICFTU merely because it offered them financial aid.

We favour affiliation to the All African Trade Union Federation, towards whose growth we should be more energetic in contributing, instead of spending so much local interest on ICFTU that we have no time left in assisting to build up our own African Labour Front. The real remote cause for the split lies in the fact that there is unfortunately a small group of labour leaders who view the movement as a business, and have no interest in preserving labour unity. This group will sacrifice everything to achieve their personal interest, and, being in reality representatives of employers and vested interests among the workers, they will do from time

M

to time precisely the opposite of the wishes of workers, even if it is at the expense of splitting their unity.

The most immediate cause we can today recall, as to how the split started after the Enugu Conference are as follows:

(i) Mr. Zudonu, Vice-President of TUC(N), went on a trip to America and made a statement branding elements of the submerged All Nigeria Trade Union Federation (ANTUF) as communists, whom he stressed must be destroyed. The fight, he continued, was between communists and anti-communists. This statement, which violated of course the whole spirit of the Enugu Merger Conference, was capable of provoking division in the TUC(N), and was spotlighted during a meeting of TUC(N) at Lisabi Hall in September 1959.

It was resented by affiliated unions, and Mr. Borha the General Secretary was asked, and he promised, to get Mr. Zudonu to withdraw it, but nothing of the sort was done, even up to the present day. From there, leaders of the TUC started on a policy of raiding unions, black-listing unionists who were not in their favour, and antagonising every one who formerly belonged to ANTUF.

(ii) Mr. Imoudu became a figure-head President not worthy of consultation; and meetings were called outside his participation. A Finance Committee was tactically established for running financial affairs without his knowledge. Monies and transport, were operated without his views or awareness, and affiliated unions were kept in the dark about large expenses said to have been made on behalf of the TUC(N) by its leaders. A policy of recklessness or 'I don't care', was developed by leaders of the TUC(N) concurrently with the receipt of these huge sums of money from ICFTU. Articles appeared in *The Daily Telegraph* above the signature of TUC(N) leaders, attacking their trade union colleagues whose unions were affiliated to TUC(N) and even hitting the President, M. A. O. Imoudu himself, below the belt.

(iii) During the election of officers at the Enugu Merger Conference, only Mr. M. A. O. Imoudu was elected into office of the new organisation as President while all other officers of the ANTUF were thrown out. It was later that we discovered that the ICFTU had given leaders of the former NCTUN a sum of £200 to buy votes at the Conference. Evidence of this type of corruption is now available.

(iv) *Secret Correspondence*. A few months after the merger conference, secret letters between the officials of the TUC(N), ICFTU and the British TUC were made available to us. . . .

Finally the climax came when it was accepted that the April Conference would be called. Yet in this same month, two singular actions were adopted to provoke a split and mis-understanding. First, while Mr. Imoudu was in the country, leaders of the TUC(N) refused to allow him as President to be one of the trustees of Congress and to endorse cheques. They insisted on Mr. S. I. E. Ese the Deputy President, who has always been going up and down Brussels to bring in monies from the ICFTU. Second, they suspended Mr. Imoudu as President of Congress. From these, it became clear that they had declared voluntary war on anyone who did not agree with their affiliation to ICFTU, a matter on which Mr. Imoudu was the leading figure.

Imoudu fixed a Conference in Lagos where everyone would attend to give account of their stewardship from April 19–21, and invited them. They deliberately fixed their date outside his date, from April 20–23 in Kano, and apart from an advert in front pages of newspapers, they would neither invite Mr. Imoudu nor all affiliated unions formerly in the ANTUF. They complicated the problem of unity by these tactics, and ensured that those coming to Lagos would not come to Kano, and that was our surprising experience of how the ground-work for an immense split in our united front was laid.

To achieve unity again we must return to neutrality in foreign affiliation and join the All-African Trade Union Federation, on a basis of equality with all African trade union centres.

GET leaders of labour to curb some of their financial greed and return to selfless service for Nigerian workers;

ACCEPT the necessity of organising a strong militant and democratic trade union movement, devoid of foreign affiliation, devoted to a concrete programme embodying the present demand and need of the workers of our country while merely maintaining mutual fraternal relations with both ICFTU and WFTU if decided in a national Conference of all trade unions;

CONVINCE ourselves that we must seek dependence on our own workers over financing our movement and refuse to serve as auxiliaries to foreign trade unions;

INSIST that every leader secures a union which he serves in Nigeria, instead of being maintained from America and Europe without attachment to any Nigerian trade union;

STEER CLEAR from the advice of US Consulate, labour department officials, Moral Rearmament and all external forces which poke their noses in our labour affairs;

WORK for posessing a trade union newspaper, to defend labour and present its independent point of view;

START our labour education programme on our own, with the assistance of only neutral agencies as UNESCO and ILO;

COMMENCE with the reorganisation of all trade unions on industrial basis and ensure that the workers themselves are given full participation in their trade unions and not the leaders alone, thus enabling trade union democracy to flourish;

OPERATE the Check-off system as a means of financing our trade unions instead of resorting to ICFTU to do so leading to its corresponding control.

FINALLY

(i) The NTUC agrees in principle to unity in the Labour Movement, i.e. the two organisations, NTUC and TUC(N), should come together.

(ii) The NTUC is in principle opposed to international affiliation (i.e. ICFTU, WFTU, IFCTU) except the AATUF. However, it is quite prepared to accept the verdict of Nigerian workers on the issue.

(iii) Towards these ends, the NTUC suggests that there should be a conference of representatives of all registered trade unions at a place easily accessible to the majority of the trade unions to take decisions on the matters.

(iv) Decision of the proposed conference shall be binding on all trade unions.

(v) The conference should be presided over by an independent chairman acceptable to the NTUC and TUC(N).

(vi) Voting at the conference shall be by secret ballot.

M. A. O. IMOUDU
President

S. U. BASSEY
Secretary-General

APPENDIX III

LETTER SIGNED BY AN OFFICIAL OF THE WFTU, ADDRESSED TO CHARLES HEYMAN, HEAD OF THE GHANA TUC's INTERNATIONAL DEPARTMENT

WORLD FEDERATION OF TRADE UNIONS
Our ref.: A.S./D.R.N.C. 1018

Prague, 10 July 1961

Brother Charles HEYMAN.
Director of African Affairs
and International Department
of the Trades Union Congress,
Hall of Trade Unions
Headquarters Secretariat,
P.O. Box 701,
Accra,
Ghana.

Dear Brother Heyman,

Although I shall be seeing you in a few days' time, I send this letter in advance so that you can consider the problems in which we both are interested and consult Brother Tettegah and others, if necessary. I am entrusting it to Brother Mabhida to hand it to you personally. There are still some people, not only the Chinese, who seem to have doubts about Brother Tettegah's loyalty because they fail to see that anyone who once was so close to the reactionary imperialist intriguers and saboteurs in Brussels could have had a truly sincere change of heart. They fail to appreciate the subtlety of tactics which is indispensable if we want to achieve the unity of the African trade union movement and to have any notable success in the near future.

It has now been decided to appeal to you to use the great influence of the Ghanaian Trades Union Congress for ensuring that matters concerning the relationships between the All-African Trade Union Federation and the WFTU should not be publicly discussed at the forthcoming Fifth World Trade Union Congress in Moscow.

As you know, the Draft Programme of Trade Union Action declares under section III: 'The WFTU considers the creation of the All-African Trade Union Federation to be a great success of the forces fighting for the unity of the trade union movement in Africa' and assures the All-African Trade Union Federation and the African workers that 'in the field of fighting for the definite liquidation of colonialism they have a sincere friend – the WFTU.'

You know also that we fully agree with our Ghanaian brothers that for the promotion of our joint political aims the major part of the All-African Trade Union Federation's financial burdens is borne and will be borne by the WFTU.

It is, however, imperative that our financial arrangements should not be exposed to the class enemy who would exploit them for hostile propaganda by malicious interpretation. It should therefore be urgently impressed on prospective participants at the Congress, above all on our African brothers, that the financial implications of our relationship must in no circumstances be disclosed or even hinted at, neither in connection with the Draft Programme of Trade Union Action nor in connection with any other part of the agenda.

As I told you in March, we were having serious difficulty in getting funds for the Casablanca meeting unless the Ghanaian Trades Union Congress could guarantee that disaffiliation from the ICFTU would be made obligatory for all affiliates of the AATUF. The Chinese were then reluctant to agree that it might be necessary to ask their friends in Kamerun and Brazzaville to give up ties with us in order to ensure that we could get the ICFTU out from Africa. They have even been pushing Imoudu to affiliate to the WFTU. That will have to change now, although Imoudu and other Nigerian friends of ours will still be urged to attend the Congress in Moscow in December.

Brother Tettegah's efforts to establish a united front between the AATUF and the WFTU have done much to strengthen his position here and have provided ammunition for me in the discussions with the Chinese. My personal view is that he should not press the united front prematurely: we still may get many waverers into the AATUF if we work on them patiently and persistently. Some here have said that we would make a tactical error if we pressed the issue of disaffiliation too far.

We are taking steps to prevent the Dakar conference; but as a further precaution, we think you should be ready, if necessary, to send some of your best men to work among any delegates who may attend. They should be kept divided which will not be difficult if we charge the ICFTU with being an organisation of the imperialists which deliberately divides African trade unions and is out to wreck the unity of the African working class. Our primary task is to get the ICFTU out of Africa and destroy its supporters in Africa.

In this connection we would like to ask our Ghanaian brothers to consider the financial uncertainty which will inevitably be felt in the near future by a number of African trade unions and organisations which at present are still ICFTU affiliates. But in our considered opinion the time has not yet come to divulge even to trusted comrades in these unions and organisations that, owing to the WFTU's moral and financial backing of the All-African Trade Union Federation, their financial future will in fact be secure.

Lastly, I hope I shall hear from you good news about your progress with Bassey, Ochwada and the others. I am already in trouble over the money I gave you for this purpose, as I have not been able to show much progress so far. Give something to Mabhida in any case.

Sending you fraternal greetings

IBRAHIM ZAKARIA

INDEX